NEW CONFUCIANISM

NEW CONFUCIANISM:
A CRITICAL EXAMINATION

EDITED BY
JOHN MAKEHAM

First published 2003 by
PALGRAVE MACMILLAN™
175 Fifth Avenue, New York, N.Y. 10010 and
Houndmills, Basingstoke, Hampshire, England RG21 6XS
Companies and representatives throughout the world

PALGRAVE MACMILLAN is the global academic imprint of the
Palgrave Macmillan division of St. Martin's Press, LLC and of
Palgrave Macmillan Ltd. Macmillan® is a registered trademark in
the United States, United Kingdom and other country.
Palgrave is a registered trademark in the European Union and
other countries.

Library of Congress Cataloging-in-Publication Data
    New confucianism: a critical examination/Edited by John Makeham.
      p.cm.
    ISBN 1–40396–140–9
      1. Neo-Confucianism. 2. Philosophy, Chinese. I. Makeham, John,
1955–

B5233.N45 N48 2000
181'.112—dc21   2002029246
ISBN: 978-1-4039-6140-2

A catalogue record for this book is available from the British Library.

Design by Newgen Imaging Systems (P) Ltd., Chennai, India.

First edition: February, 2003
10 9 8 7 6 5 4 3 2 1

Transferred to Digital Printing 2010

Contents

INTRODUCTION

John Makeham

Nathan Sivin once opined "It is hard to think of any idea responsible for more fuzziness in writing about China than the notion of Confucianism."[1] This is because the term "Confucianism" has been variously applied to so many different things, some of the more common being the philosophical and ethical teachings of a number of thinkers (including Confucius), a tradition of scholarship, a religion, a social ethic, and a state ideology. One scholar has even argued that since the sixteenth century, Confucianism has become a metonym of " 'real' Chineseness" in the West.[2] This century, in China, it has been used derogatively by some as a catchall term subsuming all that is rotten in China's "feudal" past, while others have championed it as the *summum bonum* of traditional Chinese culture.[3] For most of the twentieth century, however, Confucianism (understood as a single orthodox synthesis) has been portrayed as moribund and effectively spent as a viable philosophical and cultural resource, with scholars charting its demise and final disintegration to the late nineteenth and early twentieth centuries.[4] Despite this, since the 1980s, Taiwan and China have witnessed the most sustained resurgence of scholarly and intellectual interest in Confucianism (both as an ideology and as a body of philosophies) of the twentieth century.[5] This claim is supported by the large number of publications, conferences, research projects, research centers, and postgraduate theses devoted to aspects of Confucianism. This phenomenon prompts reexamination of the view that the demise of scriptural Confucianism[6] in the late nineteenth and early twentieth centuries has actually meant the death of Confucianism as a viable philosophical and cultural resource.

Contemporary New Confucianism (*dangdai xin Rujia* 當代新儒家; *dangdai xin Ruxue* 當代新儒學; *xiandai xin Rujia* 現代新儒家; *xiandai xin Ruxue* 現代新儒學, hereafter, New Confucianism) is a movement promoted and/or researched by prominent Chinese intellectuals based in China, Taiwan, Hong Kong, and the United States of America. (In English, the term "New Confucian" is to be distinguished from "Neo-Confucian," which refers to certain Confucian thinkers of the Song, Yuan, and Ming dynasties, in particular.)[7] New Confucianism has emerged as a neo-conservative philosophical movement, with religious overtones, which claims to be the legitimate transmitter and representative of orthodox Confucian values. By the early 1990s, a broad consensus had been reached by scholars in Taiwan, Hong Kong, and China that New Confucianism was a movement that could be traced to the early part of the twentieth century, that it boasted distinct phases of internal development, a cohort of representative thinkers, and clearly defined lineages of intellectual transmission. Particularly noteworthy, in the late 1980s and early 1990s, is the high critical regard in which New Confucianism had come to be held by a large number of mainland Chinese scholars. For example, in 1987, Fang Keli 方克立 maintained that of all the schools of thought in modern China, New Confucianism ranks second only to Marxism in terms of its creative theoretical qualities, influence, and longevity.[8] Two years later, Zheng Jiadong 鄭家棟 described the New Confucian "school" (paibie 派別) as being the longest developing and most influential conservative school of thought and cultural movement in modern·Chinese history.[9] By 1992, Luo Yijun 羅義俊 was even prepared to write that "It is only due to the establishment of this great Confucian school [i.e., New Confucianism], that the true lifeblood and spirit imbuing the vitality of Chinese culture has remained unsevered and sustained."[10]

Successfully transcending the geographical and political boundaries of China, Taiwan, and Hong Kong, since the mid-1980s, New Confucianism has increasingly played a leading role in bridging the cultural and ideological divide separating mainland and overseas Chinese scholars by providing a shared intellectual discourse. The wider influence of this discourse is evident not just in the way it has shaped philosophical research and debate in the region, but also in its contribution to broad cultural and intellectual issues, with some protagonists identifying "exclusive" links between "Confucian values" and East Asian economic prosperity. New Confucianism has also proven to be the most successful form of philosophical appropriation, reinvention, and "creative transformation" of "Confucianism" in contemporary China, Taiwan, and Hong Kong.

Despite the movement's importance, there is only one detailed study of New Confucianism written in English.[11] By contrast, a tremendous amount of research and writing on the subject of New Confucianism has been done by Chinese (mainland and overseas) scholars over the last two decades. It is about time that the fruits of this scholarship are distilled, examined, and evaluated. The purpose of this book is to examine critically the notion of New Confucianism as a philosophical school and to introduce the thought of some of its representative thinkers. On the one hand, the very existence of the movement challenges the assertion that the demise of scriptural Confucianism in the late nineteenth and early twentieth centuries has actually meant the death of Confucianism as a living philosophy. On the other hand, this observation has to be balanced against consideration of the extent to which the identity of Contemporary New Confucianism has, itself, been retrospectively created.

The book is divided into four parts of two chapters each. Part 1 is concerned with the broader historiographical problems; part 2 with the reception of New Confucianism in China; part 3 with two representative "second generation" New Confucian figures; and part 4 with two representative "first generation" New Confucians. (The book is structured on a reverse chronology, proceeding from the 1990s to the 1920s.) In chapter 1, I argue that there is little evidence that New Confucianism had attained a degree of integration or coalescence sufficient for it to be recognized and promoted as a distinct intellectual movement, or school of thought, before the 1970s. In China, discourse on New Confucianism can be traced quite precisely to 1986. I further argue that at one extreme, the term "New Confucian" has been employed in such a way that it has served to exercise a homogenizing effect, which has obscured complexities and philosophical differences. This has been at the expense of a willingness to recognize the variety of forms in which Confucian philosophy has continued to survive throughout the twentieth century (even if the study of individual "New Confucians" has, in fact, considerably enhanced the understanding of individual twentieth-century philosophers). At the other extreme, the term has been applied with such narrow proprietary rigor that it has served to elevate a select group as constituting a whole school or movement. Contributors to this volume have been invited to regard these polemical views as a point of consideration in the preparation of their individual contributions, thereby strengthening the thematic unity of the volume. As editor, my views have not been presented as the "party line" according to which contributors have been required to craft their individual contributions.

In chapter 1, I explore seven interlinked topics, beginning with a historical enquiry into the origin and early uses of the term *xin Rujia* (New Confucian). I then turn to examine a document that continues to be conventionally recognized as a watershed in the history of New

Confucianism and even interpreted as a manifesto of the movement:
the 1958 "Wei Zhongguo wenhua jinggao shijie renshi xuanyan
為中國文化敬告世界人士宣言" (Declaration on Behalf of Chinese
Culture Respectfully Announced to the People of the World). I question the appropriateness of this conventional recognition, arguing that
in the late 1950s New Confucianism still did not exist as a school or
movement. I then subject to scrutiny some of the more influential
definitions of New Confucianism, and the consequences that arise
when either a more inclusive or a more exclusive definition is favored.
After this, I explore the question of whether New Confucianism should
be considered as a philosophical or a cultural movement, arguing in favor
of the former. Next, I take a critical view of various responses to the
complex and still unresolved question faced by scholars writing in
the 1980s and early 1990s: "How should different historical phases in
the development of New Confucianism be identified and demarcated?"
Answers to this question bear directly on such notions as intellectual
lineages and orthodoxy. This leads into the following topic: "Where
does one draw the line between 'Confucian' and 'New Confucian?'" Is
there a line to draw or is the distinction purely retrospective and largely
subjective? The final part of chapter 1 introduces the so-called third
generation New Confucians and the much more tentative and recent
phenomenon of "Post New Confucianism."

Chapter 2, "The New *Daotong*," starts from the premise that New
Confucianism provides students of Chinese intellectual history with a
rare opportunity to study traditional strategies of orthodoxy formation
in a contemporary context. I begin by showing how many premodern
Chinese intellectual traditions have been retrospectively created. This
serves as a background for understanding the historical significance of
the concept of *daotong* 道統 (interconnecting thread of the way) in
Confucian discourse on orthodox lines of transmission. A brief account
is given of the key role that Zhu Xi 朱熹 (1130–1200) played in this
development. The main subject of this chapter is Mou Zongsan's
牟宗三 (1909–95) revised *daotong*. Indeed, it is tempting to compare
Mou Zongsan's role in propagating a New Confucian *daotong* to that
played by Zhu Xi in propagating what subsequently became the officially
sanctioned *daotong* of the Cheng-Zhu (Cheng Yi 程頤 [1033–1107] and
Zhu Xi) tradition of Neo-Confucianism. Both Mou and Zhu were
philosophical synthesizers[12] and system builders, and both sought to
use the *daotong* strategy to promote certain thinkers and exclude other
thinkers from their versions of the orthodox Confucian tradition.
I show that as with the early Neo-Confucian versions of the *daotong*,

Mou Zongsan's revised *daotong* simultaneously functions as a vehicle for exclusion as well as inclusion. On the one hand, this is used to privilege one particular orthodox lineage in the transmission of the *dao*, the Xiong Shili 熊十力 (1885–1968)–Mou Zongsan lineage; on the other hand, it is used to exclude figures such as Feng Youlan 馮友蘭 (1895–1990) and He Lin 賀麟 (1902–93) from the New Confucian fold. I then describe how Mou's followers in Taiwan and Hong Kong secured victory over their mainland counterparts in their claims to proprietary rights over New Confucianism by appealing to the concept of *daotong*. Related topics subsequently addressed in chapter 2 include accounts of how Xiong Shili's "spiritual" legacy was used in the construction of the new *daotong*; how Mou's *daotong* was designed to undermine the traditional authority granted to Zhu Xi as a mainstream transmitter of the *daotong*; and the key distinguishing features of Mou's revised *daotong*. The chapter concludes with an account of Liu Shuxian 劉述先, heir to the *daotong* inheritence in the so-called "post Mou Zongsan age" (post-1995), and a younger contender, Lin Anwu 林安梧.

Chapter 3 by Song Xianlin, "Reconstructing the Confucian Ideal in 1980s China: The 'Culture Craze' and New Confucianism," examines the introduction and early reception of New Confucianism in the context of the "culture craze" (*wenhuare*) of the mid-1980s. Song describes this as a process whereby New Confucianism served as a vehicle through which Confucianism became appropriated for domestic consumption in China. More broadly, chapter 3 examines various threads in the pattern of discourse on Confucianism in the period between China's implementation of its Open Door policy (from the end of the 1970s) to the "national studies craze" (*guoxuere*) of the early-to-mid 1990s. This chapter, thus, not only provides insights into how and why New Confucianism was introduced into China in the 1980s, but also into how it has paved the way for (and gradually come to be subsumed within) the broader discourse of Confucianism in 1990s China.

Song argues that the introduction and reception of New Confucianism owed more to the political and cultural realities of this period than to the priorities or appeal of any philosophical agenda. She traces these political and cultural realities to calls for the "reevaluation" of Confucianism, beginning in the late 1970s, and shows that by the mid-1980s Confucianism had come increasingly to be seen as having redeeming qualities, which could be selectively adapted and developed to suit contemporary needs. The year 1986, in particular, was a watershed, because it was in November of that year that New Confucianism was identified and funded as a key research topic under the national seventh five-year plan for the social sciences. Within a year there were nearly fifty scholars working on topics related to New Confucianism in China. This event was followed by a rapid succession of conferences on Confucius, Confucianism, and individual New Confucian thinkers, as well as a host of related publications. "For the first time in decades . . . Confucianism, in the shape of New Confucianism, was systematically introduced to Chinese readers, many of whom up to that point only associated Confucian teaching with 'harmful feudal remnants.'" Song argues that the introduction of New Confucianism into China was also aided by Deng Xiaoping's call for a "socialism with Chinese character-istics," and the government's "anti-spiritual pollution" campaign.

Mainland scholars succeeded in creating a Confucianism for Chinese audiences, a "homogenized Confucian discourse" designed for domestic consumption.[13] The distinct academic focus on the study of New Confucianism adopted by mainland scholars was due to the fact that they had to operate within the confines of a particular political space and that the "introduction of New Confucianism had to transform itself along the parameters of the concurrent political discourse." This is nowhere better illustrated than in the ideological import of the terms *xin Rujiao* and *xin Ruxue*, used in Taiwan and China, respectively, to refer to New Confucianism. The Taiwan academic, Chun-chieh Huang, for example, maintains that "Taiwan scholars do not dabble in objective descriptions of Confucianism; they hammer out their own identity in Confucian terms. . . . Their Confucian scholarship is an existential engagement in cultural endeavors. Confucianism is not so much a collec-tion of objects to be investigated than it is an existential value system within which an investigator cultivates his personality and cultural enrichment to meet the challenge of modernity."[14] Song's account con-cludes with some observations about the role played by New Confu-cianism as a catalyst for the "national studies craze" in the 1990s.

Sylvia Chan's contribution (chapter 4) on the philosopher, Li Zehou 李澤厚 (1930–), is the most controversial inclusion in this volume because Li is not conventionally regarded as a New Confucian, either by mainland or overseas Chinese scholars. For this reason, a more detailed justification for his inclusion is in order. Despite Li's fundamentally Marxist philosophical outlook, Chan argues that it is "in his answer to why we live that establishes his credentials as a New Confucian. His ethics and aesthetics are both concerned with inner sageliness. In both, he adopts the Confucian cardinal virtue of benevolence as the axis, and affirms the Confucian ideal of union with heaven as the ultimate standard for authentic living." Chan further argues that Li should be recognized as a New Confucian on the grounds that if New Confucianism is true to the Confucian tradition it "should not be dogmatic and sectarian, but should be broad enough to accommodate and creatively transform all the trends either already in the Confucian canon or which can be adapted to harmonize with Confucian teachings." This inclusivist approach to New Confucian identity is not inconsistent with the view of many mainland scholars of New Confucianism (as I explain in chapter 1). Indeed, even leading Taiwan-based New Confucian, Liu Shuxian, when discussing Li's claim that he (Li) could be described as a "contemporary New Confucian" (*dangdai xin Rujia*), was prepared to concede that "there is certainly no fixed interpretation of contemporary Confucianism; the one hundred flowers should all be allowed to bloom." He did, however, also point out that Li's philosophical approaches placed Li at a considerable remove from contemporary New Confucianism, "as understood in the narrow sense" of the term,[15] that is, the lineage principally associated with Xiong Shili, Mou Zongsan, and their disciples. Perhaps most telling of all is the fact that Li has been a regular contributor to the invitation-only workshops on "Topics in Contemporary Confucianism" convened by the Institute of Chinese Literature and Philosophy, Academia Sinica, in Taiwan, and has had several of his essays published in their book series. This is significant for two reasons. First, it attests to a current transition in both scholarly and partisan concerns as New Confucianism increasingly yields to the broader category of contemporary Confucianism. Second, it underscores the importance of the still emerging role played by syncretistic thinkers such as Li, in this period of transition and "creative transformation."

Even though the focus of this volume is retrospective, another reason warranting Li's inclusion is that he is an example of the prospective dimension of New Confucianism—an example of one possible direction that New Confucianism might take as it is increasingly subsumed by and merged within the broader phenomenon of "contemporary Confucianism." In Li's particular case, this creative transformation takes the form of a Marxist–Confucian synthesis. Although there are inevitable and unresolved tensions between his Confucianism and his Marxism, as Sylvia Chan points out, "Marxism has shaped the mode of thinking of many people in mainland China, and a number of Marxist principles are still accepted by them. Li's synthesis may thus help to bridge the two thought systems, and promote understanding and acceptance of Confucianism among mainland Chinese. Although, as I have contended, he has not been completely successful in this respect, it is a commendable pioneering attempt. . . . Li therefore can play an important role to win a following for New Confucianism in mainland China, which will be critical to the success of the global project of New Confucianism."

There are also some superficial resemblances between Li and Lin Anwu—another "transitional" New Confucian thinker (discussed in chapter 2)—such as the latter's characterization of "Post New Confucianism" as being a move away from "learning of the mind and the nature" (*xin xing lun*) to a "philosophical anthropology" (*zhexue renleixue*). The choice of the term "anthropology," in particular, recalls Li's description of his own philosophy as an ontological theory of anthropology (*renleixue bentilun* 人類學本體論), and more recently, an ontological theory of historical anthropology (*renleixue lishi bentilun* 人類歷史學本體論). Similarly, Lin's use of the term "Post New Confucian" echoes Li's description of his own philosophy as "Post Marxist." Their common concerns over alienation and the embrace of certain motifs associated with postmodernity are additional elements of resemblance.

Li also shares a number of commonalities with earlier New Confucians, such as his embrace of the philosophy of change and activity that is found in the cosmology of the *Book of Changes*. This is a "New Confucian" trait that goes back to Xiong Shili. As with Mou Zongsan, he owed much to Kant.[16] In his own ethical theory, Li tries to synthesize Confucian and Kantian ethics. Where he parts company with some of the more representative New Confucian figures—even as he extends the conversation, and the opportunities for critical self-reflection, by engaging them in critical dialogue—is his argument that New Confucianism in the twentieth and twenty-first centuries should be regarded as the fourth period in the development of Confucianism, rather than its third period, as claimed by Mou Zongsan and his disciples. As with other problematic "New Confucians"—Yu Yingshi and Qian Mu—Li is critical of the *daotong* concept (the subject of chapter 2).

Serina Chan's, "What is Confucian and New about the Thought of Mou Zongsan?" (chapter 5) examines one of the twentieth century's most important Chinese philosophers, Mou Zongsan (1909–95). Although widely recognized and even revered in Hong Kong and Taiwan since at least the 1960s, Mou's importance as a thinker really only came to the attention of mainland scholars in the late 1980s. In the West he still remains largely ignored and unheard of. Although only one chapter in this book is devoted to Mou, his name appears in many other chapters. This is because Mou is central to the very notion of what New Confucianism is. Indeed, one might well argue that without Mou there would be no New Confucian movement.

Chapter 5 provides a comprehensive, accessible, and timely introduction to the man and his thought. Serina Chan first analyzes the
theoretical framework of Mou's philosophical thought, and then argues
the case for recognizing Mou's philosophical system to be Confucian,
despite its liberal appropriation of Buddhist paradigms and Kantian
terminology. The final part of her chapter examines what is new about
Mou's thought. Like the Song Neo-Confucian philosopher, Zhu Xi
(1130–1200), Mou was a grand synthesizer. This synthesis extends
from the incorporation of key conceptual distinctions derived from
Xiong Shili's (1885–1968) writings, such as the *ti–yong* (structure–
application) polarity, to the broader tradition of Confucian thought itself,
as well as to elements of philosophical Daoist thought and Buddhism.
Perhaps most significantly, this syncreticism also extended to Mou's
attempt to merge themes in Immanuel Kant's (1724–1804) moral philosophy with his own metaphysical and moral thought system. Mou had
great respect for Kant, describing him as the only Western philosopher
who had a true understanding of the nature of morality. (This is particularly significant, as the impetus for Mou's philosophical project was
strongly motivated by his conviction that the West had come to place too
little store in morality as it became dominated by the positivist directions
being pursued in philosophy and science. Mou saw Chinese philosophical
values, especially the moral metaphysics of Mencius and certain Neo-
Confucian thinkers, as being able to provide a remedy for this imbalance.)
He translated Kant's major works into Chinese and worked hard at
extending Kant's moral philosophy and reconciling it with his own. As
Chan shows, the "fruit of this labor was the enhancement of the contemporary, philosophical status of his thought system and the establishment of
a potential bridge between Chinese philosophy and Western philosophy."

Chan singles out two of the concepts that Mou appropriated from
Chinese Buddhist thought as being particularly important: the "two-
tier mind" paradigm and the "perfect teaching" paradigm. She shows
how Mou believed that the two-tier mind paradigm under-girded a
Chinese philosophical premise common to Confucianism, Daoism, and
Buddhism: the unity of the transcendent and the immanent. According to
Mou, this paradigm represents the most fundamental difference between
Chinese and Western cultures. (Chan shows that even though Mou
affirms Kant's understanding of morality, he draws a sharp contrast
between Kant's understanding of the human mind and the two-tier mind
paradigm that is fundamental to his own thought system.)

In making her case that Mou's thought was both new and Confucian,
Chan emphasizes a fundamental continuity between his moral

metaphysics and the Mencius-Lu-Wang (Lu Jiuyuan 陸九淵 [1139–93] and Wang Yangming 王陽明 [1472–1529]) tradition of Confucianism. She also identifies four new features in Mou's thought as evidence of his further development of Neo-Confucian philosophy: its syncreticism (especially in relation to Buddhism and Kant); its highly intellectual construction; its concern with China's modernization (especially scientific development and democratic forms of governance); and its promulgation of Confucianism as the teaching that would facilitate the formation of a global culture or world creed. Readers will be able to judge for themselves the extent to which this assessment begs the question of whether the combination of being a "Confucian" thinker and contributing to "new" developments in Confucian philosophy, is sufficient reason for us to regard a particular thinker as a New Confucian. While not all readers will share Chan's sanguine faith in the continuing relevance of Mou's philosophical vision, she is surely correct in her assessment that the future of the New Confucian movement rests with intellectual and cultural developments in mainland China (as opposed to its traditional home in Taiwan and Hong Kong).

Feng Youlan 馮友蘭 (1895–1990) was the twentieth century's most influential historian of Chinese philosophy.[17] His celebrated and hugely popular *Zhongguo zhexueshi* 中國哲學史 (A History of Chinese Philosophy; 1934 [English translation, 1937])[18] has decisively shaped twentieth-century understanding of Chinese philosophy, particularly in the West. Feng was also a philosopher and original thinker in his own right. One of the most intensely debated issues in New Confucian studies is whether Feng Youlan should be identified as a New Confucian. To this day there is still no consensus. Even among mainland scholars of New Confucianism, there is no consensus, although the rationale for not wishing to deny New Confucian status to Feng Youlan is clear. As I argue in chapter 1, "Should major figures such as Feng Youlan and He Lin be excluded from the New Confucian pantheon, the proprietary rights of mainland scholars over the interpretation and definition of New Confucianism—past, present, and future—would be severely diminished. Conversely, the proprietary rights of a significant number of overseas Chinese scholars (buoyed by their connections with Mou Zongsan, Tang Tang Junyi 唐君毅 [1909–78], and Xu Fuguan 徐復觀 [1903–82], in particular) would become greatly enhanced. A fundamental and, as yet, unresolved tension and rivalry is the consequence." The issue is further complicated by the fact that individual scholars have not been consistent in their evaluations of Feng. Leading mainland scholar of New Confucianism, Zheng Jiadong, is a prominent example. In chapter 6, "A Modern Chinese Philosophy Built upon Critically Received Traditions: Feng Youlan's New Principle-Centered Learning and the Question of Its Relationship to Contemporary New Ruist ('Confucian') Philosophies," Lauren Pfister describes how even in Zheng's most recent book *Duanlie zhong de chuantong: Xinnian yu lixiang zhi jian* (Splintering Traditions: Between Commitment and Rationality; 2001), on the one hand, Zheng is prepared to identify Feng as a New Confucian, yet, on the other hand, Zheng's own notion of the "splintering of traditions" underscores just how questionable that identification really is. Pfister argues against identifying Feng Youlan as a New Confucian thinker. He shows that the conservative orientation of the New Confucians is fundamentally at odds with the "forward-looking" orientation of Feng's *lixue* (New Principle-Centered Learning), as set out in Feng's *Zhen yuan liu shu* (Purity Descends, Primacy Ascends: Six Books). He further contrasts the second generation New Confucians' (Mou Zongsan, Tang Junyi *et al.*) call to "revive" Song and Ming Confucian philosophical traditions with Feng Youlan's qualified "critical reception" of those same traditions. Pfister's understanding of the "New Confucian" (or in his terms, the "New Ruist" position), is based principally on the evidence of the 1958 Declaration. Whether the 1958 Declaration should be regarded as a New Confucian document, let alone manifesto, is a moot point, but to the extent that this document is widely identified with a new Confucian "school," Pfister convincingly shows that Feng does not belong there. Instead, he proposes that it is more appropriate to regard Feng as a representative philosopher of the "new traditionalist" phase of Chinese philosophical discussions in the twentieth century.

Since the 1970s, Liang Shuming 梁漱溟(1893–1998) and Xiong Shili have become widely recognized as first generation New Confucians and the founders of the New Confucian movement. Liang Shuming's 1922 publication, *Dong-xi wenhua ji qi zhexue* (Eastern and Western Cultures and Their Philosophies) is often described as being the first New Confucian text.[19] The metaphysical and epistemological thinking that both men subscribed to was substantially influenced by Buddhist thought. It is the role of Buddhist thought in the philosophical frameworks of these two men that is the subject of part 4. At what point does "influence" become a defining feature of a philosophical orientation? At what point is it more meaningful to describe these thinkers as Buddhist rather than as Confucian? In chapter 5 on Mou Zongsan, Serina Chan argues that despite Mou's liberal appropriation of Buddhist paradigms, these paradigms are subsumed within a broader Confucian framework. Chapter 7 by John Hanafin on Liang Shuming, argues that Liang should be regarded as a Buddhist rather than as a Confucian, hence the title, "The Last Buddhist: The Philosophy of Liang Shuming." This title should not be taken too literally, as it is a playful allusion to the title of Guy Alitto's influential study, *The Last Confucian: Liang Shu-ming and the Chinese Dilemma of Modernity*.[20] Hanafin sets himself the task of developing an alternative portrayal of Liang, and asks "whether it is more valid to categorize the spirit, views, and philosophy of Liang Shuming as Buddhist rather than as Confucian or New Confucian."

Liang came to prominence as a lay Buddhist scholar before publicly committing himself to Confucianism in 1921. The publication of his lectures on the theme of "Eastern and Western Cultures and Their Philosophies" the following year, cemented his standing as a public intellectual of national stature. The book continues to be studied today. He also became well known for his writings on, and active promotion of, rural reconstruction. While acknowledging a variety of influences in Liang's writings, Hanafin describes Liang as having "developed his fundamentally Yogācārin metaphysical and epistemological positions with the aid of Bergson's and Schopenhauer's philosophies, while at the same time looking for corresponding themes in Confucian philosophy to support his position." Drawing on the evidence of Liang's *Yindu zhexue gailun* (An Outline of Indian Philosophy; 1919), *Weishi shuyi* (The Meaning of Consciousness-Only Buddhism; 1920), *Dong-xi wenhua ji qi zhexue* (Eastern and Western Cultures and Their Philosophies [1922]), and *Renxin yu rensheng* (The Human Mind and Human Life; 1984), as well as interviews conducted late in Liang's life, Hanafin presents a detailed technical analysis of Liang's metaphysical and epistemological concepts, while demonstrating that Liang's understanding of culture and society is grounded in his metaphysical and epistemological views.

After examining Liang's conflicting and changing descriptions of himself as variously a Buddhist or a Confucian, Hanafin concludes that Liang did not relinquish his personal commitment to Buddhism (being "Buddhist in spirit") even though his philosophy of culture argued for the relative merits of Confucianism (and later Marxism) for Chinese culture at its particular stage of development. Hanafin maintains that even this concession to Confucianism was, in fact, an expression of a social concern that was grounded in Liang's Buddhist beliefs. Moreover, he argues, Liang actually believed that China's ultimate future lay in the realization of a Buddhist, rather than a Confucian, cultural ideal. He shows how Liang's views on consciousness, attachment, and the self are drawn from Consciousness-Only theory and how Liang integrated his metaphysical view of life and the self with his theory of the three stages or paths of cultural development (Indian, Western, and Chinese). Hanafin also argues that Liang similarly employed the concept of ethical reason (*lixing*)—which Liang contrasted with the intellect (*lizhi*)—to rationalize this same theory of cultural development.

As Hanafin's thesis is presented as polemic, the question of the role of Confucian elements in Liang's thought should not be ignored: the influence of Wang Gen 王艮 (1483–1540), the *Book of Changes*' philosophy of change, and elements of Wang Yangming's philosophy of mind (*xin*) and intuitive knowledge (*liangzhi*). It is one matter to claim that Liang focused on particular Confucian themes principally from the perspective of their relevance to his overall *Weishi* metaphysical and epistemological positions: "For instance, his concept of 'intuition' developed over the years from the *Weishi* notion of *feiliang*, through the Bergsonian concept of intuition, the incorporation of the Confucian notions of *ren* (benevolence), *liang zhi* (ethical knowledge), *liang xin* (ethical conscience), to *lixing* (intuition as ethical reason)." The devil's advocate, however, might retort that the transformation of this concept is evidence of a growing Confucian (Wang Yangming) influence on Liang's thought.[21] Alternatively, rather than polarize the issue by insisting on a rigid Confucian/Buddhist dichotomy, is such a blunt instrument as school affiliation the most appropriate framework to apply to a genuinely syncretistic thinker? For example, might not such observations as "Liang found a parallel to the *Weishi* notion of *citta* (mind) and *cittamātra* (mind only) in Wang Yangming's philosophy of *xin* (mind)," be better regarded as evidence of Liang's attempt to appropriate elements from different traditions to contribute to new philosophical directions? However one stands on this particular issue, the strength of Hanafin's interpretation is that by showing consistent links between Liang's theory of cultural development and his metaphysics and epistemology, Hanafin is able to argue the case for the fundamental *Weishi* orientation of Liang's thought.

Of all the contributors to this volume, only Ng Ru-kwan warrants the distinction of being deemed a New Confucian (although he may not regard himself as such), if by that term we mean someone who studied under the one or more representative New Confucians, and who is sympathetic to New Confucian philosophy. Ng is a former student of both Tang Junyi and Mou Zongsan, and his essay, chapter 8 in this volume, on Xiong Shili confirms a clear sympathy with New Confucian philosophical themes (albeit tempered with a similar keen appreciation of Buddhist philosophy). Indeed, Ng finds Xiong to have been a philosopher of such originality and importance that he is prepared to give the following assessment: "Whether judged in terms of depth and comprehensiveness in content or in term of its theoretical vigor, Xiong's philosophical achievements are great, and can be compared with those of Western philosophers such as Aristotle, Leibnitz, Husserl, Heidegger, and Whitehead. In Chinese philosophy, his scope is on par with that of Zhu Xi 朱熹 (1130–1200) and Wang Fuzhi." Ng starts from the premise that the notion of a New Confucian school is unproblematic. What he wants to affirm is the seminal role of Xiong in this school. He does this by appealing to Xiong's place in the *daotong*: "he was the first Confucian after Wang Yangming 王陽明 (1472–1529) to inherit and promote moral spirituality in general, and moral metaphysics in particular"; and by reiterating the fact that Tang Junyi, Mou Zongsan, and Xu Fuguan were all Xiong's disciples. Most significant, however, is his evaluation of Xiong's theory about the non-separability of substance and function: "This philosophy of the non-separability of substance and function is the foundation of New Confucianism."

As with Liang Shuming, Vijñāna-vāda or Yogācāra Buddhism had a profound influence on Xiong Shili, the other "founder" of New Confucianism.[22] Within two years, the largely self-taught Xiong was appointed to a lecturing position at Beijing University giving lectures on Vijñāna-vāda. For most of the next decade, however, he taught his own system of philosophy, "The New Theory of Consciousness-Only." This is also the name of his most representative and influential philosophical writing. He continued publishing philosophical works up until the early 1960s. Opinions differ as to the extent to which his philosophical orientation changed after 1949.

Whereas John Hanafin argues that Liang Shuming should be regarded as a Buddhist rather than as a Confucian, in chapter 7 on Xiong Shili, Ng Ru-kwan shows that despite appropriating important elements from Vijñāna-vāda philosophy, Xiong went on to develop these into his own Confucian onto-cosmology (*bentiyuzhoulun* 本體宇宙論), "a metaphysics in which the ontological substance transforms and permeates all things so that the ontological substance and phenomena are coherent." Ng describes Xiong's onto-cosmology as having been inspired by both Confucian and Buddhist teachings: "On the one hand, he was deeply impressed by *The Book of Changes* which claims that the universe is perpetually and vigorously changing. On the other hand, he also absorbed the Buddhist idea of quiescence. As a result, he formulated the metaphysical doctrine of an ontological substance, which is both active and quiescent." By and large, however, it would seem that it was in reaction to the notion of a quiescent and unchanging substance (which Xiong associates with certain fundamental Buddhist teachings) that spurred his embrace of the philosophy of change and process he found in the *Book of Changes*. Most important, for Xiong, substance is constantly creating and changing.

The title of Ng's chapter, "Xiong Shili's Metaphysical Theory about the Non-Separability of Substance and Function," reflects the central importance of the pair of polar concepts, *ti* and *yong*, in Xiong's onto-cosmology:[23] "The core of Xiong's thought is the theory of the non-separability of substance and function. Generally speaking, substance (*ti* 體) refers to the substance or essence of things, while function (*yong* 用) refers to the form or phenomenon of things achieved on the basis of the underlying substance." The *ti–yong* polarity has a long history in Chinese thought, with Wang Bi 王弼 (226–249) traditionally and conventionally being credited with the pairing of these two concepts.[24] Since the 1980s, as New Confucianism has taken on a genuine school identity, and as generations of intellectual and "spiritual" genealogies have been identified within the New Confucian ranks, Xiong's formulation of the *ti–yong* polarity has come to be problematized in terms of immanence and transcendence. As Serina Chan has pointed out in chapter 5, it was Mou Zongsan who claimed to have identified an important theme underlying the three main traditions of Chinese thought (Confucianism, Daoism, and Buddhism): "the unity of the transcendent (objective heaven) and the immanent (the subjective true mind of human beings). This theme represents, in his opinion, the most fundamental difference between Chinese culture and Western culture." This notion of the unity of the transcendent and the immanent, or "immanent transcendence," has become a focal point in theoretical debates between a number of third and fourth generation New Confucians and their critics. Now, although Xiong emphasized the immanence of *ti*—it did not exist apart from or outside of phenomenal entities or *yong*—he did not analyze his theory of the non-separability of *ti–yong* in terms of immanence and transcendence. Despite this, Xiong and Mou are widely understood to have contributed to a common philosophical discourse on "immanent transcendence." Debate on this topic has been messy, due to commentators employing different senses of the term "transcendence."[25]

The particular strengths of Ng Ru-kwan's contribution are threefold. First, employing his expert understanding of Buddhist philosophy, he has provided the most thorough and authoritative theoretical analysis of Xiong's version of the *ti–yong* polarity yet undertaken. Second, by emphasizing the mutual entailment requirement in Xiong's *ti–yong* formulation, he succeeds in removing any suspicion that Xiong was, in fact, promoting some explicit or implicit notion of a dualism, as we find in such classical Western formulations as Plato's theory of Forms. Third, for my purposes at least, by drawing attention to the emphasis that Xiong placed on *yong* relative to *ti*, he highlights an emphasis that is not shared with other New Confucian thinkers.

The Future

The four parts of the book are structured on a reverse chronology, proceeding from the 1990s to the 1920s. While some references have been made to developments from 1996–2002, by and large they fall beyond the main scope of enquiry. One of the principal reasons for not dealing with the post-1996 period in more detail is that since the early to mid-1990s, the conservative goals of the New Confucians have come to be bypassed by a broader range of attempts to develop syncretistic forms of modernized Confucian thought through dialogue and engagement with other traditions and ideologies: Confucianism and Western philosophy, Confucianism and various world religions, Confucianism and Marxism, Confucianism and capitalism, Confucianism and democracy, liberalism, and human rights. These are all new domains of intellectual activity. What is now required is an understanding of the larger phenomenon of the intellectual construction of Confucianism in contemporary "cultural China." The field of modern Confucian intellectual history still lacks a critical overview and comprehensive analysis of discourse on Confucianism. Studying the nature and role of discourse on Confucianism over the last two decades would enable us to understand the processes by which intellectuals have sought to rejuvenate Confucianism in order to make it a viable philosophical and cultural resource in the modern world, and to evaluate how successful they have been in achieving these goals. Only by studying the processes—the debates, discussions, and other forms of communication—that contemporary Chinese intellectuals have employed to talk about "Confucianism" can the discourse defining this subject be isolated as an object of study. Questions that warrant our attention include: "What has been the nature of the on-going process of intellectual cross-fertilization between scholars in China and overseas Chinese scholars that has been made possible by the shared discourse of Confucianism?" "To what extent has this discourse transcended geographical and political boundaries to bridge cultural and ideological divisions separating mainland and overseas Chinese scholars?" "What have been the roles played by various institutional contexts in facilitating and shaping this process?" "Why do so many Chinese intellectuals

equate 'Confucianism' with Chinese cultural identity and cultural continuity, and what is the significance of this against the backdrop of
globalization?" "What are the differing ways in which nationalist
ideologies ("nativism/localism" [*bentuhua*]) have shaped discourse on
Confucianism in China and Taiwan respectively?" "How are modern
representations of Confucian thought and values being deployed to
promote, resist, and modify new trends of thought (especially trends in
Western thought)?" "Does the Confucian revival of the 1990s in China
and Taiwan represent the beginnings of a genuine philosophical renaissance or is this resurgence in interest better explained by appeal to a
range of political and cultural factors?" "If we are witnessing a genuine
philosophical renaissance, then what new (or rejuvenated) philosophical resources does Confucianism now have as a consequence of this
extended period of 'creative transformation?' "[26]

Notes

1. Nathan Sivin, foreword to Benjamin Elman, *From Philosophy to Philology:
   Intellectual and Social Aspects of Change in Late Imperial China*, Cambridge,
   M.A.: Harvard East Asia Monograph Series, 1984, xiii.
2. Lionel Jensen, *Manufacturing Confucianism*, Durham and London: Duke
   University Press, 1997, 79.
3. In her new book (Michael Nylan, *The Five "Confucian" Classics*, New
   Haven and London: Yale University Press, 2001) Michael Nylan reserves
   use of the term "Confucianism" for "two fictive constructs implying a
   single orthodox synthesis." The first "was devised by several groups in the
   nineteenth century . . . it purported to encompass the entire semantic field
   registered by a complex of Chinese terms referring to sorts of people and
   ideas including Ru (classicists): Rujia (classical affiliation), Rujiao (classical
   teachings), Ruxue (classical learning)." Nylan associates the second
   construct ("no less fictive and probably even more reductionist") with "four
   successive political movements of the twentieth century: the May Fourth
   movement, the New Life movement, the anti-Confucius campaign, and the
   New Confucian Revival, all of which have praised or excoriated Confucius as
   symbol of an Asia-specific religious ethos" (366). See especially chapter 7.
4. Joseph Levenson, *Confucian China and Its Modern Fate: A Trilogy*, Berkeley:
   University of California Press, 1968; Mark Elvin, "The Collapse of Scriptural
   Confucianism," *Papers on Far Eastern History* 41(1990): 45–76.
5. Ironically, the largest popular resurgence of interest in Confucius and his
   teachings in China was in 1973–4 during the anti-Confucius movement.
   See Kam Louie, *Critiques of Confucius in Contemporary China*, New York:
   St. Martin's Press, 1980. •
6. Mark Elvin, "The Collapse of Scriptural Confucianism," 45, defines scriptural Confucianism as "the system of meanings, values, and explanations of

the place of human life in the universe that was based on the Classics, and closely related sources such as Mencius, as privileged repositories of truth." More recently, a younger generation of Western scholars has been critical of such definitions of Confucianism, arguing that they continue to per-petuate a fictive construct.

7. A number of Taiwan-affiliated scholars use the terms *dangdai xin Rujia* and *dangdai xin Ruxue* in the sense of "modern Neo-Confucians" and "modern Neo-Confucianism" to emphasize a continuity or connection with certain Song and Ming Confucian ("Neo-Confucian") thinkers and their thought. Mainland scholars tend to use the terms *xiandai xin Ruxue* or *xiandai xin Rujia* with an emphasis on the modern (post–May Fourth) mani-festation of Confucian philosophical thought. In New Confucian scholarship the terms *Rujia* and *Ruxue* can often be translated as "Confucianism." *Rujia* can also be translated as "Confucian" (either in the sense of "Mou Zongsan was a Confucian thinker" or in the sense of "Confucian ideas"), depending on the context. It should be noted that at different periods in Chinese history, the semantic field of the terms *Rujia* and *Ruxue* varied.

8. Fang Keli, "Guanyu xiandai xin Rujia yanjiu de jige wenti 關於現代新儒家研究的幾個問題" (Several Issues Concerning New Confucian Studies; 1987), in Fang Keli and Li Jinquan 李錦全 (eds.), *Xiandai xin Ruxue yanjiu lunji* 現代新儒學研究論集 (Collected Essays on New Confucian Studies), vol. 1, Beijing: Zhongguo shehui kexue chubanshe, 1989, 7.

9. Zheng Jiadong, "Rujia yu xin Rujia de mingyun 儒家與新儒家的命運" (The Fate of Confucians and New Confucians), *Zhexue yanjiu* (1989.3): 14.

10. Luo Yijun, "Jin shiyu nian dangdai xin Ruxue de yanjiu yu suowei menhu wenti 近十餘年當代新儒學的研究與所謂門戶問題" (The So-Called Problem of Factionalism in New Confucianism over the Past Ten-Plus Years), 18, paper distributed at the Second International Conference on New Confucianism, National Central Library, Taipei, 1992.

11. Umberto Bresciani, *Reinventing Confucianism: The New Confucian Movement*, Taipei: Taipei Ricci Institute, 2001. Bresciani's book is a comprehensive and well-informed account of the New Confucianism. Its purpose—to present a sympathetic survey of the movement from the 1920s to the present—is quite different from the more narrowly focused critical examination undertaken in our volume. For studies of some individual New Confucians, see Chung-ying Cheng and Nicholas Bunnin (eds.), *Contemporary Chinese Philosophy*, Oxford: Blackwell Publishing, 2002. The "classic" account of the movement is given in Hao Chang, "New Confucianism and the Intellectual Crisis of Contemporary China," in Charlotte Furth (ed.), *The Limits of Change: Essays on Conservative Alternatives in Republican China*, Cambridge, M.A.: Harvard University Press, 1976. Arif Dirlik has written an engaging critique of the movement in the late 1980s and early 1990s: "Confucius in the Borderlands: Global Capitalism and the Reinvention of Confucianism," *boundary* 2, 22.3(1995): 229–73. Other more general accounts include, John H. Berthrong, *Transformations of the Confucian Way*, Boulder: Westview Press, 1988, 183–200; Xinzhong

Yao, *An Introduction to Confucianism*, Cambridge: Cambridge University Press, 2000, 251–86; Liu Shu-hsien, "Postwar Neo-Confucian Philosophy: Its Development and Issues," in Charles Wei-hsün Fu and Gerhard E. Spiegler (eds.), *Religious Issues and Inter-Religious Dialogues: An Analysis and Sourcebook of Developments Since 1945*, New York: Greenwood Press, 1989.

12. From Mou's own perspective, his aim was less to synthesize than to elucidate Mencius' understanding of the mind and the nature, and to recast the Lu-Wang (Lu Jiuyuan 陸九淵 [1139–92] and Wang Yangming 王陽明 [1472–1529]) tradition of Neo-Confucian thought using Buddhist paradigms and Buddhist and Kantian terminology. Mou would argue that he was a transmitter of Confucian thought even though the transmission entailed significant repackaging. Thus, he argued that Zhu Xi was not a true transmitter of Mencian thought.

13. Michael Nylan has recently made the same point in relation to claims concerning "transnational Confucian values and institutions": "Despite the exaggerated claims made for the East Asian states' distinctive Confucian heritage, claims based on the persistence in everyday life of practices and beliefs associated with the old imperial state and society, this Confucian Revival was largely an artificial rhetorical construct, and Confucianism a foreign product to be marketed or copied for local consumption." See Michael Nylan, *The Five "Confucian" Classics*, 335, 336.

14. Chun-chieh Huang (=Huang Junjie 黃俊傑), "Confucianism in Postwar Taiwan," *Proceedings of the National Science Council, ROC. Part C: Humanities and Social Sciences*, vol. 2, no. 2, 1992, 218–19.

15. See Liu Shuxian 劉述先, "Rujia yu xiandai shijie guoji yantaohui jianshu 儒家與現代世界國際研討會簡述" (Brief Report on the International Symposium on Confucianism and the Modern World), included as an appendix in Li Minghui 李明輝 (ed.), *Rujia sixiang de xiandai quanshi* 儒家思想的現代詮釋 (Contemporary Interpretations of Confucian Thought), Taipei: Zhongguo wenzhe yanjiusuo choubeichu, Zhongyang yanjiuyuan, 1997, 274.

16. As Roger T. Ames has pointed out, however, Mou Zongsan and Li Zehou have been "attempting to promote a 'new Confucianism' fortified by the prestige and rigor of Kant, while at the same time resisting the cultural imperialism entailed by taking Kant on his own terms," thereby contributing to Chinese philosophy "as a real alternative to dominant Western sensibilities." See Roger T. Ames, "New Confucianism: A Native Response to Western Philosophy," in Shiping Hua (ed.), *Chinese Political Culture, 1989–2000*, Armonk: M.E. Sharpe, 2001, 94.

17. For an autobiographical introduction to Feng, see Feng Youlan, *The Hall of Three Pines: An Account of My Life*, trans. Denis C. Mair, Honolulu: University of Hawaii Press, 2000.

18. Feng Youlan, *Zhongguo zhexueshi* 中國哲學史, Shanghai: Shangwu yinshuguan, 1934, 800. Bodde's translation, *A History of Chinese Philosophy*, was first published in Beijing, by Henri Veitch, in 1937. The two-volume Columbia edition (1952–53) has been reprinted many times.

19. For a recent in-depth analysis of this book (with copious passages of translation), see Zbigniew Wesolowski, *Lebens-und Kulturbegriff von Liang Shuming (1893–1988). Dargestellt anhand seines Werkes Dong-Xi wenhua ji qi zhexue*, Monumenta Serica Monograph Series, vol. XXXVIII, Nettetal: Steyler Verlag, 1997. My thanks to John Jorgensen for this and a number of Liang-related references, and also for clarifying a number of matters relating to Buddhist scholarship.

20. Guy Alitto, *The Last Confucian: Liang Shu-ming and the Chinese Dilemma of Modernity*, Berkeley: University of California Press, 1979.

21. Yanming An, for example, in his article "Liang Shuming and Henri Bergson on Intuition: Cultural Context and the Evolution of Terms," *Philosophy East and West* 47.3(1997): 357, concludes that Liang's placement of *lixing* (ethical reason) in the "dominant position" vis-à-vis *lizhi* (intellect) "proves once again that Confucianism is still a fundamental element in Liang's later thought."

22. In fact, it was through the introduction of Liang that Xiong came to study under the Buddhist layman, Ouyang Jian 歐陽漸 (1871–1944)—also known by his Buddhist style, Jingwu 竟無—at the Chinese Academy for the Study of Buddhism (Zhina Neixueyuan 支那內學院) in Nanjing in 1922.

23. *Ti* and *yong* are conventionally translated as substance and function. Unfortunately this sometimes leads to certain infelicitous Aristotelian associations being read into the concept of *ti*. An alternative that avoids this problem is structure–application.

24. Nevertheless, the conventional view that the *ti–yong* model was Wang's invention is open to question. Even if it was Wang who first used *ti* and *yong* as a pair of terms in *Laozi* 38 (and even he did not use the pair as a compound), there is little doubt that the relationship expressed by the terms was not first formulated by him. Late Han thinkers had already employed near-identical terminology to *ti* and *yong* to express the same relationship that Wang Bi later expressed with *ti* and *yong* (albeit without the same metaphysical application). Thus, in his preface to *Liji*, Zheng Xuan 鄭玄 (127–200) writes: "Ritual is both *ti* and *lü* 履. Where it is integrated in one's heart, this is known as *ti* (structure); where it is practiced and put in to action, this is known as *lü* (application)." Quoted by Kong Yingda 孔穎達 (574–684) in his preface to *Liji zhengyi* 禮記正義 (The Correct Meaning of the Book of Rites), 9a, *Shisanjing zhushu* edition, Taipei: Yiwen yinshuguan, 1985. Moreover, if *Zhouyi cantong qi* 周易參同契 (Token for the Agreement of the Three According to the Zhou Book of Changes), attributed to Wei Boyang 魏伯陽 (late second century, A.D.), is a genuine late second, early third-century work, then the use of the terms, "inner structure" (*nei ti* 內體) and "external application" (*wai yong* 外用), in the first *zhang* of that work, would certainly predate Wang Bi's use.

25. See Robert Cummings Neville, *Boston Confucianism: Portable Tradition in the Late-Modern World*, Albany: SUNY Press, 2000, chapter 8, in which he provides instructive examples of some of the different senses of the term "transcendence." He also identifies some of the problems with David

L. Hall and Roger T. Ames' influential thesis that there is no transcendence in classical Confucian thought. See David L. Hall and Roger T. Ames, *Thinking Through Confucius*, Albany: SUNY Press, 1987, 12–17. See also their criticism of Mou Zongsan's characterization of the concepts of *tian* (heaven) and *tian ming* (what is ordained by heaven) as transcendent. For a criticism of the notion of "immanent transcendence" and an argument that Mou really understood such concepts as *tian* and *tian ming* to be ineffable (due to their non-empirical nature) rather than as real entities, see Feng Yaoming 馮耀明, "Dangdai xin Rujia de chaoyue neizai shuo 當代新儒家的超越內在說" (Theories of Immanent Transcendence in New Confucianism), *Dangdai* 4.1(1993): 99–102. For further criticisms of Hall and Ames' claims about transcendence and a defence of Mou's use of the term, see Li Minghui 李明輝, "Rujia sixiang zhong de neizaixing yu chaoyuexing 儒家思想中的內在性與超越性" (Immanence and Transcendence in Confucian Thought) in *Dangdai Ruxue zhi ziwo zhuanhua* 當代儒學之自我轉化 (The Subjective Turn in New Confucianism), Taipei: Zhongyang yanjiuyuan, Zhongguo wenzhe yanjiusuo, 1994, 129–48.

26. Chung-ying Cheng's "onto-hermeneutics" is one example of such new philosophical approaches. For a recent application of Cheng's onto-hermeneutics, see his "An Onto-Hermeneutic Interpretation of Twentieth-Century Chinese Philosophy: Identity and Vision," in Chung-ying Cheng and Nicholas Bunnin (eds.), *Contemporary Chinese Philosophy*, 365–404.

Part I

CHAPTER 1
THE RETROSPECTIVE CREATION
OF NEW CONFUCIANISM[1]

John Makeham

Although most of the promoters and sympathetic interpreters of New
Confucianism trace the movement to the early part of the twentieth
century, in fact there is little evidence that New Confucianism had
attained a degree of integration or coalescence sufficient for it to be
recognized and promoted as a distinct philosophical movement or
school of thought before the 1970s. Crucially, up until that time, the
"New Confucians" did not have a sense of group identity that distinguished them from other Confucian-inspired thinkers. I will argue that
a differentiation needs to be made between Confucian revivalism—a
conservative cultural phenomenon that has taken on a variety of forms
throughout the twentieth century—and a distinct philosophical
movement with its own self-identity, which promoted itself as, and
became identified as, New Confucianism. I will further argue, against
the conventional view, that this latter development did not occur until
the early 1980s. Over the next decade, the movement matured rapidly.
I will begin by examining the genesis and early uses of the term *xin
Rujia*. It was Feng Youlan 馮友蘭 (1895–1990)—himself later identified as an early New Confucian—who seems to have been the earliest
twentieth-century figure to use the term *xin Rujia*. Thus, in his famous
Zhongguo zhexueshi 中國哲學史 (A History of Chinese Philosophy;
1934) he used it to refer to Song and Ming dynasty *daoxue* 道學
(learning of the way) philosophy or the Cheng-Zhu (Cheng Yi 程頤
[1033–1107] and Zhu Xi [1130–1200]) tradition of "Neo-
Confucianism"[2] as it has become more widely known in the West
(following Derk Bodde's 1937 English translation of Feng's famous
book).[3] In his 1941 essay, "Rujia sixiang zhi kaizhan 儒家思想之開展"

(The New Unfolding of Confucian Thought),[4] He Lin 賀麟 (1902–93) also used the term *xin Rujia*. Unlike Feng, he used it to refer to a new form of Confucianism, not the *daoxue* Confucianism of the Song and Ming periods. He does not, however, employ the term with reference to specific thinkers or to an actual historical movement, but to an amorphous and yet to be realized goal. This goal was also predicated on a thorough understanding of Western culture.[5]

In his widely cited 1976 essay, "New Confucianism and the Intellectual Crisis of Contemporary China," Hao Chang (Zhang Hao 張灝) explains that *xin Rujia* (New Confucianism) is the popular term for a "brand of Chinese conservatism" that can be traced to the May Fourth period, and which since 1949 was associated particularly with "four prominent intellectuals outside Communist China": Zhang Junmai 張君勱 (Carsun Chang, 1887–1969), Mou Zongsan 牟宗三 (1909–95), Tang Junyi 唐君毅 (1909–78), and Xu Fuguan 徐復觀 (1903–82).[6] In personal correspondence, Professor Chang informed me that:

> Regarding the origin of the term "New Confucianism," I am afraid there is perhaps very little I can tell you. As I recalled, I coined the term out of a practical necessity to distinguish the twentieth-century Confucian thinkers from the Sung-Ming Neo-Confucian scholars when I wrote my article in the *Limits of Change* some twenty-five years ago. At the time, I had no convention to follow and knew of no other scholar who used the term. But that doesn't mean there is no possibility that others might have used the term before me. This is a factual question I have neglected to find out about to this day. This is all I know regarding the issue.[7]

Professor Chang is, of course, referring to the English rendering of *xin Rujia* as "New Confucian." As his 1976 article makes plain, the Chinese term, *xin Rujia*, had already been in popular circulation for some time. Writing in 1980, the Taiwanese scholar, Cai Renhou 蔡仁厚, similarly maintains that the term *dangdai de xin Rujia* had been used during the previous twenty or thirty years, by scholars generally, to refer to those scholars based in Hong Kong and Taiwan who promoted Confucian scholarship.[8]

It is perhaps impossible to determine just when the term *xin Rujia* (or one of its variants) was first used to refer specifically to those who today are widely recognized as New Confucians. Nevertheless, mainland scholar, Luo Yijun, has shown that the term can be traced to at least 1963. He has identified the following two examples from the Hong Kong journal, *Rensheng* 人生 (Life) 229(1963). The first is an article by Li Zhen 李震, entitled "Wushi nian lai Zhongguo sixiang zhi dashi 五十年來中國思想之大勢" (The General Orientation of Chinese Thought over the Past Fifty Years) in which Li specifically identifies Xiong Shili 熊十力 (1885–1968), Qian Mu 錢穆 (1895–1990), Tang Junyi, and Mou Zongsan as promoters of "New Confucian (*xin Rujia*) philosophy." The second article, by Gu Yiqun 顧翊群, entitled "Lun Rujia sixiang zhi fuxing 論儒家思想之復興" (On the Revival of Confucian Thought) identifies the following authors as being of relevance to people interested in modern New Confucian (*xiandai xin Rujia*) philosophy: "Zhang Junmai, Qian Mu, Tang Junyi, Mou Zongsan, Xu Fuguan, Xie Youwei 謝幼偉, and others." Although neither Li nor Gu elaborated on the characteristics of New Confucian philosophy, this seems to be the earliest evidence we have of Zhang, Qian, Tang, Mou, and Xu being grouped under the "New Confucian" rubric.

The significance of this event, however, needs to be tempered by three other observations. First, as Luo Yijun himself notes, the influence of Li and Gu's remarks on later studies of New Confucian thought has been negligible. "In fact, at that time in Hong Kong, Taiwan, and overseas, study of New Confucianism had yet to develop."[9] Second, to this day, scholars have still not produced evidence from the 1950s, 1960s, or 1970s writings of Mou, Tang, Qian *et al.* in which these figures acknowledge the existence of New Confucianism as a school or a movement, nor has any scholar produced evidence confirming that these influential figures, either individually or collectively, identified themselves with such a school or movement. Third, Li's and Gu's use of the term New Confucian is limited to those who had achieved prominence in the 1950s and 1960s. No attempt is made to link them or the concept of New Confucian with earlier figures. As Shimada Kenji 島田虔次 has correctly noted, the term New Confucian was first applied to Tang, Xu, and Mou (as well as Zhang and Qian) and only later retrospectively applied to their teacher Xiong Shili, and then to Liang Shuming 梁漱溟 (1893–1998), and Feng Youlan (and others).[10]

The 1958 Declaration

With the rapid proliferation of New Confucian studies since the mid-1980s, it has virtually become an unquestioned dogma that one event in 1958 marks a watershed in the movement's development. This event is the declaration that Mou Zongsan, Tang Junyi, Xu Fuguan, and Zhang Junmai co-signed and published simultaneously in the two Hong Kong journals, *Minzhu pinglun* 民主評論 (Democratic Tribune) and *Zaisheng* 再生 (Renaissance) at the beginning of 1958: "Wei Zhongguo wenhua jinggao shijie renshi xuanyan 為中國文化敬告世界人士宣言" (Declaration on Behalf of Chinese Culture Respectfully Announced to the People of the World).[11] In its emotionally charged apologetic for traditional Chinese culture and the ethico-religious and spiritual values that the authors identify with that culture, the Declaration rejects the positivist paradigm ushered in by modernity and Westernization and demands a place for Chinese cultural values on the world stage. Indeed, it argues for the cross-cultural significance of Confucianism on a global scale. Hao Chang quite correctly describes the Declaration as "an important synopsis of a conservative trend of thought still very much alive [in 1958] among contemporary intellectuals in non-communist China."[12] For today's scholars of New Confucianism, as well as for proponents of New Confucianism, the real significance of the Declaration is perhaps less the ideological platform it outlines than the fact that it can be seen to represent a group of Confucian scholars speaking collectively, thereby lending the group a cohesion and shared identity. Whether the Declaration actually "constituted a major statement of New Confucianism" remains unclear. The fact that even a scholar as critically alert as Arif Dirlik should accept this claim without question underscores just how successful the post-1980s New Confucians have been in retrospectively creating their identity.[13] To borrow Dirlik's own words, the scholarly activity around New Confucianism is, "the foremost instance during the [1980s] of intellectual discourse creating its object."[14] My concern about the Declaration stems from the manner in which it has been retrospectively identified as a watershed in the history of New Confucianism and interpreted as a mission statement of the movement. It is problematic to define the salient characteristics of New Confucianism principally on the basis of the Declaration. The cultural conservatism espoused in the Declaration was hardly new. As Hao Chang has argued, the Declaration may be regarded as "the development of a major trend of Chinese conservatism that had its origin in the 1920s."[15] I would further argue that we need to differentiate between Confucian revivalism—a conservative cultural phenomenon that has taken a variety of forms throughout the twentieth century—and a distinct intellectual movement with its own self-identity, which promoted itself as, and became identified as, New Confucianism. The real question is at what point is it meaningful to talk of coalescence and self-identity such that the New Confucians were able to distinguish themselves collectively from other Confucians. It should also be noted that the Declaration does not make a single reference to earlier twentieth-century Confucian revivalists (including Xiong Shili and Liang Shuming).[16] The ideals it outlines for Confucianism as an ethico-spiritual and cultural mainstay are vaguely formulated aspirations and are not identified with any modern movement or school (other than "Confucianism" understood in a broad and undefined sense). Nor should we overlook the fact that the term "New Confucian" (in any of its various Chinese locutions) is not used at all.

Definitions of New Confucianism

Since at least the mid-1970s, conventional accounts of New Confucianism have generally identified Xiong Shili and Liang Shuming as its earliest representatives. During the 1980s others also came to be identified as New Confucian. Indeed, much of the mainland Chinese literature on New Confucianism published during 1986–92 was concerned with retrospectively identifying which thinkers should be classed as New Confucian, a subject I will address later in this chapter. In one of the earliest and most influential definitions of New Confucian, the Taiwan scholar, Wei Zhengtong 韋政通,[17] identifies the following seven characterizations as being common to the New Confucian identity.

- *Confucianism is accepted as the orthodoxy and main pillar of Chinese culture. As a branch or school within Confucianism, the New Confucians place a high value on xin xing zhi xue* 心性之學. (I will translate this term as "learning of the mind and the nature." It refers to theoretical discussions of the metaphysical and ontological import of the two concepts, mind and human nature.) This is one of the most critical claims made in identifying New Confucianism as a philosophical movement (as I will show in subsequent discussions). While the emphasis on "learning of the heart and the nature" is certainly in evidence in the Declaration and in the writings of key figures such as Mou Zongsan, Tang Junyi, and Xiong Shili, the same cannot be said for others such as Zhang Junmai or Ma Yifu 馬一浮 (1883–1967). Furthermore, the "learning of the mind and the nature" of philosophers such as Feng Youlan and He Lin, for example, is quite different in premises and orientation from the "learning of the mind and the nature" of, say, Xiong Shili or Mou Zongsan.
- *New Confucians regard China's historical culture as a spiritual reality (jingshen shiti* 精神實體*) and the flow of this historical culture is where this spiritual reality is manifest.* This characterization is more widely shared by figures who are conventionally identified as New

Confucians. Nevertheless, many twentieth-century cultural conservatives also shared this view. By the 1990s it is much harder to find the new generations of New Confucians openly championing this belief.

- *New Confucians affirm the notion of daotong* 道統 *(interconnecting thread of the way) as the basis for nationhood and the source of cultural transformation.* The real issue is "Whose *daotong*?" because by the late 1980s the concept had become associated with a particular lineage of New Confucians, as will be shown in chapter 2.
- *New Confucians emphasize the need to adopt a respectful and empathetic attitude to China's historical culture.* Again, hardly a unique characteristic.
- *New Confucians have a strong sense of "origin; roots (genyuan* 根源*)."* Again, this is not a uniquely defining characterization. Morever, it is far from evident that Feng Youlan's sense of origin, for example, in any way matched that of, say, Tang Junyi.
- *New Confucians evidence a keen awareness of the crisis facing Chinese culture.* Again, this characterization is not unique to New Confucians.
- *New Confucianism is rich in religious sentiment and has a strong sense of mission to rejuvenate Chinese culture.* The religious sentiment is the most interesting part of this characterization and is in particular evidence in the writings of Mou Zongsan and his disciples. Nevertheless, as a general or shared characterization, it is unconvincing.

Although this list is purportedly based on characteristics shared by Liang Shuming, Zhang Junmai, Xiong Shili, Qian Mu, Mou Zongsan, Tang Junyi, and Xu Fuguan, its contents seem to be largely inspired by the Declaration. Moreover, as I have pointed out, if we follow many mainland scholars in also recognizing Feng Youlan, He Lin, and Ma Yifu as New Confucians, then inconsistencies become apparent. Wei himself notes some exceptions to these characterizations. For example, he states that neither Liang nor Zhang attached much importance to the concept of *daotong*.[18] In the opinion of a leading mainland scholar of New Confucianism, Luo Yijun, Wei's list is adequate as a general characterization but a more essential characterization is necessary.[19] In 1998, another mainland scholar, Yan Binggang 顏炳罡, proposed the following list of more specific attributes or characterizations.[20]

- *New Confucians believe that Confucianism is the key component of traditional Chinese culture and that they are its inheritors and transmitters.* While this is true, it is also true of most Confucian revivalists, not just New Confucians.
- *New Confucians maintain that moral values constitute the core of Chinese culture. Thus, when New Confucians promote a philosophy of culture, it is the primacy of moral values—which in turn is to be explicated in terms of a "learning of the mind and the nature"—that distinguishes New Confucian philosophies of culture.* This is perhaps closer to the mark, but, again, it fails to account for figures such as Feng Youlan.
- *New Confucians espouse a kind of vitalism, borrowing elements from Bergson's and Schopenhauer's intuitionist and vitalist theories, and Whitehead's organicism, integrating them with the notion of "the process of unceasing vital transformation (sheng sheng bu xi 生生不息)" of the Book of Changes.* This characterization can only be applied to a few New Confucians, such as Xiong Shili and Mou Zongsan.
- *New Confucians affirm a transcendent rationality (e.g., Liang Shuming's concept of lixing 理性, and Xiong Shili's concept of xingzhi 性智), which is different from ordinary, everyday rationality (e.g., Liang's lizhi 理智 or Xiong's liangzhi 量智). The latter involves ratiocination and is used in the context of our empirical experience; the former involves intuition and relates to the metaphysical. Ultimately, the latter is grounded in the former.* The real question is, how many twentieth-century Confucian philosophers (of any persuasion) were not committed to some notion of transcendent rationality based on the concept of principle (*li*)?

Despite the fact that Yan published this list after more than a decade of concerted research effort by mainland scholars of New Confucianism, the problem of definition and defining characterizations continues to be elusive. It is my contention that this is because too many philosophically incompatible thinkers have been grouped together as New Confucians.

Philosophical Movement or Cultural Movement?

Before turning to examine the identification and grouping of individual thinkers in more detail, a preliminary issue that needs to be addressed is the nature of New Confucianism as an intellectual movement. If we accept that it is, indeed, a cohesive intellectual movement (without concerning ourselves at present with the problem of when this cohesion was achieved), a question that immediately presents itself is, "Is New Confucianism a philosophical movement or a cultural movement?" Some prominent mainland scholars have described it as both. Luo Yijun, for example, defines it as a school of culture and philosophy.[21] Similarly, Hu Weixi 胡偉希 has described the New Confucianism that has developed in Hong Kong and Taiwan since the 1950s as "a cultural trend of thought (*wenhua sichao*) the focus of which was the revival of Confucian thought."[22] While it is uncontentious that New Confucianism (as conventionally portrayed) embraces both philosophical and cultural concerns[23] there is disagreement as to whether it is the cultural concerns that are subordinate to the philosophical concerns or vice versa.

The attitude of some scholars to this issue reveals a genuine ambivalence in their assessment of the character of New Confucianism. Zheng Jiadong 鄭家棟, who has emerged as one of China's leading scholars of New Confucianism, is an excellent case in point. In 1989, he maintained that while New Confucianism in its later period of development had come to evidence a general concern with such areas as culture, politics, ethics, and history, its core concerns are metaphysical issues. He insisted that the core issue of all New Confucian thought is the reconstruction of traditional Confucian metaphysics.[24] In 1992, however, he writes that Xiong Shili and Liang Shuming had been instrumental in proposing a set of issues that became central to the subsequent development of New Confucianism. These issues could be approached from two levels: those concerning human nature (beliefs, values, ultimate meaning, existence, subjectivity) and those concerning culture (Chinese cultural identity and its future development).[25] By 1997 this ambivalence is even more pronounced in Zheng's characterization, with neither the "philosophical" nor the "cultural" component emerging as primary:

> Looking at the development of New Confucianism after the May Fourth period, it seems that its representatives have been more inclined to affirm the universal significance of Confucian thought. That is, regarding Confucian thought as "the learning of the person, the mind, the nature, and conditioning circumstances (*shen xin xing ming zhi xue* 身心性命之學)" they emphasized the widespread and ongoing value that Confucian thought had for humanity. Yet, from another perspective, the main concern of New Confucians has been the transmission of our national culture (*minzu wenhua*), what it is that makes Chinese people who they are.[26]

While there are important philosophy of culture (*wenhua zhexue*) concerns evident in the writings of many of the figures conventionally identified as New Confucian—including its earliest representatives[27]—they are usually tied to underlying metaphysical concerns. Even the predominantly cultural agenda of the 1958 Declaration is explicitly premised on the groundwork of "learning of the mind and the nature" (*xin xing zhi xue*):

> As we have stated above, in researching China's cultural history and thought,[28] we want to treat it as an objective expression of the Chinese people's spiritual vitality. Yet, where is the core of this spiritual vitality? It may be said to be in the Chinese people's thought or philosophy. This is certainly not to say that China's thought or philosophy has determined China's cultural history. Rather, it is to say that only by beginning with China's thought and philosophy can one illuminate the spiritual vitality of China's cultural history . . . (10). If one wants to understand Chinese culture, then one must do this by penetrating its philosophical core . . . (12). In fact, it is precisely "learning of the mind and the nature" (*xin xing zhi xue*) which is the core of Chinese thought . . . (17). If people today are able to understand *xin xing zhi xue*, then this is where the spiritual marrow of Chinese culture is to be found . . . (21). *Xin xing zhi xue*, the core of Chinese culture (25).

Despite the ambivalence of some writers, during the 1990s most New Confucian scholarship has focused on the identity of the movement as a philosophical school.

Historical Phases in the Development of New Confucianism

Although scholars outside of China (principally those in Taiwan and Hong Kong) had, since the mid-to-late 1970s, begun to identify phases in the historical development of New Confucianism, it was not until the mid-1980s that mainland scholars first began to articulate the notion of a philosophical school called New Confucianism. A diverse range of factors can be identified as having contributed to an appropriate climate for New Confucianism to flourish in late 1980s "cultural China": the publication of a number of seminal works by so-called "second generation" New Confucians beginning in the 1960s and continuing through the early 1980s; the impact of the death of Tang Junyi 唐君毅 in 1978 and Xu Fuguan 徐復觀 in 1982 (as reflected in the many obituaries and essays devoted to evaluating their scholarship and legacy); the round-table discussions convened in Taipei by the Zhongguo luntanshe 中國論壇社

in October, 1982 (reports and extracts from which were published in the journal *Zhongguo luntan* 中國論壇), on the topic of "New Confucianism and China's Modernization," in which a number of prominent scholars participated; the 1981 conference on Neo-Confucianism convened in Hangzhou in which overseas Chinese scholars participated; the 1982 Zhu Xi 朱熹 (1130–1200) conference in Hawaii, which again brought leading overseas and mainland scholars together; the participation of eight prominent overseas Chinese scholars in the planning stages of the Singapore government's 1982 decision to introduce Confucian Ethics into the secondary curriculum Religious Knowledge course; the establishment of the Confucius Foundation in 1984 in Beijing; Du Weiming's 杜維明 (Tu Wei-ming) lectures and networking in China in the late 1970s and early 1980s; and the rise of the "culture fad (*wenhuare* 文化熱)" in mid-1980s China. The single most immediate factor was the Chinese government's support for research on New Confucianism. In November, 1986, "New Confucianism" was identified and funded as a key research project, under the national seventh five-year plan for the social sciences. Within a year there were nearly fifty scholars working on topics related to New Confucianism in China.[29]

From 1985 to about 1992, much research effort was directed at trying to identify just who should have been retrospectively identified as a New Confucian.[30] While even today no lasting consensus has been reached,[31] between seven and twelve individuals are commonly identified as representative New Confucians. Fang Keli, for example, the leading mainland scholar of New Confucian thought during this initial period of research (particularly on the organizational side of things), identified the following ten figures: Liang Shuming, Zhang Junmai, Xiong Shili, Feng Youlan, He Lin, Qian Mu, Fang Dongmei 方東美 (1899–1976), Tang Junyi, Mou Zongsan, and Xu Fuguan.[32] These figures are often referred to as first and second generation New Confucians.[33] Generally, Xiong Shili and Liang Shuming are identified as first generation New Confucians. There are, however, a number of dissenting voices. As early as 1982, Yu Yingshi had objected to classifying Xiong as a New Confucian.[34] Later he also questioned if Liang should be regarded as a New Confucian, due to Liang's Buddhist leanings.[35] Zhang Dainian 張岱年 goes even further, objecting not only to the identification of Liang and Xiong as New Confucians, but also to that of Feng Youlan and He Lin. At times, Zhang Junmai and Ma Yifu are also identified as first generation New Confucians.[36] The case of Zhang's generational affiliation is complicated by the fact that he was a co-signatory to the 1958 Declaration. Feng Youlan, He Lin, Tang Junyi, Mou Zongsan, and Xu Fuguan are most commonly identified as representing the second generation of New Confucians. Hong Kong and Taiwan-based scholars, however, tend to reject out of hand the identification of He Lin and Feng Youlan as New Confucians, principally, it seems, because of their post-1949 careers in China. Mainland scholars generally include He, but sometimes not. This is probably due to the fact that He's New Philosophy of the Moral Mind (*xin xinxue* 新心學) was little more than a proposal, a plan; it was never developed into a systematic philosophy.[37] As for Feng Youlan, to this day there is still no consensus. Indeed, one of the most intensely debated issues in New Confucian studies is whether Feng Youlan is a New Confucian. To a significant extent, the issue hinges on whether his New Principle-Centered Learning (*xin lixue* 新理學) is judged to be an extension of Song-Ming Neo-Confucian thought or to be a new philosophical direction.[38] In the opening pages of his *Xin lixue* (New Principle-Centered Learning; 1939), Feng himself declares that the system of philosophy he was seeking to introduce in that book was not a modern explication of Song-Ming Neo-Confucian philosophy but a new development of that philosophy, hence the name "new."[39] (That which Feng sought to develop were the concepts of universals and particulars, which, somewhat perversely, he saw as central to the Cheng-Zhu tradition of Neo-Confucian philosophy.)[40] Liu Shuxian's following remarks typify the attitude of many Hong Kong and Taiwan-based scholars.[41] Having first discussed Xiong Shili, Liu comments: "In appearance, Feng also promoted the teachings of the Neo-Confucians, but he only apprehended the extremely superficial. It was quite mistaken to use New Principle-Centered Learning to cobble together Master Zhu [Xi]'s teachings. After the mainland changed hands, he did not cease revising his interpretations. Later, there was even a period when he was associated with the Gang of Four. This is most regrettable. Unlike Xiong Shili and Liang Shuming, he was incapable of displaying the strength of character of a traditional scholar!"[42]

Whatever we might think about the fairness or otherwise of Liu's criticisms, his comments carry a certain weight, because Liu himself is a leading New Confucian (third generation). Nor were such "internal" criticisms a recent phenomenon.[43] The widespread and persistent nature of such (purportedly) endogenous criticisms prompted the mainland scholar,[44] Luo Yijun, to make a virtue of necessity: "Moreover, even though on matters of academic thought there were some major differences between some of the New Confucians—even to the point that they argued with one another—this, in fact, is a unique feature of the New Confucian school, and is the best explanation as to why they did not form factions to attack each other on academic grounds."[45] In 1991, however, a mere two years after these comments were first published, there is clear evidence of tensions. This episode was ignited by Yu Ying-shi's denial that Qian Mu was a New Confucian. Yu's comments are significant, not simply because of the high esteem in which Yu is held in academic circles, but more particularly because Qian Mu had been his teacher. Moreover, by this time, mainland scholars were regularly identifying Yu himself as a New Confucian.[46] Yu set out his critique in considerable detail in a long essay entitled, "Qian Mu yu xin Rujia 錢穆與新儒家" (Qian Mu and the New Confucians). In the essay, he rejects classifying Qian Mu as a New Confucian on the grounds that Qian did not set out to develop new philosophical interpretations of Confucianism to constitute a new system of thought, but rather merely researched and described Confucianism. In short, he was a historian, not a philosopher. In this respect, Yu argues, Qian must be clearly distinguished from such figures as Xiong Shili, Liang Shuming, and Feng Youlan. Yu proposes a twofold characterization of Qian's view of Confucianism. First, Confucianism encompassed a system of values that for the past two thousand years has molded every aspect of Chinese people's lives. Second, Confucianism had provided the principal impetus leading to the longevity and breadth of Chinese culture and moreover it could still provide modern Chinese culture with a spiritual foundation. Qian further believed that the subtle influence that the Confucian value system exerted on both individuals and society served a positive function. Yu also describes Qian's objections to the concept of *daotong* 道統 (interconnecting thread of the way). For Qian, the only *daotong* that should be recognized is one that was a product of the overall tradition of China's historical culture. Yu calls this the *daotong* of the historian, not the philosopher.[47] Yu was not the first to have objected to Qian's being identified as a New Confucian on the grounds that he was an historian, not a philosopher. In 1990, for example, Hong Kong scholar, Wu Rujun 吳汝鈞 (Ng Yu-kwan), a contributor to this volume, had objected to the identification of Zhang Junmai, Xu Fuguan, and Qian Mu as New Confucians on the grounds that Zhang's main activities were in politics, while Qian and Xu were primarily historians.[48] As if anticipating this line of objection, in 1989, Luo Yijun described Qian as a New Confucian historian[49] and the preface to Qian's *Guoshi dagang* 國史大綱 (Outline History of China) as a manifesto (*xuanyan*) of New Confucianism historiography.[50] Nowhere, however, does Luo establish what is distinctively "New Confucian" about Qian's thought.[51]

Confucian or New Confucian?

This, in turn, points to a far more fundamental issue confronting the historiographer of New Confucianism: Where does one draw the line between "Confucian" and "New Confucian?" Is there a line to draw or is the distinction purely retrospective and largely subjective? Writing in 1990—a time when the issue of definitions was high on the agenda of scholars of New Confucianism—Zheng Jiadong noted that up to that time, mainland scholars had adopted a very broad, inclusive approach to the study of New Confucianism, which had the effect of making the term synonymous with the "Confucian modernization movement" when, in fact, "New Confucianism only represented one particular direction in Confucian modernization." Unfortunately, Zheng fails to relate precisely what it is that characterizes this "one direction." Moreover, he proceeds to undermine his claim that New Confucianism has a unique identity by citing the example of how previously he had argued that Feng Youlan should not be classified as a New Confucian because Feng's philosophy did not address the issue of "learning of the mind and the nature," but later changed his mind because general use of the term was such that "all those whose beliefs were generally oriented towards Confucian moral ideals and values could be referred to as, or could style themselves as, New Confucians."[52] Writing in 1998, the following comments by Li Daoxiang 李道湘 suggest that little progress had been made in the intervening years: "In fact, right from its beginning, New Confucianism was not a completely united school. Right from the beginning, the attitudes of individual New Confucians towards Confucius, Mencius, and Neo-Confucianism were not identical. Such differences even included differences in the way they identified with the basic spirit of Confucianism. *New Confucianism has become a trend of thought (sichao) because New Confucians all identify with Confucianism* [my emphasis]. With a sense of collective identity they have taken up the task of reviving Confucianism and reconstructing Confucianism's historical mission."[53] Even the appeal to revival and restructuring fails to distinguish how New Confucianism is more than a "Confucian modernization movement."

For Yan Binggang, the key difference is one of further development and innovation: "Their difference is merely that contemporary Confucians emphasize the explication of moral philosophy and its overall integration while the New Confucians emphasize the further development of Confucian moral philosophy and also being innovative."[54] Yan has proposed his own three generational periodization: 1840–1919; 1919–49; 1949–today.[55] Pushing back the origins of New Confucianism to the pre–May Fourth period has enabled him to identify Kang Youwei 康有爲 (1858–1927) and Liang Qichao 梁啓超 (1873–1929) as representative of the first period. Other mainland scholars of New Confucianism, such as Li Zhenguo 黎振國, object to the inclusion of pre–May Fourth figures, Zeng Guofan 曾國藩 (1811–72), Zhang Zhidong 張之洞 (1837–1909), and Kang Youwei on the grounds that even though they were "Confucian converts," their views were very firmly planted in tradition, and that these views were a continuation of traditional forms of Confucian thought, thus it was only natural for them to continue to champion Confucianism. Li explains that this was because they had not been exposed to other traditions of thought and could not break out of their Confucian mold.[56] This is too simplistic. Kang Youwei is certainly not a Confucian of the traditional mold. Indeed, he radically (even iconoclastically) reinterpreted many aspects of Confucian thought and tradition. Why should he not be regarded as a New Confucian? Yet, on the other hand, is innovation itself a sufficient condition for New Confucian identity? Other early (first generation) Confucian figures who have been nominated for New Confucian candidature include Mei Guangdi 梅光迪 (1890–1945), Wu Mi 吳宓 (1894–1925), and Lin Zaiping 林宰平 (1879–1960).[57] When we turn to the "second generation," what is the rationale for not according New Confucian status to figures such as Chen Daqi 陳大齊 (1886–1983), Xie Youwei 謝幼偉 (1905–76), Chen Rongjie 陳榮捷 (1901–94), Zhang Qiyun 張其昀 (1900–), Hu Qiuyuan 胡秋原 (1910–), Cheng Zhaoxiong 程兆熊, Jin Yuelin 金岳霖 (1895–1984), Chen Lifu 陳立夫 (1900–2001), or Lao Siguang 勞思光?[58]

In 1991, Yu Yingshi identified three common ways in which the term New Confucian has been understood.

- Most general (widely employed by mainland Chinese scholars). According to this definition, almost any twentieth-century scholar who is not biased against Confucian learning and who conscientiously researches Confucian learning can be regarded as a New Confucian.
- More specific. This definition stipulates that only those scholars who have contributed new philosophical interpretations and developments to Confucian learning should be classified as New Confucians. Yu includes such examples as Xiong Shili, Zhang Junmai, Feng Youlan, and He Lin. (Yu puts a question mark on the case of Liang Shuming because of Liang's Buddhist inclinations.)

- Most specific. Yu claims that this is the definition most widely adopted outside China: those people who belong to Xiong Shili's "school" (*pai*).[59] This presumably includes such figures as Mou Zongsan, Tang Junyi, and Xu Fuguan.

Of course, other variations on the definition of New Confucianism have been proposed. Yu's tripartite division is useful in that he alerts us to the significant disparities between some of them. As he remarks, the generality of this first definition is so broad that it robs the term of any useful function. The second and third definitions share a common philosophical characterization, supporting the view that the touchstone for New Confucian identity is a particular philosophical orientation. The second definition is the one favored by most scholars of New Confucian thought in China, as well as a number of scholars and commentators outside China. As we have noted, the problem with this second definition is that it still begs the question of how to distinguish New Confucianism from Confucianism in the twentieth century. The third definition is attractive in that Mou and the others had been students of Xiong Shili. In turn many of their own students in Taiwan and Hong Kong have actively promoted their thought and sought to identify themselves with their teachers. Thus, on prima facie grounds, the third definition boasts a coherence and identifiable lineages that are lacking in the other two definitions. The problem for mainland scholars (and even a number of overseas Chinese scholars) is that "New Confucian" thus becomes a much more exclusive category than most are prepared to concede. If major figures such as Feng Youlan and He Lin are excluded from the New Confucian pantheon, the proprietary rights of mainland scholars over the interpretation and definition of New Confucianism—past, present, and future—would be severely diminished. Conversely, the proprietary rights of a significant number of overseas Chinese scholars (buoyed by their connections with Mou Zongsan, Tang Junyi, and Xu Fuguan, in particular) would become greatly enhanced. A fundamental and, as yet, unresolved tension and rivalry is the consequence.

Third Generation New Confucians

Despite this tension, the so-called third generation of New Confucians clearly favors one particular lineage. Guo Qiyong 郭齊勇 is typical of mainland scholars who, up until 1986, still referred to overseas Chinese intellectuals such as Yu Yingshi, Du Weiming, Cheng Zhongying 成中英, Jin Yaoji 金耀基, and Zheng Yiyuan 鄭舜元 as "Confucian revivalists."[60] Yet, within two or three years, Guo and others came to refer to these scholars as New Confucians or third generation New Confucians. This first signs of this change in assessment were already in evidence in 1986. An (unattributed) article entitled "What is New Confucianism?" (Shenme jiao xin Rujia 什麼叫新儒家) published in the June 10, 1986 edition of the Wenhuibao newspaper, identified Du Weiming and Liu Shuxian as representative third generation New Confucians. By 1989, academic recognition of the third generation of New Confucians had developed to the point that Luo Yijun was able to identify the 1982 round-table discussion convened by Zhongguo luntanshe in Taipei, on "New Confucianism and China's Modernization," as marking the beginning of the third period in the development of New Confucianism. Luo further identified the following figures as third generation New Confucians: Yu Yingshi, Liu Shuxian, Zhang Hao (=Hao Chang), Lin Yusheng 林毓生, Du Weiming, Lao Siguang, Cai Renhou, and Wang Bangxiong 王邦雄.[61] While Lin Yusheng, Zhang Hao, Lao Siguang, and Yu Yingshi would not be classified as New Confucians today, Liu Shuxian, Du Weiming, Cai Renhou, and Wang Bangxiong generally still are. Also writing in 1989, Fang Keli similarly identified the sudden rise of the third generation New Confucians as a phenomenon of the 1980s. In his article, he reports on a conference he had attended in Hong Kong in 1988 on the thought of Tang Junyi, convened by the Hong Kong Fazhu wenhua xueyuan 法住文化學院. The conference included an exhibition of books gathered under the rubric of "New Confucian writings." In addition to the writings of a range of scholars conventionally identified as first and second generation New Confucians, the writings of sixteen or so younger scholars were also exhibited. Fang describes members of this "new generation" of New Confucians as either having been students of the first and second generation scholars or as having been influenced by their thought. He interprets this as significant in that it demonstrates that this group had achieved a clear collective identity. Fang divides the group into two: the Hong Kong Fazhu group, identified as students of Tang Junyi, all of whom had studied at New Asia College and who were then mostly teaching at the Chinese University of Hong Kong, and the Taiwan Ehu 鵝湖 group, identified with the students of Mou Zongsan.[62] (This group is centered on the Ehu yuekanshe 鵝湖月刊社, the society responsible for publishing the journal, *Ehu yuekan* [Legein Monthly].) Fang also includes two scholars in this latter group who were at the time based in the (now defunct) Institute of East Asian Philosophy in Singapore, Liu Guoqiang 劉國強 and Feng Yaoming 馮耀明, because they had published in *Ehu yuekan*.[63] Three years later, Luo Yijun identified distinct subgroupings within the Ehu group based on teacher–disciple affiliations: the Zhang Junmai "group" (*men* 門), the Qian Mu group, the Fang Dongmei group, the Tang Junyi group, the Mou Zongsan group (the dominant subgroup), and the Xu Fuguan group. Each of these groups, he maintains, is characterized by its engagement in three core activities: the transmission, promotion, and interpretation of their respective teacher's scholarship.[64]

Although there is no definitive list of third generation New Confucians, by and large it is restricted to those who had studied under, or who can claim some connection with, Mou Zongsan, Tang Junyi, Xu Fuguan, and Zhang Junmai. There are, of course, some important exceptions, such as Liu Shuxian, a student of Fang Dongmei. Despite not being able to establish a "genealogical" connection with Tang, Xu, Zhang, or Mou,[65] Liu has arguably been the most prominent of the third generation promoters of New Confucianism, challenged only by Du Weiming (Tu Wei-ming). Mainland scholars such as Fang Keli have been keen to attribute to Du a seminal role in arousing interest in New Confucianism in China,[66] as is evidenced by Du's lecture tours, stints as visiting scholar, conference presentations, and behind the scenes networking in 1980s China. Yet, there is some question as to whether Du is a New Confucian at all, despite having studied under Mou while at Donghai University. Writing in 1982, as part of his involvement with the ill-starred "Singapore Project," he says: "the emergence of Confucian ethics in the last ten or twenty years, during the period following the Second World War, represents a new phase and a new reality. . . . We are now in the third generation of this serious rethinking of Confucian ethics."[67] Significantly, he does not use the term New Confucian to describe himself. By the mid-1980s, he sometimes identifies himself as belonging to a third generation of the post–May Fourth promoters of Confucianism;[68] and sometimes as an active participant in the New Confucian movement.[69] Most often, however, he seems to be more interested in a future revival of Confucianism than in New Confucianism per se. Following Mou Zongsan, he refers to this revival as the third period of Confucianism. (Writing in 1962, Mou Zongsan proclaimed that while a third period of Confucianism was needed, it had still to be realized.[70] For Mou, this third period of Confucianism would follow the first and second periods of pre-Qin and Song-Ming Confucianism, respectively.) In discussing his notion of a third period of development for Confucianism, Du writes: "If the second period of development for Confucianism [which for Du is the eleventh to the mid-nineteenth

centuries] was in response to Indian culture—or the challenge of
Buddhist culture—in which the creative response was to absorb Indian
culture and in doing so propose a uniquely Chinese model of thought,
then the possibility of Confucianism having a third period of development will be determined by whether it can respond creatively to the challenges of Western culture." He proceeds to describe how such a creative
response would need to encompass three areas other than philosophy: a
religio-spiritual dimension grounded in an understanding of transcendence; a social, political, and economic dimension; and a "deep psychology" (such as Freudian psychology).[71]

Significantly, like Mou, Du regularly expresses caution about the
very possibility of there being a third period of development for
Confucianism. He sees it as an ideal, a goal, the precise character of
which has yet to be formulated,[72] much less partially realized. During
the 1990s, developments in New Confucian philosophy and, more
generally, modern Confucian thought, have done little to undermine such
caution. In Taiwan, the pluralist agendas of those younger scholars associated with the Ehu Monthly Society (the Society responsible for organizing
and co-organizing four major conferences on New Confucianism in
1990, 1992, 1994, and 1996), is one such development.[73] Another is a
greater willingness for proponents both of New Confucianism and
modern Confucian thought to engage in dialogue with other traditions
and ideologies.[74] Most recently, the phenomenon of so-called "Post
New Confucianism" has emerged. For mainland scholars, Fan Guiping
范桂萍 and Gan Chunsong 干春松, the Post New Confucian age is a
development that signals the rejection of New Confucian moral idealism, as Chinese intellectuals adopt a new inclusive attitude to China's
cultural heritage: "That is, when people affirm the contemporary value
of China's cultural tradition, they are already beginning to transcend
blatant sectarian biases, and—against the backdrop of world culture—
are emphasizing the comprehensive assimilation of all forms of traditional wisdom: Confucian, Daoist, Mohist, and all the various schools
of philosophers."[75] Taiwanese scholar and New Confucian reformer
Lin Anwu 林安梧—who started to use the term in 1994—also characterizes "Post New Confucianism" as a reaction to an excessive emphasis
on inner moral cultivation at the expense of practice or social application.
He does not, however, see this as entailing a rejection or overthrow of
core Confucian values, but rather the adaption of Confucianism to the
postmodern condition: "The development from old Confucianism to
New Confucianism, and then to Post New Confucianism, is a critical,
successive, and creative development. . . . It is not a development

involving severance, segregation, or overthrow. [I describe it as such] precisely to show that the key to Confucianism's being Confucianism is that that which it emphasizes comes from the impetus of putting into practice our subjective, inner root-nature. This is 'humaneness,' as was pointed out by venerable master Confucius, some two thousand years ago."[76] For Lin, humaneness is the exemplary *social* virtue. Although I return to the issue of Post New Confucianism in chapter 2, the fuller study of these and related developments will be the subject of a sequel volume.

At the one extreme, the "New Confucian" label has exercised a homogenizing effect that has obscured complexities and philosophical differences at the expense of exploring the variety of forms in which Confucian-inspired philosophy has continued to survive throughout the twentieth century (even if the study of individual "New Confucians"—Xiong, Liang, Mou, etc.—has, in fact, significantly enhanced our understanding of particular twentieth-century philosophers and thinkers). At the other extreme, the label has been applied with such narrow proprietary rigor that it ends up elevating a select group as constituting a whole school or movement. I have argued that although most of the promoters and sympathetic interpreters of New Confucianism trace the movement to the early part of the twentieth century, in fact, there is little evidence that New Confucianism had attained a degree of integration or coalescence sufficient for it to be recognized and promoted as a distinct philosophical movement, or school of thought, before the 1970s. I have further argued, against the conventional view, that this latter development did not occur until the early 1980s. Over the next decade, the movement matured rapidly. It is only with the advent of this "third generation" that we can speak of New Confucianism as having cohesion and self-identity, thus making the "third" generation the first real generation of New Confucians. By the early 1990s, a broad consensus had been reached by scholars in Taiwan, Hong Kong, and China that New Confucianism was a movement that could be traced to the early part of the twentieth century, that it boasted distinct phases of internal development, a cohort of representative thinkers, and clearly defined lineages of intellectual transmission. The most successful of these lineages will be examined in chapter 2 where I show that the retrospective identification of lineage necessarily entails exclusion. This exclusion is so severe that, on a narrow definition, ultimately the only ones who qualify for New Confucian status are Xiong, Mou, and Liu Shuxian. While I find that their's offers the most compelling case for school identity, it seems unnecessarily reductionist, not to mention self-serving, to make the term New Confucian exclusive to one lineage of thinkers. Equally questionable are the proprietary claims over the entire "orthodox" Confucian tradition, made in the name of *daotong* (interconnecting thread of the way). Rather than thinking of New Confucianism as being a single line of intellectual orthodoxy, or even a complex intellectual movement comprising many threads of thought, I would prefer to think in terms of twentieth-century Confucian or Confucian-inspired philosophies that embrace a variety of forms of intellectual expression. To privilege New Confucianism seems unjustified.[77]

Notes

1. I would like to express my thanks to Professors Liu Shuxian (Liu Shu-hsien) and Li Minghui (Lee Ming-huei) of the Institute for Literature and Philosophy, Academia Sinica, Taiwan, for their constructive criticisms of an earlier draft of this paper. Professors Liu and Li, naturally enough, do not accept my "retrospective creation" thesis or many of the other views I express in this chapter. They nevertheless showed the good humor of allowing me to present it as a seminar paper while I was a visiting scholar at the Institute in January, 2002.

2. Professor Liu Shuxian informs me (personal communication) that Feng had already employed this term in a similar sense in his 1924 Colombia University dissertation, "A Comparative Study of Life Ideals." I have not seen the dissertation.

3. Feng Youlan, *Zhongguo zhexueshi*, Shanghai: Shangwu yinshuguan, 1934, 800. Bodde's translation, *A History of Chinese Philosophy*, was first published in Beijing, by Henri Veitch, in 1937. Feng also used the term "New Confucianism" to refer to Song and Ming *daoxue* philosophy in his English publication, *A Short History of Chinese Philosophy* (ed. Derk Bodde), New York: Macmillan, 1948.

4. The article was published in the first issue of the journal, *Sixiang yu shidai* 思想與時代 (Thought and the Times), and has been republished in Luo Yijun 羅義俊 (ed.), *Ping xin Rujia* 評新儒家 (Evaluating New Confucianism), Shanghai: Shanghai renmin chubanshe, 1989, 30–44.

5. He Lin, "Rujia sixiang zhi kaizhan," 33. For a discussion of the role of Western philosophy in He Lin's revitalized Confucianism, see Jiwei Ci, "He Lin's Sinification of Idealism," in Chung-ying Cheng and Nicholas Bunnin (eds.), *Contemporary Chinese Philosophy*, Oxford: Blackwell Publishers, 2002, 200–6. Ci's essay is perhaps the first English-language study of He Lin's philosophy.

6. Hao Chang, "New Confucianism and the Intellectual Crisis of Contemporary China," in Charlotte Furth (ed.), *The Limits of Change: Essays on Conservative Alternatives in Republican China*, Cambridge, M.A.: Harvard University Press, 1976, 276.

7. E-mail correspondence, December 13, 2000.

8. Cai Renhou, *Xin Rujia de jingshen fangxiang* 新儒家的精神方向 (The Spiritual Direction of the New Confucians), Taipei: Xuesheng shuju,

1981, 15. Most recently, Lao Siguang has claimed that already by 1958 New Confucianism had come to be regarded as a school of thought in Hong Kong, with Mou and Tang as its chief representatives. See his *Siguang renwu lunji* 思光人物論集 (Lao Siguang's Essays on People), Hong Kong: Chinese University Press, 2001, 109. Unfortunately, Professor Lao provides no evidence of just who at that time regarded New Confucianism to be a school.

9. Luo Yijun, "Jin shiyu nian dangdai xin Ruxue de yanjiu yu suo wei menhu wenti 近十餘年當代新儒學的研究與所謂門戶問題" (The So-Called Problem of Factionalism in New Confucianism over the Past Ten-Plus Years), 1, paper distributed at the Second International Conference on New Confucianism, National Central Library, Taipei, 1992. In this connection it may be noted that in his 1973 article in the Chung Chi Student Monthly, Ng Yu-kwan 吳汝均 (a contributor to this volume) identifies Ma Yifu, Liang Shuming, Xiong Shili, Tang Junyi, and Mou Zongsan as representative mainstream twentieth-century Chinese philosophers. Nowhere in the article, however, does he describe them as New Confucians or as having a group or school identity. See his "Dangdai Zhongguo zhexue 當代中國哲學" (Contemporary Chinese Philosophy), *Chongji xueshengbao*, February 14, 1973, 8. (Chung Chi College is one of the four colleges forming the Chinese University of Hong Kong.)

10. Shimada Kenji, *Shin Jukka tetsugaku ni tsuite: Yū Jūriki no tetsugaku* 新儒家哲學 について: 熊十力の哲學 (On New Confucian Philosophy: The Philosophy of Xiong Shili), Kyoto: Tōhōsha, 1987, 146, n. 10.

11. I have used the version reprinted in Feng Zusheng 封祖盛 (ed.), *Dangdai xin Rujia* 當代新儒家 (Contemporary New Confucianism), Beijing: Sanlian shudian, 1989, 1–52. An abridged and cumbersome English translation-cum-synopsis is appended to the second volume of Carsun Chang's (Zhang Junmai), *The Development of Neo-Confucian Thought*, New York: Bookman Associates, 1962, 455–83. A complete (and more faithful) English translation was published in an issue of the Taiwan journal, *Chinese Culture*, under the name, "A Manifesto on the Reappraisal of Chinese Culture." (The copy I have seen, which is held in the library of the Institute for Literature and Philosophy, Academia Sinica, Taiwan, is an off-print that does not include the date of publication. Based on the introduction of the document, my guess is that it was published ca. 1960–61.) Most pertinent is that a fifth person, Xie Youwei (Hsieh Yu-wei 謝幼偉; 1903–76), is listed as being one of the original authors. The second paragraph of the pamphlet states: "With the agreement and suggestions of Professors Mou and Hsu, Prof. Tang drew up the first sketch of this treatise while still on tour in the United States of America and sent it to Prof. Hsieh Yu-wei in Taiwan for consultation. After several revision [sic.] this booklet took its final shape." It is surely significant that in the retrospective creation of the New Confucian identity, although the four signatories of the earlier Chinese version of the Declaration are granted a pivotal role in the movement, Xie Youwei is quite ignored. New Confucianism's modern creators seem quite content to leave this anomaly unexplained. In addition to Hao Chang's essay on New Confucianism, see also the summary by Liu Shu-hsien, "A Critical Review of Contemporary

Neo-Confucian Thought with a View to Modernisation," in Tu Wei-ming, *The Triadic Concord: Confucian Ethics, Industrial Asia, and Max Weber*, Singapore: The Institute of East Asian Philosophies, 1991.

12. Hao Chang, "New Confucianism and the Intellectual Crisis of Contemporary China," 276.

13. This impression is further strengthened by comments made in the most recent and authoritative English-language contribution to Western understanding of contemporary Chinese philosophy, appropriately titled *Contemporary Chinese Philosophy*, 11. In his introduction, coeditor, Nicholas Bunnin asserts that the Declaration gave "rise to the Movement of Contemporary New Confucianism."

14. Arif Dirlik, "Confucius in the Borderlands: Global Capitalism and the Reinvention of Confucianism," *boundary* 2, 22.3(1995): 235, 238. In the main, this is a particularly incisive and insightful article. A similarly uncritical portrayal of the Declaration is chapter 2 of Umberto Bresciani's *Reinventing Confucianism: The New Confucian Movement*, "The Basic Tenets of the New Confucian Movement," in which these "tenets" are identified exclusively with the content of the Declaration.

15. Hao Chang, "New Confucianism and the Intellectual Crisis of Contemporary China," 277.

16. One might, however, argue that this omission needs to be understood in the political and ideological context of the 1950s. At that time, both Xiong Shili and Liang Shuming (as well as Feng Youlan and He Lin) were pursuing careers in communist China. This fact, in turn, introduces further complexities into the notion of New Confucian identity.

17. Wei Zhengtong, "Dangdai xin Rujia de xintai 當代新儒學的心態" (The Contemporary New Confucian Mind), *Zhongguo luntan* 15.1(1982): 44.

18. We may also note that Wei Zhengtong later seems to have abandoned this early set of characterizations. In his 1993 publication, *Sixiang de tanxian* 思想的探險 (Exploring Thought), Taipei: Zhengzhong shuju, 95, he concurs with Yu Yingshi's 余英時 characterization, according to which only the Xiong Shili "school" is recognized as New Confucian (see below): "Yingshi's analysis is correct. Not only is Qian Mu not a New Confucian, but, strictly defined, Liang Shuming, Zhang Junmai, and Xu Fuguan cannot be counted as New Confucians either."

19. Luo Yijun, "Dangdai xin Rujia de licheng he diwei wenti 當代新儒家的歷程和地位問題" (Issues on the Course and Status of New Confucianism), in his *Ping xin Rujia*, 2.

20. Yan Binggang, *Dangdai xin Ruxue yinlun* 當代新儒學引論 (Introduction to New Confucianism), Beijing: Beijing tushuguan, 1998, 70 ff.

21. Luo Yijun, "Dangdai xin Rujia de licheng he diwei wenti," 1.

22. Hu Weixi, *Chuantong yu renwen: Dui Gang-Tai xin Ru de kaocha* 傳統與人文: 對港臺新儒的考察 (Tradition and Humanism: Investigations into New Confucians in Hong Kong and Taiwan), Beijing: Zhonghua shuju, 1992, 1.

23. Fang Keli, "Guanyu xiandai xin Rujia yanjiu de jige wenti 關於現代新儒家研究的幾個問題" (Several Issues Concerning New

Confucian Studies), in Fang Keli and Li Jinquan 李錦全 (eds.), *Xiandai xin Ruxue yanjiu lunji* 現代新儒學研究論集 (Collected Essays on New Confucian Studies), vol. 1, Beijing: Zhongguo shehui kexue chubanshe, 1989 (written in 1987), 2, 4, is critical of those who restrict it to a philosophical school or movement, yet, he provides little argument to support his view, forcing him to makes distinctions like "New Confucian in the broad sense of the term." Elsewhere in the same article (5), he seems to renege on this claim by characterizing the New Confucians as philosophers.

24. Zheng Jiadong, "Xiandai xin Ruxue de jiben tezheng 現代新儒學的基本特徵" (Basic Characteristics of New Confucianism), in Fang and Li (eds.), *Xiandai xin Ruxue yanjiu lunji*, vol. 1, 70, 74 ff.

25. Zheng Jiadong, "Xiandai xin Ruxue de luoji tuizhan jiqi yinfa de wenti 現代新儒學的邏輯推展及其引發的問題" (The Logical Development of New Confucianism and the Issues Generated), 8, paper distributed at the Second International Conference on New Confucianism, National Central Library, Taipei, 1992.

26. Zheng Jiadong, *Dangdai xin Ruxue shilun* 當代新儒學史論 (Essays on the History of New Confucianism), Nanning: Guangxi jiaoyu chubanshe, 1997, 11. Elsewhere in the same book—in which several of his essays are critical of the metaphysical emphasis of New Confucian philosophers, thus seeming to concede (implicitly, at least) the priority of metaphysics—he claims that Liang Shuming's championing of Confucianism was in order to find a path for the future of Chinese culture and not because of the appeal of Confucian "learning of the mind and the nature" or matters of "ultimate concern" (104; by this, Zheng is referring to "meaning of life" concerns). He argues that it was only in this sense that Liang came to be regarded as the founder of New Confucianism.

27. Here, I am thinking in particular of Liang Shuming's *Dong-xi wenhua ji qi zhexue* 東西文化及其哲學 (Eastern and Western Cultures and Their Philosophies), in *Liang Shuming quanji* 梁漱溟全集, vol. 1, Shandong: Shandong renmin chubanshe, 1994, which is based on lectures he had been giving at Beijing University beginning in 1920.

28. The authors of the Declaration consistently use the term *xueshu* 學術 in a sense that is much closer to "thought" than to "scholarship."

29. Fang Keli, "Guanyu xiandai xin Rujia yanjiu de jige wenti," 1.

30. In his essay "Guanyu xiandai xin Rujia yanjiu de jige wenti," 1–2, written in 1987, Fang Keli outlines some of the early accounts in China about who should have been classified as New Confucian and who should have not.

31. Also writing in this period, Luo Yijun, "Lun dandai xin Rujia de licheng he diwei," 27, has argued that despite the distinct intellectual differences between the figures conventionally identified as New Confucian, in seeking to retrace the history of the school our purpose should be to identify what these thinkers have in common, not their individual differences. As I have already pointed out in connection with Wei Zhengtong's proposed list of New Confucian characteristics, identifying what thinkers have in common also poses particular problems.

32. Fang Keli, "Guanyu xiandai xin Rujia yanjiu de jige wenti," 5.

33. Even on this point, there is disagreement among mainland scholars. For example, in his *Xiandai xin Ruxue gailun* 現代新儒學概論 (A General Account of New Confucianism), Nanning: Guangxi renmin chubanshe, 1990, 15–16, Zheng Jiadong identifies the following figures with the first three generations of New Confucians: (1) Liang, Zhang, and Xiong; (2) Feng, He, and Qian; (3) Mou, Tang, and Xu.

34. This was at the roundtable discussion involving the participation of a number of prominent overseas Chinese scholars, entitled "Dangdai xin Rujia yu Zhongguo de xiandaihua 當代新儒家與中國的現代化" (New Confucianism and China's Modernization) published in *Zhongguo luntan* 15.1(1982): 7. Zhang Dainian 張岱年, "Guanyu xin Rujia yanjiu de xin 關於新儒家研究的信" (A Letter Concerning Research on New Confucianism), *Zhexue yanjiu* (1990.6): 109, has similarly argued that Xiong's *Xin weishilun* 新唯識論 (New Consciousness-Only Treatise) would be better regarded as a Neo-Buddhist tract than a New Confucian work. Only in his later years, Zhang maintains, did Xiong abandon Buddhism and return to Confucianism.

35. Yu Yingshi, *Xiandai Ruxuelun* 現代儒學論 (Essays on Modern Confucianism), Shanghai: Shanghai renmin chubanshe, 1998, 192. Originally this essay, "Qian Mu yu xin Rujia 錢穆與新儒家" (Qian Mu and the New Confucians) was published in Yu's *You ji feng chui shuishang lin* 猶記風吹水上鱗 (Ripples on Water), Taipei: Sanmin shuju, 1991.

36. Although Ma's writings are included in the series, *Xiandai xin Ruxue lunzhu jiyao* 現代新儒學論著輯要 (Key Edited Writings of New Confucianism), Beijing: Zhongguo guangbo dianshi chubanshe, 1992–95, more often than not he is omitted from most conventional accounts of New Confucianism. Ma's particular volume is titled, *Moran bushuo sheng ru lei: Ma Yifu xin Ruxue lunzhu jiyao* 默然不說聲如雷: 馬一浮新儒學論著輯要 (A Thunder-Like Reticence: Key Edited Writings of Ma Yifu), Beijing: Zhongguo guangbo dianshi chubanshe, 1995.

37. Writing in 1998, Yan Binggang, *Dangdai xin Ruxue yinlun*, 58, says that it remains unclear if He Lin should be classified as a New Confucian because his main contributions were not in that area, but in translating and introducing Western philosophy. Although true, this comment is beside the point. As with Feng Youlan, Xiong Shili, and Liang Shuming, in particular, we need to distinguish between different phases in their philosophical careers. Most of He Lin's translation work was undertaken post-1949. His "New Philosophy of the Moral Mind" phase occurred in the decade before this. Yang Junyou 楊君游, cited in Fang and Li (eds.), *Xiandai xin Ruxue yanjiu lunji*, vol. 1, 345, for example, argues that He Lin should not be classed as a New Confucian, precisely because his interest in New Confucian ideas was very short-lived.

38. Other issues include his attitude to intuition and his views on whether the cosmos is morally normative. In his early writings (and at a time when Henri Bergson [1859–1941] was fashionable in China), Feng Youlan was opposed to the idea of intuition being the most appropriate force to shape thought and the emotions, arguing instead for the primary role of rational

judgment. See his *Yizhong renshengguan* 一種人生觀 (One View of Life), section (*zhang*) 7, Shanghai: Shangwu yinshuguan, 1924. Some commentators have seized on Feng's remarks in his 1985 publication, *Zhongguo zhexue jianshi* 中國哲學簡史 (A Shorter History of Chinese Philosophy), Beijing: Beijing daxue chubanshe, 387, that after he had written his *Xin lixue* (New Principle-Centered Learning) in 1939, he also came to appreciate the importance of intuition (*fu de fangfa* 負的方法; literally "obverse method," in contradistinction to *zheng de fangfa* 正的方法, logical analysis). See, for example, Zheng Jiadong, "Xiandai xin Ruxue de jiben tezheng," 79 ff. While the Neo-Confucians (including the Chu-Zhu tradition) regarded the cosmos to be morally normative, Feng argued that it only contained within it morally normative principles and was itself not morally normative. See his *Xin lixue* in his *Sansong tang quanji* 三松堂全集 (Complete Writings from the Hall of Three Pines), Henan: Renmin chubanshe, 1986, vol. 4, 100.

39. Feng Youlan, *Xin lixue*, 5.
40. See, for example, his comments in *Sansong tang zixu* 三松堂自序 (Prefatory Comments from the Hall of Three Pines), Beijing: Sanlian shudian, 1984, 247; and his *Zhongguo xiandai zhexueshi* 中國現代哲學史 (A History of Modern Chinese Philosophy), Hong Kong: Zhonghua shuju, 1992, 206–7.
41. Liu has emerged as the most active contemporary New Confucian intellectual. He holds a professorial position at Academia Sinica in Taiwan, where he now lives. In 1999 he retired from his position as Chair of Chinese Philosophy at the Chinese University of Hong Kong.
42. Liu Shuxian, *Zhuzi zhexue sixiang de fazhan yu wancheng* 朱子哲學 思想的發展與完成 (The Development and Completion of Zhu Xi's Philosophical Thought), Taipei: Xuesheng shuju, 1995 revised (original 1982), 483.
43. For example, He Lin, *Dangdai Zhongguo zhexue* 當代中國哲學 (Contemporary Chinese Philosophy), Nanjing: Shengli chubangongsi, 1947, 36, criticized Feng Youlan for concentrating on the Cheng-Zhu views on *li* 理 (principle/pattern) and *qi* 氣 (psychophysical energy) while paying insufficient attention to their views on *xin* 心 (mind) and *xing* 性 (the nature), and also for preferring Cheng-Zhu thought over Lu-Wang (Lu Jiuyuan 陸九淵 [1139–93] and Wang Yangming 王陽明 [1472–1529]) thought. For a discussion of He Lin's reconciliation of the Cheng-Zhu and Lu-Wang "schools," see Jiwei Ci, "He Lin's Sinification of Idealism," 190–6.
44. It should also be noted that Luo is one of the very few mainland scholars of New Confucianism who might also qualify as a genuine promoter of New Confucianism.
45. Luo Yijun, "Dangdai xin Rujia de licheng he diwei wenti," 2.
46. This act was consecrated with the inclusion of an edited selection of Yu's writings in the series, *Xiandai xin Ruxue jiyao*, entitled, *Neizai chaoyue zhi lu: Yu Yingshi xin Ruxue lunzhu jiyao* 内在超越之路: 余英時新 儒學論著輯要 (The Road to Immanent Transcendence: Edited Collection of Yu Yingshi's Key New Confucian Writings), Beijing: Zhongguo

guangbo dianshi chubanshe, 1992. It should be noted that the planning for this series had been in place since 1987.

47. Yu Yingshi, "Qian Mu yu xin Rujia," 83–193, *passim*.

48. Wu Rujun, "Tang Junyi xiansheng yu dangdai xin Rujia," 7.

49. Luo Yijun, *Ping xin Rujia*, preface, 2.

50. Luo Yijun, "Lun dangdai xin Rujia de licheng he diwei," 32–3.

51. He does not do this even in his more detailed response to Yu Yingshi, "Jin shiyu nian dangdai xin Ruxue de yanjiu yu suowei menhu wenti."

52. Zheng Jiadong, *Dangdai xin Ruxue shilun*, 300, 301–2.

53. Li Daoxiang, Xiandai *xin Ruxue yu Song Ming lixue* 現代新儒學與宋明理學 (New Confucianism and Song-Ming Neo-Confucianism), Shenyang: Liaoning chubanshe, 1998, 297. The view that Confucianism is in need of rejuvenation contrasts sharply with that of Li Zehou 李澤厚, "Guanyu Ruxue he xin Ruxue 關於儒學和新儒學" (On Confucianism and New Confucianism), Fudan daxue lishixi 復旦大學歷史系 (ed.), *Zhongguo chuantong wenhua zai jiantao* 中國傳統文化再檢討 (A Critical Re-Appraisal of China's Traditional Culture), Hong Kong: Shangwu yinshuguan, 1987, vol. 2, 7, who claims that, "As an ideology of social control for several thousand years, Confucianism is no longer the thought of a particular class, but rather it has become the main component in the nature of the Chinese people (*Zhonghua minzu xing*), or the people's nature (*guomin xing*), or what we can term 'cultural psychology.'" Unlike the New Confucian figures, for this very reason, he concludes: "Obviously, Confucianism is certainly not exhausted; it is not something that needs quickly to be saved or rejuvenated and promoted." Despite this, the ready identification of Confucianism with "the nature of the Chinese people" and "the people's nature" is also espoused by many so-called New Confucians.

54. Yan Binggang, *Dangdai xin Ruxue daolun*, 67–8. Yan objects to the identification of Zhang Junmai as a New Confucian on the grounds that while he was a Confucian, he lacked innovation, and was uncritical of many aspects of the Confucian tradition. See 58–61 ff.

55. Yan Binggang, "Shi lun xin Ruxue de yanbian 試論新儒學的演變" (An Account of the Development of New Confucianism), in Fang and Li (eds.), *Xiandai xin Ruxue yanjiu lunji*, vol. 1, 51–5.

56. Li Zhenguo, "Xiandai xin Ruxue yu chuantong Ruxue bentilun de chongjian 現代新儒學與傳統儒學本體論的重建" (New Confucianism and the Restructuring of Traditional Confucian Ontology), in Fang and Li (eds.), *Xiandai xin Ruxue yanjiu lunji*, vol. 1, 148.

57. Jing Haifeng 景海峰, "Dangdai xin Ruxue sichao jianlun 當代新儒學思潮簡論" (A Brief Account of the New Confucian Intellectual Movement), *Shenzhou daxue xuebao* (renwen kexue ban) (1987.1): 61.

58. Lao Siguang is sympathetic to many of the "New Confucian" ideals, but is not generally considered to be a New Confucian. In a number of respects, his 1952 essay, "Zhongguo wenhua zhi weilai yu Ruxue jingshen zhi chongjian 中國文化之未來與儒學精神之重建" (The Future of Chinese Culture and the Rebuilding of the Confucian Spirit), in his *Ruxue jingshen yu shijie wenhua luxiang* 儒學精神與世界文化路向 (The Confucian

Spirit and the Direction of World Culture), Taipei: Shibao chubanshe, 1986, might even be regarded as a precursor to the 1958 Declaration. Lao avers that "China's cultural spirit is able to be represented only by the Confucian spirit" (169); "Not only has the Confucian spirit indeed been the mainstream of the Chinese cultural spirit, but as to its actual system, only it is fit to represent the [future] direction of Chinese culture" (170); and that moral spirit and moral subjectivity are the main concerns of Confucian thought while knowledge is the main concern of Western thought (171–2). Where Lao probably removed himself from contention as a New Confucian candidate are his beliefs that Cheng-Zhu Confucianism represents the pinnacle of Confucian thought, and that there has been an over emphasis on the primacy of moral subjectivity in Confucian thought. In a recent publication, Lao explains that he was not a signatory to the 1958 Declaration because despite a close relationship with Mou Zongsan, there was some distance between himself and Tang Junyi in their respective evaluations of Confucian thought. See Lao Siguang, *Siguang renwu lunji*, 109.

59. This contrasts significantly with a position that Yu had held in 1982 when he objected to classifying Xiong as a New Confucian on the grounds that his thinking was quite different from that of Tang, Xu, and Mou, despite having been their teacher. Instead, Yu proposed that the most representative New Confucian thinkers were Tang Junyi, Mou Zongsan, and Xu Fuguan. He also objected to classifying Zhang with Tang, Xu, and Mou on the grounds that his thought was very different from theirs. See "Dangdai xin Rujia yu Zhongguo de xiandaihua" 15.1(1982): 7.

60. Guo Qiyong, "Xiandaihua yu Zhongguo chuantong wenhua chuyi 現代化與中國傳統文化芻議" (My Views on Modernization and China's Traditional Culture), *Wuhan daxue xuebao* (Shehui kexue ban) (1986.5): 9 ff.

61. Luo Yijun, "Lun dangdai xin Rujia de licheng he diwei," 42.

62. The distinctions Fang proposes are a little hard to sustain given that Mou also taught at New Asia College during 1968–74.

63. Fang Keli, "Disandai xin Rujia lüeying 第三代新儒家掠影" (A Sketch of the Third Generation New Confucians), *Wenshizhe* (1989.3): 45–6.

64. Luo Yijun, "Jin shiyu nian dangdai xin Ruxue de yanjiu yu suowei menhu wenti," 6.

65. Liu did, however, have a close relationship with Mou Zongsan and Xu Fuguan during the six years he spent teaching at Donghai University in Taichung (1958–63). Although Mou left for Hong Kong in 1960, Liu relates that even before 1958, he had participated in some of the informal study sessions that Mou conducted in his (Mou's) own home in Taichung. Both Mou and Xiong Shili were close friends of Liu's father. See Liu Shuxian, *Chuantong yu xiandai de tansuo* 傳統與現代的探索 (Investigations into Tradition and Modernity), Taipei: Zhengzhong shuju, 1994, 9, 47 ff.

66. Guan Dong 關東, "Xiandai xin Ruxue yanjiu de huigu yu zhanwang 現代新儒學研究的回顧與展望" (New Confucian Studies in Retrospect and Prospect), *Zhexue yanjiu* (1990.3): 80, which is an interview with Fang Keli.

67. Tu Wei-ming (=Du Weiming), *Confucian Ethics Today: The Singapore Challenge*, Singapore: Federal Publications, 1984, 108.

68. Du Weiming, "Chuangzao de zhuanhua 創造的轉化" (Creative Transformation [1987]), in *Rujia chuantong de xiandaihua: Du Weiming xin Ruxue lunzhu jiyao* 儒家傳統的現代化: 杜維明新儒學論著輯要 (The Modernization of Confucian Tradition: Edited Collection of Du Weiming's Key New Confucian Writings), Beijing: Zhongguo guangbo dianshi chubanshe, 1992, 146–7.

69. Tu Wei-ming, "Towards a Third Epoch of Confucianism" (1986), in his *Way, Learning and Politics: Essays on the Confucian Intellectual*, 141, confirms this impression.

70. Mou Zongsan, *Shengming de xuewen* 生命的學問 (Vital Learning), Taipei: Sanmin shuju, 1970, 62.

71. Du Weiming, "Rujia chuantong de xiandai zhuanhua 儒家傳統的現代轉化" (The Modernization of Confucian Tradition), in *Rujia chuantong de xiandaihua: Du Weiming xin Ruxue lunzhu jiyao*, 69.

72. Cheng Zhongying 成中英, "Dangdai xin Rujia de jieding yu pingjia 當代新儒家的界定與評價" (The Boundaries and Evaluation of New Confucianism), in Luo Yijun (ed.), *Ping xin Rujia*, 134, similarly insists that New Confucianism is a philosophy that is still in the process of developing and does not have a fixed or permanent nature.

73. See Wang Qishui 王其水, "Ehu xi: Taiwan xin Ruxue de xin quxiang 鵝湖系: 臺灣新儒學的新趨向" (The Ehu Group: New Directions in New Confucianism in Taiwan), *Kongzi yanjiu* (1998.2): 76–81.

74. In his criticism of what he perceives to be the damaging influence of the "formalism and subjectivism" of Kant's moral philosophy leading to the "dogmaticization" of Mou Zongsan's influential teachings, Lin Anwu, "Dangdai xin Ruxue ji qi xiangguan wenti zhi lijie yu fanxing (shang) 當代新儒學及其相關問題之理解與反省 (上)" (Understanding of and Reflections on New Confucianism and Issues Relating to It), *Ehu yuekan* 19.7(1994.1): 20, proposes not only a broader engagement with a wide range of New Confucian thinkers (including Feng Youlan and He Lin), but also with the various "schools" of Marxism, Three Principles of the People (Sun Yat-sen), liberalism, and the Taiwanese Scholastic (aka "Shilin Catholic") philosophers. Since the mid-1990s many of these areas of engagement have, in fact, been undertaken, with both mainland and Taiwanese scholars writing books and articles on the connections between New Confucianism and a range of subjects including: Marxism, Post Modernism, Buddhism, Islam, Christianity, and religion generally.

75. Fan Guiping and Gan Chunsong, "Hou xin Rujia shidai: Guanyu chuantong wenhua yanjiu zhuanxiang de pingjie 後新儒家時代: 關於傳統文化研究轉向的評介" (The Post New Confucian Age: Concerning the Evaluation of a Change in Direction in Studies of Traditional Culture), *Zhexue dongtai* (1997.3): 25–6.

76. Lin Anwu, "Mou Zongsan xiansheng zhi hou: Zhoushu, zhuanzhi, liangzhi yu jiezhou: Dui Taiwan dangdai xin Ruxue de pipan yu qianzhan 牟宗三先生之後: 咒術, 專制, 良知與解咒: 對臺灣當代新 儒家的

批判與前瞻" (Post Mou Zongsan: Spells, Autocracy, Innate Knowledge and the Removal of Spells: Critique of and Future Prospects for New Confucianism in Taiwan), *Ehu yuekan* 23.4(1997.10): 11–12.

77. Indeed the whole linear notion of intellectual transmission and orthodoxy is questionable when discussing our retrospectively identified New Confucians. Li Minghui (Lee Ming-huei) informs me that in his forthcoming volume, *Der Konfuzianismus im modernen China*, Leipzig: Leipziger Universitätsverlag, 2002, he uses the metaphor of a "circle" (as in the Vienna circle). Both this and a retreat from the narrow "New Confucian" label are laudable.

CHAPTER 2

THE NEW *DAOTONG*

John Makeham

Many premodern Chinese intellectual traditions and "schools" (especially philosophical and religious ones) share the common characteristic of being retrospectively created. New Confucianism provides students of Chinese intellectual history with a rare opportunity to study this traditional strategy of orthodoxy formation in a contemporary context. One of the earliest and most influential examples of the practice is Sima Tan's 司馬談 (ca. 180–110 B.C.) essay on the essential characteristics of the six "schools" (*jia* 家) of pre-Qin thought, in which four of the "schools" he identifies—the Legalists, the School of Names, the Daoists, and the Cosmologists—are retrospectively created. Sima Tan's taxonomy has exercised a lasting influence on the historiography of classical Chinese thought. Even today, standard textbooks still largely adhere to his classifications. The authority of his taxonomy was consolidated when it was subsequently adopted by bibliographers, Liu Xiang 劉向 (79–8 B.C.), in his *Bielu* 別錄, and his son, Liu Xin 劉歆 (46 B.C. to A.D. 23), in his *Qilüe* 七略. The Lius contributed to the genealogical dimension of the classifications by identifying and assigning individual writers to particular categories. In his *Hanshu* "Treatise on Bibliography (*Yiwen zhi* 藝文志)," Ban Gu 班固 (32–92) expanded the number of classifications to ten and, in the case of the Confucians, pushed their genealogy back to the time of predynastic cultural heroes, Yao and Shun.

In later periods, the practice of retrospective creation was further stimulated by the practice of lineage building. Developments during the Six Dynasties period (222–589), in particular, are especially significant. Albert Dien, for example, maintains that the "Six Dynasties is one

characterized by unusual considerations of pedigree in the appointment
of office," where lineage rather than material wealth or property was the
prerequisite for favored treatment. "These favored lineages emerged
during the troubled years from the end of the Han to the early Chin,
through the institution of the Nine Grades system. . . . Very quickly the
distinction between those who qualified and those who did not became
set, especially in the South."[1] Scott Pearce even singles out pedigree as
the defining characteristic of this age: "Although the medieval Chinese
world was not ruled by oligarchy, nor dominated by a prepotent aris-
tocracy, it does contrast with earlier and later periods in the inordinate
attention that men of this age gave to pedigree. . . . Pedigree was an
intangible, an ideal that informed the mentality of this age."[2]

By the eighth century, we find genealogical discourse being used to
shape the concept of a Chan school of Buddhism. There is a growing
consensus in modern scholarship that Chan was not a monolithic tradition but was made up of a number of competing ideologies and
lineages, each of which claimed a direct genealogical connection with
Bodhidharma (early sixth century). As David W. Chappell notes, a
"major legitimizing device from the eighth century on was the 'transmission of the lamp' histories of mind-to-mind transmission from
enlightened masters."[3] These texts articulated complex genealogies, often
going back to the Indian patriarchs and the early Buddhas. In addition to
their function as "catalysts for the enlightenment of readers," John
McRae identifies two other functions: "(1) to glorify the sages of the past
and thereby legitimize the status of their living disciples and (2) to
rationalize the origins and existence of the Chan school itself."[4]

Also active in the late eighth and early ninth centuries is the major
Confucian thinker, Han Yu 韓愈 (768–824). In his essay, "Yuan dao
原道" (Tracing the Way to Its Source),[5] he outlines what was later to
become one of the most potent forms of genealogical discourse in Chinese
intellectual history, the so-called *daotong* 道統 or "interconnecting
thread of the way" (although Han Yu did not refer to it as such.) In
this essay, he identifies a lineage of Confucian sages and luminaries
responsible for handing down the "way and virtue" from antiquity to
Mencius. He relates that after Mencius the transmission became inter-
rupted, implying that he was the first after Mencius to have taken up
the mantle of transmission. Han Yu employs the genealogical strategy
to bolster the claims he makes for the Confucian way, thereby supporting his criticisms of the rival paths of Daoism and Buddhism,[6] just as
early forms of Chan used genealogical discourse to distinguish themselves from their rivals.

In the Northern Song, Cheng Yi 程頤 (1033–1107) claimed that he was the first to have taken up the mantle of transmitting the *dao*—the learning of the sages—having rediscovered its significance after an extended hiatus since the classical period. Elsewhere, he also includes his elder brother as a transmitter.[7] The great Neo-Confucian thinker, Zhu Xi 朱熹 (1130–1200), accepted this and refined it with his own modifications and additions. He coined the term *daotong* to describe this passing on of the way. *Daotong* has been variously translated, some of the more common renderings being, "succession to the way"; "line of continuity with the way"; "transmission of the way"; "legacy of the way;" "orthodox tradition"; and "tradition of the way." Like the word "tradition" (or, more closely, the German *Überlieferung*, with its active verbal sense of "what comes down from the past;" "handed down from the past"), *daotong* certainly has a sense of taking possession of and handing on of that which is transmitted (*traditum*). Thomas A. Wilson, however, has cautioned against the conventional translation of *daotong* as "tradition of the Way," proposing instead "genealogy of the way": "*Daotong* does not signify a *tradition* as such, but rather a filiative lineage of sages who were regarded as the sole transmitters of the true Confucian Way." For the proponents of the *daoxue* 道學 (learning of the way; Dao School; Cheng-Zhu tradition of learning) lineage, "Authority is believed to derive from a remote origin that has been lost or forgotten.[8] ... The solution is to recover this origin by means of genealogical practices that separate the main lineage from collateral lines and privilege the main lineage (*ta-tsung*) as the true transmission."[9] Failure to distinguish the correct lineage of the *dao* meant being unable to know "which of the many former Confucians correctly understood the Dao" thereby putting "one at risk of sinking into heterodoxy."[10] Based on the evidence of his preface to Zhu Xi's *Lun Meng jingyi* 論孟精義 (The Essential Meaning of the Analects and Mencius; 1172), Zhu's own understanding of *daotong* is more faithfully translated as "the interconnecting thread of the way."[11] This sense is still evident in contemporary use of the term, although, as I go on to show, New Confucians have employed the term in both broad and specific applications. Zhu is believed to have coined the term *daotong* in 1181[12] and began propagating it in the 1189 preface to his commentary on *Zhongyong*. Both there and in his preface to *Daxue* (written one month earlier), Zhu portrays the Chengs as having played a pivotal role in the restoration of the *daotong*. Zhu, of course, was not the first to have described how the transmission of the way had been disrupted after Mencius. Two aspects of Zhu's appropriation of the *daotong* conceit are especially pertinent.

First, Confucius, Zengzi, Zisi, and Mencius are identified as the last in a long line of early transmitters. By privileging this group, Zhu was able to present the *Analects*, *Daxue*, *Zhongyong*, and *Mencius* as an integrated body of texts, premised on the line of transmission from Confucius to Mencius. Second, by writing commentaries on these four books and identifying the Cheng brothers as the modern inheritors of the *daotong* transmission, Zhu sought to imply that he, too, was an heir to that transmission.[13] As Wilson has shown in his book, beginning in the Song and continuing into the Qing Dynasty, the concept of *daotong* was employed as a strategy to confirm certain Confucians as true transmitters of the way and exclude others on the basis of their being propagators of heterodox teachings. The concept continues to be employed for that purpose today.

In the opening chapter I referred briefly to the as yet unresolved tension and rivalry that exists between mainland scholars and overseas scholars concerning proprietary rights over New Confucianism. Events of the 1990s confirm that it is the overseas camp that has emerged victorious. In what follows, I will describe how Mou Zongsan 牟宗三 (1909–95), and his followers in Taiwan and Hong Kong, secured this victory by appealing to the concept of *daotong*.

Liu Shuxian 劉述先 has accurately summed up the perspective of many overseas Chinese scholars concerning why they consider themselves to be the legitimate heirs to New Confucianism:

> However, when we overseas talk of New Confucianism our field of vision is quite different from that of the mainland scholars. Our aim is not to pursue old historical traces, but rather to grasp a still vibrant trend of thought. When viewed from a philosophical perspective, in particular, after the mainland changed hands, He [Lin 賀鄰 (1902–93)] and Feng [Youlan 馮友蘭 (1895–1990)] had both already embraced Marxist thinking and fundamentally negated their earlier points of view. They have not exerted a single iota of influence on the development of overseas New Confucian thought. So, of course, they are ineligible to be considered as New Confucians. The case of Xiong Shili 熊十力 [1885–1968], however, is entirely different. Tang [Junyi 唐君毅 (1909–78)], Mou [Zongsan], and Xu [Fuguan 徐復觀 (1903–82)] were all his students. Even Liang Shuming's 梁漱溟 [1893–1998] influence pales in comparison to that of Xiong. As the publicly acknowledged founding figure of this trend of thought, his thought must be discussed. . . . In its narrow sense, the definition of Contemporary New Confucian philosophy is naturally based on [the thought of] Tang and Mou and the traditions of New Asia [College]. If, however, we take a more liberal view, then why should the definition be so narrowly focused? . . . In fact, that which Xiong

bequeathed was a spiritual inspiration. There was certainly nobody who genuinely transmitted his learning (*xuewen*).[14]

Explicitly and otherwise, Liu raises a host of issues in this passage. Most germane to our present inquiry is the claim that Xiong left a "spiritual" legacy—a regular refrain in Liu's writings. As early as 1982 Liu had maintained that "One may say that Mr Xiong initiated a spirit; it was this spirit that Tang, Mou, and others fastened on to." Liu then proceeds to claim that if Xiong Shili had not initiated what he did, then there would not have been a Tang and a Mou after him.[15] Ten years later, the spiritual legacy claim was made even more forcefully: "That which is transmitted by overseas, Hong Kong, and Taiwan New Confucians is definitely not the system of Mr Xiong's [thought], but rather his spirit. This is already as clear as daylight. . . . Later on [i.e., in the 1960s, 1970s, and 1980s], the major works of New Confucians in Hong Kong and Taiwan were published one after the other. In spiritual terms they carried on Mr Xiong's [legacy]; in terms of academic endeavor and intellectual brilliance they far surpassed Mr Xiong."[16]

What was Xiong's spiritual legacy and why was it so pivotal? Liu provides the answer by citing the following anecdote—one strikingly reminiscent of the Chan "encounter dialogue"—as related by Mou Zongsan. Once when Xiong and Feng Youlan were discussing the concept of *liangzhi* 良知 (innate moral knowledge), Xiong berated Feng as follows: "'You claim that *liangzhi* is a hypothesis. How can you say that? *Liangzhi* is as real as real can be. Moreover, it is a presence (*chengxian*呈現). This presence needs to be intuited directly and confirmed directly.' Mr Feng was stunned and speechless. Mr Mou commented: 'Up until then, it had never been heard that *liangzhi* is real, that it is a presence. Like a thunderclap which immediately rouses the deaf and stirs the hard of hearing, Mr Xiong's words had the effect of raising a person's level of enlightenment to the level of the Song and Ming Confucians.'"[17] Liu cites this example to explain why, despite his fame, Feng Youlan's influence as a philosopher was minimal, while Xiong Shili, who was unknown to society at large, was able to establish the New Confucian school (*xuepai*). Of especial interest is the reference to the "sudden enlightenment" experience and Xiong's nodal role in linking Neo-Confucian and New Confucian thought.

Contrary to what one might have expected, a number of mainland scholars echo these views. Zheng Jiadong's 鄭家棟 following comments (also published in 1992) might even be read as a gloss on Liu's foregoing remarks. Zheng relates that Mou Zongsan had completed the work that Xiong had hoped to complete but was unable to do so. According to Zheng, this enabled "learning of the mind and the nature" (*xin xing zhi xue* 心性之學) to become a system of thought that, "for the first time," could be grasped logically both in respect of its external structure and its inner "philosophy (*yili* 義理; normative principles)." He further states that Mou's development of Xiong's thought was limited to a common "spiritual direction; in fact, in terms of their respective learning and inherent spiritual temperament there was quite a distance between them. . . . Mr Mou was principally concerned with addressing the self-transcendence of the ethical life and its empathetic resonance with heaven, earth, and the ten thousand things. Mr Xiong placed more emphasis on the creative capacity of 'noumenal reality' (*benti* 本體; *shiti* 實體), strength (*gangjian* 剛健), 'creation and its transformation' (*shenghua* 生化), 'arousing the ten thousand things,' 'ceaseless creativity,' and 'instigating the myriad transformations and bringing the ten thousand things completion.'"[18] In the same year, Luo Yijun 羅義俊 similarly described Tang, Mou, and Xu as being the transmitters of Xiong's legacy. "However, what they transmit is not the specific perspective of Xiong's scholarship but rather the desire to open up a spiritual direction for the future path of Chinese culture."[19]

While clearly not denying or even marginalizing the nodal role ascribed to Xiong in linking New Confucianism with Neo-Confucianism, mainland scholars have a strategic commitment to being more catholic in their recognition of other similarly nodal figures (viz. Liang Shuming, Ma Yifu 馬一浮 [1883–1967], Feng Youlan, He Lin). This is expressed both in general and specific formulations. The former tend to be couched as blanket statements about the general character of New Confucian thought: "New Confucian thought has grown directly out of Song-Ming Confucianism and has its own system and unique scholarly characteristics."[20] "Veneration of Neo-Confucianism (*Song Ming lixue*) is the common spiritual orientation of the New Confucians. The fundamental spirit of Confucianism, as understood by them, is, in fact, the spirit of Neo-Confucianism. That is to say, they regard Confucian 'learning of the heart and the mind' as the source and mainstream of Chinese scholarly culture."[21] The specific formulations relate to individual thinkers. Zheng Jiadong, for example, argues that New Confucian metaphysics—which for him (in 1989, at least) is the central characteristic of New Confucianism—can be divided into two broad factions: the Liang-Xiong-Mou group members who are the chief representatives of a Neo-Lu-Wang (Lu Jiuyuan 陸九淵 [1139–93] and Wang Yangming 王陽明 [1472–1529]) tradition, and Feng Youlan who is the chief representative of a Neo-Cheng-Zhu (Cheng Yi 程頤 [1033–1107] and Zhu Xi [1130–1200]) tradition.[22] This classification of individual twentieth-century Confucians as Cheng-Zhu partisans, Lu-Wang partisans, or syncretists did not begin in the 1980s. Already in his *Dangdai Zhongguo zhexue* 當代中國哲學 (Contemporary Chinese Philosophy), He Lin had described Liang Shuming as the leading partisan of the Lu-Wang faction, Xiong Shili as the systematizer and synthesizer of Lu-Wang "learning of the moral mind" (*xinxue*), and Ma Yifu as drawing on both the Lu-Wang and Cheng-Zhu traditions.[23] As noted in chapter 1, He Lin also criticized Feng for concentrating on the Cheng-Zhu views on *li* 理 (pattern; principle) and *qi* 氣 (psychophysical energy), while paying insufficient attention to their views on *xin* 心 (mind) and *xing* 性 (the nature), and also for preferring Cheng-Zhu thought over Lu-Wang thought.[24]

Daotong: The Interconnecting Thread of the Way

This Cheng-Zhu/Lu-Wang distinction is a continuation of a polemic that may be traced to Yuan and Ming period discussions of "the differences and similarities of Zhu and Lu (*Zhu-Lu yitong* 朱陸異同)."[25] It is no coincidence that protagonists should choose to frame the issue of the Neo-Confucian roots of New Confucianism within the discourse of "the interconnecting thread of the way (*daotong*)."

It is tempting to compare Mou Zongsan's role in propagating a New Confucian *daotong* to that played by Zhu Xi in propagating what subsequently became the officially sanctioned *daotong* of the Cheng-Zhu tradition of Neo-Confucianism. Both Mou and Zhu were philosophical synthesizers and system builders, and both sought to use the *daotong* strategy to promote certain thinkers and exclude other thinkers from their versions of the orthodox Confucian tradition. As I will show below, Mou's *daotong* was designed to undermine the traditional authority granted to Zhu Xi as a mainstream transmitter of the *daotong*.

In his mature writings, Mou uses the term *daotong* in two different, but related senses. The first sense refers to what might be termed the "content" of the way (*dao*) that has been preserved in and transmitted through China's traditional culture (the reality or "presence" of which has been "personally experienced" and set down in specific teachings by past sages and enlightened philosophers): "China's tradition of 'learning of the moral nature' (*dexing zhi xue* 德性之學) is called *daotong*."[26] Here, *dexing zhi xue* is synonymous with "learning of the mind and the nature" (*xin xing zhi xue*). The "truth" or "meaning" disclosed by *xin xing zhi xue* is that ultimate meaning (the transcendent: *daoti* 道體; *benti* 本體) is immanent in each person collectively (*xingti* 性體) and individually (*xinti* 心體)—everyone can realize this ultimate meaning. Mou distinguishes this sense of *daotong* (ethico-religious value system based on intuitive knowledge of our innate moral nature and its transcendent underpinning or mode of being) from *zhengtong* 政統 (democratic system of governance) and *xuetong* 學統 (scientific learning).[27] Traditional Chinese culture had developed neither *zhengtong* nor *xuetong* (in the forementioned sense), but will need to do so in the future.[28] What China's traditional culture did have, however, was a rich and vibrant *daotong*. Indeed, it is this *daotong* that makes China's traditional culture unique, so much so that the two are inseparable. Elements of this conception of *daotong* are also evident in section 4 of the 1958 Declaration (see chapter 1), although there the emphasis is on the unity of the cultural matrix rather than its ethico-religious core:

> Here, in referring to Chinese culture, we are referring to its "single stemmed-ness" (*yi ben xing* 一本性). This "single stemmed-ness" is what is referred to as "Chinese culture." In its origins, it is a single system. This single stem does not deny its many roots. This is analogous to the situation in ancient China where there were different cultural areas. This did not, however, impede the main thread of its single line of transmission (*yimai xiangcheng zhi tongxu* 一脈相承之統緒). The Yin overthrew the mandate of the Xia yet continued the Xia culture, and the Zhou overthrew the mandate of the Yin yet continued the Yin culture, thus constituting the unified succession and continuity of the cultures of the three dynasties. After this, the Qin succeeded the Zhou, the Han succeeded the Qin, and right up to the Tang, Song, Yuan, Ming, and Qing, even though politically there were periods of division and unity, overall the constant way (*chang dao* 常道) was that of great unity (*da yitong* 大一統). Moreover, the periods of political division and unity never adversely affected the general convergent trend of China's culture and thought. This is what is referred to as the "successive transmission of the interconnecting thread of the way (*daotong*)." . . . In the China that existed up until one hundred years ago, Chinese culture was fundamentally a single cultural system that had been successively passed down from dynasty to dynasty. . . . Chinese culture has always existed as an interconnected main thread (*yiguan zhi tongxu* 一貫之統緒).[29]

While we cannot be sure how much of this passage was written by Mou, the ideas expressed are largely consistent with Mou's conception of the unified cultural system in which meaning/value was vouchsafed by the ethico-religious core of that culture.[30] This meaning or value or truth was made accessible through an apprehension of our moral nature, through the learning of the mind and nature.

The second sense of *daotong* relates to the transmission of this interconnected cultural thread and its ethico-religious core. In particular, it concerns those sages and enlightened Confucian philosophers who had understood the connection between, on the one hand, their mind, nature, and ultimate meaning, and, on the other hand, the genealogy of enlightened men who had transmitted and enhanced this understanding through their teachings. Yu Yingshi has argued that unlike traditional genealogical accounts of *daotong* since Song times, the New Confucian formulation is based on the notion of an awareness of the relationship between our minds and nature as the locus of immanent moral value and their transcendent, ontological underpinning, *daoti* 道體 (also variously known as *tiandao* 天道, *tianming* 天命, *benti* 本體, *shangdi* 上帝, and the like).[31] I would question the accuracy of this generalization. In the case of Mou Zongsan, both genealogical and ultimate meaning concerns are in evidence. The following passage from Mou's *Zhongguo zhexue de tezhi* 中國哲學的特質 (The Characteristics of Chinese Philosophy) is a typical example of how these two concerns are interwoven:

> Chinese Confucianism traces its main lineage to Confucius and Mencius. Accordingly, the heart of this great tradition of Chinese thought rests firmly in the high regard that it accords to subjectivity (*zhutixing* 主體性). It is also because of this that Chinese thought can be broadly termed learning of the mind and the nature (*xin xing zhi xue* 心性之學). Here "the mind" stands for "moral subjectivity" (*daode de zhutixing* 道德的主體性). ... This is the nucleus of Chinese thought and so Mencius is in the orthodox lineage of the learning of the mind and the nature. Song-Ming Confucians such as Zhou [Dunyi 周敦頤 (1017–73)], Cheng [Yi 程頤 (1033–1107)], Zhang [Zai 張載 (1020–77)] and Zhu [Xi] by and large have not followed the Mencian route, but have come via the route of the *Xici* 繫辭 commentary to *Changes* and *Zhongyong*.[32]

Zheng Jiadong has identified three key aspects to Mou's revised *daotong*.[33] The first is Mou's reaffirmation of Confucius' seminal role. The evidence Zheng musters in support of this first aspect is a little strained because he downplays Mou's portrayal of Confucius as continuing (or reestablishing) the *daotong*. Despite this, Mou clearly sought to present Confucius as the founder of the "Confucius tradition" (*Kongzi zhi chuantong*), a new phase in the interconnecting thread of the way (*daotong*). This phase is characterized by Confucius' new "teaching of humaneness," a teaching that enabled "the original interconnecting thread of the way" (*dao zhi ben tong* 道之本統) to be reestablished. Mou describes this new phase as highlighting "inner sageliness" (*nei sheng* 內聖),

which for Mou is another term for moral metaphysics.[34] As Zheng suggests, Mou is, in fact, arguing that any account of the *daotong* should begin with Confucius and not with Yao, Shun, Yu, Tang, Wen, Wu, and the Duke of Zhou. This revised *daotong* challenges the *daotong* genealogy outlined in Zhu Xi's preface to *Zhongyong* (and which was adopted and championed by Zhu's later followers).

The second aspect is Mou's classification of the *Analects*, *Mencius*, *Zhongyong*, and the *Xici* commentary to *Changes* as the texts of the *daotong*. Mou separates *Daxue* from the mainline of the *daotong* on the grounds that it is primarily concerned with a system of education rather than moral metaphysics. This, in turn, supports his charge that the Cheng-Zhu tradition deviated from the mainline,[35] allowing Mou to propose a tripartite division in the so-called "second period of Confucianism," the Song-Ming period. The first lineage (literally "thread" [*xi* 系]) in this division consisted of Zhou Dunyi, Zhang Zai, Cheng Hao 程顥 (1032–85), Hu Hong 胡宏 (1105–55), Lu Jiuyuan, Zhang Shi 張栻 (1133–80), and Liu Zongzhou. The second consisted of Cheng Yi and Zhu Xi. The third consisted of Lu Jiuyuan and Wang Yangming. Mou links the first and third lineages because of their joint emphasis on a core group of texts: *Analects*, *Mencius*, the *Xici* commentary to *Changes*, and *Zhongyong*. Mou, thus, distinguishes two Song-Ming Neo-Confucian traditions: a major tradition represented by the first and third lineages and a minor (or inferior) tradition represented by the "divergent" (*qichu* 歧出) and "collateral" (*pangzhi* 旁枝) second lineage.[36] Mou's contemporary followers, such as Cai Renhou 蔡仁厚 and Liu Shuxian, have continued to adhere faithfully to his revised Neo-Confucian *daotong*.[37] Yu Yingshi argues that this practice of determining which Song-Ming Confucians continued to transmit the *daotong* after Mencius; who among them had realized the *daoti* 道體 (ontological reality of the way);[38] and what had been their path to that realization, is "the most important internal evidence that the New Confucians have for reconstructing the *daotong*."[39]

The third aspect is Mou's use of the *daotong* to affirm the historical role of Xiong Shili's philosophy. Although Xiong himself said very little about the concept of *daotong*,[40] "As far as Mr Mou was concerned, the significance of Mr Xiong's philosophy did not lie in his having established a school of thought but rather in maintaining the continuity of the single thread of Confucian *daotong*."[41] Mou himself stated that "Only the lifelong learning of my teacher, Mr Xiong Shili, inherited and advanced the humaneness teaching of the Confucian sages as well as the aims and intentions of the various great Confucians of the late

Ming."[42] Comments such as this have been echoed and developed by Mou's followers. In his obituary for Xiong Shili, Cai Renhou claimed that "After the fall of the Ming, Chuanshan 船山 [Wang Fuzhi 王夫之; 1619–92] died, learning was severed, and the way perished for three hundred years." Cai then proceeds to identify Xiong as having been the first to take up the "thread (*xu* 緒)" left by Wang Fuzhi, thereby reestablishing a connection with Confucius' distant teachings.[43] (The parallels with early Neo-Confucian accounts of the hiatus in the transmission of the *daotong* from Mencius to the Cheng brothers are unmistakable.) Liu Shuxian similarly describes Xiong as being the first person after the May Fourth period to have "mastered the fundamental wisdom of Neo-Confucianism" and to have "applied his energies to reviving the thought of this tradition. ... After the Song and Ming periods, the Qing Confucians lost the thread of the *daotong* once again, and it was not until the Republican period that Xiong Shili opened up the beginnings of contemporary New Confucianism."[44]

Having established Xiong Shili as a nodal figure linking Neo-Confucianism and New Confucianism, New Confucian proponents and scholars of New Confucianism have been particularly concerned to describe the movement's twentieth-century developments. Liu Shuxian, for example, has regularly emphasized that, in his role as transmitter of the *daotong*, Xiong opened up a new direction in Confucian thought: "In every period since the time of Xiong Shili, there have been talented and wise gentlemen who have applied themselves to stopping the decline in Confucianism, resulting in contemporary Neo-Confucianism's (*dangdai de xin Rujia*) having now already become a trend of thought that cannot be completely ignored in international scholarship."[45] This new direction is often referred to as the third period of Confucianism. As the earliest New Confucian to use this term, and given his connection with Xiong, it is perhaps understandable that Mou is singled out as an exemplary New Confucian. Jing Haifeng, for example, suggests that early figures such as Xiong Shili, Liang Shuming, and Ma Yifu had been unable to formulate a clear sense of unity and continuity: "Only with Mou Zongsan's thesis of a third period of Confucianism can New Confucianism be finally considered to have established a historical position for itself."[46] Other commentators have been less willing to tarnish Xiong's legacy (presumably out of a concern that it would also diminish Mou's authority). Having related that the *daotong* was reestablished by a handful of luminaries during the twentieth century, Cai Renhou (a disciple of Mou) introduces Mou as follows: "In his early years Mr Mou studied at Peking University as a student of Mr Xiong from Huanggang.[47] After this, he spread Mr Xiong's teachings in a number of our universities and his reputation spread to the four quarters. . . . Compared with those among his contemporaries who have lost their ancestral tablets and whose origins are a disparate mix, there is a great distance."[48] Even Zheng Jiadong, who is a mainland scholar of New Confucianism rather than a New Confucian partisan, maintains that "It can be said of the Confucian lineage of Zisi, Mencius, Lu Xiangshan, and Wang Yangming, that with Mou Zongsan its process of modernization was completed."[49] Elsewehere, Zheng has sought to bolster Xiong's (and hence Mou's) authority by criticizing Liang Shuming for lacking a sound metaphysical foundation in this moral philosophy, thereby failing to address the issue of *xinxing benti* 心性本體 (the ontological dimension of "learning of the mind and the nature"): "Yet it was precisely this that was the nucleus of Lu-Wang philosophy.[50] Without this there is no way to explain the goodness of morality or the inner foundation for the epistemological method of that which enables one to seek within one's ontological mind (*benxin* 本心). . . . The real founder of New Confucian ontology was Xiong Shili."[51]

As with the early Neo-Confucian versions of the *daotong*, Mou Zongsan's revised *daotong* simultaneously functions as a vehicle for exclusion as well as inclusion. Earlier, we have already noted Liu Shuxian's attempt to highlight a qualitative difference between the enlightened minds of Xiong and Mou, on the one hand, and Feng Youlan, on the other hand. Elsewhere, he has criticized Feng Youlan and He Lin while singling out Xiong, Tang, Mou, and Xu as the legitimate inheritors of Wang Yangming's philosophy. (He excludes Qian Mu on the grounds that Qian was a historian and that his *Guoshi dagang* 國史大綱 [Outline of China's History] is outdated.)[52] In the preface to his book on Zhu Xi's philosophy, he notes that in writing the book he drew on Tang's *Zhongguo zhexue yuanlun* 中國哲學原論 (Essays Tracing the Source of Chinese Philosophy) only minimally because Tang had tried to reconcile the differences between the Cheng-Zhu and Lu-Wang traditions, despite there being irreconcilable differences and contradictions. He contrasts Tang's attitude to this with the pro-Lu-Wang and anti-Zhu attitude of Mou Zongsan in Mou's *Xinti yu xingti*, and a pro-Zhu sympathy he detects in Qian Mu's *Zhuzi xin xue'an* 朱子新學案 (New Studies of Zhu Xi).[53] Thus, not only has the Cheng-Zhu/Lu-Wang distinction been used externally to distinguish Feng Youlan from the Xiong-Liang-Mou-Tang-Xu-Zhang camp, it has also been used internally by Mou's followers to distance Mou from potential second generation "contenders."

Liu Shuxian's commitment to the goal of establishing Mou as the legitimate successor to Xiong (and the *daotong* lineage associated with Xiong) is never in doubt. In some respects, this is surprising because Liu had not been a student of Mou but of Fang Dongmei 方東美 (1899–1976).[54] Equally surprising is Liu's refusal to recognize Fang as a New Confucian, even though many other scholars (both in China and overseas) have done so.[55] What is not surprising, however, is Liu's appeal to the Cheng-Zhu/Lu-Wang distinction to justify excluding his teacher from the ranks of New Confucianism: "As for my teacher, Mr Fang Dongmei, he promoted the teachings of the early Confucians (*yuanshi Ru*). He maintained a consistently veiled criticism of the Song-Ming Confucians and had no direct connection with this line [i.e., Neo-Confucian thought]."[56] It is possible that the real explanation for Liu's attitude to his teacher was that Fang's writings were incompatible with the Xiong-Mou tradition of moral philosophy.[57] Certainly, Fang's critical attitude to the Confucian *daotong* mentality puts a significant distance between him and Mou.[58] Given Liu's attitude to Qian Mu, it is perhaps not entirely coincidental that Qian should also have been critical of the *daotong* mentality.[59]

A potentially more serious threat to Mou's revised *daotong* is Xiong Shili's own writings, or at least his publications from the 1950s and the 1960s. Many of his publications from this period substantially revise his earlier views on a wide range of issues. In his *Yuan Ru* 原儒 (Tracing Confucianism; 1956), Xiong not only rejects the sages who preceded Confucius but also the Confucians who came after Confucius in the Spring and Autumn and Warring States periods. The only Confucian he respects is Confucius. In his *Ming xin pian* 明心篇 (A Treatise on Understanding the Mind; 1959), Xiong claims that Confucius' inner sage learning of the mind (*neisheng xinxue*) stopped being transmitted after Mencius, and that the Song and Ming Confucians were not in the main line of transmission. In his *Qian kun pian* 乾坤篇 (The Explication of Creativity and Procreativity; 1961), he denies that even Mencius had been able to transmit all of Confucius' main teachings. We may further note that there are elements in Xiong's earlier writings that are also inconsistent with Mou's philosophy. Although Xiong, like later New Confucians, regarded *xin xing zhi xue* to be the life blood of Confucian thought, his understanding of *xin xing zhi xue* was different from that of Mou and Tang. Whereas Mou placed more emphasis on the transcendence aspect of *benxin* 本心 (ontological mind) or *xingti* 性體 (principle of creativity immanent in humans), Xiong placed more emphasis on the creativity of the *xinti* 心體 (moral subjectivity), reflecting the influence of Henri Bergson and Xiong's understanding of the *Book of Changes*. This difference in emphasis is also reflected in Xiong's criticisms of the Song-Ming Confucians for purportedly losing this aspect of Confucius' thought.[60]

These inconsistencies have not daunted the enthusiasm of the so-called third generation New Confucians, the group that gradually assumed an identity in the 1970s and 1980s. It is also this group that, together with post-1985 mainland scholars, retrospectively created the very idea of New Confucianism as a philosophical school with its own self-identity. As I have argued in chapter 1, it is only with the advent of this "third generation" that we can speak of New Confucianism as having cohesion and self-identity, thus making the "third" generation the first real generation of New Confucians. The price that has been paid for the *daotong* conceit is a much more circumscribed cohort of "orthodox transmitters" of the way.

Zheng Jiadong identifies Liu Shuxian as being the most straightforward in his acceptance of Mou Zongsan's philosophical teachings, and one who is very much in the Xiong-Mou tradition. By contrast, of Du Weiming he writes: "In fact, Mr Du's so-called 'Confucianism's third period of development' should really be understood to refer to a broadly encompassing cultural movement . . . He is very far removed from the transcendent 'learning of the mind and the nature' theoretical system of Xiong and Mou. Overall it can be said that Du Weiming's main concern is not to build some sort of [philosophical] system, but rather to show how Confucianism—as an intellectual resource—can possibly have an influence on modern people's lives and society." As such, Du is really a Confucian revivalist rather than a New Confucian. Next, Zheng cites Cheng Zhongying's criticisms of New Confucianism's failure to address real-life problems and its overemphasis on subjectivity at the expense of objectivity. Zheng cites these three examples in response to his own question: "Does New Confucianism still exist as a unified school in the post–Xiong-Mou period? Or is it that we only have New Confucian learning (*xin Ruxue*) [i.e., scholarly and academic in nature], and no New Confucians (*xin Rujia*) [i.e., being applied to real life]?" Clearly he is pessimistic. He concludes:

> When considered as a particular school, New Confucianism (*xin Rujia*)— with Xiong and Mou as its main representatives, and also including Xiong's students Tang Junyi, Xu Fuguan, and their followers—has already become, or is in the process of becoming, history. Amongst the new generation of Confucians, those scholars who defend their masters' teachings with great intensity have, in fact, consciously or unconsciously, departed

from their teachers' original starting point. The basic characteristic of New Confucianism (*xin Rujia*) does not reside in learning (*wei xue* 為學) but in promoting the way (*hong dao* 宏道). When the day passed that scholarship and the search for knowledge become the guiding concern, New Confucianism lost the unique determining feature that made it a particular school, and it melted into the horizon of Contemporary New Confucianism's (*xin Ruxue*) multiple developments.[61]

Zheng's complaint that "learning" in the New Confucian agenda had come to replace the "promotion of the way," is but a resurfacing of the old tension between "honoring the moral nature (*zun dexing* 尊德性)" and "following the path of inquiry and study (*dao xuewen* 道學問)." Since Song times, these two hermeneutic styles[62] have been portrayed as alternating trends in the practice and pursuit of the Confucian way; sometimes viewed as complementary, at other times antithetical. The reality for most thinkers, however, has been a blend of the two styles.[63] Although the rhetorical appropriation of the dichotomy reached its zenith in the late eighteenth to mid-nineteenth centuries, with Han Learning–Song Learning polemics, it is not surprising to see the two concepts being redeployed in the late 1990s' discussions of New Confucianism. At an innocuous and superficial level, this is evident in the distinction between the *xin Rujia* (New Confucian identity) and *xin Ruxue* (scholarship on New Confucianism), a distinction that effectively functions as a shorthand way to distinguish between the overseas and mainland Chinese intellectuals who publish on New Confucian subjects. (The superficiality of this particular distinction is brought home when one reflects on the wealth of scholarship so readily in evidence in Mou Zongsan's writings.) Yet, the distinction is also strategically employed in matters of more pressing consequence. This is well illustrated in the case of rival pretenders to the *daotong* inheritance: Lin Anwu and Liu Shuxian.

In the early-to-mid 1990s, Taiwanese New Confucian, Lin Anwu, had become more vocal in his dissatisfaction of what he perceived as an excessive emphasis on the "cultivation of the mind and the nature (*xin xing xiuyang* 心性修養)" at the expense of "ethical praxis" (*daode shijian* 道德實踐).[64] Although this dichotomy differs from the "moral nature"/"study and inquiry" dichotomy, there is a common element in each pair: "cultivation of the mind and the nature" and "honoring the moral nature." In 1994, Lin coined the term "Post New Confucianism" referring to a broad philosophical reorientation that would promote a move away from inner ethical cultivation toward ethical practice.[65] Since then, in many of his publications he has sought to refine his thought in regard to this new orientation. In 1997, he began to characterize this new direction, variously, as a move away from metaphysical discussion of the mind and the nature (*xin xing lun* 心性論) to a "philosophical anthropology" (*zhexue renleixue* 哲學人類學); from an idealist ontology to a materialist methodology; and from ethics to social criticism. The appropriation of the term "anthropology" is presumably to draw attention to a renewed focus on distinctly human problems. For Lin, the biggest task facing Post New Confucianism in a postmodern world is to address the problem of human alienation.[66]

The death of Mou Zongsan, in 1995, provided a new impetus (and freedom) to promote the idea of a Post New Confucian philosophy in what Lin terms the "post Mou Zongsan age."[67] At a conference on the philosophy of Mou Zongsan, convened by the Ehu yuekanshe in June 1996, Lin had described Mou as belonging to a collateral line (*bie zi wei zong* 別子為宗) of Confucianism, not the main line. (Mou himself had used this expression to separate the Cheng-Zhu line of Neo-Confucianism and so portray it as deviating from the main line.)[68] In his clearest explanation of what he meant when he referred to Mou as "the biggest collateral line" Confucian, his major objection seems to be to the influence of the Kantian distinction between noumena and phenomena on Mou's system of thought that in turn, undergird Mou's own transcendent-immanent distinction. He even pays Mou the following backhanded compliment: "Mou's theses are so brilliant. They constitute an extremely well-integrated Idealist (*xinxue*) system of thought. They really have enabled Mr Mou to have become the founding teacher (*zongshi* 宗師) of a generation. In this respect, I feel that Mr Mou is the biggest collateral Confucian."[69]

Behind Lin's challenge to Mou, lies an implicit alternative *daotong*, the philosophical character of which is shaped by a particular interpretation of the concept of *qi* 氣 (psycho-physical energy). According to Lin, this particular interpretation avoids the ontological bifurcation of *li* (pattern) and *qi* responsible for the sort of transcendent-immanent distinction that lies at the center of New Confucian metaphysics. While some commentators have observed that Lin does not clearly articulate which philosophers represent this alternative orthodoxy,[70] others have cogently argued that the figure Lin has foremost in his mind is Wang Fuzhi 王夫之 (1619–92), as is attested in Lin's early study of the latter.[71] We expect Lin to make the association between himself and Wang more explicit in his future writings. At present, he has still not shaken-off his image as an *enfant terrible* and iconoclast. Although Lin is a prodigious publisher of books and essays, his most trenchant critics charge him with displaying more show than substance, maintaining that until he can produce a work of theoretical sophistication and academic rigor, many will continue to ostracize him.

By contrast, for some years now, Liu Shuxian may be seen to have assumed the mantle of *de facto* successor to the Xiong-Mou lineage (although Professor Liu would vehemently deny the claim). His efforts to promote New Confucianism (and Confucian thought more generally) have been tireless. For much of the 1990s (until his retirement from the Chinese University of Hong Kong in 1999), he simultaneously held two posts: one as chair of the Philosophy Department at the Chinese University of Hong Kong and one as a researcher in the Institute for Literature and Philosophy, Academia Sinica, Taiwan. As such, he has been particularly well positioned to promote the cause of New Confucianism. Since 1993, he has codirected three three-year state-funded projects on New Confucianism. Publications from the first two three-year projects have been included in the book series, *Dangdai Ruxue yanjiu congkan* 當代儒學研究叢刊 (New Confucian Studies Series), published by Academia Sinica. Li Minghui 李明輝 states in his preface to one of the books in the series, that the first of these three-year projects was not only the largest project on Confucianism ever undertaken by Academia Sinica, but also the largest ever undertaken in Taiwan. He further relates that it was modeled on the major state-funded project on New Confucianism directed by Fang Keli and Li Jinquan in China in the mid-1980s and early 1990s.[72]

Liu Shuxian's campaign is conducted under the banner of "spiritual Confucianism," simultaneously signaling an ethico-religious agenda with "world religion" ecumenical overtones, a reiteration of the "spiritual" legacy of Xiong and Mou, and a clear reaffirmation of his commitment to the "honoring the moral nature" style of New Confucianism. While his recent comments concerning Lin's Post New Confucianism are summary and dismissive, the very fact that he should deign to make them at all is revealing:

> Over the past few years, since the death of Mr Mou in 1995, New Confucian thought has been undergoing a type of deformation. The signs of this are clearer today than ever before. . . . In developments within the realm of learning, there has been a movement away from "honoring the moral nature" towards "following the path of inquiry and study." Even within the Mou school, there have appeared divisions between the young men of the Ehu camp. Lin Anwu's "Draft Structure of a Post New Confucian Philosophy", which he proposed at the Third International Conference on New Confucianism [held in Hong Kong in 1994], is a very clear example.[73]

Liu has also used the banner of "spiritual Confucianism" to distance himself from the "Confucian capitalism" thesis that has been pushed by Du Weiming and others since the late 1980s.[74] Despite this difference, Liu and Du have each realized the strategic importance of attempting to galvanize intellectual support for the notion of a broader East Asian Confucian identity. Yet, intellectual support may not be enough. John H. Berthrong has reiterated an important issue now confronting the third and fourth generation New Confucians: Will they "be able to move out from their academic posts in order to provide a Confucian interpretation of modern life that will have real appeal to modern and East Asian peoples?" Although the more skeptical observer will dismiss the possibility of a middle-class Confucianism emerging "within the nexus of changing economic structures of East Asia," more modest possibilities should not be ruled out. As Berthrong further observes, "Reforming Buddhists in Taiwan have accomplished just this kind of inspired religious marketing by engaging educated lay people in what can only be called socially relevant Buddhism."[75] Indeed, some academics I have spoken to in Taiwan argue that the success of popular Buddhist marketing, in part at least, lies in the appeal to traditional "Confucian" values. If there is to be a future for a socially relevant Confucianism, it surely cannot ignore the small but growing lobby of those in China and Taiwan who have been calling for "secularized" and grass-roots forms of Confucianism.[76]

Notes

1. Albert E. Dien (ed.), *State and Society in Medieval China*, Hong Kong: Hong Kong University Press, 1990, introduction, 21, 22.
2. Scott Pearce, "A Survey of Recent Research in Western Languages on the History of Early Medieval China," *Early Medieval China* 1(1994): 134.
3. David W. Chappell, "Hermeneutic Phases in Chinese Buddhism," in Donald S. Lopez (ed.), *Buddhist Hermeneutics*, Honolulu: University of Hawaii Press, 1988, 196.
4. John R. McRae, *The Northern School and the Formation of Early Ch'an Buddhism*, Honolulu: University of Hawaii Press, 1986, 79–80.
5. Han Yu, "Yuan dao 原道" (Tracing the Way to Its Source), *Changli xiansheng ji* 昌黎先生集 (Han Yu's Collected Writings), *Sibu beiyao*, Shanghai: Zhonghua shuju, 1936.
6. Peter K. Bol, *"This Culture of Ours": Intellectual Transmission in T'ang and Sung China*, Stanford: Stanford University Press, 1992, 129–30.
7. See the passages cited and translated in Peter K. Bol, "Cheng Yi as a Literatus," in Willard J. Peterson, Andrew H. Plaks, and Ying-shi Yu (eds.), *The Power of Culture: Studies in Chinese Cultural History*, Hong Kong: The Chinese University Press, 1994, 177.

8. This characterization does not hold true in the case of Zhu Xi. See, for example, his preface to *Zhongyong, Sishu zhangju jizhu* 四書章句集注 (Section and Sentence Commentaries and Collected Annotations on the Four Books), Beijing: Zhonghua shuju, 1983.

9. Thomas A. Wilson, *Genealogy of the Way: The Construction and Uses of the Confucian Tradition in Late Imperial China*, Stanford: Stanford University Press, 1995, 75.

10. Thomas A. Wilson, "Genealogy and History in Neo-Confucian Sectarian Uses of the Confucian Past," *Modern China* 20.1(1994): 6, 7, 14.

11. In this preface, Zhu writes: "Yet, ever since the Qin and Han, none in the Confucian category has been up to the task of participating in learning about the transmission of this way." Later in the same preface he refers to "the thread (*xu* 緒) which has not been transmitted (*chuan*) for one thousand years" and the "main thread (*tong* 統) transmitted (*chuan*) by the clear-sighted sages and worthies."

12. Hoyt Cleveland Tillman, *Confucian Discourse and Chu His's Ascendancy*, Honolulu: University of Hawaii Press, 1992, 138.

13. On the subject of Zhu Xi and *daotong*, see Wing-tsit Chan, *Chu Hsi: New Studies*, Honolulu: University of Hawaii Press, 1989, 320–35.

14. Liu Shuxian, "Pingxin lun Feng Youlan 平心論馮友蘭" (A Balanced Account of Feng Youlan), *Dangdai* 35(1989.3): 63.

15. Liu Shuxian, cited in "Dangdai xin Rujia yu Zhongguo de xiandaihua 當代新儒家與中國的現代化" (New Confucianism and China's Modernization), *Zhongguo luntan* 15.1(1982): 17.

16. The quotation is from Liu's essay, "Duiyu Xiong Shili xiansheng wannian sixiang de zai fansi 對於熊十力先生晚年思想的再反思" (Some More Reflections on Mr Xiong Shili's Thought in His Later Years), *Ehu* (1992.3): 1–2.

17. Mou Zongsan, *Shengming de xuewen* 生命的學問 (Vital Learning), Taipei: Sanmin shuju, 1970, 126, cited by Liu Shuxian, "Pingxin lun Feng Youlan," 56–7. Mou also relates this story in his *Wushi zishu* 五十自述 (My Story at Fifty), Taipei: Ehu chubanshe, 1989, 86.

18. Zheng Jiadong, "Xiandai xin Ruxue de luoji tuizhan ji qi yinfa de wenti 現代新儒學的邏輯推展及其引發的問題" (The Logical Development of New Confucianism and the Issues Generated), 26, paper distributed at the Second International Conference on New Confucianism, National Central Library, Taipei, 1992.

19. Luo Yijun, "Jin shiyu nian dangdai xin Ruxue de yanjiu yu suowei menhu wenti 近十餘年當代新儒學的研究與所謂門戶問題" (The So-Called Problem of Factionalism in New Confucianism over the Past Ten-Plus Years), 15, paper distributed at the Second International Conference on New Confucianism, National Central Library, Taipei, 1992.

20. Luo Yijun (ed.), *Ping xin Rujia* 評新儒家 (Evaluating New Confucianism), Shanghai: Shanghai renmin chubanshe, 1989, preface, 4.

21. Fang Keli, "Guanyu xiandai xin Rujia yanjiu de jige wenti 關於現代新儒家研究的幾個問題" (Several Issues Concerning New Confucian Studies; 1987), in Fang Keli and Li Jinquan (eds.), *Xiandai xin Ruxue yanjiu lunji* 現代新儒學研究論集 (Collected Essays on New

Confucian Studies), vol. 1, Beijing: Zhongguo shehui kexue chubanshe, 1989, 3.

22. Zheng Jiadong, "Xiandai xin Ruxue de jiben tezheng 現代新儒學的基本特徵" (Basic Characteristics of New Confucianism) in Fang and Li (eds.), *Xiandai xin Ruxue yanjiu lunji*, vol. 1, 75. It should be noted, however, that by 1990 Zheng was already showing a clear bias toward Xiong (at the expense of Liang) in his purported role as a seminal New Confucian. This is because Zheng (like many others) had come to regard Xiong and Xiong alone as the "founder of New Confucian ontology." See his *Xiandai xin Ruxue gailun* 現代新儒學概論 (A General Account of New Confucianism), Nanning: Guangxi renmin chubanshe, 1990, 139.

23. He Lin, *Dangdai Zhongguo zhexue*, Nanjing: Shengli chubangongsi, 1947, 9–19, passim. Li Daoxiang, *Xiandai xin Ruxue yu Song Ming lixue* 現代新儒學與宋明理學 (New Confucianism and Song-Ming Neo-Confucianism), Shenyang: Liaoning chubanshe, 1998, 223–5, argues that despite his bias to certain Lu-Wang philosophical positions, He Lin himself still sought to reconcile the Cheng-Zhu and the Lu-Wang traditions.

24. He Lin, *Dangdai Zhongguo zhexue*, 36.

25. See, for example, Thomas A. Wilson, *Genealogy of the Way*, chapter 6.

26. Mou Zongsan, *Shengming de xuewen*, 61.

27. Mou's *santong* 三統 (three unities) thesis is expounded in three of his writings, in particular: *Lishi zhexue* 歷史哲學 (The Philosophy of History; 1995), *Zhengdao yu zhidao* 政道與治道 (The Way of Government and the Way of Rule; 1961), and *Daode de lixiang zhuyi* 道德的理想主義 (Moral Idealism).

28. See, for example, his *Shengming de xuewen*, 60–3; *Daode de lixiang zhuyi* 道德的理想主義 (Moral Idealism), Taichung: Donghai daxue chubanshe, 1959, 152–7.

29. I have used the version of the Declaration reprinted in Feng Zusheng 封祖盛 (ed.), *Dangdai xin Rujia* 當代新儒家 (Contemporary New Confucianism), Beijing: Sanlian shudian, 1989, section 4, 10–11.

30. Mou would have embellished this account by also acknowledging the contributions of exceptional individuals such as Confucius. Confucius was exceptional because of his teaching of humaneness that enabled the *daotong* to be reestablished and revitalized. See, for example, *Xinti yu xingti* 心體與性體 (Ontological Mind and Ontological Nature), Taipei: Zhengzhong shuju, 1968, 1: 192–3, 245.

31. Yu Yingshi, "Qian Mu yu xin Rujia 錢穆與新儒家" (Qian Mu and the New Confucians), republished in Yu Yingshi, *Xiandai Ruxuelun* 現代儒學論 (Essays on Modern Confucianism), Shanghai: Shanghai renmin chubanshe, 1998, 202.

32. Mou's *Zhongguo zhexue de tezhi*, Taipei: Xuesheng shuju, 1965 (third edition), 66–7. In his *Cong Lu Xiangshan dao Liu Jishan* 從陸象山到劉蕺山 (From Lu Xiangshan to Liu Jishan), Taipei: Xuesheng shuju, 1979, 216–17, he claims that after Mencius, other than Wang Yangming 王陽明 (1472–1528) and Liu Zongzhou 劉宗周 (1528–1645), hardly anyone had been able to receive what Mencius had transmitted

regarding the learning of inner sageliness (i.e., learning of the mind and the nature).

33. Zheng Jiadong, *Dangdai xin Ruxue shilun* 當代新儒學史論 (Essays on the History of New Confucianism), Nanning: Guangxi jiaoyu chubanshe, 1997, 22–43.

34. Mou Zongsan, *Xinti yu xingti*, 1: 192–3, 262.

35. Mou Zongsan, *Xinti yu xingti*, 1: 19; 3: 369, 383.

36. Mou Zongsan, *Xinti yu xingti*, 1: 11–19.

37. See, for example, Cai's comments in *Song Ming lixue: Nan Song pian* 宋明理學：南宋篇 (Song-Ming Neo-Confucianism: Southern Song Volume), revised third edition, Taipei: Xuesheng shuju, 1993 (originally published 1980), 1–9; Liu Shuxian, *Zhuzi zhexue sixiang de fazhan yu wancheng* 朱子哲學思想的發展與完成 (The Development and Completion of Zhu Xi's Philosophical Thought), Taipei: Xuesheng shuju, 1995 (revised third edition; original 1982), 479.

38. A good example of the exclusionary dimension to this practice is the following assessment of Zhu Xi made by Liu Shuxian, *Zhuzi zhexue sixiang de fazhan yu wancheng*, 478 (see also 527): "Indeed, there remained a gap separating Zhu from achieving a personal experience (*tiyan* 體驗) of the ultimate (*zhongji* 終極). There is no denying this fact." This is curiously reminiscent of the comments about Yan Yuan's 顏淵 similar failure, finally, to achieve sagely enlightenment, assembled in Zhu's *Lunyu jizhu* 論語集注 (Collected Annotations to the Analects) commentary to *Analects*, 9.11.

39. Yu Yingshi, "Qian Mu yu xin Rujia," 203.

40. See the examples cited in Li Minghui 李明輝, "Dangdai xin Rujia de daotong lun 當代新儒家的道統論," in *Dangdai Ruxue zhi ziwo zhuanhua* 當代儒學之自我轉化 (The Subjective Turn in New Confucianism), Taipei: Zhongyang yanjiuyuan, Zhongguo wenzhe yanjiusuo, 1994, 155–6.

41. Zheng Jiadong, *Dangdai xin Ruxue shilun*, 38.

42. Mou Zongsan, *Shengming de xuewen*, 38.

43. Cai Renhou, *Xin Rujia de jingshen fangxiang* 新儒家的精神方向 (The Spiritual Direction of the New Confucians), Taipei: Xuesheng shuju, 1981, 277, 279.

44. Liu Shuxian, *Zhuzi zhexue sixiang de fazhan yu wancheng*, preface, 1990, 4, 425, 481. Liu Shuxian, "Lun Rujia sixiang yu xiandaihua, houxiandaihua de wenti: da Bao Zunxin xiansheng 論儒家思想與現代化，後現代化的問題：答包遵信先生" (On the Issue of Confucianism, Modernization, and Post-Modernization: In Reply to Mr Bao Zunxin), *Zhongguo luntan* 27.2(1988): 78, says he is following Du Weiming in identifying Xiong as the founding figure of Third Epoch Confucianism or New Confucianism, and in regarding Xiong to be the first *daotong* inheritor after the Ming.

45. Liu Shuxian, *Zhuzi zhexue sixiang de fazhan yu wancheng*, preface, 1990, 4. In his English-language publications, Liu similarly uses the term "contemporary Neo-Confucianism" to refer to New Confucianism.

46. Jing Haifeng, preface to *Dangdai xin Rujia*, 2.

47. Mou studied at Peking University from 1927 to the summer of 1933. Mou met Xiong for the first time in the winter of 1932 (but not as a student studying under Xiong) and stayed in close contact with him during the following ten years. See Yan Binggang 顏炳罡, *Dangdai xin Ruxue yinlun* 當代新儒學引論 (Introduction to New Confucianism), Beijing: Beijing tushuguan, 1998, 197, 384–5; *Mou Zongsan xueshu sixiang pingzhuan* 牟宗三思想評傳 (A Critique of Mou Zongsan's Thought), Beijing: Beijing tushuguan chubanshe, 1998, 9.
48. Cai Renhou, *Xin Rujia de jingshen fangxiang*, 323–4.
49. Zheng Jiadong, "Xiandai xin Ruxue de luoji tuizhan jiqi yinfa de wenti 現代新儒學的邏輯推展及其引發的問題" (The Logical Development of New Confucianism and the Issues Generated), 24, paper distributed at the Second International Conference on New Confucianism, National Central Library, Taipei, 1992. This same *daotong* mentality is reiterated by Fang Keli, "Guanyu xiandai xin Rujia yanjiu de jige wenti," 2–3, even though he does not single out Mou for individual attention. Thus, he describes the New Confucians as "striving to carry on the *daotong* of Kong-Meng-Cheng-Zhu-Lu-Wang so as to reconstruct the Confucian value system and so enable Confucianism to achieve its 'third period of development' today."
50. That is, the tradition of philosophy associated with Lu Xiangshan and Wang Yangming.
51. Zheng Jiadong, *Xiandai Ruxue gailun*, 139. In his *Dangdai xin Ruxue shilun*, 17, 18, Zheng further claims that there is no concept of *daotong* (in a strict sense) in Liang Shuming's thought. Moreover, "it seems that he did not discuss the *daotong* issue." Despite the fact that he discussed *liangzhi* (ethical knowledge) and *lixing* 理性 (ethical reason) as aspects of his epistemology, "mainly they were discussed from the aspect of their actuality (and not their transcendent aspect). It may also be said that by *liangzhi* and *lixing*, he was only referring to moral reality and not cosmic reality." These comments should not, however, be taken as an indication that Zheng was unwilling to accord Liang New Confucian status; rather, he wants to establish the relative importance of Xiong over Liang.
52. Liu Shuxian, "Dangdai Ruxue fazhan de xin qiji 當代新儒學發展的新契機" (A New Turning-Point in the Development of New Confucianism), in Zheng Jiadong 鄭家棟 and Ye Haiyan 葉海煙 (eds.), *Xin Rujia pinglun* 新儒家評論 (Critical Essays on New Confucianism), Beijing: Zhongguo guangbo dianshi chubanshe, 1995, 1.
53. Liu Shuxian, *Zhuzi zhexue sixiang de fazhan yu wancheng*, preface, 1–2.
54. For Liu's early association with Mou, see chapter 1, this volume.
55. Most recently, however, he has changed his stance on this issue, arguing that Fang should be identified as a first generation New Confucian. See his preface to Umberto Bresciani, *Reinventing Confucianism: The New Confucian Movement*, 2.
56. Liu Shuxian, *Zhuzi zhexue sixiang de fazhan yu wancheng*, 483. Similarly, Fang Keli argues that because Fang Dongmei belonged neither to the Neo Cheng-Zhu tradition nor the Neo Lu-Wang tradition, he cannot be classifed as a New Confucian. See Fang Keli, "Xiandai xin Ruxue de fazhan licheng

現代新儒學的發展歷程" (The Historical Development of New Confu-cianism), in Fang Keli and Li Jinquan (eds.), *Xiandai xin Rujia xue'an* 現代新儒家學案 (Studies of New Confucians), vol. 1, Beijing: Zhongguo shehui kexue chubanshe, 1995, 33.

57. Fang Keli, "Guanyu xiandai xin Rujia yanjiu de jige wenti," 3 (written in 1987), maintained that like Feng Youlan, Fang Dongmei held Cheng-Zhu learning in high regard, thus his approach differed from the Lu-Wang emphasis of Mou Zongsan.

58. On Fang Dongmei's critical attitudes to the *daotong* mentality, see the first four of his lectures in his *Xin Rujia zhexue shiba jiang* 新儒家哲學十八講 (Eighteen Lectures on New Confucian Philosophy), Taipei: Liming wen-hua shiye gongsi, 1983.

59. See the passages discussed in Yu Yingshi, *Xiandai Ruxue lun*, 190–1. As Li Minghui, "Dangdai xin Rujia de daotong lun," 149–50, has noted, how-ever, Qian's views on *daotong* were not consistent.

60. For a discussion of these differences, see Zheng Jiadong, *Dangdai xin Ruxue shilun*, 16–17.

61. Zheng Jiadong, *Dangdai xin Ruxue shilun*, 96–101.

62. Which, respectively, can be quite neatly correlated with Tzvetan Todorov's typologies of "finalist" and "operational" interpretation. On Todorov's identification of these as the two major types of interpretation in the history of hermeneutics, see his *Symbolism and Interpretation*, trans. Catherine Porter, New York: Cornell University Press, 1982, Part II.

63. See Donald J. Munro's stimulating account of the "imperial style of inquiry," a style that would seem to correspond to Todorov's "finalist" typology. See his *The Imperial Style of Inquiry in Twentieth Century China: The Emergence of New Approaches*, Ann Arbor: Center for Chinese Studies, The University of Michigan, 1996.

64. Lin Anwu, "Dangdai xin Ruxue ji qi xiangguan wenti zhi lijie yu fanxing (shang) 當代新儒學及其相關問題之理解與反省 (上)" (Reflections on and Understanding of New Confucianism and Related Issues), *Ehu yuekan* 19.7(1994.1): 13.

65. See Lin Anwu, "Guanyu Rujia zhexue zhong de shijian gainian zhi liqing: Cong lao Rujia, xin Rujia, dao Hou xin Rujia de fansi 關於儒家哲學中的實踐概念之釐清：從老儒家，新儒，到後新儒家的反思" (Clarifying the Concept of Praxis in Confucian Philosophy: Reflec-tions on Old Confuciansim, New Confucianism, and Post New Confu-cianism), *Ehu yuekan* 20.6(1994.12): 18–19.

66. Lin Anwu, "Mou Zongsan xiansheng zhi hou: Zhoushu, zhuanzhi, liangzhi yu jiezhou: Dui Taiwan dangdai xin Ruxue de pipan yu qianzhan 牟宗三先生之後：咒術，專制，良知與解咒—對臺灣當代新儒家的批判與前瞻" (Post Mou Zongsan: Spells, Autocracy, Innate Knowledge, and the Removal of Spells: Critique of and Future Prospects for New Confucianism in Taiwan), *Ehu yuekan* 23.4(1997.10): 11.

67. Lin Anwu, "Ruxue geming: Hou xin Rujia zhexue de wenti xiangdu: Xuyan 儒學革命：後新儒家哲學的問題向度：序言" (Confucian Revo-

lution: The Orientation of Problematics in New Confucian Philosophy),
Ehu yuekan 24.12(1999.6): 42.

68. For a detailed account of the expression and Mou's application of it to
Zhu Xi, see Cai Renhou, *Song Ming lixue: Nan Song pian*, 391–6.

69. Lin Anwu, "Hou xin Rujia zhexue de siwei xiangdu 後新儒
家哲學的思維向度" (The Orientation of Thought in New Confucian
Philosophy), *Ehu yuekan* 24.7(1999.1): 12.

70. Chen Lixiang, "Hou xin Rujia zhexue de siwei xiangdu: lundian zhi
shengsi 後新儒家哲學的思維向度：論點之省思" (The Orientation of
Thought in New Confucian Philosophy: Reflections on Arguments), *Ehu
yuekan* 25.1(2000.4): 59.

71. Li Zongding 李宗定, "Guanyu Lin Anwu jiaoshou 'Hou xin Rujia zhexue
de siwei xiangdu' ji dian yiwen 關於林安梧教授 '後新儒家
哲學的思維向度'：幾點疑問" (Several Queries Concerning Professor
Lin Anwu's "The Orientation of Thought in New Confucian Philosophy"), *Ehu yukan* 25.2(2000.5): 51–4. The study referred to
is Lin's *Wang Chuanshan renxingshi zhexue zhi yanjiu* 王船山
人性史哲學之研究 (A Study of Wang Chuanshan's Philosophy on the
History of Human Nature), Taipei: Dongda tushu gongsi, 1987, especially
section 5.

72. Li Minghui (ed.), *Rujia sixiang zai xiandai Dongya: Zonglun pian*
儒家思想在現代東亞：總論篇 (Confucian Thought in Contemporary
East Asia: Papers on General Topics), Taipei: Academia Sinica, 1998.

73. Liu Shuxian, "Lun dangdai xin Rujia de zhuanxing yu zhanwang
論當代新儒家的轉型與展望" (Change and Prospects for New
Confucianism), *Zhexue zazhi* 31(2000): 33–4.

74. Liu Shuxian, "Lun dangdai xin Rujia de zhuanxing yu zhanwang," 32–4.

75. John H. Berthrong, *Transformations of the Confucian Way*, Boulder:
Westview Press, 1998, 205.

76. See, for example, Jiang Guobao 蔣國保, "Rujia shisuhua de xiandai yiyi
儒家世俗化的現代意義 (The Modern Significance of Confucianism's
Secularization)," *Kongzi yanjiu* 57(2000): 26–35, 46; Wang Qishui, "Ehu
xi : Taiwan xin Ruxue de xin quxiang," 76–81.

PART II

CHAPTER 3
RECONSTRUCTING THE CONFUCIAN IDEAL IN 1980S CHINA: THE "CULTURE CRAZE" AND NEW CONFUCIANISM

Song Xianlin

In the 1980s, China underwent a period of drastic change. One of the most discussed phenomenon on the cultural front was the "culture craze" (*wenhua re* 文化熱). Fueled with ammunition from a range of imported "isms," participants in the cultural debates attempted to map out national and Western cultural territories. Many intellectuals attempted to redefine what is meant by Chinese culture and to rediscover the "national essence" through their study of New Confucianism. This essay examines New Confucianism in the context of the culture craze of the 1980s China. I argue that this seemingly philosophical exercise was principally brought about by cultural and political necessity; that the studies on New Confucianism were intentionally directed toward practical ends; and that the newly created "Confucian discourse" helped to reconstruct and re-imagine the Confucian ideal in post-Mao Chinese society, later serving as a catalyst for the "national studies craze" (*guoxue re* 國學熱) of the 1990s.

The Controversy over Western Influence and Cultural Tradition

One of the consequences of the Open Door policy was an acute awareness by Chinese intellectuals of the gap between the economic development in the modern West and China, after the Cultural Revolution. When Chinese intellectuals, for the first time in several decades, started to see

China in contrast with the "outside world," they became increasingly agonized and humiliated just as their predecessors had at the turn of the century. They were unwittingly caught in the middle of a cultural dilemma: either attempt to modernize China in line with the outside world or endeavor to preserve the cultural traditions that had been the very basis for Chinese cultural pride. On the one hand, the urgent need to realize the Four Modernizations (*sige xiandaihua* 四個現代化) led many intellectuals to embrace Western civilization, and to take it upon themselves to "catch up" to the West's level of technological power; on the other hand, they felt it was their duty to preserve the "national essence" in the face of what was perceived to be an outside threat, and so sought solace in China's cultural heritage.

The debate over the emergence of Obscure Poetry (*menglong shi* 朦朧詩) was the first manifestation of this dilemma. The immediate step taken by the government in the wake of the death of Mao Zedong 毛澤東 (d. 1976), in the late 1970s, was the "Emancipation of Thought." As a result of this new social, cultural, and political environment, there appeared a new poetry that was later referred to as Obscure Poetry. By proclaiming "I do not believe!" a group of young poets started their creative experiment with what were seen as Western Modernist techniques. To an "ultra stable culture,"[1] in which the inviolability of tradition is absolute, new occurrences never come easily. Even the so-called Great Cultural Revolution, which was an attempt to "smash the old world and create a new world," did not completely achieve its objectives.[2] Though primarily "I do not believe!" was a direct reaction to the poetic legacy of the Cultural Revolution, poets instantly found themselves caught in a debate over the issue of inheriting cultural tradition and learning from the West. Critics and poets were engaged in open polemic to validate or invalidate what was perceived as Western modernist poetic technique. The government-owned literary journal, *Shikan* 詩刊, ran the first critical forum in its August 1980 issue, and was later joined by more than forty other literary and cultural periodicals from all over the country.

In order to argue for the need to modernize Chinese society, those defending the new poetry saw the need to redefine "modernism." By describing Western Modernism as the "product of the development of human civilization at a certain historical stage," they tried to justify the poets' efforts to learn from the West. "As a widespread and prolonged artistic phenomenon," Xu Jingya 徐敬亞 believed that Western Modernism "was not to be disposed of by claims of 'decadence' or 'formalism.'"[3] Similarly, another critic, Xu Chi 徐遲, asserted the validity of modernism in Chinese literature by calling it "a historical necessity."

In his controversial article, "Modernization and Modernism," he insisted that modernism in literature is a natural by-product of social and economic modernization. In his muddled arguments, he claimed that if a society was to become modern, then it was necessary to have modernism in literature.[4] For those arguing against the impact of Western Modernism, however, it was considered unhealthy to the development of Chinese poetry to learn from Western poetic techniques. Chinese poetic writing should be built on China's own cultural heritage. In their overt arguments against what was seen as Westernization, their choice of words was militant and unreserved. Zang Kejia 臧克家 said that Obscure Poetry was doing nothing but "learning from the 'dregs' of foreign literature."[5] By degrading Western Modernism as "decadent" and "diseased," these critics accused the new poetry of having degenerated from Chinese tradition and "deviated from the national style."[6]

Almost all of the hundreds of articles on this cultural debate during 1980–84 highlighted the confrontation between what was perceived as Western Modernism and what was claimed as the Chinese cultural tradition. While many agreed that the "revolutionary legacy" of Mao's era did not represent the Chinese cultural tradition, confusion and strained arguments permeated the debates that initiated "the cultural craze." Attempts to define and redefine such terms as "national style" and "national heritage" soon led to more serious attempts to rediscover and re-imagine the spaces where Western Modernism and Chinese cultural tradition operate. Explorations were undertaken to articulate the indigenous qualities and characteristics of Chinese culture. In literature, there appeared works by A Cheng 阿城 and Han Shaogong 韓少功, later known as the "Seeking Roots 尋根" school; and in the field of philosophy, scholars started to reexplore traditional philosophical territory through tentative forays into Confucianism.

Reiterating Confucianism

It was against this backdrop that the word Confucianism came to be used again, in the Chinese press. While it was fashionable for scholars such as Gan Yang 甘陽 and Jin Guantao 金觀濤 to introduce and translate interpretative and critical discourses from the West, other scholars sought to rediscover what was meant by the "national essence." Like the emergence of Obscure Poetry, the word "Confucius" appeared on August 12, 1978, in the *Guangming Daily* 光明日報 as a reaction to the cultural environment of the Cultural Revolution. For the first time in over a decade the word Confucius was mentioned not to bring up its negative connotations of feudal society, but to call for a "reevaluation." In a conference organized by Shandong University in October 21–30, 1978, the issue of reevaluating Confucianism was also raised. Argument was focused upon the Gang of Four's attitude towards Confucius, and it was proposed that "Confucius should not be completely negated" but rather that "he should be divided into two," so that his positive and negative qualities could be distinguished. In subsequent articles in various newspapers and in symposia on Confucius held in October 1980 and April 1983, the theme of Confucius' reevaluation gained prominence. Zhang Dainian 張岱年 pointed out that the age of venerating Confucius and the age of anti-Confucius movements were both in the past. Instead, now was the age for studying Confucianism with scientific Marxist philosophy.[7] The books published before the mid-1980s are introductory in nature and circumscribed by the political discourse of the time. In the earliest publication on Confucius from this period, *The System of Confucian Philosophy*, Cai Shangsi 蔡尚思 concluded that "the political views of Confucius, although not without merit, in general are an elegy of a crumbling old system, and belong to the ranks of the backward and the conservatism."[8]

Interestingly enough, the term Confucianism was not seriously engaged in the ongoing cultural debates over tradition and Westernization until a year or so later. Unlike the literary endeavors to seek cultural "roots" in traditional ways of living, cultural philosophers took a different path in discussing Confucianism. With the memories of the Anti-Li Biao and Anti-Confucius 批林批孔 campaign still fresh, and the ongoing purge of "spiritual pollution 精神污染" (late 1983–early 1984), Chinese intellectuals discovered that it was more palatable to approach the subject of national essence indirectly by citing overseas discussions of New Confucianism. This strategy was clearly an example of a practice in Chinese society at that time to make commodities more saleable by first exporting them and then reimporting them (*chukou zhuan neixiao* 出口轉內銷). In September 1984, in a conference held in Confucius' hometown, Qufu, to celebrate Confucius' two thousand five hundred and thirty fifth birthday, thousands participated in the ceremony to unveil a statue of Confucius that had been destroyed during the Cultural Revolution. The establishment of the Academy of Chinese Culture (*Zhongguo wenhua shuyuan* 中國文化書院) and of the Chinese Confucius Research Institute (*Zhonghua Kongzi yanjiusuo* 中華孔子研究所) in 1985, marks the real beginning of engaging Confucianism in the ongoing cultural debates. Though the objective of the Academy of Chinese Culture was to research Chinese culture as a whole, Confucianism was given prominence as part of the whole in its agenda. Headed by the well-known philosopher, Tang Yijie 湯一介, the establishment of the Academy of Chinese Culture was considered one of the landmarks of the New Enlightenment Movement (*xin qimeng yundong* 新啓蒙運動)[9] and the 1980s culture craze.[10] One of its first academic endeavors was to publish a series of research works on Chinese culture in Hong Kong, Taiwan, and Overseas (*Gang-Tai haiwai Zhongguo wenhua yanjiu luncong* 港臺海外中國文化研究論叢), and introduce the works of some second and third generation New Confucians to Chinese readers. With the involvement of prominent overseas scholars such as Tu Wei-ming 杜維明 and Cheng Chung Ying 成中英, Confucianism—under the name of New Confucianism, an overseas intellectual school—became legitimized in mainstream discussions of tradition and Westernization. Tu Wei-ming's visit to Beijing in 1985 has been regarded as the beginning of "the return of New Confucianism to its homeland."[11] Although the works introduced at this time did not come exclusively from scholars outside mainland China, initially the active participation by New Confucians outside China certainly contributed to the gloss and validity of the study of Confucianism.

By the mid-1980s, the main objective for scholars who studied Confucianism shifted from reevaluation. In an opening address at the Symposium on Confucius in June 1985 in Beijing, the chairman of the Chinese Confucius Research Institute, Zhang Dainian, called for a scientific investigation into Confucius and Confucianism in order "to promote the democratic essence of Confucianism and fight against its feudal dross."[12] He credited Confucius as having been the founder of the spiritual civilization of feudal China, and linked the ongoing spiritual civilization campaign with the attempt to critically inherit the Chinese cultural legacy. In June 1985, the influential academic journal *Dushu* published Xue Yong's 薛涌 interview with Tu Wei-ming, "Cultural Value and Social Change," in which Tu brought up the topic of the third period of development of Confucianism. Subsequently, the renaissance of Confucianism—its so-called third period of development—was introduced into the ongoing cultural debates as a New Confucian agenda.[13] From the mid-1980s onwards, evaluations of Confucius and Confucianism became more positive. Although still talking about the stagnating influences of Confucianism in preventing Chinese culture and society from moving forward in modern history, Chen Lai 陳來, a philosophy professor in Beijing University, called for the "rational reorientation" of Confucianism in contemporary multicultural China.[14] In the same way that the concept of a Confucian renaissance was presented to Chinese audiences, the perception of Confucian culture as the essence of Chinese culture was introduced by way of research into first generation New Confucians such as Liang Shuming. In discussing Liang's *Dongxi wenhua ji qi zhexue* 東西文化及其哲學 (East and West Cultures and Their Philosophies), Zhao Dezhi 趙德志 concluded that "the characteristics of Chinese traditional culture are, in fact, the characteristics of Confucian thought." And again, through the voice of He Li 賀麟, Zhao asserted that "The fate of Confucian thought is tied up with the fate of the nation's future; these two cannot be separated."[15] By the late 1980s, Confucius became "the great thinker, educationist, statesman, philosopher, and historian," and was crowned "the founder of Chinese traditional culture." Confucianism, once portrayed as the ideology responsible for all China's feudal evils, was now credited with a uniquely Chinese psychological structure and way of thinking, and—as the mainstay of traditional Chinese culture—as having exercised a determinant influence on the main customs, rituals, and value systems of Chinese society.[16] By introducing the subject of New Confucianism into intellectual discussions, scholars involved in the Academy of Chinese Culture and in the Studies on Modern New Confucian Thought (*xiandai xin Rujia sichao yanjiu* 現代新儒家思潮研究) project, a major research project funded under the national seventh five-year plan for the social sciences, reclaimed the universality of Confucius' teachings, re-accredited to Confucius the honor of founding Chinese traditional culture, and reasserted the spiritual and psychological influence of Confucianism upon the Chinese nation. Summing up the transformation of Confucianism in the shape of New Confucianism in mainland China, in 1990 Fang Keli 方克立 wrote:

> Following the open-door reforms in mainland China, all sorts of trends of thought came swarming from the outside. This theory [New Confucianism] originated in China. Holding the flag of preserving China's national cultural spirit and seeking to reconcile the problems which exist between tradition, modernization, and Westernization, naturally New Confucianism will not pass by the opportunity to return to its homeland. Relying mainly on the efforts of some overseas Chinese scholars, New Confucianism actively promotes the renaissance and the third period of development for Confucianism, and has become an influential school of studies in the cultural debates in 1980s China.[17]

The discourse of government officials concerning the study of Confucianism also went through a similar transformation. In August 1987 in Qufu, Shangdong province, for the first time in the history of the People's Republic of China, an international symposium was held on Confucianism. The Honorary Chairman of the Confucius Foundation, Vice-Premier of the State Council, Gu Mu 谷牧, addressed the conference, and officially declared Confucianism to be "one of the crystallizations of national Chinese culture. . . . Although its founder, Confucius, was born in China, culture and thought are the common wealth of all humankind, and are not bound by national boundaries. . . . In order to make China progress, the only correct way is to start from the needs of reality, critically inherit those periods of excellence in traditional Chinese culture and thought, including that of Confucianism, and at the same time, critically assimilate the reasonable elements of other cultures."[18] If Gu Mu's speech in 1987 was still reserved and cautious, his public address at the October 1989 Symposium on Confucianism celebrating the two thousand five hundred and fortieth birthday of Confucius, clearly indicated a metamorphosis of discourse, describing Confucius as "an erudite scholar of high moral integrity, who devoted all his life to culture and education, and established the Confucian school. This makes him an important founder of traditional Chinese culture. Confucius and the Confucian school have played a very positive role in Chinese history, and have exerted a deep influence upon East Asia." Commenting on the Confucian emphasis on harmony (*he wei gui* 和為貴), Gu Mu also linked this philosophy with harmonizing human relationships, environmental protection, and ecological balance, concluding that it still has a practical significance today.[19] Another indicator marking this metamorphosis in attitude is the meeting of Jiang Zemin 江澤民 with some representatives of the symposium, as meetings with top government officials always signify official consent.

Thus, Confucius and Confucianism went through a remarkable process of reiteration and reimagination in both academic and official discourse. Both of Gu Mu's speeches emphasize the universality of Confucianism, but in his second speech he also referred to its contemporary relevance and practical significance. With official support, in a matter of ten years Confucius and Confucianism were transformed from feudal evils to the locus of Chinese national essence. As a result, Confucius and Confucianism became homogenized to stand for the mainstay of traditional Chinese culture. In this sense, by the late 1980s, both academic and official discourses converged to join overseas Chinese New Confucians in a shared "Confucian discourse."[20]

Confucianism and Modernization

The relationship between Confucianism and modernization dominated much of the emerging Confucian discourse. One of the main propositions to emerge from the International Symposium on Confucianism in 1987 was that there was a connection between Confucianism and modernization. Some argued that "the core value of Confucian ethics is the modernization of the person in human relationships."[21] Confucianism was also seen as "a motivating force for personal integration, socio-communal participation, and moral leadership"; as having contributed to the modernization of some East Asian countries; and as having developed an intrinsically modern and progressive system of educational theory and practice that could help enlighten the modern world.[22] China's Four Modernizations were also discussed in connection with the modernization of Confucianism. In the preface to Cheng Chung Ying's 成中英 book, *The Modernization of Chinese Culture and Globalization*, Tang Yijie reiterated his call for the internationalization of Chinese culture: "Let Chinese culture out to the world, and let the world's cultures into China."[23] He argued that without the modernization of Chinese culture it would be impossible to realize China's Four Modernizations, and that a modern culture should be founded upon a solid national culture. With his logic, the modernization of traditional Confucianism became a prerequisite for the politically instigated Four Modernizations in contemporary China.[24]

Li Zehou 李澤厚, by contrast, approached Confucianism from a diachronic perspective. Amid arguments on the topic of Confucianism and modernization, he claimed that the former is far from dead, and that the study of Confucianism is not a matter of "rehabilitation" as it is a living reality beyond the manipulation of human will. Confucius is alive amongst "you, me, him, and the mentality of the Chinese people." For Li, Confucianism is no longer an ideology of a certain class; it has become a major part of the Chinese national character or "psycho-cultural construct" (*wenhua xinli jiegou* 文化心理結構). In contrast to the New Confucians, he believed that it is pointless to argue for the preservation of Confucianism. What this living psycho-cultural construct needs now is understanding and reform.[25]

The maverick culturalist, He Xin 何新, also supported explorations into New Confucianism to find ways to realize China's modernization. In a peculiar way, he focused his argument not on the universality of Confucianism but on its particularity. In his opinion, Deng Xiaoping's theory of "socialism with Chinese characteristics" is a great breakthrough and a development of scientific socialist theory. For He, the term "Chinese characteristics" does not only imply national particularity, but also refers to the historical particularity that has been conditioned by Chinese cultural tradition. Because New Confucianism values China's traditional cultural spirit and value systems, the emergence of New Confucianism could be interpreted as presaging the renaissance of Eastern culture: "the sun is rising again from the East!"[26]

Although sharing similar aspirations to modernize Chinese culture, some other protagonists in the culture craze clearly had a different perspective. As the most venerated school of teaching in Chinese history, Confucianism also came to be portrayed as the locus of the cultural evils that had prevented China from becoming modern. Many young scholars who had been through the disastrous Cultural Revolution era and who acutely felt the humiliation of being "left behind," were naturally suspicious of the notion of Confucius as the new cultural savior. Their strategy was, first of all, to distance Confucianism from the concept of "tradition." In his article, "Tradition, Temporality, and the Future," Gan Yang, a scholar educated in Western philosophy, introduced the concept of "temporality" to the understanding of tradition. Temporality is three dimensional, embracing the past, present, and future. If we equate tradition with the past, then we inevitably have to bear the cost of losing what is present. If we see tradition as perpetually in-the-making, then the act of carrying tradition forward will definitely not be restricted to the reproduction of what existed in the past. To Gan Yang, it is impossible to "return Confucianism to its original appearance." Confucianism no longer has an original appearance. It has been interpreted and reinterpreted throughout the centuries, and is forever changing. Chinese cultural tradition is not Confucianism, and we should unequivocally say no to the dream of making Confucianism the mainstay and core of modern Chinese culture. As to the issue of inheriting tradition, he believed that the best way to carry tradition forward is precisely by promoting "anti-tradition."[27]

Some other scholars agreed with Gan Yang's quasi-postmodern position in discussing the value of Confucianism. Zhu Riyao 朱日耀, Cao Deben 曹德本, and Sun Xiaochun 孫曉春 proposed that because Confucianism was the philosophy of culture in feudal China, the renaissance of Confucianism is irrelevant to the needs of China's modernization.[28] Other scholars, such as Bao Zunxin 包遵信, argued that Confucianism was simply incompatible with China's modernization. "As the mainstay of China's traditional culture, the structure and value system of Confucianism are incompatible with modernization." In his article, "Confucian Tradition and Contemporary China," he dissected Mao's teachings and practices, tracing them back to Confucian philosophy, and attributing most of them to Mao's learning of traditional Confucian ideology. According to Bao, the cultural disasters of recent history were the direct legacy of what Mao and his colleagues had inherited from Confucianism. The Confucian tradition, a closed, non-critical system of thought, Confucianized even Marxism in China, creating "modern [Confucian] scholasticism (*xiandai jingxue* 現代 經學)." In his critique of "wholesale Westernization," he asked, "What is wholesale Westernization? . . . Aren't Marxism and Leninism imported from the outside?"[29] Bao Zunxin was also greatly concerned with the call for "Chinese characteristics" by academics, questioning what it entailed and how it was defined.[30]

At each pole of this group of scholars arguing against the value of traditional culture were Gao Xuguang 高旭光, who applied the famous Chinese Marxist theory that tradition would follow the course of birth, development, and death,[31] and Liu Xiaobo 劉曉波, who took on Li Zehou in his ostentatious onslaught on traditional culture. In Gao Xuguang's opinion, the formation and development of all traditional concepts go through three steps: formation, repeated strengthening, and gradual death. Quoting Marx and Engels extensively, he concluded, "Judging from the circumstances of present day China, indeed there are many negative, old, and decayed traditional concepts. They seriously hinder the rapid development of politics, economics, culture, and the like. If not reformed quickly, the construction of our modernization cannot be smoothly carried out."[32] Liu Xiaobo, on the other hand, argued for a complete destruction of "the theory of the people as the foundation of the nation (*minben sixiang* 民本思想)," the "Confucius-Yan Yuan personality" (*Kong Yan renge* 孔顏人格), and "the unity of heaven and humans" (*tian ren he yi* 天人合一). Attempting to engage in dialogue with Li Zehou, Liu Xiaobo protested that the theory of "the people as the foundation of the nation" is an illusionary group consciousness, it denies the equality of individuals, and condones hierarchical systems of sociopolitical order. The ideal Confucian personality, he contended, amounts to nothing more than a "self-enslaving personality" (*zijue de nuxing renge* 自覺的奴性人格), and the subjugation of Chinese intellectuals—with their great sense of duty and responsibility—to their rulers. As for Li Zehou's ultimate ideal state of the unity of heaven and humans, Liu Xiaobo, branded it as "the ultimate level of enslavement" (*nuhua jijing* 奴化極境), as he believed that its emphasis on wholeness, stability, and harmony, when applied in society, has not only prevented the Chinese people from developing analytical skills, but has also snubbed individuality and creativity.[33]

The cultural debates in the 1980s were not only a reaction to the impact of Western culture, but also a reaction to the leading ideology of the late 1970s. The attempts to reconsider and reevaluate the

Cultural Revolution in the process of discovering Western culture, were deeply located in the social and political arena of the time. If the earlier discussions of tradition and Westernization were operating under the gray space where there were constant calls against "spiritual pollution" by the political leadership of the country, the study of New Confucianism certainly seems to have enjoyed more leverage. It is not surprising that the government should find some of the issues discussed by New Confucians to be relevant to its own agenda. It is interesting to see how some of the issues in the cultural debates paralleled the policies of Deng Xiaoping's government. Reintroducing the Confucian teaching of "pacifying the country, stabilizing society, and regulating the people" (*an guojia ding sheji xu renmin* 安國家，定社稷, 序人民) seemed to coincide with the government's policy of promoting "stability and unity, and building the Four Modernizations (*anding tuanjie, jianshe sihua* 安定團結, 建設四化)," while highlighting the positive side of Confucianism—both historical and the present (e.g., the Singaporean practice of Confucian capitalism [*Rujia zibenzhuyi* 儒家資本主義])—as the national essence also appeared to converge with Deng Xiaoping's calling for "socialism with Chinese characteristics." Research into the spiritual civilization of Chinese history seemed to respond to the government's campaign against "spiritual pollution" and to its need to locate the "socialist spiritual civilization" in the face of Western impact and the debilitating legacy of the Cultural Revolution. It is little wonder that the project to "Study Modern Confucian Thought" should have been credited as a key national social sciences project in the seventh five-year plan of November, 1986.

The Object of Study

With central governmental support legitimizing and re-enforcing Confucianism as a part of China's heritage worthy of serious study, the reimported "New Confucianism" thus became an object of cultural studies in the 1980s. This seventh five-year plan funded research project to study modern New Confucian thought involved about fifty scholars from more than ten provinces over China, and over the following decade these scholars produced many volumes of research publications. Confucianism in the shape of New Confucianism was systematically mass introduced to Chinese readers, many of whom, up to that point, had only associated Confucian teachings with "harmful feudal remnants." As there were few resources to draw upon, the project virtually started "from scratch."[34] According to the research done by the scholars involved in the project, during 1986–89 alone, some two hundred and fifteen articles on New Confucianism were published in various journals, newspapers, and anthologies.[35] Another study reports that during 1986–96, sixty-one books by New Confucians, and fifty-four books on New Confucianism were published.[36]

In their attempt to define what New Confucianism entails, scholars in mainland China came to the following consensus: "Modern New Confucianism appeared in the 1920s and still has vitality today. It is characterized by a mission to carry on the 'interconnecting thread of the Way' (*daotong* 道統), to revive Confucianism, and by its belief in the idealist philosophy of the Song and Ming dynasties, especially Confucian moral metaphysics (*xinxing zhi xue* 心性之學). Its object is to take Confucianism as its main foundation, and to incorporate, assimilate, and have a masterly knowledge of Western studies in the hope of finding the way to China's modernization. It is an academic school of thought, and can also be seen as a cultural and ideological trend."[37]

In its meticulous wording, this definition is significant in two respects. First, it deliberately avoids issues that might have been politically sensitive in mid-1980s China. For instance, two of (Taiwan scholar) Wei Zhengtong's 韋政通 characterizations of New Confucianism as "taking Chinese historical culture as a spiritual entity which manifests itself in the process of historical culture" and "emphasizing a respectful and sympathetic understanding of historical culture"[38] would have undoubtedly invited unwanted attention to the project. Presenting New Confucianism as an academic school would have been conducive to making the study appear less politically oriented. Second, such a broad definition was an important step to ensuring its all-inclusive nature, and making it possible for these scholars to: (1) study earlier scholars like Liang Shuming, Xiong Shili, Feng Youlan, and He Lin, who did not belong to the overseas Declaration group; (2) include those third generation scholars living overseas; and (3) allow a discursive space for the future development of Confucianism in mainland China. If the definition were too narrowly focused, it would not have been possible for the study to shift its focus, in the future, to mainland New Confucians. As it so happened, later in the 1990s some mainland scholars began to hold up the banner of "mainland New Confucians": "without the succession and creation (*chuancheng he chuangxin* 傳承和創新) of mainland scholars, without the emergence of mainland New Confucianism bred on the works of overseas New Confucians, the third period of development for Confucianism would be the dream of a returning bird lost on its way. . . . The emergence of mainland New Confucianism does not mark the systematic cultural annotation of traditional Confucian philosophy. This task has been practically completed by the overseas scholars of New Confucianism. The emergence marks the creative transformation of traditional Confucianism in politics and law" in mainland China.[39] By the mid-1990s, even the self-confessed Marxist scholar, Li Zehou, admitted that he did not mind being called a New Confucian, although he insisted that there were differences between himself and the overseas New Confucians.[40] Some other prominent scholars like Luo Junyi 羅義俊 and Jiang Qing 蔣慶 also openly identified themselves as New Confucians.[41]

It may appear that the New Confucians outside mainland China and the scholars involved in the seventh five-year plan funded research project shared the same sense of duty that was deeply embedded in the Confucian ideology of being concerned for the fate of the country and the people (*youguo youmin* 憂國憂民). The immediate agendas being pursued by these two groups, however, were quite different and were framed in different rhetoric. To the earlier generations of New Confucians, Western culture was seen as passé and should be replaced with Chinese culture. Chinese culture, whose essence is Confucianism, should shoulder the task of saving the world from degeneration: "The culture of the future of the world lies in the renaissance of Chinese culture."[42] The mainland New Confucian, Feng Youlan 馮友蘭, believed that "Chinese philosophy by itself is enough to save the world."[43] The New Confucians outside China, who wrote their Declaration in 1958, called on the world for "equal treatment"[44] at a time when they were "completely without hope." While their concern with Confucianism was focused on reviving and reinterpreting Chinese culture to seek a way out for the benefit of China's future, the scholars who came to study New Confucianism in China thirty years later had more urgent concerns. Their study of the past was directed more toward the benefit of the present. When the overseas New Confucians such as Tu Wei-ming were operating on a global stage, mainland scholars focused on practical domestic issues. In the words of Tang Yijie, they were busy making Confucianism "serve the needs of our modern society."[45] While the objectives of both groups of scholars were pragmatic, New Confucians outside the mainland were more concerned with the savior role that Confucianism could play in the modern world, whereas the mainland scholars were much more inclined to explore the possibility of making the age-old cultural heritage serve the needs of present day China. "Give it a modern interpretation. Develop it. Make it serve the needs of our modern society."[46] In a book published in 1995, Tang Yijie further elucidated, "Even though the culture craze in the mid-1980s discussed 'cultural problems,' its objective was very clear. It aimed at extending the Open Door policy in the areas of economy and technology, politics and ideology, and pushing forward the realization of full-scale modernization in mainland China."[47] Some other scholars, trying to distance themselves from the call for "Confucian capitalism" in China, also conceded that studying Confucianism had an immediate relevance: "The revival of Confucianism does not stand for eulogizing traditional culture alone, but is a theory directed at the realities of today's China."[48] Moreover, the study of China's historical legacy was to "serve real life reforms," therefore this effort cannot be the same as that of the overseas New Confucians as their social background is different.[49]

Though attempts to clarify how Confucianism could "serve" the interests of the Four Modernizations seem to be nebulous, the purpose of studying Confucianism was not. Pragmatic necessity lent philosophical research a cultural orientation. The urgent need to curtail official corruption and to fill the void left by the Cultural Revolution seems to have been a major objective. "Modern New Confucians stress the development and reestablishment of traditional moral civilization and humanist values. In order to overcome the crisis and loss of meaning in life caused by lopsided instrumentalism and scientism, it naturally has remedial merit."[50] At a time when the government was also promoting a "socialist spiritual civilization" and combating "spiritual pollution," scholars were seeking to revamp and reinterpret Confucian concepts to fill the void talked about by hundreds of people in the "discussions on the meaning of life" initiated by Pan Xiao 潘曉 in the early 1980s. Self-proclaimed mainland New Confucian, Jiang Qing 蔣慶, even went so far as to argue for the restoration of Confucianism as a "national religion" to replace Marxism and Leninism: "Marxism and Leninism cannot be compared with Confucianism as the Chinese orthodox culture. They can't represent the Chinese national life force and religious spirit. Therefore, Confucianism naturally should replace Marxism and Leninism as 'the national religion' and recover its position in history."[51]

No doubt, scholarship had to operate within the political space tolerated by the system of the time. The introduction of New Confucian discourse had to conform to the parameters of contemporary political discourse. In the introductory sections of publications on New Confucianism, scholars repeatedly asserted that New Confucianism was an object of study, or the object of academic exchange with scholars of Chinese cultural studies in Hong Kong, Taiwan, and overseas.[52] They saw their major task being to "critically assess, investigate, generalize, and learn from" a cultural and philosophical trend of thought[53] and to benefit the Four Modernizations.[54] Wherever possible, the needs of the Four Modernizations were projected as the ultimate objective for academic research activities into New Confucianism. Fang Keli was adamant that mainland scholars did not advocate the road of "Confucian capitalism," and that what they were exploring was the socialist road to modernization with Chinese characteristics. Their research activities were carried out within the boundaries of "the Four Fundamental Principles" (*si xiang jiben yuanze* 四項基本原則).[55] Many of the scholars emphasized the importance of Marxism as the guiding principle and methodology in their research.[56] According to Fang Keli, of all the modern schools of thought in recent Chinese history, New Confucianism is second only to Marxism in terms of its theoretical creativity and influence, and its capacity to survive,[57] and is one of the three major ideological trends in addition to Marxism and Western liberalism.[58] As the works of New Confucianism come from scholars who love Chinese historical culture and devote themselves to the renaissance of national culture, they are, therefore, worthy of study.[59] At a time when the government was calling on all people of Chinese descent to care for the fate of the Chinese nation, it seemed only appropriate that the efforts of these patriots were appropriately recognized. Tang Yijie seems to have thought that the development of Confucianism was not at odds with the development of Marxism, because Marxism and the revival of Confucianism are intertwined. In order to adapt Marxism to China's "national conditions," it is necessary to inherit the rational part of tradition. Therefore, attempts to develop the rational part of tradition are, in a way, attempts to develop Marxism.[60]

It is not surprising that mainland scholars of New Confucianism repeatedly emphasized the difference of their own viewpoints from that of New Confucian thinkers, and at times, painstakingly distanced themselves from New Confucian thought. Fang Keli, as one of the two professors in charge of the seventh five-year plan funded research project on New Confucian thought, held that New Confucianism is a school of the bourgeois class because it advocates "Confucian capitalism."[61] From a theoretical perspective the researchers in the project stand against the cultural conservative view and idealism of New Confucianism, and fundamentally diverge from its negation of the May Fourth spirit, and its attacks upon Marxism, Leninism, and socialism.[62] Song Zhiming believed that the philosophy of New Confucianism is the natural product of the declining philosophy of the bourgeois class, and is determined by the nature of the Chinese society at its time.

Quoting Mao Zedong's definition of culture, he pointed out that New Confucianism itself is highly selective in its study of Confucianism, as New Confucian philosophers sought to create a Chinese–Western philosophy with Confucian substance and Western function.[63] Wu Lingling 伍玲玲, a scholar from Nanjing University, even proposed that the next stage of development of Confucianism should be one "with socialist characteristics."[64]

It is, however, important to point out here that scholars did generally maintain a critical edge in their introductory research. Many were dubious about the savior role that Confucianism could play in building China's future. As mentioned earlier, these scholars actively participated in the ongoing cultural debates, and were highly critical of the cultural conservatist approach employed by the New Confucians. Zheng Jiadong maintained that overseas New Confucians believe that "moral idealism is above political democracy," and they often confuse political democratic freedom with freedom of will in the domain of morality. Citing the Declaration, Zheng claimed that putting morality and personality above political democracy shows that these New Confucians have not gone beyond the way of traditional Confucian thinking: "Ideas of moral communitarianism and equality of character will of course lead to an affirmation of the democratic system."[65]

Realms of Convergence: Reconstructing the Confucian Ideal

Like its reinvention on the world stage, talked about by Arif Dirlik, New Confucianism in mainland China is subject to appropriation and interpretation through processes of negotiation. While overseas New Confucians were striving "to endow Confucianism with a presence and a voice in a global culture,"[66] the mainland scholars, sharing the commonalities of a homogenized Confucian discourse, succeeded in creating a Confucianism for Chinese audiences. Given the historical and political constraints, the introduction of New Confucianism into mainland China and its engagement in the cultural debates were necessarily selective. Although the introduction of New Confucianism appeared to be comprehensive and extensive, as measured by publication output, certain sections of Confucian teaching were more highlighted than others. The pragmatic approach toward New Confucianism focused on morality and human relationships.

The reconstruction of the Confucian ideal is a case in point. Many works were devoted to explaining what the Confucian ideal entails. The most highlighted aspects were Confucian morality and the ideal personality.[67] Even when discussing the ways of approaching New Confucianism, scholars involved in the major research project funded under the national seventh five-year plan for the social sciences set a high value on the moral integrity of the New Confucians. The pursuit of noble character came to be regarded as the prime example of Chinese cultural tradition. Some went so far as to suggest that the study of New Confucianism should start with the personal integrity of the scholars involved, and disregard those who were lacking in moral values.[68]

One young scholar, Song Zhiming, in his *A Study on Modern New Confucianism*, appears to have based the objects of his study purely on the patriotic qualities of the scholars themselves. In this book, Song chose to talk about New Confucianism through the works of Liang Shuming, Feng Youlan, Xiong Shili, and He Lin. For Song, what distinguishes these scholars has to do with their aspiration to save China, revitalize national spirit, and develop traditional culture. Their decision not to have fled China also makes them admirable patriots.[69]

According to Werner Meissner, the introduction of New Confucianism as a subject of study in the 1980s served two purposes. The Confucian love of order, "obedience to one's superior, the devotion to the state and the protection of the family . . . helps to promote the desperately needed social order and stability."[70] At a time of drastic social, cultural, and, most of all, economic change, to reestablish the notion of social order after the chaos of the Cultural Revolution undoubtedly served the interests of a government desperately in need of a stable social environment to push for economic reform. Also, "Confucianism as a Chinese ideology could help to provide the people with some sort of national identity. National Confucianism could serve as a bulwark against the ideological impacts from the West following rapid modernization."[71]

The sense of crisis felt by intellectuals who were worried that China was facing the danger of being "expelled from world-membership" (*kaichu qiuji* 開除球籍), compelled them to seek solace in the space of traditional culture. As it happened, through a very subjective process of introduction, Confucius' teachings were renegotiated according to the social realities of contemporary China. For mainland Chinese audiences, the invented "Confucian discourse" that spoke of traditional Chinese culture as a whole, made it possible for them to go through a process of what Dirlik has termed "cultural re-signification"[72] in the 1990s. The temporarily homogenized traditional culture provides a space for the identification of national identity for both Chinese intellectuals and the government. It was precisely within the comfort of this locus that after June the Fourth in 1989, the study of national culture further developed and extended itself to other schools of thought in Chinese history, giving rise to the national studies craze in the early 1990s.

By appropriating Confucianism for domestic consumption, intellectuals of mainland China not only reaffirmed the image of the exemplary Confucian scholar, but also gained a new position of discursive power: transmitters of the great cultural heritage. Like some of the overseas New Confucians who identified themselves as transmitters of the "interconnecting thread of the Way" (*daotong* 道统), intellectuals empowered themselves with a newly found Confucian discourse. Sanctioned by the official policy of "respect knowledge and respect science," Chinese intellectuals reestablished themselves as the bearers and interpreters of China's cultural heritage.

Speaking from their regained position of authority, they were able to pick and choose from a body of knowledge and appropriate it for a domestic audience. Those passages and concepts which, in their minds, did not serve the needs of contemporary China were edited out. Their version of the essence of the Chinese nation not only excluded references to traditional Confucian attitudes to laborers, but also to the "small people (*xiao ren* 小人)." Curiously, when talking about the ideal personality of the "gentleman" (*junzi* 君子), the much-detested "small people" seem to have vanished from the rhetoric. The Confucian insistence upon the great character divide between gentleman and small person almost disappeared in the published research. Moreover, with only a few exceptions,[73] the destructive role that Confucianism had played historically in oppressing women is hardly mentioned. According to Li Zehou's commentary on *The Analects*, the passage, "women and underlings are especially difficult to handle: be friendly, and they become familiar; be distant, and they resent it" (following Simon Leys' translation) "quite accurately describes certain characteristics of women's personality."[74] In the lineage of his great master, he also finds that women have these characteristics and insists that this attitude is a class above the European persecution of women as witches in the Middle Ages.[75]

The outcome of the study of New Confucianism in mainland China in the 1980s is nothing but spectacular. In a matter of some five years, Confucianism, clothed in a new robe called New Confucianism, made a grand entry onto the cultural stage: "Five years ago, to many people, 'New Confucianism' and 'New Confucians' were completely new terms. Today, however, not only have they made a grand appearance in our newspapers, journals, and books, but they are also fast developing into a new area and new focal point in the cultural studies of Chinese modern thought."[76] Thus on the cultural horizon in mainland China, a new image of Confucianism emerged from the works which introduced New Confucianism. With the help of overseas New Confucians, Confucianism underwent a process of transformation through which it acquired a refreshing and rejuvenated facelift. Like a phoenix completely resurrected from the ashes,[77] Confucianism was reproduced to articulate the national characteristics of Chinese culture. Through the process of negotiation and renegotiation with images of traditional, overseas, and mainland Confucianism, and with the constant changing social and political environment, intellectuals in mainland China were able to present to their Chinese audience a tailor-made New Confucianism.

Conclusion

The introduction of New Confucianism to a mainland Chinese audience in the 1980s was part of a cultural New Enlightenment movement during a time of transition, in a society confronted by the outside world. Initially, the philosophical attempt to rediscover Confucian thought was necessitated by the cultural debates on Westernization and modernization. The pragmatic need to search for ways to cope with an identity crisis brought about by cultural and social change compelled Chinese intellectuals to redefine and rediscover what is entailed by Chinese cultural tradition. Tolerated and operating within the political and cultural climates, assisted by the New Confucians living outside China, and inspired by the successes of the economies of "the four little dragons," Confucianism was reintroduced in the clothes of New Confucianism, and appropriated for domestic consumption. The representation of New Confucianism, in a way, catered for a specific cultural market in the mainland.

New Confucianism was a principal object of study during the culture craze. The mass introduction exercise not only facilitated the involvement of Confucianism in ongoing cultural debates, but also helped to clarify such concepts as "tradition," "traditional culture," and "traditional Chinese culture"—concepts that became so muddled up in the debates on Obscure Poetry and New Literature—and laid down the foundation for further studies in national culture. Although some people believe that it was the strong economic development that strengthened the new identification with national culture, one cannot deny that the introduction of New Confucianism did serve as a catalyst for the national studies craze of the 1990s.

It is interesting to observe, as an afterword, that the introduction/ reintroduction of Confucianism in the clothes of New Confucianism, like the government's campaigns for spiritual civilization, did little to revive a "humanist spirit." By the mid-1990s, writers and scholars were occupied with "a crisis of the humanist spirit" (*renwen jingshen weiji* 人文精神危機). The efforts to reassert the "ideal Confucian personality" and to revive traditional value systems bore few fruits in social reality. If one takes Tang Junyi's 唐君毅 reductionist definition of "humanist spirit" or "moral self" (*daode ziwo* 道德自我) as the essence of Chinese culture, then this very "essence" was seriously endangered ten years after the mass reinvention of the national cultural legacy. As the process of marketization accelerated, the practice of labeling people *Rushang* 儒商 (Confucian businessman) achieved nothing more than adding a touch of gloss in the name of the traditional cultural essence. To some late comers in the cultural debates, such as Ge Hongbing 葛紅兵, the whole practice of rediscovering Confucianism reveals more about the weakness of the intellectuals themselves than of Chinese culture. Intellectuals, in his mind, are like "spiritual vagrants" (*jingshen liulangzhe* 精神流浪者) who, having lost their own cultural identity at the time of disintegration of discursive power, sought new clothes from all sorts of "isms" to empower themselves in discourse. Their experiments with New Confucianism or Neo-Marxism are acts of desperation.[78]

Notes

1. Sun Longji 孫隆基, *Zhongguo wenhua de shenceng jiegou* 中國文化的深層結構 (The Deep Structure of Chinese Culture), Hong Kong: Jixian she, 1985, 8.
2. This point was argued by Liu Xinwu 劉心武 in 1988, "Jin shinian Zhongguo wenxue de ruogan texing 近十年中國文學的若干特性" (Some Characteristics of Chinese Literature over the Past Decade), *Wenxue pinglun* (1988.3): 5–12.
3. Xu Jingya, "Jueqi de shiqun 崛起的詩群" (The Rise of Poets), in Bi Hua 璧華 and Yang Ling 楊零 (eds.), *Jueqi de shiqun* 崛起的詩群 (The Rise of Poets), Hong Kong: Dangdai wenxue yanjiushe, 1984, 99.
4. Xu Chi, "Xiandaihua yu xiandaipai 現代化與現代派" (Modernization and Modernism), *Waiguo wenxueyanjiu* (1982.1): 115–17.
5. Zang Kejia 臧克家, "Shi yao sanshun 詩要三順" (The Three Requirements of Poetry), *Shikan* (1981.2): 51–2.
6. Zhang Ming 章明, "Lingren qimen de menglong 令人氣悶的朦朧" (Stifling Obscurity), in Bi Hua and Yang Ling (eds.), *Jueqi de shiqun*, 151–3.
7. Song Zhongfu 宋仲福, Zhang Jihui 趙吉惠, and Pei Dayang 裴大洋, *Ruxue zai xiandai Zhongguo* 儒學在現代中國 (Confucianism in Contemporary China), Zhengzhou: Zhengzhou guji chubanshe, 1991, 355.
8. Song Zhongfu *et al.*, *Ruxue zai xiandai Zhongguo*, 363.

9. According to Xu Jilin 許紀霖, the publication of the *Zouxiang weilai* 走向未來 (Towards the Future) series and *Dushu* 讀書, combined with the establishment of the Academy of Chinese Culture, are landmarks of the New Enlightenment movement in China. See Xu Jilin, "The Fate of an Enlightenment—Twenty Years in the Chinese Intellectual Sphere (1978–98)," trans. Geremie Barmé with Gloria Davies, *East Asian History* (2000.20): 169–86.

10. In Tang Yijie's opinion, the establishment of the Academy of Chinese Culture, together with the publication of the *Zouxiang weilai* series and *Dushu* are the three key elements in the culture craze. See Tang Yijie, *Zai feiyou feiwu zhijian* 在非有非無之間 (Between Not Having and Not Non-Having), Taibei: Zhengzhong shuju, 1995, 154–5. Li Minghui 李明輝, however, believes that five major phenomena distinguish the culture craze: the *Towards the Future* series; the *Wenhua: Zhongguo yu shijie* 文化：中國與世界 (Culture: China and the World) series; the establishment of the Academy of Chinese Culture; the introduction of New Confucianism; and "Seeking Roots" literature. See Li Minghui, "Jiedu dangqian dalu de Ruxuere 解讀當前大陸的儒學熱" (Deciphering the Present Confucian Studies Craze in Mainland China), in Li Minghui (ed.), *Rujia sixiang zai xiandai Dongya: zonglun pian* 儒家思想在現代東亞：總論篇 (Confucian Thought in Contemporary East Asia: Papers on General Topics), Taibei: Zhongyang yanjiuyuan Zhongguo wenzhe yanjiusuo choubeichu, 1998, 82–3.

11. Liang Yuansheng 梁元生, "Qiantu weibu de fenghuang: Xin Ruxue yu dangdai Zhongguo 前途未卜的鳳凰：新儒學與當代中國" (Uncertain Phoenix: New Confucianism and Contemporary China), in Li Minghui (ed.), *Rujia sixiang zai xiandai dongya: zonglun pian*, 108–10.

12. Song Zhongfu *et al.*, *Ruxue zai xiandai Zhongguo*, 356.

13. The very first public call for the renaissance of Confucianism by mainland scholars did not occur until 1989, in the Taiwanese journal *Ehu Yuekan* 鵝湖月刊 (1989.8-9): 29–37.

14. Chen Lai 陳來, "Duoyuan wenhua jiegou zhong de Ruxue jiqi dingwei 多元文化結構中的儒學及其定位" (Confucianism in a Multicultural Structure and Its Position Therein), *Zhongguo luntan* (1988.313): 21–3.

15. Zhao Dezhi 趙德志, "Xiandai xin Rujia manlun (xu) 現代新儒家漫論 (續)" (On Modern New Confucianism: A Sequel), *Shehui kexue jikan* (1988.2): 24–5.

16. Song Zhongfu *et al.*, *Ruxue zai xiandai Zhongguo*, 390–417.

17. Fang Keli 方克立 and Li Jinquan 李錦全, "Congshu zhubian de hua 叢書主編的話" (Editors' Note to the Series), in Han Qiang 韓強, *Xiandai xin Ruxue xinxing lilun pingshu* 現代新儒學心性理論評述 (On the Moral Metaphysics of Modern New Confucianism), Shenyang: Liaoning daxue chubanshe, 1992, 2.

18. Song Zhongfu *et al.*, *Ruxue zai xiandai Zhongguo*, 357.

19. Zheng Jiadong 鄭家棟, "Jin wushinian lai dalu Ruxue de fazhan jiqi xianzhuang 近五十年來大陸儒學的發展及其現狀 (1950–1996)" (The Development of Mainland Confucianism and Its Present Situation

[1950–96]), in Li Minghui (ed.), *Rujia sixiang zai xiandai Dongya: Zonglun pian*, 27.

20. See Arif Dirlik "Confucius in the Borderlands: Global Capitalism and the Reinvention of Confucianism," *boundary* 2, 22.3(1995): 229–73.

21. Wu Dingbo, "1987 Controversy Over the Evaluation of Confucius," *Journal of Chinese Philosophy* 16.3, 4(1989): 431.

22. *Ibid.*, 431–2.

23. Tang Yijie 湯一介, "Zhongguo xinwenhua de chuangjian 中國新文化的創建" (The Creation of China's New Culture), *Dushu* (1988.7): 9.

24. Tang Yijie, *Zai feiyou feiwu zhijian*, 150–1.

25. Li Zehou, "Guanyu Ruxue he xin Ruxue 關於儒學和新儒學" (About Confucianism and New Confucianism), *Zhongguo chuantong wenhua zai jiantao* 中國傳統文化再檢討 (The Second Self-Criticism of Chinese Traditional Culture), Hong Kong: Shangwu yinshuguan, 1987, 6–7.

26. He Xin, "Dui xiandaihua yu chuantong wenhua de zai sikao 對現代化與傳統文化的再思考" (More Thoughts on Modernization and Traditional Culture), *Shehui kexue jikan* (Shenyang) (1987.2): 21–7.

27. Gan Yang, "Chuantong, shijianxing yu weilai 傳統, 時間性與未來" (Tradition, Temporality, and Future), *Dushu* (1986.2): 3–10.

28. Zhu Riyao, Cao Deben, and Sun Xiaochun, "Chuantong Ruxue de lishi mingyun 傳統儒學的歷史命運" (The Historical Fate of Traditional Confucianism), *Jilin daxue shehui kexue xuebao* (1987.3): 6.

29. Bao Zunxin, "Liang'an xuezhe tan Zhongguo wenhua 兩岸學者談中國文化" (Scholars from Both Sides of the Strait Discuss Chinese Culture), *Zhongguo luntan* (1988.312): 64.

30. Bao Zunxin, "Rujia chuantong yu dangdai Zhongguo 儒家傳統與當代中國" (Confucian Tradition and Contemporary China), *Zhongguo luntan* (1988.313): 27–31.

31. Gao Xuguang, "Lun chuantong guannian 論傳統觀念 (On Traditional Ideology)," *Zhongguo luntan* (1988.311): 11–15.

32. *Ibid.*, 15.

33. Liu Xiaobo, *Xuanze de pipan* 選擇的批判 (Critique of Choice), Taibei: Fengyun shidai chuban gongsi, 1989.

34. Guan Dong 關東, "Xiandai xin Ruxue yanjiu de huigu yu zhanwang 現代新儒學研究的回顧與展望" (The Past and Future of Modern New Confucianism), *Zhexue yanjiu* 哲學研究 (1990.3): 80.

35. Fang Keli and Li Jinquan (eds.), *Xiandai xin Ruxue yanjiu lunji* 現代新儒學研究論集 (Collected Essays on New Confucian Studies), vol. 2, Beijing: Zhongguo shehui kexue chubanshe, 1991, 369–87.

36. Zheng Jiadong, "Jin wushinian lai dalu Ruxue de fazhan jiqi xianzhuang," 50–79.

37. Fang Keli and Li Jinquan (eds.), *Xiandai xin Ruxue yanjiu lunji* 現代新儒學研究論集 (Collected Essays on New Confucian Studies), vol. 1, Beijing: Zhongguo shehui kexue chubanshe, 1989, 2.

38. Wei Zhengtong, "Dangdai xin Rujia de xintai 當代新儒家的心態" (The Psychological State of Contemporary New Confucians), in Luo Yijun

羅義俊 (ed.), *Ping xin Rujia* 評新儒家 (On New Confucians), Shanghai: Shanghai renmin chubanshe, 1989, 165.

39. Gan Chunsong 干春松, *Xiandaihua yu wenhua xuanze* 現代化與文化選擇 (Modernization and Cultural Choice), Nanchang: Jiangxi renmin chubanshe, 1998, 192.

40. *Ibid.*

41. Li Minghui, *Rujia sixiang zai xiandai Dongya: zonglun pian*, 6–7.

42. Liang Shumingg 梁漱溟, *Dongfang wenhua jiqi zhexue* 東方文化及其哲學 (Eastern Cultures and Their Philosophies), Beijing: Shangwu yishuguan, 1987, 199.

43. Feng Youlan, *Sansongtang xueshu wenji* 三松堂學術文集 (Collected Academic Essays from the Hall of Three Pines), Beijing: Sanlian shudian, 1984, 643.

44. Mou Zongsan 牟宗三, Xu Fuguan 徐復觀, Zhang Junmai 張君勱, and Tang Junyi 唐君毅, "Wei Zhongguo wenhua jinggao shijie renshi xuanyan 為中國文化敬告世界人士宣言" (Declaration on Behalf of Chinese Culture Respectfully Announced to the People of the World), in Feng Zusheng 封祖盛 (ed.), *Dangdai xin Rujia* 當代新儒家 (Contemporary New Confucianism), Beijing: Sanlian shudian, 1989, 52.

45. Tang Yijie 湯一介, "Is It Possible to 'Modernize' Confucianism?" Conference paper, translated by Archibald McKenzie, at Chinese Studies Association of Australia Conference, University of Sydney, July 1991.

46. *Ibid.*

47. Tang Yijie, *Zai feiyou feiwu zhijian*, 155–6.

48. Guan Dong, "Xiandai xin Ruxue yanjiu de huigu yu zhanwang," 85, 128.

49. Li Shuyou 李書有, "Xin Ruxue sichao yu women de Rujia lunli yanjiu 新儒學思潮與我們的儒家倫理研究" (New Confucian Thought and Our Studies on Confucian Ethics), *Nanjing daxue xuebao* (1987.1): 128–9.

50. Guan Dong, "Xiandai xin Ruxue yanjiu de huigu yu zhanwang," 84.

51. Gan Chunsong, *Xiandaihua yu wenhua xuanze*, 192.

52. See Luo Yijun, *Ping xin Rujia*, 4; and Tang Yijie, "Zongxu 總序" (Preface to the Series), in Feng Zusheng (ed.), *Dangdai xin Rujia*, 1.

53. See Fang Keli and Li Jinquan (eds.), *Xiandai xin Ruxue yanjiu lunji*, vol. 1, unnumbered opening page.

54. See Tang Yijie, "Zongxu," 4; and Song Zhongfu *et al.*, *Ruxue zai xiandai Zhongguo*, 5.

55. Guan Dong, "Xiandai xin Ruxue yanjiu de huigu yu zhanwang," 83–4.

56. Fang Keli and Li Jinquan (eds.), *Xiandai xin Ruxue yanjiu lunji*, vol. 1, 6, 338–9; Guan Dong, "Xiandai xin Ruxue yanjiu de huigu yu zhanwang," 84; Song Zhiming 宋志明, *Xiandai xin Rujia yanjiu* 現代新儒家研究 (Studies of Modern New Confucians), Beijing: Zhongguo renmin daxue chubanshe, 1991, ii.

57. Fang Keli and Li Jinquan (eds.), *Xiandai xin Ruxue yanjiu lunji*, vol. 1, 6.

58. *Ibid.*, "Congshu zhubian de hua," 1.

59. *Ibid.*, 11.

60. Liu Shuxian 劉述先, *Dalu yu haiwai: chuantong de fanxing yu zhuanhua* 大陸與海外：傳統的反省與轉化 (Mainland and Overseas: Reflections

on Tradition and Its Transformation), Taipei: Yongchen wenhua shiye gongsi, 1989, 10.

61. Fang Keli and Li Jinquan (eds.), *Xiandai xin Ruxue yanjiu lunji*, vol. 1, 338.
62. Guan Dong, "Xiandai xin Ruxue yanjiu de huigu yu zhanwang," 83.
63. Song Zhiming, *Xiandai xin Rujia yanjiu*, 4–8.
64. Fang Keli and Li Jinquan (eds.), *Xiandai xin Ruxue yanjiu lunji*, vol. 1, 336.
65. Zheng Jiadong, "Rujia yu xin Rujia de mingyun 儒家與新儒家的命運" (The Fate of Confucians and New Confucians), *Zhexue yanjiu* (1989.3): 21.
66. Arif Dirlik, "Confucius in the Borderlands: Global Capitalism and the Reinvention of Confucianism," 260.
67. The most telling case would be Zhu Yilu 朱義祿, *Rujia lixiang renge yu Zhongguo wenhua* 儒家理想人格與中國文化 (The Ideal Confucian Personality and Chinese Culture), Shengyang: Liaoning jiaoyu chubanshe, 1991.
68. Fang Keli and Li Jinquan (eds.), *Xiandai xin Ruxue yanjiu lunji*, vol. 1, 339–40.
69. Song Zhiming, *Xiandai xin Rujia yanjiu*, 8.
70. Werner Meissner, "New Intellectual Currents in the People's Republic of China," in David C.B. Teather and Herbert S. Yee (eds.), *China in Transition: Issues and Policies*, London: Macmillan Press Ltd., 1999, 19.
71. *Ibid.*
72. Arif Dirlik, "Markets, Culture, Power: the Making of a 'Second Cultural Revolution' in China," *Asian Studies Review* 25.1 (2001): 1–33.
73. See Zhu Yilu, *Rujia lixiang renge yu Zhongguo wenhua*, 122–63.
74. Li Zehou, *Lunyu jindu* 論語今讀 (Contemporary Reading of The Analects), Hefei: Anhui wenyi chubanshe, 1998, 418.
75. *Ibid.*, 418–19.
76. Fang Keli, "Zongxu," 1.
77. Liang Yuanshen employs this image in his article "Qiantu weibu de fenghuang: xin Ruxue yu dangdai Zhongguo."
78. Ge Hongbing, *Zhang'ai yu rentong: dangdai Zhongguo wenhua wenti* 障碍與認同：當代中國文化問題 (Obstacles and Identification: Contemporary Chinese Cultural Problems), Shanghai: Xuelin chubanshe, 2000, 275–85.

CHAPTER 4

LI ZEHOU AND NEW CONFUCIANISM

Sylvia Chan

Introduction: Is Li Zehou 李澤厚 (1930–) a New Confucian?

As John Makeham has pointed out in the introductory chapter, there is as yet no consensus as to who is or is not a New Confucian. To most adherents of New Confucianism outside mainland China, Li Zehou, an avowed Marxist or "post-Marxist," would be the last person to be accorded a place in the New Confucian canon. It is their common perception that Marxists and communists are responsible for destroying the Confucian tradition in China. By a curious twist of fate, Li has been pejoratively called a New Confucian in mainland China in the 1980s and 1990s by those who are probably no less anticommunist but even more anti-Confucian.[1] The mainland Chinese scholars who identify themselves with New Confucianism, or who at least maintain scholarly neutrality toward that school of thought, have generally preferred to avoid the sensitive issue of Confucianism versus communism, and have widened the category to include non-anticommunist philosophers such as Feng Youlan 馮友蘭 (1895–1990). Even so, many of them are still evasive as to whether Li is a New Confucian.

Li Zehou himself is critical of the brand of New Confucianism developed by Xiong Shili 熊十力 (1885–1968) and inherited by his disciples Mou Zongsan 牟宗三 (1909–95) and others.[2] He also declared that he could identify himself with Confucianism, but never with New Confucianism.[3] What then is the justification for including him in this volume?

It is now widely recognized that Confucianism is by no means a homogeneous body of teachings, but that as certain ancient texts were passed down through generations of scholars over many centuries, they received various interpretations, in which new elements were introduced, and non-Confucian ideas were creatively adapted and assimilated. Xunzi's 荀子 (298–238 B.C.) introduction of materialist and legalist elements, Dong Zhongshu's 董仲舒 (179–104 B.C.) assimilation of yin–yang cosmology, and the adaptation of Buddhism by Neo-Confucians of the Song Dynasty are some of the most noted cases in point. Thus, what is known as Confucianism today actually consists of many strands of thought, some of which are mutually contradictory. In a word, the spirit of tolerance of diversity is characteristic of the Confucian school. New Confucianism, if it is true to the Confucian tradition, should not be dogmatic and sectarian, but should be broad enough to accommodate and creatively transform all the trends either already in the Confucian canon, or which can be adapted to harmonize with Confucian teachings.

In order to have a working definition of Confucianism, I shall venture to identify certain shared beliefs and concerns among Confucians. I believe that Confucianism can be summed up as a teaching about inner sageliness (*nei sheng* 內聖) and outer kingliness (*wai wang* 外王). This ideal is defined in the opening passage of the *Great Learning* (*Daxue* 大學) as "illustrating the illustrious virtue, loving (regenerating) the people, and resting in the highest good." It goes on to explain that illustrating the illustrious virtue to the myriad things under heaven has to be done by steps, beginning with cultivation of one's moral self (*xiu shen* 修身), then regulation of one's family (*qi jia* 齊家), then ordering of the state (*zhi guo* 治國), and finally bringing about universal peace (*ping tianxia* 平天下).[4] Confucians of all times believe that these four goals are interrelated and that self-cultivation is the basis for the other three. They therefore treat Confucianism primarily as a philosophy of ethics. They all hold that the cardinal Confucian virtue is benevolence (*ren* 仁). It is benevolence that enables people to live a richer and more fulfilling life—the goal of self-cultivation—and makes them more loving of their fellow beings. Moreover, they also subscribe to a basic Confucian moral metaphysics, namely, that the moral order is somehow in harmony with the cosmic order, the latter also being underpinned by benevolence. While upholding these general principles, Confucians have had many different opinions concerning details. For instance, they have argued over whether the universe is dualistic (noumenal/phenomenal; spiritual/material; *ti/yong* 體/用, and so on) or monistic, and hence whether "objective" knowledge is essential to moral cultivation. The difference between the Cheng-Zhu 程(頤)-朱(熹) School of Principle (*lixue* 理學) and the Lu-Wang 陸(象山)-王(陽明) School of Mind (*xinxue* 心學), in this respect, is well-known.[5] Confucians have also differed over the standards and ways whereby families or society should be regulated and states should be governed. Mencius 孟子 (ca. 372–289 B.C.) emphasized the innate goodness of human nature and recommended rule by virtue, while Xunzi regarded human nature as basically evil and proposed rule by law.[6] Cheng Yi 程頤 (1032–85) believed in the absolute submission of wives to husbands,[7] while Kang Youwei 康有為 (1858–1927) advocated absolute sexual equality, going so far as to recommend the abolition of conventional marriage and allowing men and women to enter into short-term, but renewable, "alliance" contracts.[8] These differences do not make any of them any more or less Confucian, so long as they all upheld the four goals outlined in the Great Learning. I shall demonstrate that Li Zehou's philosophy is mainly concerned with ethics; that his aesthetics—on which he has written a great deal—is ethics on a higher level, or a kind of religio-ethics; and that for him the highest standard a moral person can reach is inner sageliness and outer kingliness. What is new about Li and all New Confucians is that they all try to uncover the relevance of Confucianism to mankind in the modern and postmodern eras, and particularly to China today on its tortuous path to modernization. In doing this, they inevitably have to look at Confucianism from new perspectives and infuse new meaning into it. They are saddened to see that in the last one and a half centuries, as China has encountered many setbacks in its course of modernization, Confucianism has been wrongly blamed for China's woes and vehemently rejected. To many New Confucians, the abandonment of Confucianism in mainland China since 1949 has plunged the nation into a deep cultural crisis, from which it is their mission to rescue China. Li Zehou is somewhat different in this respect. Although he is in complete agreement with other New Confucians that Confucianism continues to be of value to China today, he does not think that the anti-Confucian movement in the twentieth century has succeeded in killing off Confucianism. He argues that criticism of Confucianism has been confined to a superficial and intellectual level by only a small number of radical Chinese intellectuals, and that it has had so little effect that Confucianism has been preserved in social customs and mores, and has continued to shape the values, emotions, behavior, and mode of thinking of the people, including those of its critics. His conclusion is that Confucian elements have so "settled" (*jidian* 積淀) in the Chinese mind—what he calls the cultural-psychological formation (*wenhua-xinli jiegou* 文化心理結構) of the Chinese people—that Confucianism has become a way of life in China, rather than a system of thought.[9] Because Confucianism is still very much alive, he argues, the task of thinkers and scholars today is to critically examine the Confucian elements in the people's cultural-psychological formation and work out in what way some of those elements can be creatively transformed to be of use to China today.[10] But before I discuss how Li executes the task he sets himself, a brief outline of his own philosophy is necessary, in order to clarify the meaning of some analytical categories he employs.

The Theoretical Framework and Analytical Categories of Li's Philosophy[11]

Li's first effort to develop his own philosophy was made while he critically examined Kant's philosophy. The result was the book *Pipan zhexue de pipan: Kangde shu ping* 批判哲學的批判—康德述評 (Critique of Critical Philosophy: A Critical Discussion of Kant; hereafter *On Kant*).[12] Later, he published *Wode zhexue tigang* 我的哲學提綱 (An Outline of My Philosophy). This book contains long excerpts from *On Kant* and four other articles: "A Theoretical Outline of Kant's Philosophy and the Construction of Subjectivity" (1980);[13] "Further Explanation of the Concept of Subjectivity" (1983);[14] "A Third Outline of Subjectivity" (1985);[15] and "A Dialogue on Philosophy" (1989),[16] together with an old article on the origins of the human species written in 1964. The choice of the word "Outline" in the title suggests that these articles are short, laying down general principles in bold strokes, but sparing in systematic elaboration. Since he immigrated to the United States of America in the 1990s, he has published more articles to develop his philosophy further.

Li used to call his philosophy an ontological theory of anthropology (*renleixue bentilun* 人類學本體論). Lest it should be confused with Feuerbachian idealist humanist anthropology, he explains that his anthropology is the study of the human species as social, super-biological (*chao shengwu* 超生物) beings and subjects of social praxis in a concrete historical process. He has recently modified it to become an ontological theory of historical anthropology (*renleixue lishi bentilun* 人類學歷史本體論), to emphasize further the historically specific nature of both the material base of human society and the level of development of the mental powers of human beings. In his view, the ultimate reality of the world consists of two aspects: material and spiritual. He calls the former technological-social formation (*gongju-shehui jiegou* 工具-社會結構), or the technological aspect of ultimate reality (*gongju benti* 工具本體), and refers to the latter as cultural-psychological formation, or the psychological aspect of the ultimate reality (*xinli benti* 心理本體). The former refers to the material conditions into which individuals are born: the natural environment, the physical structure of the human body, and the level of technological development at any given historical period. The latter refers to the mental powers individuals have: cognition, emotion, and volition (*zhi qing yi jiegou* 知情意結構), which Li also refers to as subjectivity (*zhutixing* 主體性), and even as human nature (*renxing* 人性). The cultural-psychological formation, according to Li, is an abstract framework (*kuangjia* 框架) or form (*xingshi* 形式) whereby consciousness is organized, in much the same way as sensory perceptions are organized by Kant's categories of understanding. This framework or form comes from the "sedimentation" of concrete sense experiences of individuals in their praxis in the course of history, but transcends empirical experiences to assume universal validity. He believes that philosophy should concern itself with the study of human beings' cultural-psychological formation, and leave the study of technological-social formation to scientists. He therefore gives his philosophy another name: a philosophy of subjectivity in praxis (*zhutixing shijian zhexue* 主體性實踐哲學).

As a Marxist by training and by conviction, Li Zehou affirms the primacy of technological-social formation over subjectivity. He regards the primates' invention of tools for use in production as the defining moment of the human species. Through collective labor, a gradually "humanized" body was developed over the course of thousands of years to enable humans to meet the challenges of increasingly complex social praxis. Human beings began to have, for instance, hind limbs suitable for walking erect, a more developed brain, and a vocal cord capable of producing many sounds. This is an important aspect of what Li calls "humanized nature" (*renhua ziran* 人化自然). He is, thus, critical of the "linguistic turn" of modern philosophy, saying that language, being a product of social praxis, cannot be an ontological category. So far, his philosophy is Marxist historical materialism through and through. Nevertheless, he emphatically repudiates the Marxist social theory of class struggle, arguing that it has been proven wrong by the practice of many Marxist states and political parties. He also rejects the kind of determinism sometimes attributed to Marxism. He believes that the psychological-cultural formation, although born out of material production, enjoys relative autonomy. Thus, he prefers to style his philosophy "post-Marxist," to highlight differences from the official Chinese version of Marxism.

In Li's philosophy, the three components of cognition, volition, and feeling in the cultural-psychological formation are not accorded the same importance. For Li, as for Confucians and Kant, the moral will is of a higher order than epistemology. Li maintains not only that practical reason is prior to pure reason in time, but also that the latter is "regulated" (*zhiyue* 制約) and "guided" (*zhidao* 指導) by the former. He even says that logic and grammar are derived from moral laws.[17] It is, therefore, not surprising that his philosophy does not talk much about epistemology. It is clear, too, that Li considers aesthetics to be of an even higher order than ethics. He thinks that the highest plane (*jingjie* 境界) a moral person can reach is the Confucian ideal of complete union of self with the cosmic order, or heaven, which is an aesthetic experience.

Li's philosophy was first developed in the late 1970s and the early 1980s, and bears the hallmark of the intense intellectual ferment of that time. In the period immediately after Mao's death, the most pressing problem facing China was to search for a new path to build a strong and wealthy modern nation after the dismal failure of Mao's experiment. In order to do this, it was necessary to undertake a thorough reexamination of the ideology, social and political theories, and cultural values underpinning that failed experiment. Such a reexamination once again revived the perennial debate on Western learning versus Chinese learning, and modernity versus tradition. During this period, Li wrote a large number of studies on Chinese thought, which are collected in his three interpretative intellectual histories.[18] These studies can be seen as his contribution to that debate. It is his argument that since the material-technological formation is basic to any human society, it is the *ti* 體, or the foundation. China's modernization of the material base must be achieved by adopting Western technology, managerial methods, and institutions. The state ideology is also the Western theory of Marxism. For these elements to work in China, however, they must be so adapted as to meet China's needs and harmonize with China's cultural and social norms. If those norms are incompatible with modernization, they must be reformed. He thus reverses the famous dictum of the nineteenth-century Confucian reformist Zhang Zhidong (張之洞 1837–1909), "*Zhongxue wei ti, xixue wei yong* 中學為體, 西學為用" (Chinese learning as foundation and Western learning for use), and proposes "*Xi ti, Zhong yong* 西體中用" (Western learning as foundation but adapted to Chinese use).[19]

Li's dictum of *Xi ti, Zhong yong* is not as antitraditional as the Chinese authorities have made it out to be. Even in the heady days of antitraditional fever of the early 1980s, Li never endorsed the fashionable idea of "wholesale Westernization," and consistently made a balanced assessment of Confucianism in his three intellectual histories. In the 1990s, he has continued to publish a large number of articles on Confucianism and Chinese tradition in Taiwan, Hong Kong, and mainland Chinese journals. These articles show that he still holds to his former views. If anything, he has come to perceive more positive features in Confucianism after his move to the United States of America. He has even modified Lin Yusheng's advocacy of a "creative transformation" to "transformative creation" (*zhuanhuaxing de chuangzao* 轉化性的創造) of tradition, saying that the former term would give the wrong impression that China's tradition must be so transformed as to conform to that of the West.[20]

Li's Theory of Ethics

In his explanation of the origin of moral consciousness, Li is strongly influenced by the pre-Qin philosopher, Xunzi. Following Xunzi, Li believes that moral norms, rites, and taboos, known collectively as *li* 禮 (rites) in ancient Confucian texts, were essential for the survival of the human species at the beginning of civilization, and therefore coercively imposed on society. While concrete norms, rites, and taboos change with time, the rational recognition of the need to control antisocial instincts for the collective good has been so "condensed" (*ningju* 凝聚) in human consciousness that it has produced the will to act morally. Moral consciousness is thus "condensed reason" deposited in the human cultural-psychological formation. This is contrary to the Mencian theory, upheld by Neo-Confucians and most New Confucians, that moral consciousness is endowed by heaven, and hence innate. Li, however, speaks highly of Mencius' recognition that even the naturally endowed moral sense needs continuous cultivation. He contends that Mencius' method of self-cultivation, that is, the art of "nurturing the flood-like vital force" (*haoran zhi qi* 浩然之氣) is actually the consciously induced condensation of reason.[21] He further argues that the most valuable contribution that Confucius and Mencius made to ethics was their exposition of the concept of benevolence. Confucius and Mencius, Li submits, have elevated this concept from its original meaning of graded love based on blood ties to universal love based on humanitarianism, and further made it the basis of selfhood, a quality whereby a moral person (*junzi* 君子) realizes his individual authentic humanity (*geti renge* 個體人格).[22] He argues that the affirmation of morality as self-legislated and as an ontological category is the greatest contribution that Mencius made to

Confucianism,[23] and this has made Confucian ethics an ethical theory of the highest order, on par with that of Kant.[24]

In his own ethical theory, Li tries to synthesize Confucian and Kantian ethics. He believes that the formation of the moral will marks a watershed in the process of "humanizing" the animal nature of human beings. Once free moral will is built into the cultural-psychological formation, it assumes the nature of Kant's categorical imperative and is not subject to the law of causality. Li's favorite hypothetical case is that of Albert Einstein sacrificing his own life to save the life of a senile and decrepit old man in a fire. From the utilitarian point of view, Einstein's altruism would seem irrational, but Li thinks that it is a shining example of what moral reason can do to bring out the best in a person.

This is, of course, Kantian, but Li disagrees with Kantian ethics in two important respects. First, as absolutist as Kant's ethics may appear, it still recognizes the need for incentives for moral action. Kant therefore postulates a cosmic order that proportions happiness to moral accomplishment, and this involves the belief in the existence of God.[25] Confucian ethics, on the other hand, does not require the assistance of a transcendental God, because it postulates that the human world and the cosmic order are regulated by the same moral principle, *dao*, or *tian dao* 天道 (the heavenly principle). The latter is thus more appealing to Li Zehou the atheist.

Second, Kant's categorical imperative is a priori, and entirely separated from the experiential world of sensibility and feeling. It also presupposes that people's biological nature is immoral or amoral. The Mencian school of Confucian ethics, on the other hand, is based on the belief in the innate goodness of human nature. It postulates no conflict between the body and soul and requires no suppression of the desire of the flesh but only its submission to the control of reason. More important still, the Confucian cardinal virtue of benevolence is firmly rooted in feelings of love and compassion, experienced by people in their daily life. Because love between parents and children is the most "natural" and spontaneous, Confucianism makes filial piety the central link of benevolence, from which radiates love (loyalty) for one's sovereign and one's kinsfolk and friends. Confucian ethics can thus be understood and practiced by everybody. Even though Li argues that the moral will comes from condensed reason, in his ethics as well as aesthetics he repeatedly stresses the importance of reason being softened by feelings and feelings being moderated by reason. The ideal state of the human mind, to him, is when there is a complete fusion of reason and feeling (*qing li jiaorong* 情理交融).[26]

One can infer from this that Li has great faith in the goodness of what people spontaneously feel. Here, he is in complete accord with Mencius, who also believes that the beginning of benevolence is the spontaneous feeling of compassion on seeing a child about to fall into a well.[27] In his belief in the limited role of reason in ethics, he echoes Mencius' remark that the knowledge possessed by men without the exercise of thought is moral knowledge (*liangzhi* 良知).[28] On the other hand, he, like Mencius, believes that spontaneity alone is not sufficient to sustain one's moral sense, and that education is necessary. He repeatedly stresses the importance of education, calling it a science of the future,[29] although he is vague about what kind of education he has in mind. Whatever it may be, it is clearly not the kind of sudden enlightenment gained through meditation or quiet sitting that the Lu-Wang school of the mind advocates; nor is it the method recommended by the Cheng-Zhu school: gradual attainment of a comprehensive understanding of the principle of heaven (*tian li* 天理), the transcendental moral principle, through laborious "investigation of things" (*ge wu* 格物).

In his later writing, Li proposes to distinguish two kinds of ethics: social and religious. The former is a minimum ethical standard based on the rule of law that every member of society has to conform to. The latter is purely a private matter. Although not everybody can be expected to have religious ethics, Li believes that the promotion of social ethics can uplift some people to a standard such that they will practice religious ethics. He even advocates a return to the Confucian tradition of fusing social and religious ethics, by reviving the worship of "heaven, earth, the country (the emperor), one's parents, and one's relatives and friends (teachers)," because these religio-ethical rituals are, according to him, based on the universal feelings of love that people have for what they worship. He believes that the strong element of personal feelings involved in Confucian ethics can help to palliate people's sense of alienation, loss of meaning, and loss of autonomy before an impersonal and inescapable network of power in our age, the malaise poignantly raised by existentialism and postmodernism.[30] Li has come to attach such increasing importance to feeling (*qinggan* 情感) in his philosophical anthropology that he even comes to regard feeling as the ultimate reality (*benti* 本體) of the human world. Because feelings are personal and diffused, he contends that his philosophy has thus dissolved the category of ultimate reality, thereby freeing individuals from any hegemonic discursive formations about metaphysics.[31]

Li Zehou's Aesthetics

In the late 1950s, Li made his name as a leading aesthetician when he took part in the Party-initiated campaign to criticize the "bourgeois idealist" aesthetics of the British-trained aesthetician Zhu Guangqian (朱光潜, 1897–1986). In the post-Mao era, he wrote on the philosophical aspects of aesthetics[32] as well as applied aesthetics.[33] His theory of subjectivity was enthusiastically embraced by the art circles, making him the most influential aesthetician in China in the 1980s.[34]

Li's aesthetics is closely related to his theory of subjectivity. It is his opinion that with the development of technology in modern times, people's material needs are met by and large. But a more affluent material life has not made people any happier. On the contrary, as the modern age evolves into the postmodern age, the feeling of alienation and of a spiritual void has become more unbearable. He therefore argues that the question of remolding our cultural-psychological formation has become one of the major challenges of our times. Even though he sticks to his materialism in thinking that the cure for spiritual ills lies largely in further development of the economy,[35] he nevertheless believes that education, including aesthetic education, has an important role to play in this respect.[36] He therefore advocates developing Marxism along the tradition of Kant and Schiller, rather than of Hegel.[37]

Li's philosophical aesthetics seem to have undergone some change in emphasis. In his major work on philosophical aesthetics, *Meixue sijiang* (Four Lectures on Aesthetics), he emphasizes the pivotal role of social praxis in the genesis of aesthetic judgment. The influence of Marxist materialism is evident. His appropriation of Kant, on the other hand, is only superficial. Although he employs Kant's categories in *Critique of Judgment* to characterize aesthetic judgment as arising from a coincidence of purposiveness and lawfulness, he uses these terms in a different sense, either deliberately or out of misunderstanding. It is beyond the scope of this article to explain clearly what lawfulness and purposiveness mean for Kant. Suffice it to say that for Kant both purposiveness and lawfulness refer to nature and are indeterminate concepts. For aesthetic judgment to be possible, it has to be hypothesized that nature has the purpose of making our aesthetic judgment possible. Such a hypothesis will explain why particulars in nature seem to manifest a certain regularity (lawfulness) that matches the form of our power of aesthetic judgment, and this enables aesthetic judgment.[38] Li, however, takes the lawfulness of nature in its materialist sense, that everything in nature is governed by a determinate law. Lawfulness is therefore the same as "truthfulness" (*zhen* 真). He also takes purposiveness to mean the purpose(s) of human praxis. The underlying yet unstated assumption of his aesthetics is the inherent goodness of the purpose of praxis (*shan* 善). This is logical, since he regards praxis, particularly tool-making, as that which makes the human species possible. When people as conscious beings "freely" apply nature's laws to make things, truthfulness coincides with goodness, which is the essence of beauty. This comes, of course, from Marx, who said that in so doing, "man . . . forms things in accordance with the laws of beauty."[39] Li, however, explains this in terms of the Confucian union of heaven (nature, truthfulness) and people (goodness of purpose) (*tian ren heyi* 天人合一).[40] As metaphysical as this may sound, at the experiential level he gives quite a straightforward materialist explanation to the genesis of aesthetic instincts, instincts that make people distinguish the beautiful from the not-beautiful. According to Li, such instincts, like moral consciousness, are not innate, but have entered into the cultural-psychological formation as a result of the human species shedding its animalistic qualities in the process of transforming nature. Then, it came to recognize as beautiful the rhythms of certain movements, or the shapes of certain objects, which they had become familiar with in praxis.[41] Aesthetic judgment is thus seen as "humanized nature" par excellence.

In the 1990s, however, he discussed aesthetics more in terms of "naturalized humanity" (*ren ziranhua* 人自然化).[42] According to Li, naturalized humanity has three levels of meaning: (1) living close to and maintaining a harmonious relationship with nature; (2) engaging in physical exercise to bring out the fullest potential of the human body; and (3) bringing our existence into accord with nature through such practices as *qigong* and yoga, which may result in tuning into nature's secrets and obtaining certain superhuman powers, such as reading with one's ears, for instance. It may thus be said that even in Li's religious ethics, there is an implied division between a lower and a higher level. To be close to nature and to develop one's physical body to its full potential, or to love one's country, parents, and kin do not require much religious piety and faith, and can be realized by a large number of people, while to live in a state of complete freedom in accord with heaven is not something the average person can hope to attain.

In naturalizing our humanity, Li says that if we extend our human nature (*xing* 性) to the fullest extent, we can come to know heaven and realize a union with heaven (nature) (*jin xing yi zhi tian* 盡性以知天). Again, he gives this Confucian dictum a new interpretation. The "xing" here, he explains, is not the same as the neo-Confucian "xing," or moral nature, but the nature of the subject having aesthetic experience. In aesthetic experience, he argues, the overwhelmingly social nature of the cultural-psychological formation is neutralized by the "natural qualities" (*ziran xing* 自然性) of the individual. What these "natural qualities" are, he has never explained, but proceeds to say that at this high level of aesthetic experience, reason, sensibility, feeling, desire, imagination, and subconsciousness all come together to produce in each individual a unique creativeness. This creativeness not only enables aesthetic creation and enjoyment, but can spark "free intuition" (*ziyou zhiguan* 自由直觀), a kind of non-logical mode of thinking that he says can lead to scientific discoveries. He calls this "revelation of truth by beauty" (*yi mei qi zhen* 以美啟真). Moreover, this absolutely free state of aesthetic enjoyment is one in which one can "follow what one's heart desires without transgressing what is right" (*cong xin suo yu bu yu ju* 從心所欲不逾矩), an ideal attained by Confucius only at the advanced age of seventy.[43] In this state, purposiveness (one's heart's desire) completely coincides with lawfulness (what is right). Thus, this is both an aesthetic and moral experience, which Li describes as "storing goodness in beauty" (*yi mei chu shan* 以美儲善).

"Naturalization of humanity" is, in my opinion, one of the most speculative and most interesting ideas Li has put forward. One gets the impression that here he is talking of the Marxian vision of unalienated and all-round-developed human beings freely realizing all human potentials at the "end of history." There is thus a strong element of utopianism in the concept. If the Marxian utopian society is to be achieved through class struggle to eliminate class oppression—the source of alienation and loss of freedom—then having disowned the Marxian theory of class struggle, Li proposes to reach his utopia through aesthetic enjoyment. This is altogether a sweeter and more pleasant vision than that of Marx, but is no less amorphous than the vision of sagely enlightenment criticized by him.

One thing is clear. The connection Li makes between aesthetics and ethics goes beyond Kant. Although Kant made the same connection, his equation of the supersensible power aroused in the judgment of the sublime with our supersensible moral volition is vastly different from the connection Li makes. On the other hand, it is the Confucian tradition that posits such a close connection between the two, often treating them as synonymous. According to Li, in the *Analects* the word beauty appears fourteen times, of which ten assume the meaning of "virtue" or "goodness."[44] Even today, the Chinese government calls the virtuous behavior it wants to promote among its citizens the "four beauties" (*si mei*

四美).⁴⁵ Whether Confucianism elevates aesthetics to a position higher than ethics is a moot point. Tang Yijie 湯一介, for instance, argues that in Confucianism aesthetics is of a lower order than ethics but higher than epistemology.⁴⁶ Still, Li's shift of emphasis from "humanized nature" to "naturalized humanity" is significant. If the former is firmly rooted in the tradition of Western humanism that takes men as the measure of all things, the latter moves close to the Confucian teaching of a mutual harmony between men and nature.

The Fourth Period of Confucianism

In recent years, Li has attracted much attention for his controversial argument that New Confucianism in the twentieth and twenty-first centuries should be regarded as the fourth period in the development of Confucianism, rather than its third period, as alleged by Mou Zongsan and his disciples.⁴⁷ Central to the third period theory is the concept of *daotong* 道统, the subject of chapter 2 in this volume. Suffice it to say here that while the theory no doubt serves the purpose of self-aggrandizement of its proponents, it also turns Confucianism into a closed system. Moreover, it runs counter to the Confucian teaching that everybody has equal potential to comprehend and practice the Confucian ideal of inner sage and outer king, and is incompatible with the modern spirit of intellectual equality and freedom. The belief that the thread of transmission of the true Confucian way is extremely fragile, and often broken off for many centuries, does not inspire much confidence in its universal validity either. All in all, the *daotong* theory is so counterproductive that it has been disowned even by some of those who might otherwise identify themselves with New Confucianism.⁴⁸

Li's rejection of the concept of *daotong*, however, is based on the argument that it distorts history. With regard to the first period of Confucianism, there is little disagreement between him and the third period proponents as to who were the foundational representatives of Confucianism, although the latter may not wholeheartedly endorse the teachings of Xunzi. On the other hand, Li is more inclined to see Confucius not as an innovator but as a creative transmitter of an ancient culture handed down to him from antiquity. He argues that the key Confucian concepts and tenets expounded in the foundational Confucian texts of the classical period could be traced to the culture of tribal societies in the Shang and Zhou dynasties, many centuries before Confucius. Li calls this culture a "tradition of shamanism and historiography" (*wu shi chuantong* 巫史傳統).⁴⁹

It is well known that ancestral worship was already practiced in the Shang and Zhou dynasties.[50] Li argues that the elevation of dead ancestors into gods and the transformation of the most revered tribal leader of the past into the supreme heavenly deity (*tian shen* 天神), marks the beginning of the blurring of the natural and the supernatural worlds that underpins Confucian metaphysics and cosmology. In ancestral worship, the communion between men and heaven was effected through the medium of shamans performing rituals. Shamanic rituals were mostly performed to achieve some practical goals, especially collective goals, such as praying for rain or for victory in battle, and not for salvation of the human soul. It was in the course of ritual performance that the divine will was revealed to men, as function, not as substance, for there was no separate existence of an objectified anthropomorphic god from ritual practice. This, Li says, was the origin of the kind of pragmatic reason (*shiyong lixing* 實用理性) that characterizes Confucianism. It also explains why there is no transcendental God in Chinese religion. Shamans also engaged in divination and were at the same time court historians, chronicling divination and other important tribal events. For rituals/divinations to be effective, they had to be performed with the right attitude: reverence (*jing* 敬), awe (*wei* 畏), loyalty (*zhong* 忠), and sincerity (*cheng* 誠) toward the spirits. As people able to read the divine will and foresee the future, the shamans/diviners were tribal political leaders or their advisers. This gave rise to the idea that rulers should be virtuous. When the Duke of Zhou (Zhou Gong 周公 eleventh century B.C.) "instituted the rites and composed music" (*zhi li zuo yue* 制禮作樂), Li says, he simply rationalized and institutionalized shamanic and divination rituals passed down from times immemorial, thereby laying the foundation of the great tradition of Chinese culture. In this tradition, virtues of reverence, awe, etc. and rites to differentiate seniority and status were established as norms to regulate the behavior of tribe members as well as their rulers. At the same time, divination manuals were rationalized (demythologized) to become the basis for the construction of a humanized cosmology found in the *Book of Changes* and other classical texts. In this cosmology, heaven is represented as humane, generous, and having inexhaustible energy, forever producing, transforming, and nourishing all under heaven. Heaven is also moral, rewarding virtue and punishing evil. Men can thus attain happiness and avert disaster if they strive to be in harmony with the heavenly way. These are very positive and activist world and cosmic views, Li says, that are ingrained in the Chinese mind. He maintains that the non-distinction between the human, the natural and supernatural worlds, pragmatic reason, and

LI ZEHOU AND NEW CONFUCIANISM / 119

a culture of optimism and contentment (*leguan wenhua* 樂觀文化) are the three characteristics of the deep structure of Confucianism.[51] As Confucianism dominates Chinese culture, these three are also characteristic of the entire Chinese culture.[52]

This article on shamanism and historiography, I believe, is of more than historical interest. Li has repeatedly called for a return to foundational Confucian texts (*yuan dian* 原典) to oppose the tendency in New Confucianism to regard neo-Confucian writings of the Song and Ming dynasties as the fountainhead for present-day development.[53] He wants to establish that the tenets in classical Confucianism have all come from everyday life and not from the metaphysical speculations of closeted philosophers. He can then argue that his interpretation of Confucianism along a materialist-historicist line—as practical teaching closely related to people's lives—is truer to the Confucian spirit than the metaphysical and moralistic direction that advocates of the third period are traveling along. He has never concealed his dissatisfaction with their one-sided emphasis on inner sageliness at the expense of the outer kingliness ideal. Moreover, he feels that even their ethics is fraught with problems. Their teaching that sagely enlightenment has to be gained by individuals having some mystical power to intuit the heavenly way is almost impossible for the average person to follow. His proof is that even the proponents themselves, Xiong Shili and Mou Zongsan among them, were in actual life far from being sages.

The proponents of the third period would, of course, reject Li's criticism that they have neglected the outer king ideal. In spite of their criticism of the antitraditionalism of the May Fourth Movement, they have all endorsed the movement's goal of modernizing China through adopting Western science and democracy. They have all tried to prove that Confucianism is not incompatible with science and democracy. In fact, Mou Zongsan has developed a famous theory of how one's innate moral mind–heart (*liangzhi* 良知) can "open out into" (*kaichu* 開出) knowledge of science and democracy, through "self-diremption" (*ziwo kanxian* 自我坎陷).[54] Such a speculative theory is not something that even scholars who generally have sympathy with Mou's New Confucianism can all support. Yu Yingshi 余英時 (1930–), for example, has convincingly pointed out the untenability of Mou's borrowed Hegelian concept. The difficulty, as Yu points out, is that while in Hegel, the absolute spirit effects self-diremption at the level of the phenomenal world, in the finite minds of men, in New Confucianism there is no differentiation between the noumenal and the phenomenal world, which self-diremption must pre-suppose. From this theoretical impasse arise practical difficulties. The *daotong* theory implies that only very few sages can hold fast to the moral mind–heart. It therefore follows that "self-diremption" can only occur in the minds of those few people, on whose shoulders would thus rest the monumental task of introducing science and democracy to China. This would clearly be an absurd proposition. If, on the other hand, it should be proposed that through the effort of the New Confucians, most Chinese people could regain their moral mind–heart and open it "out into" science and democracy, New Confucians then would have to convince us how they, as private scholars, can successfully lead the broad masses of the Chinese people onto the Confucian way. Moreover, Yu says, the Chinese people have been searching for science and democracy long before New Confucianism came into being. Does it mean that they already possessed the innate moral mind–heart even though they may not realize it? If this should be the case, then this would render redundant the effort of New Confucians to realize their outer kingliness.[55] To Yu's incisive criticism, Li Zehou adds that the self-diremption theory destroys the coherence of Mou's own system. If Mou regards people's innate moral mind–heart as the original state of being, which is complete and perfect in itself, embracing the entire perfect cosmic order, how can he, Li asks, explain that this complete and perfect state needs "self-diremption" in order to acquire something else? Another internal theoretical contradiction in Mou and in all New Confucians, Li points out, is their theory of immanent transcendence. Li maintains that this term is an oxymoron, because transcendence can only mean transcending the phenomenal world and can therefore not occur in a philosophy refusing to accept a separation between the noumenon and phenomenon.

Having dismissed Mou's novel theory of "self-diremption" of the innate moral mind–heart, Li comes to the conclusion that New Confucianism is really a copy of Song-Ming Neo-Confucianism without much innovative development, and should therefore be regarded as a contemporary form of Neo-Confucianism and a continuation of the third period of Confucianism. Since this line of development can teach nothing to help realize either the inner sage or the outer king ideal, Li believes that it has led Confucianism to a dead end, from which only a completely new direction of development can deliver it. The new direction, Li implies, is the one he has been following in his philosophy of subjectivity in praxis, and his new development should be regarded as the fourth period of Confucianism.

Li further contends that the development of Confucianism made by Confucians in the Han Dynasty, particularly by Dong Zhongshu, was the second period.[56] The *daotong* theory, however, does not recognize them as authentic transmitters of Confucianism at all. This view is, of course, hard to justify on historical grounds, for Han Confucians were responsible for elevating Confucianism to state orthodoxy in the reign of the Han Emperor Wu Di (漢武帝 r. 141–87 B.C.), in which position Confucianism had remained for the next two thousand years. Dong Zhongshu's eclecticism, however, had drawn criticism from Confucians even before the *daotong* theory had become established.[57] His cosmology borrows heavily from the pseudo-scientific theory of yin–yang and the five elements, and even includes superstitious beliefs such as portents, while his social and political theory is extremely authoritarian. One may well wonder what it is in Dong's philosophy that attracts the rationalist-materialist and liberal Li Zehou. There is, however, no denying that Dong was the first Confucian to assimilate and to "Confucianize" many influential schools of thought in his time—including Legalism, Daoism, and the yin–yang school—to construct a coherent and all-embracing metaphysical system to try to explain everything in the natural and human worlds. Li thinks very highly of Dong's synthesis, describing it as a "transformative creation." According to Li, Dong's creativeness lies in his infusion of the concept of benevolence into heaven, the way, and yin–yang, thereby constructing a feeling cosmos, a cosmos full of love for all animate and inanimate things.[58] Under the thick mass of Dong's mystical speculations and irrational suppositions lie materialistic and rationalist concerns for the ordering of human affairs and a humanist glorification of men. From the *Book of Changes* Dong took the belief in a benevolent and active cosmic order, in which not only does heaven ceaselessly reproduce and nourish life, moreover, by acting in accordance with the heavenly way men can "assist the transforming and nourishing powers of heaven and earth and form a triad with them" (*can tiandi, zan huayu* 參天地, 贊化育). Here, men are put on par with heaven and earth, and are told to match their behavior with their supreme position in the universe. For all its authoritarianism, the system puts the onus on rulers to act in harmony with heaven and earth and set moral examples to their subjects. Li maintains that Dong preserved and developed the essence of the rationalist-activist school of Confucianism founded by Xunzi and expounded in the *Book of Changes* and the *Doctrine of the Mean*. It is the emphasis on the outer king ideal, the celebration of men's capabilities, and the activist and optimistic world outlook found in these texts that appeal strongly to Li. He believes that New Confucianism should attach greater importance to this legacy, which is a healthy antidote to the quietist inward-looking tendency of Song-Ming Confucianism.

Li, of course, rejects the concrete content of Dong's outer king ideal, that is, his authoritarian political and social order supported by the so-called three bonds and five constants (*san gang wu chang* 三剛五常). In his opinion, the fourth period of Confucianism should be an open system that can assimilate modern Western ideas to replace some of its outmoded ones. Of Western ideas, he considers Marxism, liberalism, existentialism, and postmodernism to be particularly useful.[59]

It is easy to see why Li wants to borrow from Marxism. We have seen how his philosophy has been deeply influenced by Marxism. He contends that his taking the material conditions of the human world as the point of departure for his philosophy is in accord with the teachings of Confucius, Mencius, and Xunzi.[60] He also thinks that Marx's exposition on freedom and on human nature, in stressing the individual's value and dignity, is specially relevant to China, where the state ideology often devalues the individual in the name of promoting the collective good. In this respect, Li believes, Marxism shares the same concern as liberalism, but is superior to the latter in that Marxism views such questions as human rights as being determined by historically specific networks of social/power relations, while the liberal concepts of atomized, free-floating individuals and of "natural" human rights (*tianfu renquan* 天賦人權) are ahistorical and asocial. Li endorses the former view and rejects the latter, but believes that the liberal theory of democracy and rule of law should be the cornerstone of today's outer king ideal. Even here, he argues, the impersonal rule of law should be mellowed by the Confucian emphasis on harmonious interpersonal relationships. He envisages, for example, that China could perfect and extend its existing system of mediation of civil disputes so as to avoid an excessively litigious society, or that the street committees in China's cities, which were set up in Mao's time to spy on urban residents, could be transformed to provide community services and promote a communitarian spirit.[61] In economics, he believes that liberalism's free market economy has proven to be superior to the Marxist command economy, but thinks that laissez-faire individualism should be balanced by concern for social justice, and that the Confucian way of the mean could be employed to achieve such balance.[62]

Conclusion

Mou Zongsan characterizes Confucianism as a "learning about living."[63] Li's philosophy takes "we live" as its point of departure and goes on to answer the questions of how we should live and why.[64] Therefore his philosophy can be said to be in the Confucian tradition. At the ontological level, however, Li's philosophy has little to do with Confucianism, being derived from Marxist materialism. His theory of the cultural-psychological formation is clearly at odds with the Neo-Confucian/New Confucian view that the moral mind is the authentic state of being. His view of how people should live, too, is strongly influenced by Marxist materialism, in his unswerving faith in social progress and in modernization through modern science and technology. Even though all other New Confucians believe in modernization, to my knowledge, none of them has shown as much unreserved enthusiasm for modern technology as Li. This in itself is not necessarily incompatible with Confucianism, and can indeed find support in the practical strain in the Confucian outer king ideal. Though Li has to borrow extensively from Western theories to develop his outer-king ideal, he has tried to incorporate Confucianism in it. His proposed application of Confucianism to the political, legal, and social arenas may seem modest, but is practical and practicable.

It is, however, in his answer to why we live that establishes his credential as a New Confucian. His ethics and aesthetics are both concerned with inner sageliness. In both, he adopts the Confucian cardinal virtue of benevolence as the axis, and affirms the Confucian ideal of one's union with heaven as the ultimate standard for authentic living. True, he has given a new interpretation to this ideal, which may not be accepted by other Confucian scholars, but this should not detract from his contributions to Confucianism, which was originally an open system and should remain so.

This is not to deny that there are some intrinsic weaknesses in Li's writings. His exposition is unsystematic. He is in the habit of writing large numbers of short articles over many years that essentially repeat the same themes and arguments but sometimes may introduce, without warning, new elements contradictory to his earlier assertions. These inconsistencies reflect a deep-seated problem: that he has never quite resolved the inevitable tension between Confucianism and his Marxism, and indeed between his liberalism and Marxism. While he embraces the activism and optimism in the cosmology of the *Book of Changes*, arguing that it is compatible with the modern spirit of pushing ahead and achieving, he has not considered how he can resolve the conflict between its conservative theory of cyclical development and his Hegelian–Marxian view of linear development and progress. Both his endorsement of the religio-ethical Confucian teaching and his liberal politics require his affirmation of the absolute autonomy of the individual as moral agent and political actor, which he indeed goes to great lengths to do.

Yet, he does not explain how individual autonomy can be reconciled with the theory of cultural-psychological formation, which is clearly not an autonomous event, but occurs willy-nilly to individuals in a given historical and social context. When questioned about this, he even maintained that "sedimentation" is initiated individually, and that this accounts for individual artistic styles as different as Cézanne's and van Gogh's.[65] One would find it very hard to square such an argument with everything he has said about the cultural-psychological formation in his major philosophical works. One gets the impression that because he is so eager to gain the acceptance of other New Confucians and liberals that he retreats from his Marxism whenever he encounters or anticipates their objection, even at the expense of theoretical coherence. While his contention that Han Confucianism is the second period of development accords well with history, one wonders why he does not follow Qian Mu in regarding Qing Confucianism to be the fourth period in the development of Confucianism, which, in my opinion, is a more accurate account of the history of Confucianism.[66] His disregard of the contributions of Qing Confucians is puzzling in view of his strong emphasis on the practical application of Confucianism.

In spite of all this, Li should be taken more seriously than he has been by those who are committed to bringing about a Confucian renaissance. For all the prominence New Confucianism has gained in recent years in academic circles, interest in it has been confined to a small number of—albeit very vocal and high profile—academics. If the declared objective of this movement is to make Confucianism relevant to modern-day life, it should try much harder to get its message across to a much wider audience and to broaden its appeal. Most foundational New Confucian texts, however, in their emphasis on mystical enlightenment of the initiated, are esoteric, difficult for the ordinary person to understand, and even more difficult to practice. Li's writing, on the other hand, is lively, and he has a gift of explaining difficult philosophical concepts and theories in plain language, although in so doing, he also tends to be too simplistic. More important, his exposition of Confucianism is more down-to-earth—with the exception of the speculative concept of "naturalized humanity"—and more closely related to the Chinese people's thinking and way of life. Although many New Confucians may find Li's Marxism unpalatable, Marxism has shaped the mode of thinking of many people in mainland China, and a number of Marxist principles are still accepted by them. Li's synthesis may thus help to bridge the two thought systems, and promote understanding and acceptance of Confucianism among the mainland Chinese. Although he has not been completely successful in this respect, it is a commendable pioneering attempt. By historicizing and contextualizing Confucianism, he is also more attuned to the postmodern suspicion of essentialism. Li was the most influential thinker in China in the 1980s and continues to be read widely in mainland China and Taiwan today. His brand of Confucianism may thus turn out to be more appealing to a greater number of people than New Confucianism narrowly defined. He may yet play an important role in winning a following for New Confucianism (broadly defined) in mainland China, a development that might be critical to the success of the global project of New Confucianism.

Notes

1. Liu Xiaobo 劉曉波 is Li Zehou's most vitriolic critic in this respect. Liu Xiaobo, *Xuanze de pipan—yu sixiang lingxiu Li Zehou duihua* 選擇的批判—與思想領袖李澤厚對話 (Critique of Choice: In Dialogue with the Intellectual Leader Li Zehou), Taipei: Fengyun shidai chubanshe, 1989.
2. Li Zehou, "Lüe lun xiandai xin Rujia 略論現代新儒家" (A Brief Discussion of Contemporary New Confucianism), in Li Zehou, *Zhongguo xiandai sixiangshi lun* 中國現代思想史論 (An Interpretative Intellectual History of Contemporary China; hereafter *Xiandai sixiangshi lun*), revised edition, Taipei: Fengyun shidai chubanshe, 1990, 377–93; "Shuo Ruxue si qi 說儒學四期" (Essay on the Fourth Period of Confucianism), in *Jimao wu shuo* 己卯五說 (Five Essays Written in 1999; hereafter *Wu shuo*), Beijing: Zhongguo dianying chubanshe, 1999, 2–13.
3. "He wei 'xiandai xin Ruxue' 何謂 '現代新儒學'" (What is 'New Confucianism'), in Li Zehou, *Shiji xin meng* 世紀新夢 (New Dream of the Century; hereafter *Xin meng*), Hefei: Anhui wenyi chubanshe, 1999, 110.
4. For the Chinese text of *Daxue* and its English translation, see *Confucius, Confucian Analects, The Great Learning & The Doctrine of the Mean*, trans. James Legge, New York: Dover Publications, 1971 (hereafter *Confucius*), 356–9. I have modified Legge's translation.
5. See, among others, Sui-chi Huang, *Essentials of Neo-Confucianism, Eight Major Philosophers of the Song and Ming Periods*, Westport, CT: Greenwood Press, 1999, 173–81; Fung Yu-lan, *A History of Chinese Philosophy*, trans. Derk Bodde, Princeton: Princeton University Press, 1953, 585–92, 605–10.
6. For a perceptive exposition of these two rival schools of Confucianism, see Benjamin I. Schwartz, *The World of Thought in Ancient China*, Cambridge, M.A.: The Belknap Press of Harvard University Press, 1985, 255–320.
7. To the extent that he recommended that impoverished widows should rather choose to die of starvation than remarry. See Ren Jiyu 任繼愈, *Zhongguo zhexueshi* 中國哲學史 (*A History of Chinese Philosophy*), 3:229, Beijing: Renmin chubanshe, 1979, 229.

8. Laurence G. Thompson (trans. and ed.), *Ta T'ung Shu: The One-World Philosophy of K'ang Yu-wei*, London: Allen & Unwin, 1958, 149–68.

9. See among others, "Shi tan Zhongguo de zhihui 試談中國的智慧" (A Tentative Discussion of China's Wisdom), in Li Zehou, *Zhongguo gudai sixiangshi lun* 中國古代思想史論 (An Interpretative Intellectual History of Ancient China; hereafter *Gudai sixiangshi lun*), Beijing: Renmin chubanshe, 1986, 290–303; "Man shuo 'xi ti zhong yong' 漫說'西體中用'" (Some Random Thoughts on "Western Learning as Foundation But Adapted to Chinese Use"), *Xiandai sixiangshi lun*, 402–7, 425–7.

10. Creative transformation (*chuangzaoxing de zhuanhua* 創造性的轉化) of tradition was coined by Lin Yusheng and subsequently borrowed by Li. Lin Yusheng, *The Crisis of Chinese Consciousness, Radical Antitraditionalism in the May Fourth Era*, Madison, WI: University of Wisconsin Press, 1979, 35, 94, 105.

11. The following summary of Li's philosophy is based on his book *Wode zhexue tigang* (An Outline of My Philosophy; hereafter *Tigang*), Taipei: Fengyun shidai chubanshe, 1990. References to other sources will be specified.

12. The first edition was published by Renmin chubanshe in Beijing in 1979.

13. *Tigang*, 167–88.

14. *Tigang*, 189–208.

15. *Tigang*, 209–21.

16. *Tigang*, 1–41.

17. *Tigang*, 28, 225.

18. Li Zehou, *Gudai sixiangshi lun; Zhongguo jindai sixiangshi lun* 中國近代思想史論 (An Interpretative Intellectual History of Modern China; hereafter *Jindai sixiangshi lun*), Taipei: Fengyun shidai chubanshe, revised edition, 1990; and *Xiandai sixiangshi lun*.

19. "Man shuo 'Xi ti Zhong yong,'" *Xiandai sixiangshi lun*, 397–433.

20. "Zai shuo 'Xi ti Zhong yong' 再說'西體中用'" (Another Discussion of "Western Learning as Foundation But Adapted to Chinese Use"), *Xin meng*, 178. The meaning of his and Lin's term is essentially the same. As his new coinage is awkward and tautological, I shall continue to use "creative transformation" except when citing Li's own words.

21. "Kongzi zai pingjia 孔子再評價" (A Second Assessment of Confucius), *Gudai sixiangshi lun*, 50–1.

22. *Ibid.*, 15–29, 43–51.

23. *Ibid.*, 48–9.

24. "Song Ming lixue pianlun 宋明理學片論" (A Sketchy Discussion of the School of Principle of the Song and Ming Dynasties), *Gudai sixiangshi lun*, 257.

25. *Tigang*, 142–3.

26. See, among others, "Song Ming lixue pianlun," 236–7; "Shuo ziran renhua 說自然人化" (An Essay on Humanized Nature), *Wu shuo*, 153–5; "Shuo Ru Fa huyong 說儒法互用" (An Essay on Mutual Borrowing between Confucianism and Legalism), *Wu shuo*, 85–6.

27. *Mencius* IIA.6.

28. *Mencius* VIIA.15.

29. *Tigang*, 205; "Zhexue tanxun lu 哲學探尋錄" (Philosophical Inquiries), *Xin meng*, 17.
30. "Yu Wang Desheng de duitan 與王德勝的對談" (A Dialogue with Wang Desheng), *Xin meng*, 285–7.
31. *Ibid.*, 288–90, "Zhexue tanxun lu," *Xin meng*, 26–8.
32. *Huaxia meixue* 華夏美學 (Chinese Aesthetics), Hong Kong: Sanlian shudian, 1988; *Meixue si jiang* 美學四講 (Four Lectures on Aesthetics; hereafter *Si jiang*), Hong Kong: Sanlian shudian, 1989.
33. *Mei de licheng* 美的歷程 (The Journey of Beauty), Beijing: Zhongguo shehui kexue chubanshe, 1989.
34. His influence was spread partly through his friend Liu Zaifu 劉再復 who applied the concept of subjectivity to literary studies. Liu Zaifu, "Lun wenxue de zhutixing 論文學的主體性" (On Subjectivity in Literature), *Wenxue pinglun* (1985.6): 11–26, (1986.1): 3–19.
35. "Shuo ziran renhua," *Wu shuo*, 158.
36. "Zhexue tanxun lu," *Xin meng*, 16–18; *Si jiang*, 24–6; *Tigang*, 157–60, 205, 220.
37. *Tigang*, 152–3.
38. I rely on Werner S. Pluhar's interpretation for my explanation of Kant's categories. Immanuel Kant, *Critique of Judgment*, trans. Werner S. Pluhar, Indianapolis: Hackett Publishing Co., 1987. "Translator's Introduction," liv–lix.
39. Karl Marx, *Economic and Philosophical Manuscripts*, quoted in Maynard Solomon (ed.), *Marxism and Art*, Detroit: Wayne State University Press, 1979, 26.
40. *Si jiang*, 48–57.
41. *Ibid.*, 44.
42. "Shuo ziran renhua," *Wu shuo*, 156–66. My subsequent discussion of this concept is based on this essay.
43. *Confucius*, 147. I have modified Legge's translation.
44. *Si jiang*, 34.
45. The term refers to beauty of the mind (*xinling mei* 心靈美), beauty of language (no coarse language) (*yuyan mei* 语言美), beautiful (good) behavior (*xingwei mei* 行為美) , and beautiful environment (*huanjing mei* 環境美).
46. Tang Yijie, "Zai lun Zhongguo chuantong zhexue de zhen shan mei wenti 再論中國傳統哲學的真善美問題" (Further Discussion on the Problem of Truth, Goodness, and Beauty in Traditional Chinese Philosophy), *Xinhua wenzhai* (1990.7): 17–18. Tang, here, gives a different interpretation of the quotation from the *Analects*.
47. Li's article "Shuo Ruxue si qi" (hereafter, "Si qi") is the most systematic exposition of his theory of the fourth period. *Wu shuo*, 1–31. In refuting the third-period theory, Li Zehou singles out that expounded by Du Weiming (Tu Wei-ming) 杜維明, probably because Du is its most famous exponent. For Du's exposition, see "Ruxue disan qi fazhan de qianjing wenti 儒學第三期發展的前景問題" (The Prospect of Development of the Third Period of Confucianism), in Luo Yijun 羅義俊 (ed.), *Ping xin*

Rujia 評新儒家 (Evaluating New Confucianism), Shanghai: Shanghai renmin chubanshe, 1991, 98–133.

48. The most noted examples are Qian Mu 錢穆 and his disciple Yu Yingshi 余英時. See Yu Yingshi, "Qian Mu yu xin Rujia 錢穆與新儒家" (Qian Mu and the New Confucians), in Yu Yingshi, *Qian Mu yu Zhongguo wenhua* 錢穆與中國文化 (Qian Mu and Chinese Culture), Shanghai: Shanghai yuandong chubanshe, 1996, 51–3.

49. "Shuo wu shi chuantong 說巫史传统" (An Essay on the Tradition of Shamanism and Historiography), *Wu shuo*, 32–70. My discussion of this tradition is based on this article, unless otherwise specified.

50. K.C. Chang, *Art, Myth and Ritual: The Path to Political Authority in Ancient China*, Cambridge, M.A.: Harvard University Press, 1983, 37–42. Li's discussion of the tradition of shamanism and historiography has apparently drawn heavily from K.C. Chang's work, particularly from this book.

51. "Chu ni Ruxue shenceng jiegou shuo 初擬儒學深層結構說" (A First Draft of an Essay on the Deep Structure of Confucianism; hereafter "Shenceng jiegou shuo"), *Wu shuo*, 168–88.

52. "Shi tan Zhongguo de zhihui," *Gudai sixiangshi lun*, 306–22.

53. "Si qi," *Wu shuo*, 2–3, 10.

54. Mou Zongsan, *Xianxiang yu wuzishen* 現象與物自身 (Phenomena and Things-in-Themselves), Taipei: Xuesheng shuju, 1975, 121–4. I follow Yu Yingshi in using the Hegelian term "self-diremption" to translate Mou's concept of *ziwo kanxian*. Yu Yingshi, "Qian Mu yu xin Rujia," 77.

55. *Ibid.*, 76–80.

56. My subsequent discussion of Dong Zhongshu is based on "Qin Han sixiang jian yi 秦漢思想簡議" (A Brief Discussion of Qin and Han Thought) and "Xun Yi Yong jiyao 荀易庸記要" (Essentials of Xunzi, Commentaries on the Book of Changes, and the Book of the Mean), *Gudai sixiangshi lun*, 106–76.

57. For example, Huan Tan 桓譚 (ca. 40 B.C.–28 A.D.) and Liu Zongyuan 柳宗元 (773–819).

58. "Shuo Ru Fa huyong," *Wu shuo*, 83.

59. "Si qi," *Wu shuo*, 20–9.

60. Here, Li cites *Analects* 8.9, and *Mencius* I.3. "Si qi," *Wu shuo*, 21.

61. "Shuo Ru Fa huyong," *Wu shuo*, 97–103; "Shenceng jiegou shuo," *Wu shuo*, 125.

62. "Si qi," *Wu shuo*, 27.

63. Mou Zongsan, *Shengming de xuewen* 生命的學問 (Vital Learning), Taipei: Sanmin shuju, 1970.

64. *Tigang*, 6–7, 223–9.

65. "Yu Wang Desheng de duitan," *Xin meng*, 307.

66. Qian Mu, *Zhongguo sixiangshi* 中國思想史 (An Intellectual History of China), 3rd edition, Taipei: Zhonghua wenhua chuban shiye weiyuanhui, 1957, 125.

PART III

CHAPTER 5

WHAT IS CONFUCIAN AND NEW ABOUT THE THOUGHT OF MOU ZONGSAN?

N. Serina Chan

This chapter is a study of Mou Zongsan's 牟宗三 (1909–95) philosophical system. It seeks to accomplish three objectives. The first objective is to present the theoretical framework of Mou's thought system. I will do this with the aim of introducing the subject to a Western readership largely unfamiliar with New Confucian thought. The other two objectives focus on the "New Confucian" label used to identify Mou's thought. I will first establish that Mou's philosophical system is Confucian, despite its liberal appropriation of Buddhist paradigms and Kantian terminology. I will then examine what is new about his system. In order to present a rounded perspective, I will also address some of the criticisms made by scholars regarding the new features of his system. While I will draw largely on the writings of Mou, other references will be used as appropriate.

Mou had a remarkably long and creative career in philosophy that spanned over sixty years. He continued to lecture and publish even when he was suffering from ill health during the last few years of his life. Mou graduated from the philosophy department of the University of Beijing in 1933 at the age of 25. He took up various teaching posts in mainland China before migrating to Taiwan in 1949, prior to the communist takeover of the mainland. His early philosophical and intellectual interests (prior to his migration to Taiwan in 1949) included the *Book of Changes*, the philosophy of English mathematician and philosopher Alfred N. Whitehead (1861–1974), and logic.[1] His study of logic led him to an appreciation of pure reason (theoretical reason). He studied *Principia Mathematica*, a monumental work produced jointly by Whitehead and Bertrand Russell (1872–1970), had doubts about Russell's realism, and came to realize that logic is pure reason displaying itself. This realization was instrumental in his understanding and appreciation of *Critique of Pure Reason*, the first critique by Immanuel Kant (1724–1804).[2] In 1932, Mou met his mentor, Xiong Shili 熊十力 (1885–1968), with whom he maintained close contact during the following ten years. Mou's interest and thinking shifted gradually from abstract conceptualization far removed from practical living to issues concerning the development of Chinese culture. He reckoned quietly and sadly with the tumultuous times in which he lived. In his autobiography, *Wushi zishu* (My Story at Fifty), he attributed this shift to his personal hardships following the Japanese invasion of China in 1937 and to Xiong's influence on him.[3] He held Xiong in great esteem and was inspired by his "primitiveness," a primitiveness in which ancient Chinese wisdom meshed with strong ethnic sentiments and exhibited what Mou called "a unity of the ethnic and cultural life [of the Chinese people]."[4] Xiong published the first version of his masterwork entitled *Xin weishi lun* 新唯識論 (New Consciousness-Only Treatise) in 1932 (classical Chinese version), revising and translating it into vernacular Chinese over the next decade. From 1942 to 1944 he added a third section to the book. The expanded vernacular version was published in 1944 and represents the mature version of Xiong's ontological construction of Confucianism, which is largely in line with the Lu-Wang school of Neo-Confucian thought—the school of thought associated with the Neo-Confucian thinkers Lu Xiangshan 陸象山 (1139–93) and Wang Yangming 王陽明 (1472–1529). Mou lived with Xiong in a college in Chongqing from the end of 1941 to the fall of 1942. He wrote that during this period, Xiong "admonished and encouraged me day and night and enlightened me a great deal."[5] The fact that Mou's philosophical system echoes much of the philosophical thinking as laid out in *Xin weishi lun* (1944), attests to the influence of Xiong in shaping Mou's thought. The purpose of *Xin weishi lun*, as stated by Xiong, is "to enlighten those scholars in pursuit of metaphysical truth so that they will realize that the ontological basis (*benti* 本體) of all things is not something that lies in objects external to one's mind or resides in knowledge of things external to mind, but is something that one realizes within in response [to ones's inner moral effort]."[6] These words also articulate the underlying idealistic theme of Mou's philosophical system. Mou's system, however, differs vastly from Xiong's in terms of methodology and theoretical framework. As I will show later in this chapter, Mou's philosophical system moves beyond Xiong's traditional *ti–yong* 體用 (structure–application) paradigm. It adopts formal Buddhist paradigms, and Mou reconciles it with the moral philosophy of Immanuel Kant. The result is a contemporary Confucian philosophical system: a philosophical system laid out systematically and cast in Buddhist and Western philosophical terms and categories, yet staunchly Confucian (or Neo-Confucian, as some might argue) in spirit. I use "Confucian" here according to Mou's definition to mean the system of thought attributed to Confucius and Mencius and further developed and expounded by Neo-Confucian thinkers.

After leaving mainland China in 1949, Mou devoted his long career to the development and propagation (through published works and decades of lecturing at universities in Hong Kong and Taiwan) of a contemporary Confucian philosophical system that would point the way for the healthy development of Chinese culture. He opposed Marxist materialism vehemently. Additionally, he was highly critical of the strong positivistic influences from the West and its accompanying preoccupation with what is external and verifiable.[7] He maintained that Chinese culture has to be reconstructed scientifically and democratically, but that such reconstruction has to be founded on Confucian moral values for it to be spiritually rooted and enduring.[8] Along this line, he believed that an important mission of Chinese intellectuals in modern times is to elucidate clearly mainstream Chinese and Western thought systems and to reconcile and harmonize the two. In his last written note to his students, composed while hospitalized in December 1994, four months before his death, he urged them to work hard at this task.[9] His own knowledge and understanding of Western philosophy enabled him to identify the main themes of Kant's moral philosophy as having the potential of being extended to merge with his own metaphysical and moral thought system.[10] Kant is one of the most influential thinkers of post-classical times. His three critiques were among many Western works introduced into China around the turn of the twentieth century. Mou maintained that Kant was the first Western philosopher to have a grasp and understanding of the true nature of morality.[11] He translated Kant's major works into Chinese and worked hard at extending Kant's moral philosophy and reconciling it with his own. The fruit of this labor was the enhancement of the contemporary, philosophical status of his own thought system and the establishment of a potential bridge between Chinese and Western philosophy.

As mentioned earlier, Mou studied logic and Kant's *Critique of Pure Reason* before devoting himself to the development of a contemporary Confucian philosophical system. He built his system systematically and progressively, based on critical studies of the three main traditions of Chinese thought—Confucianism, Daoism, and Buddhism—and of Kant's moral philosophy. While there were no sharp turns in his philosophical thinking, Mou did not think that he had reached a mature phase, philosophically, until after the age of fifty.[12] His major works, all written during this mature phase, include: (1) *Daode de lixiangzhuyi* 道德的理想主義 (Moral Idealism; 1959; revised and new preface, 1978), which presents his vision of a Confucian modernity for China; (2) *Caixing yu xuanli* 才性與玄理 (Material Human Nature and the "Profound Principles" [of the Wei-Jin Period]; 1963), a critical study of the "profound learning" (*xuanxue*) of the Wei-Jin period (220–420) in China; (3) his three-volume magnum opus, *Xinti yu xingti* 心體與 性體 (Ontological Mind and Ontological Human Nature; vols. 1 and 2, 1968; vol. 3, 1969), which combines with *Cong Lu Xiangshan dao Liu Jishan* 從陸象山到劉蕺山 (From Lu Xiangshan to Liu Jishan; 1979) to form a four-volume critical study of Song-Ming Neo-Confucianism; (4) *Foxing yu bore* 佛性與般若 (Buddha Nature and Prajñā; 1977), a critical study of Buddhist thought in China, focusing on the paradigm of *yuan jiao* 圓教 (perfect teaching); (5) *Yuan shan lun* 圓善論 (A Treatise on the Highest Good; 1985), a significant work that elucidates Mencius' concept of the innate goodness of human beings (*xing shan* 性善) and brings Mou's thought system to completion with the concept of *yuan shan* 圓善 (due correspondence between virtue and happiness); and (6) translations of Kant's major works—*Groundwork of the Metaphysics of Morals* and *Critique of Practical Reason* (both translated in 1982); *Critique of Pure Reason* (translated in 1983); and *Critique of Judgment* (translated in 1992 and 1993).

Mou's philosophical system has exerted a great influence academically in Taiwan, Hong Kong, and, over the last decade, mainland China. University students and researchers in all three places have studied it intensively and evaluated it critically. Scholars and educators in mainland China have adopted an increasingly receptive attitude toward Confucian thought and Western thought (including the moral philosophy of Kant) since the country opened its door to the rest of the world in the late 1970s. In late 1986, the mainland Chinese government formally recognized New Confucian thought as a high-priority category in the social sciences.[13] In 1990, the Ministry of Education recognized as a top-priority item "experimentation and research into the teaching of traditional Chinese virtues."[14] Moral education and Confucian values have since become a regular discussion and research topic in the ministry's monthly research publication entitled *Jiaoyu yanjiu* 教育研究 (Educational Research). It is noteworthy that despite Mou's vehement opposition to Marxism, a recent article in this journal quoted his comments on the inner subjective nature of Confucian morality—that morality is not something imposed from the outside, but is a consciousness that issues from within a person.[15]

The Theoretical Framework of the Thought of Mou Zongsan

Being a moral idealist, in the original preface to his *Caixing yu xuanli* (1963), Mou states that "cultural development is but the purification and deepening of life and the expression of reason."[16] By "reason" he means moral reason in Confucian terms or practical reason in Kantian terms. In *Daode de lixiangzhuyi* (1959), he states that culture is "the expression of the spirit of sages and other great characters from antiquity to the present time."[17] Mou's view of culture is both "universalist" and "particularist." He believes that there are universal truths and values that can be appreciated by the entire humanity, but that no one culture expresses all of these truths and values. Rather, each culture tends to express in its particular way some of these truths and values, and cultures enrich one another by offering different paths to the realization of universal truths and values. In this regard, he is of the view that Chinese culture has tended to focus on life as a whole and emphasize moral values that nurture and settle life, while Western culture (along the Greek tradition) has tended to focus on nature and emphasize theoretical reason and knowledge about the external world.[18] The modern age, in Mou's eyes, is marked by an excessive dominance of Western values. On the one hand, he is highly positive about Western values as expressed in the building of modern national states, the development of science, and the realization of democracy. He firmly upholds these as values that should be adopted by China. On the other hand, he is adamant that these values have been unchecked and pushed to the extreme, resulting in excesses, imbalances, and calamities to humanity. He disapproves of Western imperialism and vehemently condemns Marxism. Moreover, he laments that modern people have become spiritually ill in that they are oblivious to their inner source of truth, value, and moral creativity and are concerned mainly with what feels good and what is technically right and socially conforming rather than with what is rational and moral. He attributes the perceived spiritual ills to the displacement of morality by science; the preoccupation with what is external and quantifiable, and the tendency toward scientism—the use of science as the only measure of truth and value.[19]

In *Zhongguo zhexue shijiu jiang* (1978)—his summary discussion of Chinese thought—Mou argues that scientific truth is but one of two types of truth and warns of the danger of scientism.[20] The other type of truth as conceived by him is of a higher order, deals with life as a whole, and is where human beings can find abiding happiness and peace of mind.[21] His main preoccupation was with the development of this other type of truth as contained in Confucian thought and the structuring of this body of truth into a contemporary moral and metaphysical philosophical system. Toward this end he conducted extensive research into the three main traditions of Chinese thought and examined the historical cross-influences among them in order to arrive at a comprehensive understanding of China's philosophical past. He maintained that such comprehensive understanding is essential for any new development of Chinese thought.[22] Decades of intensive study and committed research led him to identify two important metaphysical paradigms in Chinese thought, which he used to erect his own philosophical system. The first one is the paradigm of *yi xin kai er men* 一心開二門, which I will render as the "two-tier mind" paradigm. The second one is the paradigm of *yuan jiao* 圓教, which Mou would render as the "perfect teaching" paradigm.[23]

Mou asserts that although Buddhist in its most developed theoretical expression, the "two-tier mind" paradigm is also implicit in Confucian and Daoist teachings and therefore should be expounded as a common philosophical paradigm in Chinese thought.[24] For Mou, Mencius' teaching represents a development of Confucius' teaching, and the teaching of the Lu-Wang school of Neo-Confucian thought represents a correct interpretation and elucidation of Mencian thought. In this regard, he notes that the Cheng-Zhu school of Neo-Confucian thought—the school propounded by Zhu Xi (1130–1200) and Cheng Yi (1033–1107)—does not subscribe to the "two-tier mind" paradigm and that its understanding of the innate goodness of human beings and their innate moral nature departs fundamentally from Mencian thought.[25] He further argues that because of this basic departure, the Cheng-Zhu school deviates from orthodox Confucian thought and has been wrongly enshrined as orthodox Neo-Confucianism.[26]

Specifically, the "two-tier mind" paradigm refers to the Mahāyāna Buddhist understanding of the human mind as consisting of the true mind and the discriminating mind. According to this understanding, the discriminating mind is the ordinary thinking mind that interprets sense perceptions and operates cognitively at the phenomenal level. It is the mind that sees the world in dualities—up and down, right and wrong, desirable and undesirable, and so on—and chooses a course of action based on sense perceptions. On the other hand, the true mind is the mind that perceives the "emptiness" of the phenomenal world. It sees the phenomenal world as the world of experiences, governed by natural causality and investigated by the sciences. "Emptiness" means that everything in the phenomenal world arises as a result of causes and conditions and has no real independence and permanence, hence no real "self," to speak of.[27] For example, a tree comes about as a result of a seed (the cause) receiving water, sunlight, and nutrients from the soil (conditions). A tree is "empty" in that it is nothing but the aggregate of the seed and conditions that bring about the seed's growth.

Neo-Confucians of the Lu-Wang school share a similar understanding of the human mind. While their conception of the discriminating mind agrees with that of the Mahāyāna Buddhists, they approach the true mind from a moral perspective and in accordance with Mencius' conception of xin 心 or more specifically, ben xin 本心, which refers to human beings' innate moral mind endowed with the four incipient virtues of empathetic compassion, rightness, propriety, and wisdom (Mencius 2A.6; 6A.10).[28] Mencius describes the four incipient virtues or moral beginnings as ren xing 人性, human beings' innate goodness or innate moral capability from which moral behavior issues (Mencius 2A.6; 4B.19; 6A.2; 7A.15). For Mencius, a person's innate goodness (xing) and his innate moral mind (xin) are one and the same and they represent an active, innate propensity for moral behavior.[29] He also thinks of this innate moral propensity as that which sets human beings apart from other animals (Mencius 4B.19; 6A.3, 8; 7B.16). Wang Yangming terms it liang zhi 良知 (moral consciousness). Because Mencius' conception of the innate goodness of human beings and their innate moral mind is not easy to grasp, Mou devotes a major part of his Yuan shan lun (1985) to its elucidation.[30] Xiong's Xin weishi lun (1944) subscribes to the "two-tier mind" paradigm with its own set of terminology.[31]

Both Mahāyāna Buddhists and Neo-Confucians of the Lu-Wang school understand the true mind and the discriminating mind as different but united. The two minds are different levels of the same mind: when it does not discriminate, it is the true mind; when it discriminates, it is the discriminating mind.[32] Mou elucidates this with the Buddhist metaphor of the sea and the wave. The larger body of seawater and the wave are different but not separate: they are homogeneous and united, with the wave issuing from the larger body of seawater and capable of returning to it. Likewise, the true mind and the discriminating mind are homogeneous and united, with the latter issuing from the former and capable of returning to the former.[33] This also means that the discriminating mind depends on the true mind for its existence, that it has its origin in the true mind.[34]

In line with Neo-Confucian thinking, both Xiong and Mou define the true mind ontologically—that it is the *tian dao* 天道 (heaven or the way of heaven) immanent in human beings. Mou uses the concept of *ti* 體 to stand for the ultimate ontological reality. He recasts heaven (*tian*), the Mencian innate goodness (*ren xing* or *xing*), and the Mencian innate moral mind (*xin* or *ben xin*) ontologically as *tian ti* 天體, *xing ti* 性體, and *xin ti* 心體, respectively. For him, these three terms represent the same ultimate ontological reality seen from different perspectives. It is *tian ti* when seen as the absolute transcendent creative principle of the universe on which the existence of everything depends. It is *xing ti* when seen as this creative principle immanent in all human beings. Lastly, it is *xin ti* when seen as the subjective innate moral mind of an individual.[35]

Mou thinks that the "two-tier mind" paradigm is of crucial importance because it provides the transcendental basis for cultivating the divinity present in every human being. Divinity refers to the innate potential of every human being to become a sage (in the context of Confucianism), a Buddha (in the context of Buddhism), or a divine being (in the context of Daoism).[36] The paradigm also brings out what Mou sees as an important theme underlying the three main traditions of Chinese thought—the unity of the transcendent (the objective heaven) and the immanent (the subjective true mind of human beings). This theme represents, in his opinion, the most fundamental difference between Chinese culture and Western culture.[37] He thinks that Confucius hints vaguely at this unity when speaking of knowing heaven at the age of 50, presumably as a result of conscientious practice of *ren* 仁 (empathetic compassion). This point is debatable. But Confucius does describe heaven in terms of the ongoing change of seasons and the flourishing of the myriad living things (*Analects* 17.19).[38] Mencius suggests a unity of heaven and human beings when he speaks of "all the ten thousand things are there in me" (*Mencius* 7A.4) and of "realizing fully one's mind [moral mind] in order to know one's true nature [moral nature or *xing*]" and "knowing one's true nature in order to know heaven" (*Mencius* 7A.1).[39] The *Doctrine of the Mean* espouses following the way of the mean as well as reaching the ultimate height and brilliance (*Doctrine of the Mean* XXVII).[40]

Because transcendence and immanence are dual, opposing concepts, analytical discussions cannot embrace both at the same time. The discussion of transcendence and immanence in *Thinking Through Confucius*, a work by David L. Hall and Roger T. Ames, epitomizes this limitation of analytical, dualistic thinking. The authors find Mou's use of the term "transcendence" problematic because according to them, what is immanent cannot be transcendent at the same time.[41] Xiong's *Xin weishi lun* (1944) proposes that the transcendent is immanent in all things within the universe. He uses the Buddhist metaphor of the sea and the foam to illustrate this unity. (As mentioned above, Mou uses a similar metaphor of the sea and the wave to illustrate the unity of the true mind and the discriminating mind.) The larger body of seawater is *ti* 體 (basic ontological substance), while the foam is *yong* 用 (manifestation or function). The foam and the larger body of seawater are one homogeneous whole made up of the same water. The foam issues from the larger body of seawater and is united and homogeneous with it. Thus, we can not only say that the seawater is transcendent to the foam (the existence of the foam depends on it) but also that it is immanent in the foam (the seawater is what constitutes the foam). Because the foam and the larger body of seawater are united and homogeneous, the transcendent and the immanent are united and homogeneous.[42] In discussing the "perfect teaching" paradigm later in this chapter, I will cover the non-analytic teaching method of "dialectic," which aims to nullify the opposition between dualistic concepts.

In Western philosophy, there is no theoretical model akin to the "two-tier mind" paradigm. In the introduction I mentioned that Mou maintains that among Western philosophers, Kant was the first to have a grasp and understanding of the true nature of morality. Mou also thinks that the "two-tier mind" paradigm is crucial to understanding the differences between Confucianism and Kant's moral philosophy.[43] What is morality? In line with Mencius and the Song-Ming Neo-Confucians, Mou defines morality in terms of the innate moral consciousness of human beings and their capacity to act humanely toward one another. The cardinal Confucian concept of *ren* (empathetic compassion) is what distinguishes human beings from other animals (*Mencius* 4B.19; 6A.3; 7B.16). The stress is not on external dogmas, but on one's ability to become aware of one's behavior and to reflect upon what one should do, as opposed to what one is inclined to do. Confucius points out that *ren* (empathetic compassion) is manifested in "feeling uneasy" about one's morally inadequate behavior (*Analects* 17.21).[44] Mou thinks that morality not only uplifts human beings spiritually, but also prescribes a regular guide for the normal functioning of society.[45] He emphasizes that morality is where human beings express higher values and determine right from wrong:[46] "When the moral mind is present within one, moral principles prevail and one attains to a higher order of value determined not just in terms of gratification or personal advantage."[47] Thus understood, morality is inner-directed and is present only when human beings assume their subjectivity. Mou points out that when human beings are reduced to objects for scientific study, they lose their subjectivity and their morality. This is because scientific study can uncover only material and objective sources of motivation but not the inner moral consciousness.[48]

Kant understands morality in terms of practical reason[49] or reason in its practical use.[50] He states that "[e]verything in nature works in accordance with laws" and that "[o]nly a rational being has the capacity to act *in accordance with the representation* of laws, that is, in accordance with principles, or has a will."[51] For him, the practical reason and the will of perfectly rational beings coincide, and their actions are invariably good (moral).[52] He concedes, however, that human beings are rational beings that are not perfectly rational and that, for them, therefore, the objective laws of reason (laws that are valid for all rational beings, regardless of subjective conditions) are moral laws—commands or imperatives of reason that express what they ought to do.[53] He also maintains that moral laws of rational beings are categorical imperatives—actions prescribed by reason unconditionally as ends in themselves because they are good in themselves and absolutely necessary for all rational beings.[54] This unconditional nature of moral imperatives means that the moral content of an action contains no conditions to which it would be limited and therefore cannot be established from any contingent or empirical grounds.[55] ("Only experience can furnish [contingent grounds]" according to Kant.[56]) Kant is making two very important points here. The first point is that moral conduct is without material or empirical motive and subject to no contingent grounds. It is good in itself and is carried out from duty—"the necessity of an action from respect for [moral] law"[57]—alone, and never from inclination, self-interest or incentives of the will (be it happiness, perfection, self-realization, or any other self-seeking purpose), or interest for others.[58] The second point is that moral worth is independent of effect (what the moral conduct effects or accomplishes).[59] These are very crucial points, for they rule out the determination of morality in terms of the matter or content of an action: "[W]hen moral worth is at issue, what counts is not the actions, which one sees, but those inner principles of actions that one does not see."[60]

This leads to Kant's thesis that the form and principle of moral action—namely, the action's universality or suitability for functioning as a universal law—alone determines the moral worth of the action.[61] To illustrate, if I help an old lady carry a heavy load across the road, the action in itself has no moral significance. Moral significance lies in the presence of a good will arising out of my recognition that it is how everyone in the same situation should act, whether one is inclined to do so or not. Morality is not relevant if I help the lady for an empirical reason rather than out of sheer good will—as is the case where I help the lady in order to conform with the expectation of her or others, to win the appreciation or praise of others, to comply with a code of behavior conditioned within me, or to feel good about myself. Kant's stress on the universal and imperative nature of morality resonates with the teachings of Confucius and Mencius. The Confucian golden rule commands one not to do to others what one would not want others to do to one (*Analects* 12.2). Mencius asserts the innate goodness of human beings in terms of their moral consciousness. He places the value of righteousness above one's life (*Mencius* 6A.10). In his view, a ruler's love of goods and of women will not impede the implementation of benevolent rule if the ruler shares the goods with his people and sees to it that all of his people have spouses (*Mencius* 1B.5).

Although Mou affirms Kant's understanding of morality, he draws a sharp contrast between Kant's understanding of the human mind and the "two-tier mind" paradigm fundamental to his own thought system. Kant insists upon the separation between God (the transcendent) and human beings. He maintains that only God possesses intellectual (transcendental, non-sensible) intuition and has knowledge of the noumenal world (the world of things in themselves as they really are, not as they appear to us phenomenally). According to him, human beings possess sensible and not intellectual intuition and can have knowledge of the phenomenal and not the noumenal world. Mou, on the other hand, expounds the unity of the transcendent and the immanent using the "two-tier mind" paradigm. In his book entitled *Zhi de zhijue yu Zhongguo zhexue* 智的直覺與中國哲學 (Intellectual Intuition and Chinese Philosophy; 1971), he argues on the basis of the "two-tier mind" paradigm that human beings can have intellectual intuition by virtue of the *xinti* (ontological moral mind, the true mind) innate in them. Thus, for Mou, human beings possess both intellectual and sensible intuition and can have knowledge of both the phenomenal and the noumenal worlds. A person's *xinti* or true mind is united with all things in one homogeneous noumenon that has no distinction between self and non-self. As conceived by Mou, *xinti* has two important functions. One is to manifest itself as moral consciousness that guides the individual's choice of action. The other is to derive from itself the discriminating mind that enables experience and knowledge, through a process Mou terms "self-negation of moral consciousness"—that is, moral consciousness negates its inherent non-discriminating state in order to allow the discriminating mind to arise and to effect action.

Kant advances three postulates from human beings' upholding of moral laws: (1) the existence of freedom—namely, freedom from natural causality, which is a precondition for the existence of free will, a will independent of empirical conditions;[62] (2) the immortality of the soul; and (3) the existence of God.[63] Morality (what one ought to do) presupposes free choice of action or free will. Free will, according to Kant, belongs to the noumenal self—the self as it is, independent of empirical conditions and in contrast to the phenomenal self, which is the self governed by natural causality and known and experienced by human beings.[64] Kant understands human beings to be imperfectly rational. Perfectly rational beings always act according to their reason; human beings do so only some of the time and follow their inclinations or other empirically based motives at other times. He postulates the immortality of the soul to allow for the "endless progress" of the human will toward "holiness," where the will conforms completely with reason.[65] In addition, he postulates the existence of God to bring about due correspondence between virtue and happiness, which, in his opinion, is something human beings rationally aspire to but cannot realize on their own.[66] Mou thinks of Kant's concepts of intellectual intuition, free will, the immortal soul, and God, as all belonging to the order of the absolute. Such is also the case with the Buddhist concept of *prajñāpāramitā* (*boreboluomiduo* 般若波羅密多) or "perfect wisdom," the Confucian concept of *tiandao* (the way of heaven), and his own concepts of *xinti* and *xingti* (the way of heaven immanent in human beings). He argues that because there can only be one absolute, all of these concepts in effect represent one and the same thing—the absolute ontological reality.[67] Thus, Mou merges Kant's concepts of intellectual intuition, free will, immortal soul, and God into his own concepts of *xinti* and *xingti*. Furthermore, he extends Kant's moral philosophy by bringing about the due correspondence between virtue and happiness not through God, but through the "perfect teaching" paradigm displayed in Neo-Confucian thought.

The "perfect teaching" paradigm is entirely absent in Western philosophy. Mou maintains that although its formal formulation was

Buddhist, its incipient conception took place during the Wei-Jin period as a result of Daoist attempts to reconcile Daoist and Confucian teachings with the concept of *wu xin wei dao* 無心為道 (practicing the way without conscious intent). He shows that notions similar to *wu* or *wu xin wei dao* can be found in the Confucian classics, and proposes that Daoist thought surrounding the key concept of *wu* be regarded as a common philosophical paradigm because it also underlies Confucian thought and Mahāyāna Buddhist thought.[68] Similarly, he proposes that the "perfect teaching" paradigm also be regarded as a common paradigm because it informs both Daoist and Neo-Confucian thought.

Adopting the criteria put forth by the Mahāyāna Buddhist sect of Tiantai, Mou points out that whether a teaching is a "perfect teaching" hinges not upon its content but upon its method of teaching. A "perfect teaching" as defined by Tiantai not only employs the non-analytic method of teaching, it also reveals the ultimate and absolute truth non-analytically. (The reasoning is that a teaching is not "perfect" if it fails to reveal the ultimate and absolute truth.) Non-analytic methods of teaching do not seek to establish a particular doctrine, but to show how teachings established analytically fail to reveal the ultimate and absolute truth. Because a "perfect teaching" employs the non-analytic method of teaching, it rises above the incompleteness and the contestability inherent in any teaching or thought system using the analytic method. This is because all concepts being dual in nature, a system which uses the analytic method—however self-sufficient, logical, and complete in itself—is able to validate only one of two sides of a conceptualized formulation and inevitably leaves out the contending side.[69] A "perfect teaching" is not an alternative system. An alternative system leaves out its opposite and cannot be said to reveal the complete, ultimate, and absolute truth; what can be contested is not the absolute.

Mou uses the term "dialectic" to describe the non-analytic method employed in "perfect teachings." Here, he refers not to the dialectical synthesis of two discrete opposites as employed by Georg Hegel (1770–1831), but to the nullification of opposition as employed in the Buddhist exposition of *prajñāpāramitā*.[70] *Prajñāpāramitā* is a Sanskrit Buddhist term, which I will render as "perfect wisdom." "Perfect wisdom" denotes the insight of the true mind. It refers to the capability of the true mind to intuit the "empty" reality of the phenomenal world: that everything arises as a result of a cause and enabling conditions and has no real independence and permanence, hence no real "self," to speak of. Because one can understand the phenomenal world only conceptually with one's discriminating mind, one sees this world in dualities. "Perfect wisdom" enables one to be mindful of the "emptiness" of the phenomenal world and not to fixate on its inherent duality. In other words, "perfect wisdom" is the letting go of dualities. While one can point to the meaning of "perfect wisdom" using concepts, its true meaning cannot be captured conceptually. One has to intuit and realize the true meaning oneself. Thus, the *Diamond Sūtra* says, "The Buddha teaches *prajñāpāramitā*. This means it is not *prajñāpāramitā*. Rather, it is called *prajñāpāramitā*." To reveal what "perfect wisdom" is, major Buddhist *sūtras*, such as the *Diamond Sūtra* and the *Heart Sūtra*, resort to dialectic using paradoxes, parables, and negation. Mou does not mention metaphors, but I think that they, too, can be used non-analytically. A prime example is the seawater and wave/foam metaphor that Mou and Xiong use to illustrate the "two-tier mind" paradigm and the unity of the transcendent and the immanent.

Dialectic as understood by Mou is rare in Western thought. The main mode of thinking in the West is critical thinking. Critical thinking is analytical and adversarial. Dialectic is non-analytic and encompassing. Dialectic aims to nullify oppositions and separations inherent in the phenomenal world as we perceive it so that the transcendent principle immanent in all things and uniting all things is revealed. In Buddhism, this transcendent principle is the "emptiness" that is inherent in all things. In Confucianism, it is the *tian dao* (way of heaven) that encompasses everything and is homogeneous with everything.

As conceived by Mou, the complete, ultimate, and absolute truth is all encompassing, ever present, and infinite. It is the ontological basis of all things and is on par with the Western concept of "first cause" or the almighty God or the Islamic concept of Allah. Yet, Mou explains that because Western or Islamic teachings of the "first cause" or God/Allah employ the analytic method, they become contestable alternative systems—in the form of Catholicism, Protestantism, and Islam—and are therefore not "perfect teachings." According to Mou, only two teachings satisfy the Tiantai criteria for being "perfect teachings." One is the Tiantai exposition of "*yuan fo* 圓佛" (the "perfect pan-Buddha"). The other is the exposition of the true mind (the way of heaven or *tian dao* immanent in human beings) by the Neo-Confucian thinkers Cheng Hao 程顥 (1032–85) and Hu Hong 胡宏 (1100–55), the latter a contemporary of Zhu Xi.

The Tiantai exposition of "perfect pan-Buddhahood" lies in the concept of *yi nian san qian* 一念三千, one thought encompassing everything within the universe and reaching the infinite. What it means is that when one realizes that Buddhahood is a state inseparable from and by virtue of all that exists within the universe, one's thoughts encompass all within the universe and one reaches the state of "perfect pan-Buddhahood." In this state of mind, due correspondence between virtue and happiness is realized dialectically because everything, be it Buddhahood or hell, happiness or suffering, is seen as homogeneous.[71]

Many Neo-Confucian thinkers have elaborated on Confucian moral dynamics analytically. Mou highly commended the elaboration by Wang Yangming (1472–1529) because it seeks to turn around Zhu Xi's thinking to conform with Mencius' exposition of *ben xin* (moral mind, moral consciousness). Wang's teaching, as summarized by Mou, posits the way of heaven as the transcendental creative principle that brings about living things in a myriad of forms. This creative principle is also immanent in human beings as their ontological basis (termed *xingti* by Mou) and manifested as human beings' moral consciousness or their innate capability to tell right from wrong (Mencius' *benxin*, also termed *xinti* by Mou). When an action is motivated by selfish or excessive desires, it is wrong. When an action is in line with the benevolent, life-nurturing principle of heaven, it is a form of moral creativity identical to heaven's creativity. Moral effort involves reflecting upon one's inner motives by resorting to one's moral consciousness and correcting wrong desires and actions to conform with the benevolent principle of the way of heaven. Wang Yangming's teaching is not "perfect teaching," however, because it is analytical and thus contestable (by Zhu Xi, for example). Mou thinks that in Confucian teachings, only the teachings of Cheng Hao and Hu Hong meet the Tiantai criteria for "perfect teaching." The other Confucian teachings might point to, but have not truly arrived at, the complete, absolute, and ultimate truth. He cites the following sayings by Cheng and Hu. Cheng Hao says, "The unchanging principle of heaven-and-earth lies in their reaching everything without conscious intent; the unchanging principle of the sage lies in his going along with every event without conscious emotions." Hu Hong says, "The way of heaven and human desires are homogeneous yet differing in their uses, moving together yet differing in their emotions." Both describe heaven as all-encompassing yet homogeneous and thus united with everything encompassed. Mou cautions that the "perfect" exposition of the true mind by Cheng and Hu serves only to reveal the ultimate goal of moral cultivation. This ultimate goal lies beyond the other Confucian teachings, which are analytical. Yet, one must have a firm grasp of these other teachings before one is able to go beyond them. As in the case with the state of "perfect pan-Buddhahood," the homogeneity or sameness between heaven and all things in effect equates virtue and happiness dialectically and enables their due correspondence.

The opposition between oneself and others is nullified dialectically. The true mind functions as one's moral consciousness and directs one's wishes and actions without any conscious discrimination between self and others. The action issuing from this moral consciousness is not only a moral and virtuous action untainted by selfish motives but is also an action in total accord with one's wishes—thus an action that brings one deserved happiness.[72]

In summary, Mou's thought system aligns closely with the Lu-Wang school of Neo-Confucian thought and is, in effect, a recasting of this school of thought in clear ontological and contemporary philosophical terms using Buddhist paradigms and Buddhist and Kantian terminologies. In recasting the school of thought, he also elucidates, amplifies, and extends it. The major elucidation centers upon Mencius' concept of innate goodness (*xing shan*). The major extension centers upon the concept of due correspondence between virtue and happiness (*yuan shan*). Mou describes the Neo-Confucian thought he expounds as both a moral metaphysics and a religion. By "moral metaphysics," a term he derived from and equates with the Kantian term "moral theology," he means an ontology that is established morally. The Neo-Confucian thought he expounds addresses ultimate reality, the nature of the human mind, and human beings' potential for moral perfection. His thought system is a moral metaphysics because ultimate reality, which forms the heart of his thought system, is a moral force—an absolute creative force (a first creative principle, the way of heaven, which is immanent in human beings as their *xinti* and *xingti*) that pervades the universe and perpetually renews and nurtures life.[73] Mou understands religions as addressing human beings' ultimate concern of how to reach perfection. For Mou, the Christian concept of God not only denotes the creator of the universe and of everything in it but also represents what Christians aspire to be united with: universal love, the absolute good, and perfection. Similarly, he thinks that the Confucian concept of *ren* (empathetic compassion), fully developed by Mencius to equate with the innate goodness of human beings (*xing*), not only denotes a first creative principle, but also provides the transcendent basis for human beings' perfection of their moral character.[74]

What is Confucian about the Thought of Mou Zongsan?

Logic dictates that the thought of Mou Zongsan must be Confucian for him to be recognized as a major New Confucian thinker. Mou thinks of himself as a Confucian thinker. He subscribes to the Neo-Confucian definition of orthodox Confucian thought as the system of thought or teachings espousing inner sageliness and outer kingliness and represented by the Ten Wings of the *Book of Changes* and the Four Books—the *Analects*, the *Mencius*, the *Doctrine of the Mean*, and the *Great Learning*.[75] This is a very broad definition and automatically renders Neo-Confucian thought and Mou's own thought system as Confucian. As summarized above, Mou's system is essentially a recasting, elucidation, and extension of the Lu-Wang school of Neo-Confucian thought in clear ontological and contemporary philosophical terms using Buddhist paradigms and Buddhist and Kantian terminologies. In elucidating the central Neo-Confucian concepts of *xin* and *xing*, which he renders as *xinti* and *xingti* to highlight their ontological status, Mou widely quotes *Mencius* and the writings of the Lu-Wang school of Neo-Confucian thought.

Mou's thought system is Confucian not just by definition but also in terms of its central theme. Many scholars would agree that the central theme of Confucian moral philosophy is centered upon the Confucian concept of *ren* (empathetic compassion). Confucius sees *ren* as manifested in "feeling uneasy" about one's morally inadequate behavior and equates insensitivity with the lack of *ren* (*Analects* 17.21).[76] Mencius describes human beings' innate nature (*xing*) in terms of goodness (*shan*) and *ren* (*Mencius* 6A.2, 3, 6, 8) and defines *ren* as that which renders human beings human and enables the *dao* (*Mencius* 4B.19; 7B.16). Both Confucius and Mencius link *ren* with the metaphysical concept of *tian* (heaven). Consistent with the Lu-Wang school of Neo-Confucian thought, Mou conceives of *ren* ontologically as *renti* and equates it with *xinti* and *xingti*, the two central concepts of his own thought system.[77] The fact that Mou upholds the central Confucian moral concept of *ren* as developed by Mencius and expounded by the Lu-Wang school of Neo-Confucian thought marks his system as Confucian.

But what about Mou's appropriation of Buddhist paradigms and Buddhist and Kantian terminologies? This renders his system syncretic and might raise questions concerning the Confucian purity of his thought. Mou makes it clear, however, that despite its syncretic nature, his thought system is purely Confucian in terms of content. He gives a high assessment of Buddhism as a philosophical system: "[Among philosophical systems], Buddhism is the most heuristic. It opens up the most new ground."[78] He maintains that understanding the major Buddhist paradigms and exploring the philosophical issues arising out of them will help further develop both Chinese and Western philosophy.[79] He also draws a clear distinction between Confucianism and Buddhism in terms of the content of thought. In the concluding pages of *Yuan shan lun* (1985), he describes Confucianism, as recast, elucidated, and extended by

him, as the great, central, and orthodox "perfect teaching" that addresses
ontological creativity squarely and positively and provides a transcendental basis for moral cultivation. In contrast, he describes Buddhism
in its perfect form as but a "perfect teaching" of deliverance (from
transmigration, suffering, and so on) that fails to address morality and
ontology in the true and proper sense.

The two traditions indeed differ fundamentally in terms of their orientation to worldly living. This fundamental difference is reflected in
their vastly different interpretation of the true mind. The Buddhists see
the true mind as an enlightened mind that is fundamentally unattached
to, unmoved by, and uninterested in worldly living. The *Diamond Sūtra*
says, "Regarding how to expound this *sūtra*: One should not dwell in
phenomena; rather, one should stay unmoved in the ultimate truth [of
emptiness]." The Buddhist true mind is not a compassionate mind.
Compassion in the Buddhist context is an expediency that enables a
bodhisattva to lead all beings away from the cycle of life and death and
into *nirvāṇa*. The Confucians see the true mind as a moral mind that
supports and nurtures life in this world. The Buddhist true mind sees
all things and events as mere phenomena brought about by causes and
conditions and is unmoved by what it sees. The Confucian mind, however, as expounded by Mou, sees them as noumena from which phenomena displaying differences are derived and it engages them morally.
Mou affirms this noumenon-cum-phenomenon as reality and describes
his thought system as "consciousness-only realism." Surely it is realism
because it deals with both phenomena and noumena, but what is
considered as noumenal or real remains a function of the mind or consciousness.[80] (Mou draws a distinction between his thought system and
Western idealism and objects to the rendering of "consciousness-only
realism" as "idealism."[81])

With regard to Kant, I mentioned in the introduction that Mou
studied Kant's philosophy even before he delved deeply into Chinese
thought. He was inspired by Kant's critical approach and impressed
with Kant's understanding of inner morality. His thought system
appears Kantian at times because of the appropriation of Kantian terms
and the frequent comparisons and contrasts made with Kant's thought.
Earlier discussion, however, should have made it clear that Mou's system
of thought does not rely on that of Kant to retain its integrity. Mou did
not use Kant's thought to build his system. Rather, he cast Neo-
Confucian thought in Kantian terminology to render it "in contemporary
terms as a moral philosophy that contains the full development of a
'moral metaphysics,' thereby according it a clear and definite place in

contemporary philosophy."[82] In the preface to *Zhi de zhijue yu Zhongguo zhexue* (1971), a work in which he reconciles and extends Kant's moral philosophy to merge with his own system, he states three philosophical aims in writing the book. One of them was to "enable the philosophical construction of Chinese philosophy." The other two are to extend Kant's philosophy objectively and to build a bridge between Chinese and Western philosophy.[83]

What is New about the Thought of Mou Zongsan?

Mou's thought system displays many new and bold features. I will discuss four main ones here. First, it is syncretic, as reflected in Mou's appropriation of Buddhist paradigms and Buddhist and Kantian terminologies. As previously mentioned, Mou thinks that although the two metaphysical paradigms that form the basic framework of his thought system are Buddhist in their most developed theoretical expression, they are also present in Daoist thought and Confucian thought and should be regarded as common paradigms. His research into the development of Chinese thought led him to two conclusions. The first is that the many contending schools of thought during the late Zhou period provided the prototypes for Chinese thought, and that Confucianism was the orthodox school of thought. The second is that Confucianism has exerted a strong influence on both the development of Chinese thought and the absorption of foreign thought systems into China.[84] He points out that the central Daoist concept of *wu* 無 (not-having) can be found in Confucian classics and that the *Book of Changes*, a Confucian classic by definition, was among the three books of "profound learning" (*xuanxue*) studied by scholars during the Wei-Jin period (220–420).[85] According to him, *xuanxue* represented a further development of Daoist thought and facilitated the absorption of Buddhism in China. He thus portrays Confucianism as the main trunk of Chinese thought and presents Daoism and Buddhism as extensions branching out from the main trunk.[86] Seen in this light, the syncretism in Mou's thought system with regard to Buddhism is more the consequence of his understanding of the historical development of Chinese thought than a product of deliberate redesign. In contrast, the syncretism with regard to Kant's moral philosophy is entirely by design and reflects Mou's commitment to reconcile and harmonize mainstream Chinese and Western thought systems.

The second new feature of Mou's system is that it is a highly intellectual construction. As mentioned earlier, Mou aims to present

Neo-Confucian thought to the contemporary reader and to bridge Chinese and Western thought. He achieves his aims not by superficially clothing Neo-Confucian thought in Western philosophical categories, but by contrasting and reconciling it with Kant's moral philosophy. He constructed his thought system systematically and intellectually through comparative studies of Chinese thought and Kant's moral philosophy and using elaborate conceptual arguments. His three-volume magnum opus, *Xinti yu xingti*, together with an additional work entitled *Cong Lu Xiangshan dao Liu Jishan* (1979), is a systematic attempt to examine and elucidate the respective thought systems of the major Song-Ming Neo-Confucian thinkers.

Mou's "intellectualization" of Neo-Confucian thought has been criticized by some scholars for putting the emphasis on intellectual, theoretical understanding rather than on actual moral practice. Di Zhicheng 翟志成, a researcher of Chinese intellectual history, has made some scathing remarks along this line and describes the "so-called New Confucian moral metaphysical systems" as "conceptual games" at "the highest point of the academic ivory tower."[87] Zheng Jiadong 鄭家棟, one of a handful of mainland Chinese scholars who specializes in the study of New Confucianism, asserts that Mou is a defender-cum-betrayer of the Confucian tradition. He explains that Mou is a betrayer of the Confucian tradition because he "unrelentingly led Confucianism down a path that turns it into rational knowledge."[88] Fang Yingxian 方穎嫻, a lecturer in the Chinese department of Hong Kong University, counters criticisms of Mou's intellectual approach on two grounds. First, the contemporary standard of scholarship and the conceptual mentality of modern people call for Mou's intellectual, theoretical approach. Second, to expound a contemporary Confucian philosophical system that would point the way for the healthy development of Chinese culture, Mou needs to change existing prescriptions about the significance of Confucian thought, and to do that effectively, he has to take a conceptual approach.[89] Lin Anwu 林安梧, a Taiwanese scholar and an active contributor to the critique of Mou's New Confucianism, thinks that the intellectual approach of seminal New Confucian thinkers not only provides a needed theoretical and philosophical grounding for, and a contemporary reconstruction of, Neo-Confucian thought but also helps to elucidate China's moral tradition. He credits such intellectual effort, especially Mou's doctrine of "self-negation of moral consciousness," with having reinvigorated and reasserted China's cultural spirit and enabled the Chinese people to overcome the "crisis of meaning" created by iconoclastic attacks on tradition prevalent since the May Fourth Cultural Movement of 1919.[90]

Because of its close engagement with Kantian philosophy, Mou's writings sometimes assume the latter's rather rational and formalistic character. While this contributes to the reconciliation between Confucian and Kantian thought, it does render Mou's thought less supple and less of a living force than classical Confucian thought. Lin, who thinks of himself as a successor-cum-critic of Mou, rightly champions for a shift of focus from theoretical reconstruction, the hallmark of Mou's moral metaphysics, to interactive participation in the living world. He even coined the term "post–New Confucianism" to promote his stream of New Confucianism based on this new focus in what he calls the "post–Mou Zongsan era."[91] Nonetheless, he concedes that "if we come to an integrated understanding of Mou's thought, we will definitely find that his main emphases are on correspondence in actual living [actual living corresponding to and resonating with the spirit of Confucian teachings] and authentic experience."[92] Indeed, one is able to note from just a casual survey of Mou's writings that he often reminds his readers that the only way to realize Confucian moral truth is through the actual practice of it as a way of life and most importantly in the form of self-watchfulness. Self-watchfulness involves a conscientious effort to reflect inwardly on one's thoughts and behavior and to correct any deviation from moral principles. Mou believes that self-watchfulness ensues from one's innate moral consciousness, and in his view, the utmost importance of this moral practice explains the Confucian emphasis on subjectivity.[93]

In his book, *A Common Humanity: Thinking about Love and Truth and Justice*, the Australian philosopher Raimond Gaita remarks that "the idea that one might be a professional lover of truth is a joke." He adds that it is "not a joke," however, "to say that the love of truth is an obligation fundamental to an intellectual or academic vocation—which is one reason why we (often, though not always) tend to think that the abandonment of such a vocation is either a sign that the person did not have one, no matter how brilliant her accomplishments may have been, or that it is a kind of infidelity."[94] Mou taught philosophy and published his philosophical writings for over fifty years. He had an accomplished career in philosophy, but philosophy for him was a vocation rather than a profession. He was certainly a dedicated lover of truth and his "three-unities" proposal for China's cultural reconstruction, which I will introduce later, reflects his strong belief that Confucian truth as reconstructed by him matters profoundly outside academia. He deeply respected moral philosophers who attempt to embody their philosophy in their way of life,[95] and his writings indicate that he aspired to be among them:

> Some people don't like to talk about morality. . . . The crux of the matter is why one should be afraid of morality. Fear of morality indicates that one has a problem. People nowadays tend to think that morality restrains. They therefore dislike morality and dislike Song-Ming Neo-Confucians, who had a very strong moral consciousness. The truth is that morality is not for restraining people. Morality is for liberating and fulfilling people. If one understand this one needs not be afraid. If one's mind is not broad or liberated, how can one be liberated from one's temperament, habits, and wrongdoing? People often talk about ideals precisely because they want to be liberated from present circumstances. To be liberated one must rely on morality.[96]

The third new feature of Mou's system is that it addresses the two main tasks of China's modernization—scientific development and democratic construction. While many scholars think that one of Mou's major contributions is in the metaphysical development of Confucian thought,[97] much of his writing can be seen as a relentless attempt to provide a systematic and theoretical grounding for his "three-unities" (santong) proposal for China's cultural reconstruction. The proposal firmly supports the May Fourth demand for science and democracy but vigorously counters iconoclastic attacks on Confucianism prevalent since the May Fourth protest.[98] It argues that even though Chinese culture used to lack science and democracy, these can be developed and are in no way incompatible with Chinese culture.[99] Specifically, it prescribes a cultural reconstruction along three different paths.[100] The first and foremost is the continuation of its Confucian moral and religious tradition (daotong). Confucianism was not a living force in communist China and it still is not. Even though the mainland Chinese people no longer reject Confucianism vehemently, they remain a long way from identifying with it culturally. Mou seeks to revive Confucianism as a living cultural force in China. He sees Confucianism as the directing force for China's cultural reconstruction, the foundation for China's modernization, and the basis for normalizing daily life. The second is the establishment and development of a scientific tradition (xuetong) to acquire theoretical and specialized knowledge and technical skills needed to meet the demands of complex, modern society[101] and to modernize the production of goods.[102] Mou fully recognizes that modernization requires that knowledge be developed for the sake of knowledge and that specialized knowledge is derived from the full development of the discriminating mind. He points out that Chinese culture used to subsume *xuetong* under *daotong* and value intuition of the true mind over the logical, conceptual thinking of the discriminating mind. To correct the thinking of Chinese intellectuals who believe that modernization requires wholesale Westernization and the abandonment of Confucian values, Mou goes to great theoretical lengths to show that modernization is entirely compatible with Confucianism using the "two-tier mind" metaphysical paradigm and his doctrine of "self-negation of moral consciousness." This paradigm depicts the human mind in its true state as being non-differentiating and in a kind of meditative state that is without thought. Such a state of mind is selfless, at one with all other beings, and infinitely compassionate because it has no thought and makes no distinction between self and others.[103] According to Mou's doctrine of "self-negation of moral consciousness," this true mind readily negates itself and descends into a cognitive, thinking mode—that is, turns into the discriminating mind—when it deals with facts and engages in the business of ordinary living.[104]

He thus argues that modernization requires a shift of emphasis to, and the full development of, the discriminating mind to grapple with, organize, and apply highly specialized knowledge but not the abandonment of compassion and other Confucian moral values. The third is the establishment of a clear understanding of China's political past with the aim of developing a democratic political tradition (*zhengtong*). Mou thinks that, as in the case with *xuetong*, Chinese culture used to subsume *zhengtong* under *daotong*. The fact that the Confucian ideal of "inner sageliness–outer kingliness"—the idealistic thinking that a ruler's inner moral cultivation and perfection would express itself outwardly in benevolent governance guided by the central Confucian concept of *ren* or empathetic compassion—failed to materialize throughout the long history of imperial China is a widely acknowledged fact among New Confucian thinkers. Mou attributes the failure to the autocratic political structure in China.[105] He frankly admits to the inadequacy of Confucian political thought[106] and points out that Confucians have never considered the autocratic political system that persisted for more than two thousand years in imperial China as the ideal system: "Confucians starting from Confucius himself have not liked the [autocratic] system. Confucius and Mencius lauded Yao and Shun because the two rulers each surrendered the rulership to a man of talent and virtue. They did not keep the rulership within the family. Later on, the Song-Ming Neo-Confucians thought the same; none of them approved of the autocratic system."[107] Mou proposes that a critical reflection of China's past political development be undertaken and a clear understanding of key democratic concepts in the West, such as liberty, rights, and citizens' duties, be developed. In *Shidai yu ganshou* (1983), he argues that, based on historical trends in the West, constitutional democracy represents the last and completing stage of political development. He urges the Chinese people to commit themselves firmly to the development of an objectively and clearly defined legal structure and a political reconstruction in the form of a constitutional democracy as is common in the West—that is, with separation of powers and checks and balances—that would ensure people's rights and orderly transfer of political power.[108]

· Mou sees modernization in the form of democratic and scientific developments as a fulfillment of the internal goals of Confucianism to attain its political ideal and to attend to the people's material well-being. [109] His assertion of the primacy of Confucianism is loud and clear: "Confucianism is the mainstream of Chinese culture. Chinese culture is a direction in life as well as a general way of life based on Confucianism. If the primacy of this culture-generating force [meaning Confucianism] cannot be maintained, then democracy, science and the rest do not really count. Modernity without Chinese culture possesses but a 'colonial' status."[110] Arif Dirlik, a specialist in the history of modern China, would label Mou's sentiments as a cultural nationalism directed against Euro-American cultural hegemony.[111] Such labeling might be correct to a certain extent. Yet, Mou's sentiments reflect his own theory of cultural development—that the philosophical system of a people directs the development of their particular culture.[112] Flowing logically from this theory of cultural development is the reckoning that if Confucianism—which Mou takes to represent Chinese philosophy—were to be displaced, then Chinese culture would be displaced. There is no question that Confucianism as an indigenous teaching in China advocates peace and harmony. It contains many universal truths about humanity and exerted a profound influence on the Chinese way of life till the turn of the twentieth century. Only when we turn from discourses of power to non-political factors will we begin to appreciate the ethos of the New Confucian undertaking to revive Confucianism and the love Mou and other New Confucian thinkers felt toward their Confucian cultural heritage.

Mou's "three-unities" proposal is rigorously logical and coherent when assessed in terms of its internal philosophical premises and paradigms. A major criticism of it is that it is weak in practicality. Lin Anwu, though applauding Mou's metaphysical reconstruction of Neo-Confucian thought, reinforces this perception by asserting that a major weakness of Confucian doctrines of practice hitherto, including those developed by New Confucian thinkers, lies in their emphasis of an inner subjective, contemplative, clannish, charismatic, and authoritarian conception of practice.[113] This criticism is rather confounded with regard to New Confucianism, for he goes on to clarify that New Confucian thinkers did not really make the emphasis. Rather, the historical emphasis has been carried forward karmically.[114] New Confuciansim, he maintains, is fundamentally different from traditional Confucianism: it aims to avoid the authoritarian, moralistic tendencies of the latter but has not attained its aim because of the karmic force of entrenched Confucian practices.[115] I do not see the logic of his attributing a deficiency in actual practice to a deficiency in New Confucian doctrines of practice, unless the attribution is an attempt to justify his "post–New Confucian" movement and to inflate its merit at the expense of New Confucianism. Mou and other New Confucian thinkers separate Confucianism as a humanistic teaching from Confucianism as politicized, institutionalized, and practiced in imperial China. Lin himself criticizes the tendency among contemporary scholars to combine the two in their conception of Confucianism[116] and praises the New Confucian thinkers not only for elucidating China's moral tradition but also for their ability to ponder China's problems from the Chinese cultural perspective.[117] What Lin seems to have in mind in his criticism of New Confucian doctrines of practice is the historical failure of subjective contemplation to translate into effective political and social action. If that is the case, the task is not to confound the failure in historical practice with a failure in theory but to do what he has undertaken to do—to identify the causes for the former, which I think Mou has largely done, and to work towards eradicating them.[118]

Han Qiang 韓強, a mainland Chinese researcher of New Confucian thought, thinks that a major deficiency in Mou's proposal is its failure to provide any workable agenda for facilitating the scientific and democratic construction of mainland China. I hold a different view in this regard. Mainland China is a country with a huge population, a large territory, and a recent history of great political and economic turmoil. It is traveling on uncharted land—developing a capitalistic market system within a communist regime. The country has been preoccupied with reforms on all fronts, but many reforms remain plagued by poor leadership, lack of expertise, mismanagement, and corruption. China's future development is a great undertaking fraught with difficulties and challenges. Progress will come only as a result of strong dedication on the part of

the political leaders and persistence through trial and error. Mou understands philosophy to be that which furnishes the direction or the wisdom
for cultural development. He further explains that this direction or wisdom cannot solve concrete and particular problems. To solve particular
problems, be they political, social, or otherwise, requires specialized
knowledge and expertise (*xuetong*) in the pertinent areas.[119] Mou aims
for his "three-unities" proposal to provide a direction, not a working
plan, for China's cultural reconstruction. As a philosopher living outside of mainland China and with the Chinese Communist Party (CCP)
insisting on its monopoly of political power on the mainland, Mou
could not have possibly come up with a realistic working plan for
China's modernization. Development does not happen in a vacuum. A
blueprint for China's development has to be based on objective, timely
assessments of conditions and key factors—such as existing power dynamics within the CCP, and the living standard and aspiration of the people.
One of Mou's main goals is to correct the thinking among many Chinese
intellectuals—Han Qiang being one of them—that Confucian values
are incompatible with the scientific and democratic construction of
China.[120]

Yu Yingshi 余英時, former Professor of Chinese History at Princeton
University, rejects the "three-unities" proposal outright as a form of
disguised elitism. His understanding is that the New Confucians put
themselves above all others by stipulating that *xuetong* and *zhengtong*
must be developed out of *daotong* and claiming that they themselves are
the only ones capable of continuing the *daotong*. He also charges that
some New Confucians—and he is able to name only Xiong Shili in
particular—display an arrogant madness. Furthermore, he asserts that
New Confucians in general exhibit a moral superiority, which, in his
analysis, is a psychological reaction to scientism.[121] Yu completely over-
looks the emphasis on universality that marks the teachings of Confucius
and Mencius as well as the thought systems of Xiong and Mou—that
moral consciousness is universal among human beings, that every
human being has the potential to realize the *dao* (the Confucian way),
and that moral laws are universal laws. Yu thinks that because New
Confucians assert that very few people have understood or realized the
dao, they are, in effect, claiming to be the only ones capable of continuing the *daotong*.[122] This is an incorrect extrapolation. They might think
that they are among the very few people who have realized the *dao*, but
they certainly believe that everyone is capable of doing so and capable
of continuing the *daotong*. Mencius describes *ren* as "the [moral] mind
of human beings" (*Mencius* 6A.11) and righteousness (*yi*, doing what is

morally right) as the proper path for human conduct (*Mencius* 4A.10).
Mou might have belonged to a moral minority, but he was ill at ease
with such a status. Rather than displaying an elitist moral superiority,
he agitated for change and devoted his life to teaching and propagating
Confucian thought (continuing the *daotong*) and to the building of a
xuetong in the area of Chinese thought. As for Xiong, he did appear
arrogant and mad in some of his later writings.[123] This is unfortunate
but should not be used to discredit the entirety of New Confucian
teachings. A driving teacher might commit the offence of drunk driving, but the behavior should not be used to discredit driving manuals
written by him when he is sober or by other driving teachers. I agree
with Yu that New Confucians react to scientism, but their reaction is
considered and rational rather than psychological. I think that it is a
grave misconception that science and the accompanying material afflu-
ence and economic freedom have rendered morality largely irrelevant
to modern living. Science greatly expands our knowledge, but it cannot
explain what is not empirical and it does not tell us how we should live.
We can use technology to kill and we can use it to save lives. Metaphysics explains what is not empirical. Moral and religious values tell us
how we should live. Metaphysics, morality, and religion are not scientific, but they are important because they guide our choice of action. In
fact, they determine what we should do with science and technology.

The fourth new feature of Mou's thought system is its promulgation
of Confucianism as the teaching that would facilitate the formation of
a global culture or world creed and enable different cultures to coexist
peacefully and with respect for one another. Mou and the other joint
authors spelled this out clearly in the concluding section of "Wei
Zhongguo wenhua jinggao shijie renshi xuanyan 為中國文化敬告世
界人士宣言" (Declaration on Behalf of Chinese Culture Respectfully
Announced to the People of the World; 1958),[124] a document retrospectively construed by many scholars in Taiwan and the mainland as
the "manifesto" for the New Confucian movement.[125] Mou and the
other joint authors were of the view that the Western domination of
the world by force and Westerners' lack of both respect for and sympathetic understanding of Chinese and other non-Western cultures did
not bode well for world peace.[126] The declaration presented their basic
stand regarding Chinese culture and its reconstruction[127] and expressed
their hope that the spiritual resources of Confucianism would contribute to the formation of a spiritual world creed to facilitate world
peace.[128] In *Daode de lixiangzhuyi* (1959), Mou portrays the Confucian
concept of *ren* (empathetic compassion) as the fountainhead of human

values, the springboard for a healthy vision for the future of humanity, and the cure for what he perceives as the spiritual ills of the modern age.[129] This is a bold assertion, given that Confucianism has yet to reestablish a strong foothold in mainland China. Du Weiming 杜維明, the best known of the North American New Confucians, has discussed some of the hurdles that have to be overcome and the steps that have to be taken in order to transform Confucianism into a teaching with global significance. In this regard, he thinks that Confucianism must not remain confined to the Chinese and East Asian cultural settings and that Confucians should strive first of all to engage in dialogues with members of other religions and to formulate a Confucian approach to world problems.[130]

These four points are the main new features of Mou's thought system relative to Neo-Confucianism. One other bold and new feature of Mou's thought system is the argument against the orthodoxy of the Cheng-Zhu school of Neo-Confucian thought. Neo-Confucianism has been traditionally understood in terms of two main contending schools—the Lu-Wang and the Cheng-Zhu schools, with the latter regarded as orthodox. Mou, however, carried out a critical examination of the thought systems of major Neo-Confucian thinkers and asserts that Zhu Xi (1130–1200) was a successor to only one of the four major Northern Song Neo-Confucian thinkers—Cheng Yi (1033–1107). That is to say, the Cheng-Zhu school has been mistakenly thought to represent the thought systems of the other three major Northern Song Neo-Confucian thinkers as well. These three other major Northern Song Neo-Confucian thinkers were Zhou Dunyi (1017–73), Zhang Zai (1020–77), and Cheng Hao (1032–85). Mou proposes a third school of Neo-Confucian thought: one that comprises the thought systems of these three major Northern Song thinkers and those of their two successors—Hu Hong (1100–55) in the Southern Song Dynasty and Liu Zongzhou (1578–1645) in the Ming Dynasty.[131] He suggests that this additional school should be grouped with the Lu-Wang school—a school started later in time by the Southern Song Neo-Confucian thinker Lu Xiangshan (1139–93) from the teachings of Mencius and developed further by the Ming Neo-Confucian thinker Wang Yangming (1472–1529)—to form a combined school. Moreover, he maintains that this combined school (which I will refer to as "the expanded Lu-Wang school") should be regarded as orthodox Neo-Confucianism true to the spirit of pre-Qin Confucianism.[132] Mou devotes the entire third volume (totaling 556 pages) of his three-volume masterwork *Xinti yu xingti* to the elucidation of Zhu's thought system. In his analysis, the much-diminished Cheng-Zhu school (now representing only Cheng Yi and Zhu Xi) cannot be orthodox. It departs from Mencius' understanding of the innate goodness of human beings (*xing*) and their innate moral mind (*ben xin*, an active moral propensity) by conceiving *xing* not in terms of *ben xin* but in terms of *li* 理 or fixed, inactive principles. Moreover, it does not fit into what Mou considers to be one of the most important common paradigms underlying Chinese thought: the "two-tier mind" metaphysical paradigm. This paradigm depicts the human mind as consisting of two different yet united tiers: the true mind (equivalent to Mencius' *ben xin*) and the discriminating mind (which is the same as the ordinary cognitive mind). As expounded by Zhu, *li* (his equivalent of the true mind) is separate from, rather than united with, the discriminating mind.[133]

Concluding Remarks

I have argued that Mou's thought system is Confucian and that it not only recasts Neo-Confucian thought but also offers many new and bold features. The "New Confucian" label of Mou's thought is therefore justified. The metaphysical paradigms of "two-tier mind" and "perfect teaching" adopted by Mou may not agree with those wanting empirical proofs for all truths. It is irrelevant at best to those taking an objective rather than subjective view of morality. Yet, I venture to assert that because Mou's thought system is about morality, it is relevant to modern living as long as morality is relevant to modern living.

New books on New Confucianism and on the thought system of Mou continue to come out of the press in mainland China and Taiwan. To many Chinese scholars in both places, Mou's thought system represents an impressive philosophical and cultural accomplishment: it recasts Confucianism in contemporary philosophical terms and argues for its relevance to the healthy development of Chinese culture.[134] Mou was a philosopher with a strong faith in the moral perfectibility of humanity. His thought system is ultimate in its reach, bold in its affirmation of Confucianism, and global in scope. For his followers, his thought system is in itself a triumphant display of practical reason.[135] At the least, it provides a fertile ground of thought for those interested in a philosophy of life and in the mysteries of the human mind. It appears to me that the future of the New Confucian movement rests with intellectual and cultural developments in mainland China. The mainland Chinese government has formally acknowledged the importance of moral education. Moreover, many mainland Chinese scholars and educators have openly embraced the subjective nature of morality and affirmed the relevance of Confucian beliefs and Confucian values to the modernization efforts of their country.[136] Mou's moral metaphysics has the potential to exert a tremendous influence in mainland China. If this eventuates, the Kantian bridge Mou constructed between his system and Western philosophy will assume a new significance for scholars worldwide.

Notes

1. Yan Binggang 顏炳罡, *Mou Zongsan xueshu sixiang pingzhuan* 牟宗三學術思想評傳 (A Critique of Mou Zongsan's Thought), Beijing: Beijing tushuguan chubanshe, 1998, 12, 307–10, 321.
2. Mou Zongsan, *Wushi zishu* 五十自述 (My Story at Fifty), Taipei: Ehu chubanshe, 1993, 66–75.
3. *Ibid.*, 85–9, 102–3.
4. *Ibid.*, 102.
5. Mou Zongsan, *Daode de lixiangzhuyi* 道德的理想主義 (Moral Idealism), Taipei: Taiwan xuesheng shuju, 2000, preface to the revised edition, 1.
6. Xiong Shili, *Xin weishi lun* (New Consciousness-Only Treatise), Taipei: Mingwen shuju, 2000, vol. 1, preface to the 1942 vernacular version, 1, 8.
7. Mou Zongsan, *Zhongguo zhexue shijiu jiang* 中國哲學十九講 (Nineteen Lectures on Chinese Philosophy), Taipei: Taiwan xuesheng shuju, 1997, 16, 446–7.
8. Mou Zongsan, *Daode de lixiangzhuyi*, 3–4, 11–12.
9. Yan Binggang, *Mou Zongsan xueshu sixiang pingzhuan*, 1.
10. Mou Zongsan, *Zhongguo zhexue shijiu jiang*, 308.
11. Mou Zongsan, *Xinti yu xingti* 心體與性體 (Ontological Mind and Ontological Nature), vol. 1, Taipei: Zhengzhong shuju, 1996, 120. *Zhongguo zhexue de tezhi* 中國哲學的特質 (The Characteristics of Chinese Philosophy), Taipei: Taiwan xuesheng shuju, 1998, 10; *Zhongguo zhexue shijiu jiang*, 46.
12. Mou Zongsan, *Zhongguo zhexue shijiu jiang*, 406–7.
13. Li Zonggui 李宗桂, "Xiandai xin Rujia sichao yanjiu de youlai he Xuanzhou huiyi de zhengming 現代新儒家思潮研究的由來和宣州會議的爭鳴" (The Origins of Research into Contemporary New Confucianism and Discussions at the Xuanzhou Meeting), in Fang Keli 方克立 and Li Jinquan 李錦全 (eds.), *Xiandai xin Ruxue yanjiu lunji* 現代新儒學研究論集 (Collected Essays on New Confucian Studies), vol. 1, Beijing: Zhongguo shehui kexue chubanshe, 1989, 333.
14. See Luan Chuanda 欒傳大, "Zhonghua minzu chuantong meide jiaoyu yanjiu baogao 中華民族傳統美德教育研究報告" (Research Report on the Teaching of Traditional Chinese Moral Values), *Jiaoyu yanjiu* 248(September 2000): 26.
15. Guo Qijia 郭齊家, "Zhongguo chuantong jiaoyu zhexue yu quanqiu lunli 中國傳統教育哲學與全球倫理" (Traditional Chinese Philosophy of Education and Global Ethics), *Jiaoyu yanjiu* 250(November 2000): 4.

16. Mou Zongsan, *Caixing yu xuanli*, Taipei: Taiwan xuesheng shuju, 1997, original preface, 1.
17. Mou Zongsan, *Daode de lixiangzhuyi*, 246.
18. *Ibid.*, 249–50; Mou Zongsan, *Zhongguo zhexue shijiu jiang*, 10, 39–43.
19. Mou Zongsan, *Daode de lixiangzhuyi*, preface, 3–5; *Zhongguo zhexue shijiu jiang*, 16, 29.
20. Mou Zongsan, *Zhongguo zhexue shijiu jiang*, 16, 20–7, 279.
21. *Ibid.*, 7–8, 15.
22. *Ibid.*, 225.
23. *Ibid.*, 319, 322–4.
24. *Ibid.*, 246, 289–91, 298, 306–8, 326.
25. *Ibid.*, 226, 303–5, 399–401; Mou Zongsan, *Yuan shan lun*, Taipei: Taiwan xuesheng shuju, 1996, 19, 36; *Xinti yu xingti*, 1:25–6.
26. Mou Zongsan, *Xinti yu xingti*, 1:17–19, 42–8.
27. Mou Zongsan, *Zhongguo zhexue shijiu jiang*, 254–5, 290–4.
28. Mou Zongsan, *Yuan shan lun*, 19, 308–13.
29. *Ibid.*, 23.
30. *Ibid.*, 1–58.
31. Xiong Shili, *Xin weishi lun*, 2:434–5.
32. Mou Zongsan, *Zhongguo zhexue shijiu jiang*, 291–6, 303–8.
33. *Ibid.*, 296.
34. *Ibid.*, 291.
35. Mou Zongsan, *Xinti yu xingti*, 1:29–33, 40–2, 44. Xiong Shili, *Xin weishi lun*, 2:437, 633–4.
36. Mou Zongsan, *Zhongguo zhexue shijiu jiang*, 246, 284–5, 289.
37. *Ibid.*, 78.
38. Mou Zongsan, *Xinti yu xingti*, 1:220.
39. *Ibid.*, 1:26–7.
40. Mou Zongsan, *Zhongguo zhexue shijiu jiang*, 78.
41. David L. Hall and Roger T. Ames, *Thinking Through Confucius*, Albany: SUNY Press, 1987, 204–5.
42. Xiong Shili, *Xin weishi lun*, 1:1–2, 92–7.
43. Mou Zongsan, *Zhongguo zhexue shijiu jiang*, 298–308.
44. *Ibid.*, 78.
45. Mou Zongsan, *Daode de lixiangzhuyi*, 152–3.
46. Mou Zongsan, *Zhongguo zhexue shijiu jiang*, 28–9.
47. Mou Zongsan, *Yuan shan lun*, 38.
48. Mou Zongsan, *Zhongguo zhexue shijiu jiang*, 30–2; *Daode de lixiangzhuyi*, 254–5.
49. Immanuel Kant, *Groundwork of the Metaphysics of Morals*, trans. and ed. Mary Gregor, Cambridge: Cambridge University Press, 1997, 19.
50. *Ibid.*, 9–10.
51. *Ibid.*, 24.
52. Kant describes a good will as "the highest and unconditional good" and "the preeminent good we call moral," *ibid.*, 14. See also 7, 10.
53. *Ibid.*, 24–5.
54. *Ibid.*, 25, 27.

55. *Ibid.*, 31.
56. *Ibid.*, 35.
57. *Ibid.*, 13.
58. *Ibid.*, 10–12.
59. *Ibid.*, 8, 13–14.
60. *Ibid.*, 19–20.
61. *Ibid.*, 27, 31.
62. Immanuel Kant, *Critique of Practical Reason* in *Practical Philosophy* (works of Kant), trans. and ed. Mary Gregor, Cambridge, U.K.: Cambridge University Press, 1996, 162.
63. *Ibid.*, 246.
64. *Ibid.*, 218.
65. *Ibid.*, 238.
66. *Ibid.*, 240.
67. Mou Zongsan, *Zhi de zhijue yu Zhongguo zhexue*, 200–1.
68. Mou Zongsan, *Zhongguo zhexue shijiu jiang*, 137, 230–3, 237; *Caixing yu xuanli*, preface to the third edition, 1–2.
69. Mou Zongsan, *Zhongguo zhexue shijiu jiang*, 320–1.
70. *Ibid.*, 354–5.
71. Mou Zongsan, *Yuan shan lun*, 276–9.
72. *Ibid.*, 317, 324–5.
73. Mou Zongsan, *Xinti yu xingti*, 1:4, 8–11.
74. Mou Zongsan, *Shidai yu ganshou* 時代與感受 (The Times and Sensibilities), Taipei: Ehu chubanshe, 1995, 399–407.
75. Mou Zongsan, *Xinti yu xingti*, 1:19; *Zhongguo zhexue shijiu jiang*, 69–70, 397.
76. Mou Zongsan, *Zhongguo zhexue shijiu jiang*, 78.
77. *Ibid.*, 414.
78. *Ibid.*, 253.
79. *Ibid.*, 262.
80. Wu Ming 吳明, "Chedi de weixinlun yu Zhong-xi zhexue huitong 徹底的唯心論與中西哲學會通" ("Comprehensive Idealism" and the Meeting of Chinese and Western Philosophies), in Li Minghui 李明輝 (ed.), *Mou Zongsan xiansheng yu Zhongguo zhexue zhi chongjian* 牟宗三先生與中國哲學之重建 (Mou Zongsan and the Reconstruction of Chinese Philosophy), Taipei: Wenjin chubanshe, 1996, 116–17.
81. *Ibid.*, 80.
82. Mou Zongsan, *Xinti yu xingti*, 1:10–11.
83. Mou Zongsan, *Zhi de zhijue yu Zhongguo zhexue*, preface, 3.
84. Mou Zongsan, *Caixing yu xuanli*, original preface, 1.
85. Mou Zongsan, *Zhongguo zhexue shijiu jiang*, 137, 227.
86. Mou Zongsan, *Caixing yu xuanli*, original preface, 1.
87. Di Zhicheng 翟志成, *Dangdai xin Ruxue shilun* 當代新儒學史論 (Critical Essays on the History of Contemporary New Confucianism), Taipei: Yunchen wenhua, 1993, preface, vii–viii.
88. Zheng Jiadong, *Mou Zongsan* 牟宗三, Taipei: Dongda tushu gufen youxian gongsi, 2000, 228.

89. Fang Yingxian, "Shengming de lixing yu lixing de shengming—Mou Zongsan xiansheng zhexue xitong de yiyi 生命的理性與理性的生命—牟宗三先生哲學系統的意義" (The Rationality of Life and the Rational Life: The Significance of the Philosophical System of Mou Zongsan), in Li Minghui (ed.), *Mou Zongsan xiansheng yu Zhongguo zhexue zhi chongjian*, 18–19.
90. Lin Anwu, *Ruxue geming lun* 儒學革命論 (Revolutionary Confucianism), Taipei: Taiwan xuesheng shuju, 1998, 22.
91. *Ibid.*, preface i–v, 25.
92. *Ibid.*, 27.
93. Mou Zongsan, *Xinti yu xingti*, 1:1 (preface), 273; *Zhongguo zhexue shijiu jiang*, 77–8, 80–1.
94. Raymond Gaita, *A Common Humanity: Thinking about Love and Truth and Justice*, Melbourne: The Text Publishing Company, 1999, 197.
95. Mou Zongsan, *Zhongguo zhexue de tezhi*, 118–19.
96. Mou Zongsan, *Zhongguo zhexue shijiu jiang*, 78–9.
97. Yan Binggang, *Mou Zongsan xueshu sixiang pingzhuan*, 220; Zheng Jiadong, *Mou Zongsan*, 225; Lin Anwu, *Ruxue geming lun*, preface, ii.
98. Mou Zongsan, *Shidai yu ganshou*, 319–27, 410; *Daode de lixiangzhuyi*, 252–3, 258.
99. Mou Zongsan, *Daode de lixiangzhuyi*, 258.
100. *Ibid.*, 3, 259–62.
101. Mou Zongsan, *Shidai yu ganshou*, 313.
102. *Ibid.*, 357–8.
103. Mou Zongsan, *Xianxiang yu wu zishen*, 123; *Yuan shan lun*, 307, 313–14, 316–17; *Zhongguo zhexue shijiu jiang*, 307–8.
104. Mou Zongsan, *Xianxiang yu wu zishen*, 122–3.
105. Mou Zongsan, *Shidai yu ganshou*, 292–5, 309–12.
106. Mou Zongsan, *Xinti yu xingti*, 1:5.
107. Mou Zongsan, *Shidai yu ganshou*, 292.
108. *Ibid.*, 385–92.
109. *Ibid.*, 300, 309, 312–13.
110. *Ibid.*, 327.
111. Arif Dirlik, "Chinese History and the Question of Orientalism," *History and Theory*, 35(4)(December 1996): 113.
112. Mou Zongsan, *Zhong-xi zhexue zhi huitong shisi jiang* 中西哲學之會通十四講 (Fourteen Lectures on the Reconciliation of Chinese and Western Philosophy), Taipei: Taiwan xuesheng shuju, 1996, 1–2.
113. Lin Anwu, *Ruxue geming lun*, 40.
114. *Ibid.*, 42.
115. *Ibid.*, 20.
116. *Ibid.*, 200–2.
117. *Ibid.*, 22.
118. *Ibid.*, 33.
119. Mou Zongsan, *Zhong-xi zhexue zhi huitong shisi jiang*, 1–2, 30–2.
120. Han Qiang, "Mou Zongsan xinxing lilun shuping 牟宗三心性理論述評 (A Descriptive Critique of Mou Zongsan's Theory of Ontological Mind

and Ontological Human Nature) in Fang Keli and Li Jinquan (eds.), *Xiandai xin Ruxue yanjiu lunji*, vol. 2, Beijing: Zhongguo shehui kexue chubanshe, 1991, 284.

121. Yu Yingshi, *Xiandai Ruxue lun* 現代儒學論 (Essays on Contemporary Confucianism), Shanghai: Shanghai renmin chubanshe, 1998, 216–23.

122. *Ibid.*, 213–14.

123. *Ibid.*, 198.

124. For a copy of the original declaration in Chinese, Feng Zusheng 封祖盛 (ed.), *Dangdai xin Rujia* 當代新儒家 (Contemporary New Confucianism), Beijing: Sanlian shudian, 1989, 1–52.

125. *Ibid.*, editorial preface, 10–11.

126. Original declaration in Chinese in *ibid.*, 39, 49.

127. Original declaration in Chinese in *ibid.*, 7–37.

128. Original declaration in Chinese in *ibid.*, 49–52.

129. Mou Zongsan, *Daode de lixiangzhuyi*, preface, 4–5.

130. Du Weiming (Tu Wei-ming), *Way, Learning, and Politics: Essays on the Confucian Intellectual*, Albany: SUNY Press, 1993, 149, 158–9; *Xiandai jingshen yu Rujia chuantong* 現代精神與儒家傳統 (The Spirit of Modernity and the Confucian Tradition), Taipei: Lianjing chuban shiye gongsi, 1996, 420–1, 436–7, 464–71.

131. Mou Zongsan, *Xinti yu xingti*, 1:51–2.

132. *Ibid.*, 49.

133. Mou Zongsan, *Zhongguo zhexue shijiu jiang*, 296, 298, 304, 399–401; *Yuan shan lun*, 19, 36; *Xinti yu xingti*, 1:25–6, 44–5.

134. Yan Binggan, *Mou Zongsan xueshu sixiang pingzhuan*, 297–9.

135. Fang Yingxian, "Shengming de lixing yu lixing de shengming—Mou Zongsan xiansheng zhexue xitong de yiyi," 19–20.

136. This can be seen in the many articles written on the topic of moral education and published in *Jiaoyu yanjiu*, a monthly journal put out by the Ministry of Education in China. Listed below are some of them: Luan Chuanda, "Zhonghua minzu chuantong meide jiaoyu yanjiu baogao," 248(September 2000): 26–7; Guo Qijia, "Zhongguo chuantong jiaoyu zhexue yu quanqiu lunli," 250(November 2000): 3–7; and Zhu Yongxin 朱永新 and Ren Sumin 任蘇民, "Zhongguo daode jiaoyu: Fazhan qushi yu tixi chuangxin 中國道德教育：發展趨勢與體系創新" (Moral Education in China: Developmental Trends and Innovation of the System), 251(December 2000): 10–14.

CHAPTER 6
A MODERN CHINESE PHILOSOPHY BUILT UPON CRITICALLY RECEIVED TRADITIONS: FENG YOULAN'S NEW PRINCIPLE-CENTERED LEARNING AND THE QUESTION OF ITS RELATIONSHIP TO CONTEMPORARY NEW RUIST ("CONFUCIAN") PHILOSOPHIES

Lauren F. Pfister

The Need to Decode Confused Attributions

In his recent book on "new traditionalism" (*xin chuantongzhuyi* 新傳統主義) Zheng Jiadong 鄭家棟 refers to Feng Youlan 馮友蘭 (1895–1990) as part of a broader movement to reinstate selective traditional concepts within the framework of a distinctively modern style of Chinese philosophizing. Much to his credit, Zheng handles the varying philosophical concerns of Feng's controversial career before and after the establishment of the People's Republic in China in 1949 with considerable objectivity, recognizing that Feng's writings display some very new interests after that watershed event. In addition, he notes Feng's consistent concern to build an interpretative bridge—or perhaps it is better to speak of him building several different bridges at various times during his long career—between the traditional concepts he coined as early as 1931 as "Chinese philosophical" ideas, and the modern "Western" and later explicitly "Marxist" philosophical concepts to which he regularly compared them.[1]

Zheng's employment of this new reference term, "new traditionalism," is a creative development of his own previous writing about the history of certain twentieth-century Chinese philosophical movements. It is a particularly apt way of referring to the various forms of philosophical expression that struggled to gain a hearing over the negatively critical and diametrically opposed modern movements among Chinese intellectuals throughout the same period. Some of these "modernists," such as Hu Shi 胡適 (1891–1962), preferred asserting a critical reconstruction of all traditional philosophy and literature on the basis of his Sinified form of pragmatism. In Hu's particular case, he also promoted a modernization process that invoked "Westernization" as the primary goal. Others, such as the Marxist intellectual Hou Wailu 侯外廬 (1903–88), preferred leveling their critiques against earlier intellectual traditions by challenging the normal interpretations of the classical canon and asserting a standard of criticism relying explicitly on dialectical materialism. "New traditionalism" suggests rightly that conservative responses to these modern critical approaches were conceived and worked out by a relatively small group of twentieth-century Chinese intellectuals. Nevertheless, the general phrase could also include Daoist and Buddhist thinkers as well as those in the Ruist camps. In fact, Zheng keeps his focus firmly on more or less conservative Ruist intellectuals, not yet extending this potentially fruitful coining of a new category into these other "traditionalist" realms.[2]

In spite of his helpful coining of this "new traditionalist" category for offering an understanding of twentieth-century conservative philosophical developments in mainland China, Zheng nevertheless has still not been able to free his discussion from issues related to an earlier frame of reference addressed under the rubric of "New Ruists (Confucians)" (xin Ru 新儒), "Contemporary Ruists" (dangdai Rujia 當代儒家), and/or "Contemporary New Ruists" (dangdai xin Rujia 當代新儒家). In fact, Zheng was one of the major intellectuals who helped to conceptualize not only this terminology, but also to give it a distinctive genealogy. In his 1990 book, Xiandai xin Ruxue gailun 現代新儒學概論 (Introductory Essays on Contemporary New Ruist Learning), Zheng explicitly spoke of "three generations" of "New Ruists." The first generation included Liang Shuming 梁漱溟 (1893–1988), Zhang Junmai 張君勱 (1887–1969), and Xiong Shili 熊十力 (1885–1968); the second, Feng Youlan, He Lin 賀麟 (1902–92), and Qian Mu 錢穆 (1895–1990); the third, Mou Zongsan 牟宗三 (1909–95), Tang Junyi 唐君毅 (1909–78), and Xu Fuguan 徐復觀 (1903–82).[3] Setting forth this chronology at the time suggested that there was an underlying consistency between these three generations of thinkers, but ten years later Zheng is willing to describe this "movement" not as a single group, but as intellectuals facing traditions that are "splintering." In fact, the plurality of these "new traditionalists" is an issue of importance for understanding the phenomena associated with the New Ruists, and so here we intend to support this "plurality" reading as it applies among the so-called New Ruists themselves.

Even in his most recent work on the "splintering tradition" of Ruism during the post-imperial period of twentieth-century China, Zheng Jiadong continues to employ the attributions still commonly found in many philosophical writings in contemporary mainland China—whether in scholarly monographs, articles, or dictionaries of Chinese philosophy—which place Feng Youlan among this distinctive group of New Ruist, and therefore "conservative," Chinese intellectuals. This claim is highly problematic precisely because of the splintering of the traditions themselves. Feng represents one of these traditions, but it is one that is largely distinctive and independent of the conservative New Ruists who are generally associated with the "Confucian Declaration" of 1958.[4] Significantly, Zheng continues in his most recent work to associate Feng's works with the New Ruists under the categories of "theoretical development and [its] final stage" and their responses to "religion."[5] Certainly, Feng did offer a new "theoretical development" of traditional Ruist concepts and argued consistently for a general position that sought to "replace religion with philosophy," but it is also the case, as we will see below, that these are specific components that distinguish Feng's own philosophy of New Principle-Centered Learning (*xin lixue* 新理學) from general trends among the key figures who published the 1958 Confucian Declaration.

While Zheng's "new traditionalism" suggests a more comprehensive and less ambivalent way of describing a distinctive and large group of twentieth-century Chinese philosophers and intellectuals, his continued use of the older terminology muddies the conceptual waters. Because of this continuing vagueness in reference and evaluation, I will seek to explain why Feng Youlan should not be considered a member of the conservative New Ruists, even though he could be counted as one of the prominent philosophers within a "new traditionalist" phase of Chinese philosophical discussions in the twentieth century. This will be argued and justified from a number of perspectives as they relate to Feng's own system of philosophy, New Principle-Centered Learning—published in six books that were presented under the title of *Zhen yuan liu shu* 貞元六書 (Purity Descends, Primacy Ascends: Six Books)—as well as in his extensive writings related to his modern conceptualization of various "histories" of "Chinese philosophy."[6]

Comparing Basic Philosophical Orientations

One of the questions that Feng continued to consider in his writings within and after the publication of the six books of his philosophical system, the New Principle-Centered Learning, was how a Chinese form of philosophy might become truly engaged with the modern world. From the mid-1930s this question related to modernization and an appropriately "modern" expression of Chinese philosophical traditions remained paramount in his mind. Significantly, the last three books in his own philosophical system—*Xin yuanren* 新原人 (New Treatise on the Nature of Humans; 1943), *Xin yuandao* 新原道 (New Treatise on the Nature of the Way; 1944), and *Xinzhi yan* 新知言 (Discussions about New Knowledge; 1946)—all approached the question of the modern expression of Chinese philosophical traditions in distinct but coordinated ways. While the first volume addressed the theoretical framework for this modern system, the second presented the New Principle-Centered Learning system as the historical summit of a Chinese philosophical progression from traditional to modern systems. The third volume argued for the modern relevance of Feng's system in the light of ongoing discussions and problems within European and North American philosophical circles.[7] In the second volume, *New Treatise on the Nature of the Way*, Feng advanced the claim in 1944 that he had discovered and presented "the new system" within his New Principle-Centered Learning system. New Principle-Centered Learning constituted the "new" and "modern" expression of the "quintessence of Chinese philosophy," identified with the seminal idea of being "inwardly sagely and outwardly regal" (*nei sheng wai wang* 內聖外王).[8] Feng later admitted that this Hegelian-like self-serving identification of his system with the "most philosophical philosophy" of that period, was an act of unbridled and irresponsible pride, especially because he began to realize as early as 1948 that this modern system was not at all the only or the most popular approach among the new traditionalist writings at the time.[9] We will explore more carefully this important theme in Feng's self-awareness in a later section.

From this perspective, one senses how Feng's concerns about Chinese philosophy were consistently forward-looking, even when they were self-consciously addressing questions in past Chinese intellectual traditions that he identified within the new category of "philosophy" or *zhexue*

哲學. Yet, it is this specific orientation in philosophizing that stands in contrast to the general philosophical orientation of those Chinese philosophers who published their conservative "Confucian Declaration" in 1958.

Prepared by exiled scholars in Hongkong and Taiwan, the 1958 "Confucian Declaration" was produced in both the English- and Chinese-language media in order to address a wide audience. This bilingual presentation displayed a linguistic and cultural orientation at that time which dominated philosophical discussions across a polarized "East/West" and "China/West" divide.[10] Nevertheless, the scholars who signed this Declaration—Tang Junyi, Mou Zongsan, Xu Fuguan, and Zhang Junmai—could all be classified as "Chinese cultural conservatives" who sought to identify the intellectual-spiritual life (*jingshen shengming* 精神生命) of "Chinese culture" in a singular formula related to Song-Ming Ruist discussions and their attendant moral efforts in the Learning of Heart–Mind and [Human] Nature (*xin xing zhi xue* 心性之學).[11] They argued that studies of "Chinese philosophy" and "Chinese culture" by twentieth-century intellectuals and scholars, both in Chinese and non-Chinese contexts, had overlooked the most significant feature of elite Chinese culture: the learning of heart–mind and [human] nature discussed and developed within the works of Song-Ming Ruist scholarship, particularly by the major figures Zhu Xi 朱熹 (1130–1200) and Wang Yangming 王陽明 (1472–1529). Precisely because of this approach to their main subject matter, the signatories to the Declaration were "backward looking" in the sense of a Ruist fundamentalism, seeking the philosophical core of their work in the achievements of previous Ruist scholarship rather than in a newly formulated modern system. This is not to say that they were not interested in the modernization of Ruist traditions, since the Declaration repeatedly insists that "democracy" as well as "science and technology" should be integrated into Chinese society. What is significant here is that the general orientation of their project is conservative and backward looking; it is a Ruist fundamentalist reorientation.

Assessing Political and Scientific Orientations

Having summarized some of the basic tenets of the 1958 Declaration, several questions arise. Who were the unnamed Chinese intellectuals and scholars that the writers of the Declaration opposed? Was Feng Youlan among them? How could such "conservative" thinkers also believe that "democracy" and "science and technology" could be integrated into their own conservative project? Did Feng Youlan agree with them in these matters?[12] Was Feng Youlan a partisan to the "Confucian Declaration" or one of those conceived as an opponent to its tenets? It should now be clear that the basic orientation of the 1958 Declaration stands in strong contrast to Feng Youlan's philosophical project, a project that presented itself as a modernizing and forward looking system. The conservative project was one that looked back and found its fundamental commitments in the writings of Song-Ming Dynasty Ruist scholars.[13] Later studies written by both Tang Junyi and Mou Zongsan about the history of Chinese philosophy differ in the way they identify the key contributions of Song-Ming Ruists, but both men continued to assert that the most important insights applicable to the twentieth-century reassertion of Ruist intellectual traditions were discovered by Ruists during these dynasties.[14] Not only was Feng Youlan's construction of his own New Principle-Centered Learning generally oriented in a "forward looking" manner in contrast to the tendency for the writers of the Declaration to be "backward looking" in orientation, moreover Feng preferred the rationalist schools associated with Zhu Xi and earlier Song Ruist scholars, while the authors of the Declaration preferred the interpretive and practical approaches adopted by the Ming Ruists, particularly Wang Yangming. As a consequence, Feng's reading of the "history of Chinese philosophy," even as early as 1931, already showed a tendency to be rationalist in orientation and more open-minded toward the variety of alternative schools of the pre-imperial period. This account of Chinese philosophical history was vigorously opposed by Mou Zongsan in his early essays on *The Special Character of Chinese Philosophy*, which were published numerous times and exercised an immense influence especially in Taiwan.[15]

Whether the question be one of their general interpretative orientation, their specific alignments with Song or Ming Ruist scholars, or their accounts of the history of Chinese philosophy, the figures associated with the 1958 Declaration and Feng Youlan are readily contrasted. Mou Zongsan's explicit criticisms of Feng's accounts regarding this last issue underscore this basic opposition. Certainly, the writers of the 1958 Declaration had Feng Youlan in mind, along with other modernists such as Hu Shi and Marxists such as Hou Wailu, when they spoke of Chinese intellectuals who had "overlooked" what they considered to be the most important theme of Ruist philosophical traditions.

What complicates this picture, however, is the fact that, like Mou and the others, Feng also referred to many Song-Ming Ruist figures in his own philosophical system, often quoting them at length in the six volumes of *Purity Descends, Primacy Ascends.* Yet, as we have already mentioned, his preferences lay with the rationalist approach of Zhu Xi. More significantly, Feng's purpose in referring to their ideas was not to reiterate or reinstate what they originally claimed as the basis for his own philosophical system, but rather to analyze what they claimed and then to "correct" it on the basis of his own "modern" convictions, and related to a formal analytic logical methodology. This "critical reception" (*jiezhejiang* 接著講) of Song-Ming Ruist philosophical traditions was made explicit in the first and fourth books of his system, and became an important element in his final history of Chinese philosophy, his seven-volume set, which can be given the more general title, *A New History of Chinese Philosophy* (1970–92).[16] Feng wanted to assert the value and importance of logic as a critical element in the modernization of Chinese philosophical traditions, one which could also prepare the way for a new and distinctive monistic metaphysics, which Feng also promoted. Yet, it is precisely this methodological feature attached to logical analysis and the "critical reception" of past Ruist traditions that is not found in the Declaration.[17] The Declaration repeatedly expressed the concern of its authors to "revive" and "reinterpret" these older traditions for a twentieth-century world, rather than producing an overall critical reappraisal and recasting of Song-Ming Ruists' philosophical claims. Consequently, if a distinctive feature of New Ruist philosophical claims was to revive the central categories of Song-Ming Ruist philosophy, Feng Youlan's "critically received" approach to Song-Ming Ruist writings shows that his own philosophical system was significantly different in orientation. Although Feng might be called a "neo-traditionalist," it would be unjustified to include him among these conservative "New Ruists."

Consequently, we should probe further into the nature of the conservatism expressed in the 1958 Confucian Declaration in order to understand these matters in a more comprehensive and precise manner. How could such conservative Ruist advocates support the modernization of Chinese Ruist philosophy by its adaptation to democratic systems of government and various scientific and technological advances? The position expressed in the Declaration on these matters is strong and clear. Democracy can work only if the moral understanding of human beings promoted by orthodox Ruist traditions is adopted as a corrective to the individualistic tendencies of modern political life. Similarly, scientific and technological progress is vulnerable to manipulation by systems that promote insensitivity to the human condition, even to the point of being inhumane. Tang Junyi, in particular, was profoundly shocked by the destructive effects of the atom bombs dropped on Hiroshima and Nagasaki, and so joined in the call made by many other intellectuals worldwide to reconsider the inhumaneness inherent in these technically advanced weapons.[18] The 1958 Declaration is distinctive in promoting a corrective to insensitivity and inhumane values, offering as an alternative its vision of human worth being grounded in the central themes of Song-Ming Ruist moral metaphysics. For Tang and Mou *et al.* there were no other alternatives: to understand Ruism properly, one must accept *xin xing zhi xue* (learning of the heart and [human] nature) as the *sine qua non* of "authentic" Chinese philosophy, and, even more broadly, as the essence of Chinese culture. It could therefore be expected that other so-called New Ruists would adopt similar stances in relation to democracy and the scientific-technological enterprises of the post–World War II period.

What one finds in Feng Youlan's own system of New Principle-Centered Learning as well as his various histories of Chinese philosophies is something quite contrary to these general trends within the 1958 Declaration. In his first book, within the six-volume set of his own philosophical system, Feng argued that "philosophy" was inherently different from "science" and so had nothing to offer to it. Any modern philosophy, Feng insisted, should be metaphysically oriented, seeking what is "true-and-real" (*zhenji* 真際), and so dealing with issues related to metaphysical reality and not with the "facts" associated with "actual" things (*shiji* 實際). This was the way toward realizing the "most philosophical philosophy."[19] Though he promoted social modernization under the influence of economic development in the second volume of his system, Feng remained adamant that "philosophy" was distinct from and "useless" to "science."[20] Another significant element informing Feng's contrast between "philosophy" and "science" was his concern to retain a particular realm of intellectual enterprise for "modern" philosophy within the "modern world." Where others might prefer an empirical or humanistic approach in addressing the general relationship between philosophy and science, Feng chose to emphasize a logico-metaphysical assessment of their relationship. Philosophy was methodologically distinct from science, using formal logic and appealing to metaphysical principles. Science was rooted in empirical investigations and, because of the limits of the inductive logic by which its theories were constructed, it could not easily attain to more general conceptualizations of the actual world, much less aspire to give accounts of the non-empirical metaphysical world.[21] When considered from a comparison of Feng's philosophical system with the relevant claims of the 1958 Declaration,

Feng's position in relation to scientific development was at best only neutral, while the Declaration promoted a more positive and affirmative position.

On the political plane, Feng's political philosophy was moored in the traditional viewpoint of being "inwardly sagely and outwardly regal." As a consequence, he tended to avoid discussions of political philosophy in any concrete sense, and only addressed "philosophical principles" undergirding the role of a political leader. Seen from this angle, his adaptation to Maoist political philosophy as a Ruist scholar after 1950, seeking to be a philosophical advisor to Mao the ruler and so submitting to his teachings under those conditions, was consistent with Feng's own relatively naïve political philosophy. In the end, Feng was forced to undergo more than one hundred self-criticisms, leading in the later 1950s to the total rejection of his New Principle-Centered Learning system as incompatible with the ideology of the new Marxist–Maoist regime.[22] While he never became a member of the Chinese Communist Party, Feng also never positively advocated a democratic alternative to Mao's communism, even though he did offer several basic criticisms of Mao's philosophy in the last volume of his final history of Chinese philosophy, a book published posthumously because of these and other critical assessments.[23] While the Declaration is positively oriented to linking Ruist moral philosophy with a humane form of democracy, Feng had no part in promoting this element of modernization in Chinese philosophical realms.

A more precise comparative picture can now be drawn between Feng Youlan's philosophical position and interests and those of the authors of the 1958 Confucian Declaration. What makes this comparison both interesting and complex is the variety of tensions that exist between them. For, while the authors of the Declaration are obviously conservative in their assessment of Ruist traditions, they were also engaged with modern political and social issues, and in many ways were more critically engaged than Feng. Consequently, there is a seeming paradox in the overall picture. Feng's basic philosophical orientation adopts a positive desire to respond to modern philosophical questions, and so he produced a special formal logical approach to philosophical problems, which matched those concerns. These kinds of problems are nowhere to be found within the 1958 Confucian Declaration. Yet, due to this very same methodological approach, Feng's commitments in political philosophical issues were relatively weak and unattached to interests in any particular political system. In addition, while the Confucian Declaration offers a sustained critique of the inadequacies of inhumane scientific and technological projects, Feng essentially sidesteps these issues, justifying this move on the basis that they really have nothing to do with philosophy in and of itself. So stark are these contrasts that one is pressed hard to establish why his New Principle-Centered Learning system should be identified with the more conservative New Ruist positions.

The New Ruists' Philosophy of Culture versus the Most Philosophical Philosophy

Another general feature—one that sets Feng Youlan's work in contrast to the orientation of the signatories to the 1958 Declaration and their later works—has to do with the claims they each develop in relation to the accessibility of the basic themes of Ruist philosophy. This general feature can be identified in their different answers to the following question: How many people could achieve the moral reorientation and philosophical awareness promoted in their own philosophical writings?

Zhu Xi had maintained, along lines previously worked out by Mencius (ca. 372–289 B.C.), that all persons could become sages, and this claim was maintained and proclaimed regularly in the works of key New Ruists, particularly Tang Junyi and Mou Zongsan. In fact, their general philosophical orientation was so optimistic in this regard that Thomas Metzger repeatedly criticizes these twentieth-century New Ruists, and Tang Junyi in particular, for being far too sanguine and not genuinely addressing the more complicated existential "predicament" regularly found in Song-Ming Ruist works concerning the cultivation of the whole person.[24] How ever one assesses Metzger's evaluation of their works, what is generally evident is that these New Ruist philosophers intend to make a universal claim about the moral transformations that humans can experience by pursuing personal cultivation.

How does Feng Youlan's philosophical system respond to the potential of humans to achieve the goal of "inward sageliness and outward regalness?" Though there are clearly times when he describes and recognizes the claims of his Ruist predecessors, which assert that "everyone can become a Yao or a Shun," Feng's own philosophical system promotes a hierarchical account of human understanding in four different "realms" (*jingjie* 境界) that privileges a comprehensive intellectual awareness of the cosmos. After describing this elevated attainment as being located in the "realm of heaven-and-earth" (*tiandi jingjie* 天地境界), Feng is able to identify only a few key figures throughout Chinese history who have attained such heights, including some of the

Song-Ming Ruists, but also Guo Xiang 郭象 (252–312), a Wei-Jin period Daoist philosopher, and Seng Zhao 僧肇 (384–414), a Wei-Jin period Buddhist thinker.[25] All indications point to Feng's philosophical system being a new elitism, the "most philosophical philosophy," and therefore not accessible to any and all human beings.

This being the case, it is manifest that Feng's New Principle-Centered Learning system is not only "forward looking" and modern in a manner unlike the claims of New Ruist philosophers, but it is also not concerned about making philosophical claims assuring that everyone would or could possibly attain the highest philosophical goal his own philosophy describes. Consequently, the New Principle-Centered Learning stands in contrast to the New Ruist philosophical claims in basic methodological and teleological orientations.

Standing Apart: Feng Youlan's Later Reflections on New Principle-Centered Learning in the Light of Developments in Twentieth-Century Chinese Philosophy

As mentioned earlier, not long after Feng had made his own bold claims concerning the "new system" he had conceived under the name of New Principle-Centered Learning, he felt obliged to point out that his modern system was not the only option within modern developments in Chinese philosophy. While he made only a short statement about this development in his English work of 1948, *A Short History of Chinese Philosophy*, this problem became a central issue in his final volume of the *New History of Chinese Philosophy*, published posthumously in Hongkong in 1992 because of its controversial assessment of Mao Zedong (1893–1976).

In the former work, Feng identified the development of a philosophical school at Beijing University during the 1930s, which was oriented "towards historical studies and scholarship, with an idealistic philosophical trend. . . . [I]n terms of Western philosophy, [this school] is Kantian and Hegelian, and, in terms of Chinese philosophy, [it] is Lu-Wang." He qualifies his own philosophical system in parallel phrases: it is directed "towards the use of logical analysis for the study of philosophical problems, with a realistic philosophical orientation, which, in terms of Western philosophy, is Platonic in the sense that the philosophy of neo-realism is Platonic, and in terms of Chinese philosophy, is Ch'eng-Chu."[26] As a consequence, Feng went on to introduce his own philosophical system as "one trend in contemporary Chinese philosophy," clearly qualifying the bolder claim he had made in his 1944 work, *New Treatise on the*

Nature of the Way, that his was *the* new modern Chinese philosophy.[27] One should add that Feng's assessment of the style and metaphysical orientation of these two trends developing during the late 1930s and extending into the 1940s was generally correct in its characterizations. Nevertheless, his own philosophical commitments underwent some drastic redevelopment two years later, when he began to work within a Maoist–Marxist oriented framework to reconsider the study of philosophy, in general, and the study of the history of Chinese philosophy, in particular.

Fifty years after writing his first account of *A History of Chinese Philosophy* (*Zhongguo zhexueshi* 中國哲學史), the elderly Feng once more addressed the modern movements in "Chinese philosophy," contrasting his own New Principle-Centered Learning philosophy with the more influential work of Xiong Shili 熊十力 (1885–1968), whose approach he characterized as a New Heart–Mind centered Learning (*Xin xinxue* 新心學). Here, once more, the contrast between his own system and that associated with the New Ruists was underscored. His was the Cheng-Zhu inclined New Principle-Centered Learning system, a philosophy that was a "new expression" of the original Principle-Centered Learning (*Lixue* 理學) generally associated with Zhu Xi. The other was a Lu-Wang oriented New Heart–Mind centered Learning that reflected influences of this alternative Song-Ming Ruist tendency referred to as Heart–Mind Learning (*Xinxue* 心學). Xiong's philosophy is presented as a radical Ruist response to various Buddhist philosophical themes, so that it "critically receives" Buddhist terminology while casting it in new meanings, which appeal to an extremely dynamic metaphysical monism. In this sense, Xiong's philosophy is similar in its critically styled methodology to Feng's works, but has a basic metaphysical difference in its claims concerning the nature of the heart–mind. Since Xiong Shili is now regularly cited as one of the major "original" philosophers of the New Ruist school, this contrast once more underscores the self-conscious differences between the philosophical orientation of the New Ruists and Feng Youlan's own system. Whether Xiong's approach and metaphysical claims are also represented in the 1958 Declaration is an important question. Generally speaking, it does not seem to be the case. Still, the New Ruists share a more intuitively orientated, culturally conservative, and relatively populist philosophical worldview, while Feng's New Principle-Centered Learning is a more logically orientated, culturally elitist, and therefore presents a less readily attainable philosophical worldview.

Beyond Political Controversies to Philosophical Clarifications

Without doubt, Feng Youlan's "Marxist turn" has fueled many arguments about the nature of his philosophical development within his own system, and also whether he should be taken as a committed philosopher at all. He made explicit claims about "losing himself" during the final years of the Cultural Revolution, and so became a willing instrument of political campaigns that harshly criticized Master Kong ("Confucius") and the Ruist traditions as a whole. Later, in the late 1970s, he claimed to have "regained his freedom," so that he was no longer intellectually driven by the fears and anxiety associated with those terrible years. Certainly, his thorough assessment and final criticism of Mao Zedong's philosophical ideas shows every indication that this was true.[28]

While there are scholars among the New Ruists who would specifically use this inconsistency in Feng Youlan's later philosophical career as a basis for outright condemnation and rejection of his philosophical claims, we have put forward other reasons for distinguishing Feng's philosophical system from those promoted by the key figures now regularly identified with the New Ruist or Contemporary New Ruist school. Feng's philosophy, expressed in his six-volume set published between 1937 and 1946 as the New Principle-Centered Learning system, stands in contrast to the basic methodological and teleological components of the 1958 Confucian Declaration as well as to the later works written by these same key figures in the New Ruist school. While his political changes of position are also an important part of his overall philosophical system, it is Feng's philosophical elitism that stands in contrast to the more populist tendencies of what Mou Zongsan has called a "moral metaphysics." As a consequence, any more precise qualification of the New Ruist school as one which follows the basic philosophical claims of the 1958 Declaration, and/or one which develops themes largely informed by the more intuitively oriented schools of Song-Ming Ruist philosophical traditions, can no longer justifiably associate Feng Youlan's New Principle-Centered Learning with this group of Chinese philosophers. While they might all be categorized under a more broadly conceived "neo-traditionalism" as recently suggested by Zheng Jiadong and discussed above, it would be inappropriate to group them together under the rubric of a more narrowly defined "New Ruism."

Notes

1. See Zheng Jiadong, *Duanlie zhong de chuantong: Xinnian yu lixing zhi jian* 斷裂中的傳統: 信念與理性之間 (Splintering Traditions: Between Commitment and Rationality), Beijing: Chinese Social Sciences Academy Press, 2001. In the seventh chapter (328–405) Zheng devotes the whole section to discussing Feng's work after 1949 as moving between "scholarship and politics."

2. So, for example, there could be good reasons to consider the work of the Buddhist layman, Ouyang Jian 歐陽漸 (1871–1944), also known by his Buddhist style, Jingwu 竟無, and the pioneering traditionalist Buddhist monk-intellectual, Taixu 太虛 (1889–1947), as appropriate candidates under the category of "New Traditionalist Buddhists," and then extended to others such as the critically receptive Buddhist thinker and expatriate Taiwanese monk-intellectual, Yin Shun 印順 (1906–). On the Daoist side, one might include Feng Youlan himself, who as early as 1931 was promoting the modern value and distinctive contribution to "Chinese philosophy" of the monistic metaphysics of Wei-Jin period Daoist intellectual Guo Xiang 郭象 (252–312), as well as the later developments and much broader reassertions of Daoist philosophy and religious studies under the authorship and editorship of Chen Guying 陳鼓應 (1935–).

3. In fact, this discussion forms the main body of the second half of Zheng Jiadong's *Xiandai xin Ruxue gailun* 現代新儒學概論 (A General Account of New Confucianism), Xining: Guangxi People's Press, 1990, 123–335.

4. Details about the content and key figures supporting the "Confucian Declaration" will be discussed later, in greater detail.

5. See Zheng Jiadong, *Duanlie zhong de chuantong: Xinnian yu lixing zhi jian*, 90–100, 259–65.

6. In another essay, I have attempted to address Feng's shifting conceptualization of "Chinese philosophy" through three stages and four particular works related to the "history of Chinese philosophy." A German translation of this essay will appear in a forthcoming issue of *Minima Sinica* (Bonn), entitled "Von den 'Drei Lehren' zur 'Chinesischen Philosophie': Die moderne Konstrucktion des Grundkonzeptes der 'Chinesischen Philosophie' in Feng Youlans verschiedenen Geschichten der chinesischen Philosophie" (From "The Three Teachings" to "Chinese Philosophy": The Modern Construction of the Basic Concept of "Chinese Philosophy" as Envisioned in Feng Youlan's Different Histories of Chinese Philosophy). A larger monograph on this topic is now being written for Harrassowitz Publishers in Germany, but will address the problem from the perspective of the first volume of Feng's first history of Chinese philosophy published in 1931.

7. For a more detailed account of this progression within the works of Feng's New Principle-Centered Learning, see my article "Feng Youlan's New Principle Learning and His Histories of Chinese Philosophy," in Chung-ying Cheng and Nick Bunnin (eds.), *The Blackwell Guide to Contemporary Chinese Philosophy*, Oxford: Blackwell Publishers, 2002, 165–87. Although

there is not yet any European language translation of the first of these three volumes by Feng mentioned previously, the second was translated by E. R. Hughes in 1947 as *The Spirit of Chinese Philosophy*, London: Kegan Paul, Trench, Trubner & Co., and the third has been rendered into both English and German. For these volumes see Chester C. I. Wang (trans.), *Feng Youlan: A New Treatise on the Methodology of Metaphysics*, Beijing: Foreign Languages Press, 1997; and Hans-Georg Möller (trans.), *Die philosophischste Philosophie: Feng Youlans Neue Metaphysik*, Wiesbaden: Harrassowitz Verlag, 2000.

8. All three of these books have been published in the second volume of *Zhen yuan liu shu*, Shanghai: China Eastern Normal University Press, 1996.

9. Feng's self-critical assessment of his earlier claims was made in an essay written late in his life in 1986, a criticism that appears to be an authentic reevaluation motivated by his own philosophical self-awareness and not by politically-instigated self criticism. See his essay *"Zhen yuan liu shu*: Cong 'zhaozhe jiang' dao 'jiezhe jiang' 貞元六書：從 '照著講' 到 '接著講'"* (Purity Descends, Primacy Ascends: Six Books: From "Discourses which Imitate Precedents" to "Discourses which Critically Address and Develop Precedents"), in Huang Kejian 黃克劍 and Wu Xiaolong 吳小龍 (eds.), *Feng Youlan ji* 馮友蘭集 (Collection of Feng Youlan's Writings), Beijing: Quanyan Publishers, 1993, 61–88. His more softened statement made four years after he had proposed his bold claim in 1944 appeared in the final chapter of the English volume he wrote, edited by Derk Bodde, entitled *A Short History of Chinese Philosophy*, Beijing: Foreign Langauges Press, 1991 [reprint], 556–67.

10. See the Chinese version of this document in *Minzhu pinglun* 民主評論 9: 1(1958), 2–21, and reprinted in *Zhonghua renwen yu dangjin shijie* 中華人文與當今世界 (Chinese Humanities and the Contemporary World), Taipei: Student Bookstore, 1978, 864–929. The original title of the piece was "Wei Zhongguo wenhua jinggao shijie renshi xuanyan 為中國文化敬告世界人士宣言" (Declaration on Behalf of Chinese Culture Respectfully Announced to the People of the World). An English version, which is not a word for word translation but an elaboration of its basic themes, was included in Carsun Chang's (the English name of the fourth signatory to the Declaration) *The Development of Neo-Confucian Thought: Volume Two*, New York: Bookman Associates, 1962, 456–83, presented under the title, "A Declaration for a Re-appraisal of Sinology and Reconstruction of Chinese Culture." How much of this orientation along "East/West" or "China/West" lines influenced the Declaration writers, and how much it continues to influence the new traditionalists, are also significant issues in the construction of the "new traditionalist" self-understanding. The problem became complicated because Chinese forms of Marxism under Mao were clearly "Western" and explicitly European and/or Russian in their Marxist orientation, while adding synthetically selective elements from various Chinese intellectual sources. This is why, as the 1958 Declaration itself makes clear, it positioned itself against two main "fronts": one involving "Western scholars" and another directed

against "Chinese scholars" who did not agree with the authors' account of "Chinese culture."

11. For a general description of the content of the Declaration and a more focused summary of the metaphysical and religious claims made in it, see my essay, "The Different Faces of Contemporary Religious Confucianism: An Account of the Diverse Approaches of some Major Twentieth-Century Chinese Confucian Scholars," *Journal of Chinese Philosophy* 22: 2(1995): 12–18. Other literature offering interpretations of the Declaration is found in the footnotes to that article.

12. Other questions related to Zheng Jiadong's chronological reconstruction of the New Ruist Movement might also be asked, but they are not specifically relevant to our discussion here. For example, since Zhang Junmai was a signatory to this Declaration, is there any clear indication that he stands, along with Liang Shuming and Xiong Shili, as a "first generation New Ruist" and is recognized as such in the Declaration? In fact, no direct or indirect indication of this self-conscious historical orientation as a movement appears in the document, raising other questions related to the origin of this conservative New Ruism. How were Liang and Xiong related to this movement, since they themselves were still in mainland China at the time and perhaps unaware of the Declaration when it was published? If they had been able to see earlier drafts of the document, would they have been willing to become its supporters? Are there independent ways to show that they did confirm the basic tenets of this 1958 Declaration?

13. This claim should not be taken to mean that the Declaration did not address modern issues, as we will see in the following section. What is underscored here is their "basic orientation," their approach to the sources for their philosophical and cultural inspiration.

14. Tang located the key insights as flowing from the work of the late Ming Ruist, Liu Zongzhou 劉宗周 (1578–1645), while Mou Zongsan identified the key trends with sources in the Song Dynasty, starting with Hu Hong 胡宏 (1105–55 or 1102–61), and flowing through Wang Yangming 王陽明 (1472–1529). Although the details clearly differ in terms of the historical periods and the key figures, the basic orientations of both claims support the "idealist" traditions of the Lu-Wang school, as it is traditionally known, as distinct from the "rationalist" traditions of the Cheng-Zhu school. In this sense, both men were clearly reconstructing their own "orthodox lineage" in a retrospective manner, and Mou in particular offered a very new and not yet widely received reading of Song Ruist traditions. Both of these positions stand in contrast to the more harmonizing position of Qian Mu in his studies of Zhu Xi completed during his years of retirement in Taiwan, where Qian argued that Zhu Xi had been successful in constructing a synthetic position that incorporated elements of both Principle-Centered Learning (*lixue* 理學) and Heart–Mind centered Learning (*xinxue* 心學). Once more, the splintering of these interpretive positions suggests that the claims of a unity in basic understanding among the members of the New Ruist advocates is not matched by the diversity of views found within the writings of the various key figures.

15. In this volume entitled *Zhongguo zhexue de tezhi* 中國哲學的特質, Mou Zongsan attacks Feng Youlan's account of the history of pre-imperial Chinese philosophy in the first few pages of the very first chapter. Disagreeing with Feng and others who claimed that his first two-volume work, *A History of Chinese Philosophy* (1934), represented an "orthodox standpoint," Mou argues that this is not manifest in the volumes themselves. According to Mou, in the first volume Feng overemphasizes some of the minor schools, especially the early logical works (including the Mohist canon, portions of the Xunzi 荀子, as well as Gongsun Long 公孫龍 and Hui Shi 惠施). In the second volume, one that Hu Shi specifically saw as taking an "orthodox position," Mou argued instead that Feng was inordinately influenced by the New Realist philosophy he had studied in North America, and so was quite wrong in his interpretations of Zhu Xi, Lu Jiuyuan, and Wang Yangming. He goes on to argue that Feng was simply imitating the "Western" styles of periodization when he divided the whole history of Chinese philosophy into the pre-imperial and imperial periods. Mou further insisted that the Song Ruists were "modern" in some important sense, but Feng had placed them within a "scholastic" periodization that Mou considered to be a misrepresentation of their importance, committing them to a "medieval age" borrowed from European history. When, then, does the "modern" period in the history of Chinese philosophy begin? Whether Mou's criticisms directly influenced Feng's change of periodization in his last account of the history of Chinese philosophies is not clear, but it is the case that Feng did change his periodization in that final work, choosing to begin the modern era with the nineteenth century. Most likely, however, this would still not have satisfied Mou, who preferred to follow Zhang Junmai's account written in the 1960s, that the Song and Ming scholars were the originators of "modern" Chinese philosophical thinking. See Mou Zongsan, *Zhongguo zhexue de tezhi*, 2–3.

16. The dates for this seven-volume work—a comprehensive revison of his previous three histories of Chinese philosophy under the new influence of a Maoist–Marxist methodology and historiography—has proven to be both philosophically controversial and historically complex. Its controversial adoption of Maoist–Marxist perspectives belies the fact that he continued to use some of the basic categories of his New Principle-Centered Learning within these volumes as well, and should be considered in the light of the "heavier" ideological elements in the first few volumes that are "lightened" in the later ones and even overturned in the final volume, where Feng explicitly criticized Mao Zedong's philosophical position in both a chapter devoted to his ideas as well as in the general conclusion to the whole work. Precisely because the elderly Feng wrote these criticisms in the very last volume of this monumental work, completed months before he died in the winter of 1990, it had to be published outside of mainland China. Consequently, the dates associated with this large set could be adjusted, depending on whether or not the final volume, which could not be published in mainland China for political reasons, should be included.

As Nicolas Standaert has shown, this is not the only problem that presents itself to readers when seeking to know what Feng wrote as part of his

New History of Chinese Philosophy. In addition, he had written two previous volumes as "drafts" for this "new edition" of the history of Chinese philosophy in the 1960s, but did so under intense ideological pressure, and so rewrote and published them in the early 1970s. These and other matters relating to Feng's massive work are described in Nicolas Standaert, "The Discovery of the Center through the Periphery: A Preliminary Study of Feng Youlan's *History of Chinese Philosophy* (New Version)," *Philosophy East and West* 45: 4(1995): 569–89.

17. One could certainly claim that the reinterpretations of the history of Chinese philosophy presented by Tang and Mou stand as "critically received" renderings of these traditions. Yet, these claims were made in the decade following the publication of the 1958 Declaration. One could also say that even these reinterpretations of Song-Ming Ruist philosophical history were understood by Tang and Mou to be the recovery of the "major achievements" of Ruist thought during these dynasties, and so although their emphasis was new—especially in the case of Mou Zongsan's reconstruction of the traditions of the Song Ruists—they were presented as the "correct" account of the "orthodox" position.

18. Tang Junyi wrote about the horrendous destructiveness of the atomic explosions in Hiroshima and Nagasaki in at least one article published in a Hong Kong journal early in the 1950s. He explicitly challenged the value system underlying the choice to drop these bombs. Rather than argue against the specific political decisions or the governments involved in those decisions, he placed the blame primarily on the unrestrained development of scientific and technological research that did not take into consideration the human or social costs such "experiments" would involve.

19. Feng discussed the basic concepts of the "true-and-real" and "actual" in the first section of his first chapter of the first volume of his philosophical system, the book taking on the name he gave to the whole system, *New Principle-Centered Learning* (*xin lixue*). This appears in the most recent edition of Feng's six books mentioned above, *Zhen yuan liu shu*, vol. 1, 21–3. His reference to the "most philosophical philosophy" (*zui zhexue di zhexue* 最哲學底哲學) appears in the introduction to this same book, 10–12. The volume by Hans-Georg Möller, mentioned earlier, rightly makes this claim a central question for understanding Feng's own philosophical system, showing how it leads Feng, especially in the highest "realm" that human beings can attain philosophically, into a kind of rational mysticism. This will be discussed briefly in the following section.

20. This also appears in the introduction to his first volume of the system, *Zhen yuan liu shu*, vol. 1, 6–7, 14–15. After his Marxist turn in the 1950s, Feng became an avid proponent of scientific and technological enterprises, but this was justified and motivated in part by changes in his philosophy of history, which had shifted from a generally "progressive" to a more firmly "dialectical" account of social development. For one expression of this perspective within his critical appraisal of Mao Zedong, see the final volume of his *New History of Chinese Philosophy*. Feng Youlan, *Zhongguo*

xiandai zhexueshi 中國現代哲學史 (The History of Contemporary Chinese Philosophy), Hong Kong: China Book Store, 1992, 176–7.

21. Some helpful essays related to these aspects of Feng's ideas are found in the annotated translation of essays on Feng Youlan's philosophy prepared by Diane B. Oberchain for the *Journal of Chinese Philosophy* 21.3–4(September–December 1994), this double volume being entitled *Feng Youlan: Something Exists—Selected Papers of the International Research Seminar on the Thought of Feng Youlan.*

22. Aspects of this period of Feng Youlan's life can be read in autobiographical and reflective biographical accounts of this period. See Cheng Weili's 程偉禮 *Xinnian de lücheng: Feng Youlan zhuan* 信念的旅程— 馮友蘭傳 (Journey of Convictions: A Biography of Feng Youlan), Shanghai: Literary Arts Press, 1994, and Yin Ding's 殷鼎 volume simply entitled *Feng Youlan* 馮友蘭, Taipei: Great Eastern Library, 1991.

23. The controversies regarding Feng's changes during Mao's rule and after Mao's death have not abated, although general trends tend to be split along the lines of mainland Chinese scholars versus those who live outside of the mainland. The former explain these changes of position as matters of personal survival and so excuse them; the latter consider the changes to be unprincipled and therefore inherently problematic. One slightly different approach was taken up by Feng Youlan's son-in-law five years after Feng had died. Cai Zhongde 蔡仲德 argued that Feng clearly describes his troubles during the Cultural Revolution—especially in the early 1970s during the anti-Confucius campaigns and later in his support of the ideology of Gang of Four—as a period when he "lost his self" and willingly became an ideological instrument of political powers. Cai further points out that Feng clearly repented in 1978 and "regained himself," so that he could write his final criticism of Mao Zedong without bowing any longer to official ideology. In my article on Feng's philosophy for the *Blackwell Companion to Contemporary Chinese Philosophy*, I have described Feng as a "Chinese Heidegger" to capture some sense of the controversies surrounding his complicity with political powers. Nevertheless, qualifications need to be made, because later Feng did admit his faults and regret his actions during the Cultural Revolution, something that Heidegger never did in relationship to his Nazi connections. For Cai Zhongde's account, see his article "Lun Feng Youlan de sixiang licheng" 論馮友蘭的思想歷程 (On the Historical Development of Feng Youlan's Ideas), *Qinghua xuebao* [Taiwan]) 25: 3(1995), 237–72. For other points of view, see also Vivienne Teoh, Ph.D. dissertation, "The Post-'49 Critiques of Confucius in the PRC with Special Emphasis on the Views of Feng Youlan and Yang Rongguo—A Case Study of the Relationship between Contemporary Political Values and the Reevaluation of the History of Chinese Philosophy," Sydney: University of New South Wales, 1982.

24. This thesis is pursued in Thomas A. Metzger, *Escape from Predicament: Neo-Confucianism and China's Evolving Political Culture*, New York: Columbia University Press, 1977, especially 29–48, in relationship to Tang Junyi, and

later in discussing other twentieth-century figures (191–236). Metzger also notes how Feng stands in critical opposition to the metaphysical and moral cultivation claims of the Song-Ming Ruists (122–3).

25. The discussion of these "realms" and their interrelationship forms the body of half of the fourth book in Feng's philosophical system, chapters 3–7 of his *New Treatise on the Nature of Humans*. See *Zhen yuan liu shu*, vol. 2, 552–649.

26. Fung Yu-lan [Feng Youlan], *A Short History of Chinese Philosophy*, 557–8.

27. Fung Yu-lan [Feng Youlan], *A Short History of Chinese Philosophy*, 559.

28. This argument has been given a more extended treatment in my chapter in *The Blackwell Companion to Contemporary Chinese Philosophy*.

PART IV

CHAPTER 7

THE "LAST BUDDHIST":
THE PHILOSOPHY OF
LIANG SHUMING

John J. Hanafin

"*Mr. Xiong [Shili] should be categorized as a Confucian, and I as a Buddhist.*"

Liang Shuming[1]

Some Preliminary Comments

The reference in my title to Liang Shuming 梁漱溟 (1893–1988) as the "last Buddhist" is a not too subtle reminder that we cannot assume that Liang was, in fact, a Confucian. Guy Alitto's 1986 publication, *The Last Confucian: Liang Shu-ming and the Chinese Dilemma of Modernity* (hereafter, *The Last Confucian*) has provided considerable currency for this assumption in the West. In this chapter, I will explore an alternative portrayal of Liang, asking whether it is more valid to categorize the spirit, views, and philosophy of Liang Shuming as Buddhist rather than as Confucian or New Confucian. This question has been a controversial topic in Chinese academic circles for a number of years.[2] Many mainland Chinese commentators who categorize Liang as a Confucian rather than as a Buddhist often regard him to be the founder of New Confucianism, and identify his *Dong-xi wenhua ji qi zhexue* 東西文化及其哲學 (Eastern and Western Cultures and Their Philosophies [1922]; hereafter, *Eastern and Western Cultures*) as a seminal work of the New Confucian "school." Liang, as it were, began it all, while Xiong Shili 熊十力 (1885–1968), Feng Youlan 馮友蘭 (1895–1990), He Lin 賀麟 (1902–93), and others carried it on.[3] Other scholars are even more forthright in claiming Liang as a New Confucian. Li Daoxiang 李道湘, for example, maintains that Liang's "turn" from Buddhism to Confucianism can be called a change in his thought. Li further maintains that when Liang returned to Confucianism it became his mission in life and subsequently there were no more changes in Liang's intellectual life. While acknowledging that Buddhism coexisted with Confucianism in Liang's life (he does not specify in what respect), Li asserts that it was the standpoint and thought of Confucianism rather than Buddhism which guided Liang. Furthermore, Li observes, although Liang was a vegetarian all his life he still believed in Confucianism and held it in high regard. Therefore, Li concludes, Liang was a Confucian and the founder of the school of thought known as New Confucianism. Moreover, without Liang, the history of the development of New Confucianism would have to be rewritten.[4] Other Chinese commentators have attempted to portray Liang as a New Confucian on the basis of personal teacher-student relations. They point to the fact that Tang Junyi 唐君毅 (1909–78) attended Liang's lectures as a student and corresponded with him afterwards.[5]

The opposing view has been expressed just as forthrightly by scholars such as Feng Zhaoqi 馮兆其 and Bai Ji'an 白吉庵 who conclude that "Liang Shuming was a Buddhist, and moreover he always was a Buddhist. Even when he appeared Confucian his spirit was still Buddhist."[6] Similarly, Yan Binggang emphatically states that Liang's way of looking at and analyzing issues was based on Buddhist theory. According to Yan, Liang used Buddhist theory, or his understanding of Buddhist theory, to discuss his own fundamental perspectives on life and the universe.[7] One reason for the controversy over Liang's position on Confucianism and Buddhism is that his philosophical thought is particularly complex. Cao Yueming, for example, believes that Liang's thought is confused, unclear and in places contradictory, thus creating genuine interpretative difficulties.[8] We might further add that the constituent elements of Liang's thought are not all that easy to unravel into identifiable strands if our principal purpose is to label them as specifically Yogācārin (*Weishi* 唯識) Buddhist, Bergsonian, Schopenhauerian, Confucian (either Wang Yangming 王陽明 [1472–1529] or Wang Gen 王艮 [1483–1540]), or Liang's own idiosyncratic innovations. Liang does, however, appear to have developed his fundamentally Yogācārin metaphysical and epistemological positions with the aid of Bergson's and Schopenhauer's philosophies, while at the same time looking for corresponding themes in Confucian philosophy to support his position. Consequently, I believe that we are able to determine whether Liang was a Buddhist in the sense of subscribing to the superiority of Buddhist philosophy and its worldview over that of Confucian philosophy. We can accomplish this by looking at what Liang himself said about his experiences of, and thoughts on, Buddhism in terms of what he believed were its intrinsic merits and superiority (or conversely, deficiencies and inferiority) in comparison to Confucianism. This will, of necessity, involve a corresponding scrutiny of Liang's understanding of the metaphysical and epistemological positions of *Weishi* Buddhism. This is because in *Eastern and Western Cultures* Liang maintains that the method he employs to investigate knowledge (*zhishi* 知識) is based on *Weishi* thought.[9] In his work, *Weishi shuyi* 唯識述義 (The Meaning of Consciousness-Only Buddhism), Liang also claims that there is only one method to his view of metaphysics—the one used in *Weishi* theory.[10] What is important to note is that Liang's understanding of culture and society is grounded in his metaphysical and epistemological views. His evaluation of the relative merits of Confucianism and Buddhism is based exclusively on these same views as I will show in what follows.

Liang on Buddhism and Confucianism

The Mahāyāna tradition of Buddhism that Liang subscribed to is known as *Weishi* (Consciousness-Only) in Chinese and Cittamātra or Yogācāra in its Indian forms. Six hundred and seven texts from this tradition were brought back to China from India by the Chinese monk Xuanzang 玄奘 (600–64) in A.D. 645, of which seventy-five were translated over a period of twenty years. Xuanzang summarized and systemized the interpretations of this school in his *Cheng weishi lun* 成唯識論 (Treatise on the Establishment of the Doctrine of Consciousness-Only). His pupil, Kuiji 窺基 (632–82), also wrote an invaluable supplement to this work entitled *Cheng weishi lun shuji* 成唯識論述記 (Notes on the Treatise on the Establishment of the Doctrine of Consciousness-Only).[11] In the seventh century, this school was one of the major movements in Chinese Buddhism, but subsequently declined in influence and suffered the loss of its major works in the Yuan period (1271–1368). In the 1880s, however, a number of Buddhist works, including Kuiji's, were brought back to China from Japan. These stimulated a Buddhist revival in China. An initiator of this revival, Ouyang Jingwu 歐陽竟無 (1871–1944), founded the Chinese Academy for the Study of Buddhism, one of the aims of which was to edit the writings of the *Weishi* tradition.[12] According to Wing-tsit Chan,

Weishi philosophy is completely alien to the Chinese tradition, being too abstract for the practical Chinese mind. Its texts are the most difficult to read and to translate, and its hair-splitting analysis does not harmonize with the Chinese tendency to synthesize.[13] If we accept Dan Lusthaus's description of Yogācāra Buddhism it would seem that it does not particularly harmonize with the Western mind either. He describes it as a "deeply complex, scholastic, philosophical form of Buddhism" that has "no vibrant present manifestations."[14] The fact that Liang subscribed to a form of complex, scholastic, philosophic Buddhism may tell us something about his intellectual disposition. It is interesting to note in this connection, too, that Liang never readily accepted criticism of his philosophy because he felt that those who criticized it simply did not understand it (this was not the case with his political ideas).[15] Nonetheless, Liang was not initially attracted to Buddhism on the basis of any superior intellectual rigor it may have appeared to possess. As we will see later, Liang believed it offered a better explanation of suffering and of the apparent pointlessness of life.

Cao Yueming maintains that the relationship between Confucianism and Buddhism in Liang's thought is extremely complicated because Liang never completely clarified the position or function of either in his theoretical system. Cao does, however, believe that this relationship cannot be adequately explained by simply representing it as a phase in Liang's intellectual life.[16] Cao is referring to Liang's claim that changes either in his theory of life (*rensheng* 人生) or in his philosophy could be divided into three periods. The first was his pragmatist period from the age of fourteen or fifteen to nineteen, when he was very much under the influence of his father. The second was his Buddhist period from the age of twenty to twenty-eight or twenty-nine when, under the influence of Buddhist literature on renouncing the world, he thought of leaving his family to become a monk. The third period was after the ages of twenty-eight or twenty-nine, when his thinking changed from Buddhism to Confucianism. This last change coincided with the publication of *Eastern and Western Cultures*.[17] This reference to a change in thinking from Buddhism to Confucianism at the time of the publication of *Eastern and Western Cultures* is one of the principal testimonies offered by Chinese commentators for Liang's purported change to Confucianism. These same commentators find further evidence of this change in the preface to the eighth edition of *Eastern and Western Cultures*, in which Liang describes the book as almost a reversion to Confucianism.[18] In analyzing these two statements by Liang one must also bear in mind that he subsequently indicated that his change in thought was essentially about what he believed was best for China in terms of its stage of development and not that Buddhism was not ultimately a superior cultural ideal.

One of Liang's earliest affirmations of his individual commitment to Buddhism was in the preface to his *Eastern and Western Cultures* where he makes the point that he had merely substituted a Confucian way of life for a Buddhist one, whereas his thinking remained Buddhist in its sympathies. In fact, he admitted that although he voiced his opposition to the Chinese people's following a Buddhist way of life, he, personally, still wished to do so. We might add that his opposition to the Chinese people following a Buddhist way of life was one based on his thesis that they had not traversed the first cultural path of human development (the Western) and were unprepared for the third path (the Indian one). Despite this, as an individual, Liang considered that the Buddhist way of life was correct.[19] Another occasion on which Liang attempted to disabuse people of the misconception that he had rejected his earlier Buddhist beliefs for those of Confucianism, was his speech at the Chinese People's Political Consultative Conference on the 5th of June 1958: "My theory of human life is fundamentally a Buddhist one of transcending the world. If there is a world then there must be transcendence of the world. These are the two aspects of positive and negative; there is nothing strange about this. With respect to the way of the world, Marxism–Leninism is absolutely correct, I am completely in agreement with it; there is no conflict. Marxism–Leninism, however, does not consider there to be such a thing as renunciation of the world, so I have already remarked to friends that although I acknowledge Marxism–Leninism, unfortunately, Marxism–Leninism does not acknowledge me."[20]

In 1980 and again in 1984, Guy Alitto, the author of *The Last Confucian*, interviewed Liang. In the course of these interviews Alitto asked Liang why the spirit that motivated him and in which he had placed his trust still had meaning in his life. Liang replied that he felt he was still empowered by Buddhism. After Liang had elaborated on the differences between Confucianism and Buddhism, Alitto asked him which of these two doctrines had held greater significance for him over the last twenty-odd years of his life. Liang replied unequivocally that it was Buddhism. To ensure that there could be no doubts about this he added "I love Buddhism! I respect Buddhism!"[21] Liang also protested to Alitto about the reference to him as a Confucian in the title of Alitto's book. In response, Alitto pointed out that in 1921 Liang had publicly announced his rejection of Buddhism and his return to Confucianism. Liang replied: "This is not a fact. Although I announced my rejection of Buddhism, in fact I did not truly reject it."[22] In a 1985 interview with a reporter from *Guoxue jikan* (Chinese Studies Collected Papers) the reporter remarked that he considered that from Liang's original investigation of culture, Liang had come to appreciate Chinese Confucian culture. In fact, the reporter said, Liang had his own peculiarly Chinese philosophy centered on Confucian ethical theory. On the contrary, Liang pointed out, he had always been a Buddhist in his thinking and this had not changed. What had in fact changed were his life and lifestyle. The reporter expressed surprise at this statement, observing that he was under the impression that Liang had always espoused and argued for Confucian thought. The reporter, however, acknowledged that in *Renxin yu rensheng* 人心與人生 (The Human Mind and Human Life; 1984) Liang had written that he saw the truth of religion that was once seen in the Buddhism of ancient India thriving again in the latest stage of communist society. This obviously indicated that Liang still maintained the view that Indian culture was humanity's final destination. Liang concluded the interview by remarking that he believed the future culture of the world would find its way back to Buddhism.[23]

Liang's comments provide compelling testimony that he subscribed to Buddhism from his youth until his death. If we accept this, and it seems we must, we still have a problem with explaining his comments about turning from Buddhism to Confucianism. For that matter, we also have a similar problem with Liang's turning from Confucianism to Marxism. What, for instance, are we to make of Liang's 1958 speech at the Chinese People's Political Consultative Conference, in which he acknowledged that with respect to the way of the world, Marxism–Leninism was absolutely correct and that he was completely in agreement with it. He also wrote that he unconditionally recognized material dialectics. The only reasonable solution to this paradoxical situation would seem to be that in some way Liang believed that Confucianism and Marxism were more appropriate vehicles for expressing a social concern that was ultimately grounded in his Buddhist beliefs. There can be little doubt that what first drew Liang to Buddhism was his deep concern regarding suffering. In fact, Liang remarks that the reason that he was attracted to Buddhist theory in his youth was because of a particular attitude he began to hold toward human life. He came to believe that human life was bound up with suffering and therefore it was a mistake to live. Suffering (Skt. *duḥkha*) is the first of the four noble truths of Buddhism. As Liang was later to point out, all suffering comes from attachment to self or things. If this attachment is light, the corresponding suffering is light; if it is deep the suffering is deep. Consequently, the depth and degree of suffering differs according to the depth and degree of attachment.[24] The cessation of suffering is achieved through the extinction (*nirvāṇa*) of life. If all that the young Liang could see in life was suffering and the mistake of living then it would seem that Buddhism was the most appropriate philosophy and worldview to adopt.[25]

It has been said that Buddhism is a world-and-life-negating philosophy and Confucianism a world-and-life-affirming one.[26] There can be little doubt that Liang held this view. For instance, in 1985, he remarked that Buddhism maintained a negative attitude toward human life in terms of seeking detachment from it; moreover, it was a fundamental idea that he had always believed to be correct.[27] He accepted, for example, that whereas Confucianism focused on issues of concern and relevance to this world, Buddhism did not; instead Buddhism sought to transcend the world. Consequently, for Liang, Confucianism could be categorized as this-worldly and Buddhism as other-worldly. This kind of thinking seemed to have had a significant influence on the reasons for Liang's apparent turn to Confucianism around 1921. For example, a world-and-life-affirming philosophy such as Confucianism would, by its very nature, tend to be more directed at relieving suffering in society (that is to say, in serving society or engaging in social activism). A world-and-life-negating philosophy such as Buddhism, on the contrary, would tend to be less so. This is the reason Liang gives for apparently "turning" to Confucianism. He began to feel that—although he claims he still remained Buddhist in spirit—as an other-worldly religion, Buddhism was incompatible with the needs of the human world and life.

The problem this poses for us is how could Liang have become a Confucian while remaining a Buddhist in spirit. Liang appears to have resolved this by appealing to a particular kind of Confucianism; one that emphasized social action and involvement. This was the Confucianism of Wang Gen 王艮 (1483–1540). Liang had a profound admiration for Wang Gen because Wang had begun as a worker in the salt fields and the majority of people under his direction were laborers. According to Liang, Wang Gen was also a social activist who acted on his ideas. Feng Youlan also describes Wang Gen's life in terms of "concreteness and practicality."[28] For Liang, the real significance of Wang Gen's Confucianism was that it was compatible with the Bodhisattva spirit of world salvation in Mahāyāna Buddhism. Can we conclude that Liang engaged in social activism under the name of Confucianism but in the Bodhisattva spirit of Mahāyāna Buddhism? As in most of his comments on Buddhism and Confucianism, Liang is giving us seemingly confusing and mixed messages. On the one hand, he claimed that whereas Confucian theory engaged with the world and with society Buddhist thinking did not. Consequently, he held that the latter was not of much use to society (yet, as we saw above, he approved of its negative attitude to life). On the other hand, he implied that the Bodhisattva ideal of Mahāyāna Buddhism, which he identified with and subscribed to, was the spur to his social activism. This, however, contradicts his statements describing Buddhism as a world-and-life-negating philosophy of renunciation and transcendence. There are times, however, when he attempts to resolve this problem by distinguishing between the Mahāyāna and Theravada (formerly known by the now discredited term Hīnayāna) traditions of Buddhism. For example, Liang believed that the Theravada tradition had been perceived in the past as embodying a selfish notion of looking solely to one's own abilities, while the Mahāyāna tradition wanted people to become involved in the world. For Liang, however, the Mahāyāna tradition's involvement with the practical world was an incomplete one. It was involvement without real involvement. That is to say, its goal was to enable all creatures to pass to the other shore.[29]

Because Liang's Buddhist metaphysics and epistemology are principally expounded in early works such as *Eastern and Western Cultures* (1922), it can be argued that these may not be truly representative of his later views. Evidence based on the writings of the late Liang does not, however, appear to support this. For example, in 1978, he wrote a short piece on Buddhism entitled "Fofa dayi 佛法大義" (The Main Ideas of Buddhism) that demonstrates a continuing interest in Buddhism. Also, in his last published work, *Renxin yu rensheng* (1984), he returns to a detailed analysis of the metaphysical and epistemological notions of the *Weishi* tradition. Furthermore, there is the evidence from his interviews that he supported his evaluations of the relative merits of Confucianism and Buddhism on the same metaphysical and epistemological grounds that he had expounded in his early years.

Liang's Metaphysics

In the previous section I have addressed the question of whether Liang considered himself to be a Buddhist rather than a Confucian, principally from the perspective of what Liang himself said or wrote about this matter. In this section and the next, I will look at this same question from the viewpoint of Liang's metaphysical and epistemological views. Do these reflect a fundamentally Buddhist perspective or a Confucian (either classical or Neo-Confucian) one? Did Liang find in Western and Chinese philosophy themes that corresponded to, and therefore reinforced his fundamentally *Weishi* beliefs, or was it the case that Liang found in Western and *Weishi* philosophy themes that buttressed a fundamentally Confucian philosophical perspective? I believe that the former is the case. For example, it is more probable that because Liang subscribed to the *Weishi* view that everything was in a state of continuous change, the more readily he focused on this same theme in the process philosophy of Bergson and in the *Book of Changes*. Again, it would seem that Liang found a parallel to the *Weishi* notion of *citta* (mind) and *cittamātra* (mind only) in Wang Yangming's philosophy of *xin* (mind) where nothing is external to the mind.

Liang divided thought into religion and philosophy. He further divided philosophy into metaphysics, epistemology, and (philosophy of) human life. All three are principally expounded in three books, *Yindu zhexue gailun* 印度哲學概論 (An Outline of Indian Philosophy), *Weishi shuyi*, and *Eastern and Western Cultures*. The fundamental Buddhist metaphysical and epistemological positions informing these three works are to be found in Xuanzang's *Cheng weishi lun*. Liang's metaphysics consists of his views on life (*shenghuo*, *shengming*), the universe (*yuzhou*), and the self (*wo*). His epistemology consists of his understanding of sensation, intellection or conceptualization, intuition, and the like, and the nature of scientific and ethical knowledge in general.

We can begin our discussion of the metaphysical dimension of Liang's philosophy by establishing the extent to which the notion of consciousness (*shi* 識) or the *ba shi*[30]—the eight forms of cognition or *parijñāna*—as understood in the *Weishi* tradition influenced, and was employed in, Liang's philosophical thought. In the forementioned works of Liang, the notion of *ba shi* is discussed extensively. That he still subscribed to this notion in his later years is evidenced by his explanation of it in reference to his Buddhist beliefs in his 1980 interview with Guy Alitto and his discussion of it in his last work, *Renxin yu rensheng*.[31] From a metaphysical or ontological perspective, what is relevant in this regard is the eighth, storehouse consciousness (*alaiye shi* 阿賴耶識; Skt. *ālaya-vijñāna*)[32] and the seventh, deliberative consciousness (*mona shi* 末那識; Skt. *manas*). I will address the other six categories of consciousness—the five senses and the sense center (*yishi* 意識; Skt. *manavijñāna*)—in the section on epistemology.[33] In the *Weishi* tradition, the storehouse consciousness is the basis, the ground or root of all things. It is the "store or totality of consciousness, both absolute and relative, impersonal in the whole, temporally personal or individual in its separated parts, always reproductive."[34] It may also be termed the absolute unconscious from which arises all consciousness.[35] The seventh, deliberative consciousness is best understood as the self-engendering and reality constituting consciousness. It is the "cause of all egoism and individualisation, i.e. of men and things."[36] The impersonal becomes personal in the deliberative consciousness. Thus, consciousness in general can be understood as both (1) an impersonal and absolute mind that as substratum, repository, or storehouse, is the basis of the perception of all that exists; and (2) a personal and individual mind that constitutes the world it inhabits.

Deliberative consciousness is the self-engendering and reality-constituting consciousness; the source of egoism and individualization. According to Liang, innate attachment to self is primarily manifested in the deliberative consciousness. Before we can understand what Liang means by this we need to look at his notion of the self, the "I" or ego (*wo*). This is based on the Buddhist doctrine of the "five aggregates" (*wu yun* 五蘊; Skt. *pañcaskandha*). As Liang explains, the five aggregates are the totality of body and mind and constitute life itself.[37] What Liang appears to mean by this is that the apparent self-dependent individual existence of the ego or personality is constituted by the phenomena comprising the five aggregates. There is no entity apart from them. Consequently, the belief in a real, self-dependent ego or personality is illusory. What we believe to be the "I" is merely a convenient linguistic term given to a composite of the five aggregates.[38] The illusionary notion of the ego is a consequence of the ongoing process of the five aggregates. On this basis, Liang further differentiates between two forms of self-attachment (briefly mentioned earlier). In his 1980 interview with Liang, Alitto asked him what he meant by self-attachment (*wo zhi* 我執; Skt. *ātmagrāha*). Liang replies that there are two forms or kinds of self-attachment. One is innate and the other a result of mental discrimination.[39] For Liang, in the first of these, attachment to self is attachment to life itself, whereas in the second, one is attached to self in the sense that one is opposed to attachment to someone or something else; the self and other are distinct and separate.[40] Liang also mentions two attachments in the sense of attachment to self and attachment to things.[41] He then appropriates and employs three notions of attachment from *Weishi*: attachment to things and two forms of attachment to self—innate and discriminatory.

Liang believed that the distinction between Confucianism and Buddhism lay in their respective attitudes to the question of the ego, self or "I" (*wo*) (which is, of course, related to their respective life-affirming and life-negating attitudes). According to Liang, this question had had its clearest exposition and analysis in the *Weishi* School. Liang argued that innate self-attachment is deep and hidden whereas self-attachment through mental discrimination is shallow. Because the former is deep it is also more powerful. It is, in fact, the basis of human life (*shenghuo*). It is also obvious that self-attachment through mental discrimination is not always active in human life. For example, when someone is in a state of deep sleep and not dreaming it seems that the cerebrum is inactive. At this time, self-attachment through mental discrimination is not apparent yet innate self-attachment is still functioning. Another example that Liang gives is of someone who has suffered a serious injury and is close to death. At this time there is no self-attachment through mental discrimination yet innate self-attachment persists. According to Liang, the difference between Confucianism and Buddhism with regard to attachment is that the latter wishes to eradicate thoroughly the two attachments to self and the attachment to things. Buddhism believes that differentiation is wrong and it seeks to restore the original non-differentiation or integrity. Confucianism, on the other hand, Liang points out, is inseparable from the idea of self. Yet, as he explains, this is only in terms of innate self-attachment and not attachment to self through mental discrimination. Confucianism holds that the former is required in order to live a meaningful life.[42] Consequently, Liang considers that neither Confucius nor Confucianism sought to eliminate innate self-attachment. Confucianism acts in the human world and does not separate itself from life, from people's primal needs for shelter, sustenance, and sex. In order to explain this fundamental difference between Confucianism and Buddhism, Liang gave the following dramatic example. If someone took a knife and cut Liang's body, Liang would feel pain. If someone were to cut Confucius' body, Confucius would similarly feel pain. If, however, someone were to take a knife and cut the Buddha's body, the Buddha would not feel pain.[43] The Buddha would not feel pain because he had eliminated innate attachment to life whereas the former two had not.[44] Nonetheless, when Liang claims that Confucianism seeks to eradicate self-attachment through mental discrimination he seems to understand this more in terms of its opposition to individualism and egoism rather than in a more strict metaphysical sense.

Liang also conflates the self or individual with the universe and life. These are identified as one essence: *weishi* (Consciousness-Only). To understand how Liang justified this, two explanations of his understanding of the notion of life are required. Liang defines life as both an unending quest for the satisfaction of desire, as well as the continuous succession of things; a thesis taken from *Weishi* Buddhism. In the latter notion, things (*shi* 事) are comprised of problems/questions/demands (*wen*) and solutions/answers/responses (*da*). The individual constitutes things by endlessly posing and resolving problems, and for the individual this continuous posing and resolving of problems, prompted by desire, is both a self-engendering and reality-constituting process. Guy Alitto describes this notion as one wherein Liang posits "an *anima mundi* comparable to Schopenhauer's concept of Will; all life was an expression of this blind force. The struggle between the individual embodiments of the Will (*ta-i-yü*) and encountered obstacles to fulfillment constituted the life process." Moreover, the "spirit—or unfulfilled Will—makes demands on the environment and overcomes the environment's obstacles to fulfillment in a continuous interaction between demand and response. The life process becomes an unending sequence of problems presented to individual expression of the Will."[45] To underpin this process Liang employs the three divisions of the eighth consciousness (*alaiye shi* 阿賴耶識): (1) the self-verifying aspect (*zi zheng fen* 自證分; Skt. *svasamvittibhaga*); (2) the perceiving aspect (*jian fen* 見分; Skt. *darśanabhaga*); and (3) the perceived aspect (*xiang fen* 相分; Skt. *nimittabhaga*). As he points out, in the *Weishi* tradition, the life-constituting process of question and response is called perceiving (*jian fen*) and being perceived (*xiang fen*). Things (*shi*) are constituted in a process of interaction between the subject or perceiver and the object or perceived. The driving force of the whole process is people's demands and desires.

Liang further describes this struggle as one between the present self and the former or prior self.[46] Life is the transcending of the prior self by the present self. The present self is active; the prior self is passive and presents an obstacle to the former. Struggle, therefore, is overcoming, striving and coping with difficulties, and resolving problems.[47] For Liang, there are three types of obstacles that people encounter when they seek to satisfy their desires. The first is the prior self—the material world. Success in achieving one's desires, in this instance, depends on the stage of development of knowledge. For example, if one wanted to fly, this would be possible only after the invention of the hot air balloon or aeroplane. The second of Liang's obstacles are people. Other minds often disagree with one's intentions and prevent their realization. Because this is completely outside the scope of a person's universe, there is no way one can control the satisfaction or frustration of one's desires. The example Liang gives is that of someone wanting another person not to hate them. If they put their case sincerely there will obviously be times when the other person has a change of heart. At other times, however, no matter how they put their case the other person will still hate them, or they will merely *say* they do not. Whereas in the first type of obstacle the stage of development of knowledge is the critical factor, in the second it is the fact that a person cannot subdue or control another person's mind that is the important factor. Liang's third type of obstacle are all those things that are absolutely unrealizable, such as individual immortality, flowers that do not wither, and so on.[48]

Liang integrated his metaphysical view of life and the self with his notion of the three stages or paths of cultural development. As I mentioned earlier, Liang maintained that the directions of Western, Chinese, and Indian culture were different. This was principally determined by their differing attitudes to life and resolution of issues. According to Liang, Western culture resolved the issue of the relation between people and things; Chinese culture resolved the issue of the relationship between people; and Indian culture resolved the issue of the relationship between people and their own selves. Consequently, the obstacle that confronted Western culture was the natural world; the obstacle that faced Chinese culture was other minds; and the obstacle that Indian culture tackled was the life (*shengming*) of the self (*ziwo*).[49]

Liang's Epistemology

In the previous section, I explained that the *Weishi* tradition divides consciousness into eight categories; two of these—the deliberative (*mona*) and the storehouse (*alaiye*)—have already been discussed in the brief account of Liang's metaphysics. For Liang, the first six consciousnesses deal with the external world and in doing so constitute life.[50] The first five categories of consciousness are: visual, auditory, olfactory, gustatory, and tactile. Each of these senses has its own sphere (*jing* 境) of objects. The sixth category of consciousness—discrimination or conceptualization (*yishi* 意識; Skt. *manovijñāna*)—takes the world as a whole as its object and is responsible for the formation of concepts. It is also responsible for taking the sphere of objects of the senses and erroneously creating the notion of externality.[51] These first six categories of consciousness have the external world as their object. This is not so in the case of the seventh category of consciousness (*mona shi*), which has as its object the eighth category, storehouse consciousness (*alaiye shi*).[52] In addition to the first six categories of consciousness, Liang also utilizes the three modes of cognition (*liang* 量; Skt. *pramāna*): (1) direct perception (*xianliang* 現量; Skt. *pratyakṣa*),[53] which is the *im*mediate apprehension of color, shape, sound, and so on; (2) intellection or reasoning (*biliang* 比量; Skt. *anumāna*); and (3) fallacy (*feiliang* 非量; Skt. *ābhāsa*).[54]

In *Eastern and Western Cultures*, Liang uses the English word "sensation"[55] to describe the *Weishi* notion of *xianliang*. It is, he says, the flavor of the tea we taste and the white of the cotton tablecloth we look at.[56] When experiencing sensations, however, we do not "know" (*xiaode*) what taste and color are; we have only the sensations of tea and white but not the significance or meaning (*yiyi*) of tea and white.[57] Therefore, the function of *xianliang* is simply sensation. As An Yangming describes it, "What *xian-liang* perceives is not an integrated sense of 'tea,' but rather some individual sense-datum. . . ."[58] In addition to employing the concepts of sensation, intellection, and intuition to distinguish between the respective functions of *xianliang*, *biliang*, and *feiliang*, Liang also utilizes the concepts of image (*yingxiang* 影像), substance (*benzhi* 本質), and sphere (*jing* 境). He uses the concept of image rather broadly. In connection with *xianliang* it represents sensation (e.g., white); in connection with *biliang* it represents a concept (e.g., a painting); and in connection with *feiliang* it represents intuition[59] (e.g., the beauty of a particular painting). The sphere of *xianliang* is *xingjing* 性境. The characteristic of this particular sphere is that it is comprised of both image and substance, the former corresponding to the latter.[60] For example, when one looks at the whiteness of cotton, whiteness is the image, while the cotton is the substance. In this sphere there is both image and substance because in sensation there cannot be an image of white if there is no white substance. Consequently, both must be present in *xianliang*.

If the function of *xianliang* is to deal with sensations, then, for Liang, the principal function of *biliang* is intellection.[61] It is, he says, "what today we call intellect (*lizhi* 理智)." Intellection is probably the best translation of Liang's notion of *biliang* if we understand by this term the exercise or activity of the intellect, or the faculty of knowing and reasoning. For example, he says that our knowledge (*zhishi*) of tea is constructed through a process wherein we see and drink tea a number of times and in doing so distinguish it from other liquids that are not tea, such as water, soup, oil, alcohol, and the like. We also note the significance of what the many kinds of teas we see and drink—such as black tea, green tea, and so on—have in common. At this time we have a most distinct, clear, and definitive concept (*gainian*) of tea. Liang goes on to explain that significance or meaning (*yiyi*) is what is termed as synthesized or integrated parts (*gongxiang* 共相; Skt. *sāmānya lakṣaṇa*) in *Weishi*. Here we can see that in the process of intellection "sense-data" become synthesized or integrated into concepts. The whole process of conceptualization is one of distinction and synthesis, abstraction and generalization.[62] The sphere of intellection is *du yingjing* 獨影境 (the sphere of image alone). As its name indicates, the characteristic of this sphere is that there is an image but no substance. Intellection produces an abstract concept, or significance (*yiyi*), through a process of distinguishing and synthesizing various kinds of sensations, without adding or taking away anything.[63]

In *Eastern and Western Cultures*, Liang does not understand *feiliang* in the sense of fallacy or illusion but rather as intuition (*zhijue* 直覺). He describes the function of *feiliang* as follows. Between the sensations of direct perception (*xianliang*) and the abstract concepts of intellection (*biliang*) there must be a stage of "intuition" (*zhijue*). This stage gives meaning to the sensational and conceptual levels of consciousness. Intuition encompasses three qualities that direct perception and intellection do not. These are *yiwei* (meaning or significance),[64] *jingshen* (spirit or essence), and *qushi* (tendency).[65] The sphere of intuition is *dai zhijing* 帶質境 (the sphere that carries substance). The characteristic of this sphere is that it has image and substance but the image does not correspond to the substance. As Liang explains: "In fact, there is no such thing as subtlety in sound itself; there is no such thing as beauty in painting itself; and there is no such thing as deliciousness in sugar itself. All of these significances (*yiwei*—subtlety, beauty, and deliciousness—are added by human intuition (*zhijue*). Thus, *zhijue* is *feiliang*."[66] According to Liang, as noted earlier, with direct perception the subject has to be in the presence of the substance (cotton) in order to receive the image (sensation of white). With intellection the image (concept of tea) can be present for the subject without the substance (the tea). With intuition the subject is in the presence of the substance (the sound, painting, or sugar) but this is not responsible for the image (intuition of subtlety, beauty, or deliciousness).

"Significance (*yiwei*)" and "intuition" have a more essential function in human cognition than merely giving subtlety to sound. Liang notes that when we normally appraise the calligraphy and painting of an eminent person, this is not simply dependent on a number of black strokes and different colors that sensations intuitively cognize. It is through intuition that we are able to become aware of the significance of the beauty and spirit of these artistic works. Moreover, significance is not the same as blank sensations and fixed concepts.[67] Here, Liang is arguing that it is significance and intuition rather than sensations and concepts that give us the illusion of movement in the world. He maintains that when we see a flying object we do not see flight. Flight is merely a kind of significance and tendency; it is not a specific thing. Direct perception has no way of cognizing flight because it can only see the image of a bird or a flag. These images are only photographs or frames. Intuition is needed to link the frames. Liang believes that, in principle, flight is like a motion picture: an illusion similar to that produced by rapidly moving through a sequence of frames. Liang considers that a bird does not fly because it exists as a succession of instants in time.[68]

In *Eastern and Western Cultures*, Liang also uses the notions of intuition and intellect (*lizhi*) to distinguish between Chinese and Western cultures. The former, he argues, is the basis of Chinese culture and the latter that of Western culture.[69] The focus of intellect is the natural world and it leads to utilitarian values and especially to an individualistic concern with one's material circumstances. The focus of intuition, by contrast, is the inner world of the spirit. It transcends utilitarianism in that it is not concerned with disputes over advantage and disadvantage. It sets great store on feelings and de-emphasizes the importance of the self. For Liang, the fact that the West takes intellect as its standard for human relations leads to a situation of indifference and ruthlessness in interpersonal dealings. Because the Chinese take intuition—which focuses on feeling (*qinggan*)—as its principle for dealing with human relations, people relate to each other in a harmonious fashion.[70]

We can see from the above that in Liang's epistemology, as it appears in *Eastern and Western Cultures*, the notions of *xianliang, biliang*, and *feiliang* are expounded alongside those of *lizhi* and *zhijue*. What this indicates is that in the subsequent development of Liang's epistemology there is a change in terminology, and a coalescence and expansion of the meaning of others. For example, *zhijue* becomes the exclusive word for intuition and *feiliang* is more or less discarded in this capacity. Then *zhijue* itself is discarded in favor of *lixing* 理性 (hereafter to be understood as *ethical* reason).[71] *Biliang*, with its fundamental meaning of intellection, reasoning, or conceptualization, coalesces with and becomes *lizhi*. About the time he wrote *Xiangcun jianshe lilun* 鄉村建設理論 (Theory of Rural Reconstruction; 1937), Liang replaces *zhijue* with *lixing*, making it the dominant philosophical concept in that book and in *Zhongguo wenhua yaoyi* 中國文化要義 (The Essence of Chinese Culture; 1949). In *Xiangcun jianshe lilun* Liang maintains that there are two kinds of rationalism (*lixingzhuyi* 理性主義). The first he terms French rationalism (*lixingzhuyi*): it is a sober, analytical rationality. The second he calls Chinese rationality (*lixingzhuyi*): it is calm and endowed with feeling.[72] These two rationalisms are based on two understandings of *li* (reason or principle). The first is the *li* 理 of the intellect (*lizhi*) and can be categorized as objective reason (*shili* 事理). It is the *li* of knowledge (*zhishi*) and is concerned with cognitive reason. It is related to science, physics (*wuli*), and logic. The second is the *li* of *lixing* 理性 (ethical reason). It is related to subjective reason or the principle of feelings (*qingli*). It is the *li* of conduct and morality that is concerned with feelings (*qing, qinggan*), and human goodness and wickedness. Liang also points out that *lixing* can be looked at in two ways: from the perspective of friendly sentiments—for example, a father's kindness and a son's filiality; and from the perspective of ethical self-improvement.[73] The former specifies that *lixing* has its beginnings in the ethical ties of friendship that stress the importance of each of the parties. The latter indicates the moral spirit of self-cultivation and yielding to others.[74]

In *Eastern and Western Cultures*, Liang used *zhijue* and *lizhi* to distinguish between Chinese and Western cultures. In *Zhongguo wenhua yaoyi*, this pair becomes *lixing* and *lizhi*. According to Liang, the difference in people's attitude to life is due to the different bases of their cultures.[75] The first attitude is one that directs force or power outwards. It originates in a *lizhi* that encompasses science, knowledge (*zhishi*), calculation, and logic. This is the basis of Western culture. The second attitude is one that directs force or power inwards. It originates in a *lixing* that involves morality, conduct, feelings, and good and evil. The former can be simply termed a corporeal (*shen* 身) culture and the latter a spiritual (*xin* 心) culture. Liang points out that the corporeal should precede the spiritual, the ethical epistemology and culture of the Chinese people ripened or flourished prematurely.[76] Finally, in *Renxin yu rensheng*, he discusses *lixing* and *lizhi* in terms of *ren xin* (the human mind). The highest form of life is the activity of human consciousness. Human consciousness is also *ren xin* 人心 (human mind). Included in *ren xin* are *lizhi* and *lixing*. The *lizhi* of *ren xin* is scientific knowledge. It soberly analyzes the exterior world and seeks to satisfy people's material desires and demands; it is also the value that ensures the continuation of human life. Nonetheless, it merely functions as a tool and is, therefore, according to Chinese thinking, *yong* (utility). *Lixing* on the other hand, is the substance (*ti*) of *ren xin*. In the human mind, *lizhi* is merely wisdom (*zhi*) whereas *lixing* is feelings (*qing*) and *yi* (meaning or intention).[77]

I have maintained that it is probable that Liang approached Confucianism from a metaphysical and epistemological *Weishi* position. His lecture notes on Confucius and Mencius further support this interpretation. In these notes, he reiterates and clarifies the *Weishi* epistemology he expounded in *Eastern and Western Cultures* and uses it to interpret Confucianism (that is, the thought of Confucius and Mencius). These lecture notes are also important as they enable us to trace: (1) the ongoing transition in Liang's epistemology from a purely rational focus to one which is just as explicitly ethical; and (2) the application of this epistemology to the interpretation of Confucius' and Mencius' ethical epistemologies. In the section on *ren* (humaneness) in *Liang Shuming Discusses Confucius and Mencius*, Liang divides knowledge (*zhi*) into three kinds with different functions. (1) The realm of corporeality: that which sensational knowledge (*ganjue*) knows (*zhi*) is substance (*shiti*), or what in *Weishi* is called *se jing* 色境 (world of visible forms). (2) Knowledge (*zhi*) as thinking, and judgment (*siwei, panduan*) as inference (*tuili*). Liang explains this as follows. If someone knows the meaning (*yiyi*) of black when she is not in the immediate presence of black, then sees something black and judges (*pan*) it to be black, then this knowledge is a concept (*gainian*). In *Weishi* this is known as *gongxiang*. The meaning (*yiyi*) of black is that which black has in common that distinguishes it from other colors. Knowledge as thinking means I know the meaning of, or have the concept of, black. Judgment as inference (a classical Buddhist epistemological category) is being able to say this is black. We are able to make inferences because we have concepts. (3) Knowledge (*zhi*) as intuition: knowing something without having to think about it. This is also knowledge of good and evil and although it appears to arise out of knowledge as thinking and inferring, it is to know something without having to think about it.

In (2), Liang's description of the process of intellection (*biliang*; although he does not use this term)[78] as the second of his three stages or modes of knowledge is much closer to the Buddhist understanding than the one he gave in *Eastern and Western Cultures*. More interesting is his definition of intuition in (3). He has developed its meaning from purely intuiting *yiwei* (meaning), *jingshen* (spirit), and *qushi* (tendency), to knowing something without thinking about it. Of equal significance is his description of intuition as knowledge that is innate, knowledge of good and evil, and knowledge that is not only a kind of *yiwei* (meaning, significance) but a kind of *qingwei* (emotional overtone). In *Eastern and Western Cultures*, Liang included *qushi* and *qingxiang* (tendency) within intuition; in his lecture notes tendency has become orientation (*fangxiang*

方向). For instance, there are foul smells and pleasant colors. When we see flowers we feel like approaching them. When we see ordure we avoid it. This is orientation, and for Liang it is absolute because our reaction is *im*mediate and not one where we consider how we should react.

From the above we can see that in Liang's lecture notes, the notion of *zhijue* has acquired additional meaning. It is innate (*xiantian*), concerned with good and evil as well as the significance of (human) feelings, emotions, and sentiments (*qingwei*), and it is an absolute, direct, or *im*mediate non-deliberated reaction in terms of inclination or disinclination (*fangxiang*). In support of his notion of *fangxiang* Liang turns to Mencius' remark that "All palates have the same preferences in taste. . . . Is mind an exception to this?"[79] For Liang, Mencius is talking about intuition. Liang observes that when we say, for example, I feel like this, you feel like this, and he feels like this we are referring to Mencius' notion of the sameness of minds. Liang then relates this to his critical distinction between rationality in terms of subjective feelings and objective facts. He argues that the *li* (reason or principle) of *fangxiang* indicated in intuition is subjective *qingli* (principle of feelings) and not objective *shili* (principle of things). Whether the *li* of objective facts is correct awaits proof but whether subjective *qingli* is correct does not depend on proof.[80] Earlier, I noted that Liang maintained that knowledge as intuition is knowing something without having to think about it. The similarity to Mencius' claim that knowledge as *liang zhi* 良知 (innate, intuitive, sense of the ethical) is knowledge that we do not have to think about[81] is obvious. In *Eastern and Western Cultures*, Liang directly equated these when he wrote that today we should refer to Mencius' *liang zhi* and *liang neng* 良能 (intuitive ability) as intuition.[82] He also equated intuition with *ren* (humaneness).[83] The concept of ethical reason (*lixing*) subsequently inherited this absorption of the Confucian concepts of *liang zhi*, *ren* 仁, and the like into intuition.[84]

Some Concluding Remarks

It seems odd that Liang Shuming—who throughout his life extolled the superiority of Buddhism—should have become known in the West as the "last Confucian" and in China as the founder of New Confucianism, in the sense that it all began with him. The evidence that Liang was a Buddhist throughout his life and that he believed it superior to Confucianism in a number of aspects, appears to me to be overwhelming. I am giving more weight to Liang's claims that he was Buddhist all his life (not taking into account his first youthful brush with pragmatism) than I am to his reference to passing from a Buddhist to a Confucian stage for the following reasons. When in 1985 the reporter from *Guoxue jikan* remarked that Liang's philosophy was centered on Confucian ethical theory, Liang emphatically denied this saying that he had *always* been a Buddhist in his *thinking*. He told Guy Alitto in the 1980s that in the previous twenty years or so Buddhism had more significance in his life than Confucianism. In June 1958, he said that his theory of life was fundamentally a Buddhist one. In *Eastern and Western Cultures* he said that only his *life style* was Confucian not his *thinking*. Even his Confucianism was in the Bodhisattva mold of Mahāyāna Buddhism. Add to this his metaphysics and epistemology, which appear to me to be *Weishi* based, determined, or informed, then the evidence is fairly strong that he was never an *authentic* Confucian. He only acknowledged that Chinese culture (Confucian) was the exemplar of the second stage of cultural development not the final and third stage to which he spiritually subscribed.

In terms of the realization of a cultural ideal, he distinguished between Western, Chinese, and Indian cultures and philosophies on the basis of how close they were to achieving this ideal. (I am equating cultural ideals with the respective attitudes of the three traditions [West, China, and India] that Liang identifies.) According to Liang, these cultural ideals are reflected in their respective philosophies. There are three attitudes or directions a culture and its corresponding philosophy (metaphysics/ ontology/philosophy of life, epistemology, and ethics) could take. It could focus on resolving the problems the natural world presented; it could concentrate its attention on the issues raised by the relation between people; or it could give its primary attention to the question of the "self." Liang believed that the first of these was the most basic and the third the most advanced. The second was an intermediate position between the first and second. Consequently, in Liang's view, Indian culture and philosophy was the most advanced and Western culture and philosophy was the least advanced. This was also the order that Liang prescribed for the development of a culture or civilization. In practice, however, it did not always work out in this way. A culture or civilization could be premature. One reason for this was the presence of outstanding creative geniuses such as Confucius and Sakyamuni. Liang also maintained that a culture was not the reflection in ideology of a specific economic form or political system but the "will" present in the spirit of a people. There can be little doubt, then, that Liang believed China's ultimate future lay in the realization of a Buddhist, rather than a Confucian, cultural ideal.

Not only did Liang believe that Buddhism was superior to Confucianism as a cultural ideal, he also maintained that, despite what people believed or said, he had always been a Buddhist. For example, in the preface to his *Eastern and Western Cultures*, Liang pointed out that he had substituted a Confucian way of life for a Buddhist one but not a Confucian way of thinking for a Buddhist one. In other words, he was committed to the view that the Buddhist way of life was correct. In his speech at the Chinese People's Political Consultative Conference in June 1958, Liang stressed that his theory of human life was fundamentally a Buddhist one of transcending the world. By this stage Liang had apparently substituted Marxism for Confucianism as the appropriate path and way of life for the Chinese nation. But whether it was Marxism or Confucianism the message was the same—his thinking was Buddhist. It seems that as Liang got older he wished, or attempted, to bring his way of life into closer conformity with his way of thinking. For example, in 1980 he told Alitto that Buddhism had been a more significant factor in his life over the last twenty or so years than had Confucianism. In the same interview, Liang remarked that he was still empowered by Buddhism and in saying so he indicated that it had all along been the primary motivating factor in his life. He even went on to say that he "loved" (*ai*) Buddhism. Again, in 1985, Liang corrected his interviewer's assumption that his philosophy was centered on Confucian ethical theory by emphatically stating that on the contrary he had always been a Buddhist in his thinking and this had not changed. There had merely been a change in his life and lifestyle. Furthermore, he was still of the opinion that the culture of the world would find its way back to Buddhism. It is clear from this that throughout his life Liang emphasized that whatever lifestyle he adopted, or thought appropriate for the times (e.g., Confucianism, Marxism), his thinking and ultimate cultural ideal (the realization of the final stage) remained Buddhist. In the final decade of his life it is clear that not only did he wish to hold a Buddhist spirit and lead a Buddhist life but he believed that he fell short of this goal. The only reason we can give for Liang's "turn" to Confucianism and Marxism (in lifestyle but not in thought) is that he considered that they were, respectively, more appropriate vehicles for expressing a social concern ultimately grounded in his Buddhist beliefs. We should remember that, in his own words, it was his profound distress at human suffering that initially attracted him to Buddhism. Liang would have been acutely aware that the goal of Buddhism was the cessation of suffering through the extinction (*nirvāṇa*) of life as attachment to self.

Although Liang's philosophy is complex, I do not consider it to be eclectic. His early and fundamental philosophical themes and theses were retained throughout his life and if we are to understand change in Liang's thought then it must be in terms of thematic development and terminological change rather than outright rejection. Liang's metaphysics and epistemology are predominantly *Weishi*. There is no essential change in these as they were expounded in works such as *Yindu zhexue gailun* (An Outline of Indian Philosophy), *Weishi shuyi*, and *Eastern and Western Cultures*, as they were later described to such people as Guy Alitto and Wang Zongyu, and as they were expressed in later works such as *Renxin yu rensheng*. I also consider that Liang focused on particular Confucian themes principally from the perspective of their relevance to his overall *Weishi* metaphysical and epistemological positions. For instance, his concept of "intuition" developed over the years from the *Weishi* notion of *feiliang*, through the Bergsonian concept of intuition, the incorporation of the Confucian notions of *ren* (benevolence), *liang zhi* (innate, intuitive, sense of the ethical), *liang xin* (innate ethical nature), to *lixing* (intuition as ethical reason).

As this study has shown, Liang's *Weishi* metaphysics and epistemology were connected with his views on culture and society as he consistently utilized them to rationalize the various distinctions he made between cultures of the West, China, and India. For example, Liang believed that the distinction between Confucianism and Buddhism was based on their respective understandings of the "I," ego or self. Basing this claim on the distinction between attachment to self through mental discrimination and innate self-attachment, Liang argued that Buddhism wished to eradicate thoroughly both forms of attachment to self. Confucianism, however, wished only to eradicate the former and not the latter. According to Liang, this was because Confucianism acted in the human world and did not separate itself from life, from people's primal needs for shelter, sustenance, and sex. Liang also utilized his metaphysics to rationalize his theory of the three stages of cultural development. For example, according to Liang, the different directions that Western, Chinese, and Indian culture took were determined by their attitudes to life and the different ways they resolved problems in terms of the particular obstacles each faced. Western culture focused on the resolution of the problem between people and things where the specific obstacle confronting people was the natural world; Chinese culture focused on the problem of the relationship between people where the specific obstacle confronting them was other minds; and Indian culture focused on the problem of the relationship between people and their own selves where the specific obstacle confronting them was the life of the self.

Liang also utilized his epistemological-ethical notions of intellect (*lizhi*) and ethical reason (*lixing*) to rationalize his theory of the three stages of cultural development. In *Eastern and Western Cultures*, Liang discusses five principal epistemological notions: direct perception (*xianliang*), intellection (*biliang*), intuition (*feiliang*), intuition (*zhijue*), and intellect (*lizhi*). In the subsequent development of his epistemology these undergo some changes. *Zhijue* replaces *feiliang* as the exclusive term for intuition; *zhijue* is then replaced by *lixing*; and the meaning of *biliang* is absorbed into *lizhi*. In *Eastern and Western Cultures*, Liang also employs two forms of the notion of "intuition." The first is the ethical *zhijue* opposed to the rational *lizhi*; it is subsequently renamed *lixing*. The second is the *zhijue* that Liang equates with *feiliang* opposed to the sensational and intellection functions of *xianliang* and *biliang*. This is not an ethical notion but an epistemological one that gives meaning (*yiwei*) to the object (*xiangfen*). It is the former that Liang goes on to develop in his later writings. In *Eastern and Western Cultures*, Liang uses *zhijue* in this ethical sense in contrast with *lizhi* to distinguish Chinese and Western cultures. The Chinese employ *zhijue*, which focuses on the inner world of the spirit and privileges feelings; this leads to harmony in human relations. The West, on the other hand, employs *lizhi*, which focuses on the natural world and leads to utilitarian values and individualism, not to mention indifference and ruthlessness in human relations. In *Zhongguo wenhua yaoyi*, *zhijue* becomes *lixing* while the term *lizhi* is retained. In this case *lixing* and *lizhi* serve to distinguish Chinese and Western cultures, respectively, as opposing attitudes. The first attitude directs energy inwards and originates in the *lixing* concerned with morality, conduct, feelings, and the issue of good and evil. The second attitude directs energy outwards and originates in the *lizhi* concerned with science, knowledge, calculation, and logic.[85]

In conclusion, I suggest that however we choose to view Liang's philosophy, its tremendous impact on contemporary Chinese thought can hardly be denied. For example, in China in the 1950s it was perceived as both a rival and threat to Marxist philosophy itself. That it was taken seriously was evidenced by a nationwide campaign against Liang (from January to December 1955) that called on the services of such prominent Chinese Marxist philosophers as Ai Siqi and Wang Ruoshui[86] and the lesser known Jin Yuelin. These critics accused him of, among other things, intuitionism, subjective idealism, and solipsism. On the evidence of what these critics considered were his essential metaphysical and epistemological positions there can be little doubt that they deemed them fundamentally Buddhist, rather than Confucian, in nature. I consider that they were correct in this regard. The testimony of Liang's writings, lectures, and interviews points to the strong probability that he developed his fundamentally Yogācārin metaphysical and epistemological positions with the aid of Bergson's and Schopenhauer's philosophies, while at the same time looking for corresponding themes in Confucianism to support his position.

Notes

1. Liang Shuming, "Jintian women yingdang ruhe pingjia Kongzi 今天我們應當如何評價孔子?" (How Should we Evaluate Confucius Today?), in Li Yuanting 李淵庭 (comp.), *Liang Shuming jiang Kong Meng* 梁漱溟講孔孟 (Liang Shuming Discusses Confucius and Mencius), Beijing: Zhongguo heping chubanshe, 1993, 199.
2. Cao Yueming 曹躍明, *Liang Shuming sixiang yanjiu* 梁漱溟思想研究 (An Investigation of Liang Shuming's Thought), Tianjin: Tianjin renmin chubanshe, 1995, 368.
3. See, for example, Li Yaoxian 李耀仙, "Xiandai xin Ruxue fazhan de xin jieduan ji qi wenti 現代新儒學發展的新階段及其問題" (The New Stage of Development in New Confucianism and Its Problems), in *Zhongguo zhihui touxi* 中國智慧透析 (A Penetrating Analysis of Chinese Wisdom), Beijing: Huaxia chubanshe, 1995, 425; and Zhu Yilu 朱義祿, "Liang Shuming," in Fang Keli 方克立 and Zheng Jiadong 鄭家棟 (eds.), *Xiandai xin Rujia renwu yu zhuzuo* 現代新儒家人物與著作 (New Confucianism—People and Works), Tianjin: Nankai daxue chubanshe, 1995, 3. Zheng Dahua 鄭大華 calls Liang the forerunner or pioneer of New Confucianism. See his "Liang Shuming yu xiandai xin Ruxue 梁漱溟與現代新儒學" (Liang Shuming and New Confucianism), in Fang Keli and Li Jinquan (eds.), *Xiandai xin Ruxue yanjiu lunji* 現代新儒學研究論集, vol. 2, Beijing: Zhongguo shehui kexue chubanshe, 1991, 58.
4. Li Daoxiang, *Xiandai xin Ruxue yu Song Ming lixue* 現代新儒學與宋明理學 (New Confucianism and Song-Ming Neo-Confucianism), Shengyang: Liaoning chubanshe, 1998, 86.
5. See, for example, Yan Binggang 顏炳罡, *Dangdai xin Ruxue yinlun* 當代新儒學引論 (Introduction to New Confucianism), Beijing: Beijing tushuguan, 1998, 147.
6. Feng Zhaoji and Bai Ji'an, "Liang Shuming Fo Ru sixiang tansuo 梁漱溟佛儒思想探索" (An Exploration of the Buddhist–Confucian Thought of Liang Shuming), *Journal of Oriental Studies* XXXIV, 2(1999): 273–92.
7. Yan Binggang, *Dangdai xin Ruxue yinlun*, 128–31.
8. Cao Yueming, *Liang Shuming sixiang yanjiu*, 244.

9. Liang Shuming, *Dong-xi wenhua ji qi zhexue* (Eastern and Western Cultures and Their Philosophies) in *Liang Shuming quanji* 梁漱溟全集, vol. 1, Shandong: Shandong remin chubanshe, 1994, 397.
10. Liang Shuming, *Weishi shuyi*, in *Liang Shuming quanji*, vol. 1, 278.
11. On Kui Ji, also known as Dasheng Ji 大乘基, see Stanley Weinstein, "A Biographical Study of Tz'u-ên," *Monumenta Serica* 15(1959–60): 130–4.
12. Wing-tsit Chan, *A Source Book in Chinese Philosophy*, Princeton: Princeton University Press, 1963, 370–4; O. Brière, *Fifty Years of Chinese Philosophy: 1898–1948*, New York: Praeger, 1965, 40. In recent years there have been several books and a number of articles published on Ouyang Jingwu and his group. For the latest, see Gabriele Goldfuss, *Vers un bouddhisme du XXe siècle, Yang Wenhui (1837–1911), réformateur laïque et imprimeur*, Paris: Collège de France, Institut des hautes études chinoises, 2001.
13. *Ibid.*, 373.
14. Dan Lusthaus, "A Brief Retrospective of Western Yogaacaara Scholarship in the 20th Century," paper presented at the 11th International Conference on Chinese Philosophy, Chengchi University, Taipei, July 26–31, 1999. Website version, cited with author's consent.
15. Yan Binggang, *Dangdai xin Ruxue yinlun*, 126.
16. Cao Yueming, *Liang Shuming sixiang yanjiu*, 23.
17. Liang Shuming, "Zishu 自述" (Self Account) in *Wo de nuli yu fanxing* 我的努力與反省 (Strivings and Reflections), n.p.: Lijiang chubanshe, 1987, 63. Discussed in Cao Yueming, *Liang Shuming sixiang yanjiu*, 23. Liang sums up his Buddhist "stage" at other times by stating that he resolved to follow Buddhism in his teens. He decided to become a vegetarian, give up any thoughts of marrying and leave his family to become a Buddhist monk. He kept to the practice of Buddhism until he was twenty-nine. Although he got married at around this time, he did not give up the "spirit" of Buddhism.
18. Cao Yueming, *Liang Shuming sixiang yanjiu*, 368.
19. Liang Shuming, *Dong-xi wenhua ji qi zhexue*, 543.
20. Quoted in Yan Binggang, *Dangdai xin Ruxue yinlun*, 127.
21. Liang Shuming, "Yu *Zuihou yige Rujia Liang Shuming yu xiandai Zhongguo de kunjing* zuozhe Ai Kai de tanhua 與最後一個儒家梁漱溟與現代中國的困境作者艾愷的談話" (A Chat with Guy Alitto the Author of *The Last Confucian: Liang Shuming and the Chinese Dilemma of Modernity*) in Liang Shuming, *Zhongguoren: Shehui yu rensheng. Liang Shuming wenxuan* 梁漱溟：社會與人生。梁漱溟文選 (Chinese People, Society and Life: Selected Papers of Liang Shuming), 805–7 (no publisher, place or date of publication given).
22. Guy Alitto, *Liang Shuming zhuan* 梁漱溟傳 (A Biography of Liang Shuming), Hunan: Hunan chubanshe, 1992, 384.
23. Liang Shuming, "Ru ye? Fo ye? 儒耶佛耶" (Confucian or Buddhist?), in Wang Shaojun 王邵軍 and Tu Maoqin 屠冒芹 (eds.), *Liang Shuming: Dongfang shengzhe* 梁漱溟：東方聖哲 (Liang Shuming: Eastern Sage), Beijing: Zhongguo qingnian chubanshe, 1994, 135–8. This article is based on Wang Zongyu 王宗昱, "Shi Rujia haishi Fojia? Fang Liang Shuming

xiansheng 是儒家還是佛家? 訪梁漱溟先生" (Confucian or Buddhist?
An Interview with Liang Shuming), *Zhongguo wenhua yu Zhongguo zhexue*
(December, 1986): 560–5.

24. Liang Shuming, "Ru Fo yitong lun 儒佛異同論" (On the Similarities and
Differences between Confucianism and Buddhism), in *Liang Shuming
quanji*, vol. 7, Shandong: Shandong remin chubanshe, 1993, 158.

25. Liang subsequently reflected on the emphasis on suffering in Buddhism
relative to Confucianism by observing that in the important Buddhist text,
the *Prajñā Sūtra of the Mind*, the term *le* (pleasures) does not occur once
while *ku* (suffering) appears three times. On the contrary, in the *Analects*,
le and *yue* (happiness) occur a number of times with no reference to *ku*
("Ru Fo yitong lun," 154).

26. "How was it that Buddhism, with its negation of the world and life, could
exercise such a force of attraction on the Chinese who . . . are devoted
to world-and-life-affirmation?" A. Schweitzer, *Indian Thought and its
Development*, London: Adam and Charles Black, 1951, 139.

27. Liang Shuming, "Ru ye? Fo ye?" 36.

28. Feng Youlan, *A History of Chinese Philosophy*, vol. 2, Princeton: Princeton
University Press, 1973, 628.

29. Liang Shuming, "Ru ye? Fo ye?" 136.

30. These eight consciousnesses can be further differentiated on the basis of
three "transformations." The first of these transformations corresponds to the
eighth consciousness (*alaiye shi*); the second transformation to the seventh or
deliberative consciousness (*mona shi*); and the third transformation to the
five senses plus the sixth or sense-center consciousness (*yi shi*). In the case of
the first transformation, "seeds" (the effects of past deeds) have the capacity
(they are endowed with the energy) to produce manifestations out of perception and conceptualization; these manifestations in turn "perfume"
(i.e., influence or affect) the seeds. The second transformation, that of the
seventh, deliberative consciousness (*mona shi*), is based on, and has as its
object, the storehouse or eighth consciousness (*alaiye shi*). It is the source
of egoism in that it erroneously believes in, and clings to, the notion of
the existence of a personal self. The third transformation, that of the five
senses in combination with the sense center (*yi shi*), involves a process
of differentiation and discrimination, out of which the external world
appears. See Wing-tsit Chan, *A Source Book in Chinese Philosophy*, 370–95;
and W. Soothill and L. Hodous (*A Dictionary of Chinese Buddhist Terms*),
London: Kegan Paul Trench, Trubner and Co., 1937. Reprinted by
Taipei: Ch'eng Wen Publishing Co., 1972, 40; Swati Ganguly, *Treatise in
Thirty Verses on Mere-Consciousness*, Delhi: Motilal Banarsidass Publishers
Private Limited, 1992; and Hsuan Tsang, *Cheng weishi lun* (Treatise on the
Establishment of the Doctrine of Consciousness-Only), Wei Tat (trans.),
Hong Kong: The Ch'eng Wei-Shih Lun Publication Committee, 1973. Wei
Tat's work is adapted from Louis de la Vallee Poussin, *Vijñāptimātratāsiddhi:
La Siddhi de Hiuan-Tsang*, 2 vols., Paris: Paul Geuthner, 1928–29.

31. Liang Shuming, "Yu *Zuihou yige Rujia Liang Shuming yu xiandai Zhongguo
de kunjing* zuozhe Ai Kai de tanhua," 805–7.

32. This is "the fundamental mind-consciousness of conscious things, which lays hold of all the experiences of the individual life; and which as storehouse holds the germs of all affairs; it is at the root of all experience . . . of all things on which sentient beings depend for existence." W. Soothill and L. Hodous, *A Dictionary of Chinese Buddhist Terms*, 292. As mind "it both stores and gives rise to all phenomena and knowledge. It is called original mind, because it is the root of all things; inexhaustible mind, because none of its seeds (or products) is lost; manifested mind, because all things are revealed in or by it; seeds mind, because from it springs all individuals, or particulars . . . it is the basis of all knowledge . . . it produces the rounds of mortality, good and evil karma, etc." (292). See also Lambert Schmithausen, *Ālayavijñāna: On the Origin and the Early Development of a Central Concept of Yogācāra Philosophy*, 2 vols., Studia philologica Buddhica Monograph series IV, Tokyo: The International Institute for Buddhist Studies, 1987.

33. Although all eight are consciousnesses, there are differences, as Liang points out in *Renxin yu rensheng*, Hong Kong: Joint Publishing, 1991, 202–3. The eighth consciousness is *xin* (the heart as the seat of intelligence); the seventh consciousness is *yi* (the thinking and calculating mind) and the first six consciousnesses are *shi* (senses). These correspond to *citta*, *manas* and *Vijñāna*, respectively. The first is the mind from which all things arise; the second deliberates or cogitates; and the third perceives and discriminates.

34. Soothill and Hodous, *A Dictionary of Chinese Buddhist Terms*, 292.

35. *Ibid.*

36. *Ibid.*, 40. On the one hand, it is clear that the seventh consciousness (*mona shi*) as the deliberative and second transformation of consciousness, creates the illusion of an individual, personal self, and in this sense is the self-engendering consciousness; on the other hand, it would seem that the five senses in combination with the sense center (*yi shi*), as the third transformation of consciousness, is the reality constituting consciousness in so much as it makes the world appear through a process of differentiation and discrimination (it has the world as its object rather than the storehouse consciousness). The assumption that the world as appearance is real and permanent is made by the seventh, deliberative consciousness (*mona shi*).

37. Liang Shuming, "Ru Fo yitong lun," 157–8.

38. It should also be noted that the five aggregates are not independent groups but interrelated. For example, whatever one senses one also perceives, and whatever one perceives one is also conscious of. The five aggregates and their interrelation in *Weishi* are: (1) Matter-form (*se* 色; Skt. *rūpa*). This includes *inter alia* the five material sense organs and their respective objects. For example, the seeing faculty of the eye, the olfactory faculty of the nose and their corresponding objects in the external world—visible form and odor, respectively. (2) Sensation (*shou* 受; Skt. *vedanā*). Sensations are experienced by contact between one of the five material sense organs and the external world. For example, the eye and nose are able to experience pleasant or unpleasant visual forms and odors, respectively. Because feelings are associated with this "aggregate," *vedanā* is sometimes

translated as "feeling." (3) Perception (*xiang* 想; Skt. *saṃjñā*). Perception is a discerning faculty that recognizes objects. (4) Volition (*xing* 行; Skt. *samskāra*). Volition directs the mind (and therefore incurs karmic effects). For example, the faculty of sight can be directed to observe what is detrimental to the individual. (5) Consciousness (*shi* 識; Skt. *vijñāna*). Consciousness is the awareness of the presence of an object. For example, visual and olfactory consciousness have the organs of the eye and the nose as their bases and visible form and odor as their objects, respectively. It should be kept in mind, however, that this is just part of what comprises the five aggregates. In matter-form, for example, there are an additional fourteen elements and phenomena. (From the perspective of Theravada Buddhism, see, e.g., Walpola Rahula, *What the Buddha Taught*, New York: Grove Press, 1974, 21–5; and Nyanatiloka, *Buddhist Dictionary*, Singapore: SBMC, 1991, 82–5.)

39. Liang Shuming, "Yu *Zuihou yige Rujia Liang Shuming yu xiandai Zhongguo de kunjing* zuozhe Ai Kai de Tanhua," 805–7.

40. Liang Shuming, "Ru ye? Fo ye?" 157–8. Here, Liang is espousing the classical Yogācārin position.

41. Liang Shuming, "Yu *Zuihou yige Rujia Liang Shuming yu xiandai Zhongguode kunjing* zuozhe Ai Kai de tanhua," 805–7.

42. *Ibid.*

43. *Ibid.*

44. In Li Yuanting (comp.), *Liang Shuming jiang Kong Meng*, 84–9, Liang also uses similar examples (e.g., a baby instead of a sleeping or injured person) to discuss the question of attachment to self. He also makes the same distinction between Confucianism and Buddhism on the basis of their attitude toward the two attachments to self.

45. Guy Alitto, *The Last Confucian: Liang Shu-ming and the Chinese Dilemma of Modernity*, Berkeley: University of California Press, 1979, 82–3.

46. Liang Shuming, *Dangdai xin Ruxue yinlun*, 378.

47. *Ibid.*; and Yan Binggang, *Dangdai xin Ruxue yinlun*, 130–1.

48. Liang Shuming, *Dong-xi wenhua ji qi zhexue*, 380.

49. Yan Binggang, *Dangdai xin Ruxue yinlun*, 142.

50. Liang Shuming, "Yu *Zuihou yige Rujia Liang Shuming yu xiandai Zhongguode kunjing* zuozhe Ai Kai de tanhua," 805–7.

51. Wing-tsit Chan, *A Source Book in Chinese Philosophy*, 390.

52. *Ibid.*, 371–2.

53. Soothill and Hodous, *A Dictionary of Chinese Buddhist Terms*, 359.

54. *Zhijue* (intuition) may be regarded as a development of *feiliang*, under the influence of Bergson's understanding of intuition.

55. Liang uses the English word "sensation" and the Chinese word "*ganjue*" to translate *xianliang*. This may, however, be misleading because the Chinese did not strictly distinguish between "sensation" (*ganjue* or *zhijue*) and "perception" (*ganjue* or *zhijue*). In *Weishi shuyi*, 284, Liang maintains that *zhijue* (perception) is a term from psychology and *ganjue* (sensation) a *Weishi* term. Nonetheless, with respect to the *Weishi* notion of *xianliang*, the important factor is immediacy: direct awareness, cognition, or experience without the

intervention of conceptualization. A traditional Western interpretation of the knowledge process (one inherited by the Chinese Marxists) was that it was comprised of the sense-perceptual (*ganxing*) and the rational (*lixing*). The first consisted of sensations and perceptions. Both sensations and perceptions were the result of the direct effects or influence of external objects on the sense organs; they differed in that while sensations were single sensory data, for example, a color, a shape, and the like, perception coordinated or synthesized these sensory data to form percepts of physical objects, for example, a chair. The latter—the rational—consisted of concepts, judgments and inferences. Concepts, as opposed to percepts, abstracted and generalized from the concrete and individual. For example, a chair is a percept if it is a particular chair that one is acquainted with. Chair, however, as it appears and is defined in a dictionary is a concept. (In *Weishi shuyi*, 285, Liang distinguishes between a *guannian* [an idea] of a specific bottle and *gainian* [an abstract concept] of a bottle to account for the above distinction.) Once concepts (or percepts for that matter) are formed, judgments can be made by affirming or denying something about them. "X is Y. X is not Y." Inferences are derived from judgments. X is Y (1st judgment). Y is opposed to Z (2nd judgment). X is opposed to Z (inference and new judgment). As Liang seems to conflate percepts and ideas (*guannian*) and include the former in his second mode or stage of knowledge (*biliang*), we cannot really equate his first stage (*xianliang*) with sense-perceptual knowledge but merely with sensations or the sensational (i.e., individual sense-data).

56. Liang Shuming, *Dong-xi wenhua ji qi zhexue*, 397.
57. *Ibid.*
58. An Yanming, "Liang Shuming and Henri Bergson on Intuition: Cultural Context and the Evolution of Terms," *Philosophy East and West* 47.3(1997): 337–62.
59. Or more correctly, the *yiwei, jingshen*, and *qushi* that comprise *zhijue*.
60. Liang Shuming, *Dong-xi wenhua ji qi zhexue*, 397.
61. The basic meaning of *biliang* is comparison and inference, that is to say, comparison of what is known and inference of what is not known (Soothill and Hodous, *A Dictionary of Chinese Buddhist Terms*, 159). *Biliang* is inference or reasoning on the basis of comparison and we can take this to mean what we generally understand as reasoning or inference.
62. Liang Shuming, *Dong-xi wenhua ji qi zhexue*, 398–9.
63. *Ibid.*, 397.
64. In discussing *biliang* Liang uses a similar term, *yiyi*. Both *yiyi* and *yiwei* can be translated as "meaning" or "significance." The difference, however, would seem to be that in connection with reference, *biliang* refers to that which is significant about paintings that makes them paintings, that is, the common characteristics paintings share that makes them paintings and allows us to form the concept of a painting. This is why Liang equates significance in this sense with concept. In discussing *feiliang, yiwei* is the meaning or significance we give to the painting in terms of its aesthetic features (e.g., subtlety), that is to say, what can only be experienced through aesthetic intuition.

65. *Yiwei* can be variously translated as "meaning," "significance," "implication," "interest," "overtone," "flavor," and the like; *jingshen* as "spirit," "mind," "consciousness," "essence," "gist," and the like; and *qushi* as "trend" or "tendency."

66. Liang Shuming, *Dong-xi wenhua ji qi zhexue*, 400–1.

67. *Ibid.*, 400. Liang also posits two kinds of intuition: sensational intuition and rational (*lizhi*) intuition. For example, the ability to comprehend the subtlety of a text is dependent on a person's rational intuition, not on anything inherent in the material symbols that make up the text, or, for that matter, on the faculty of reason alone. Another distinction that Liang makes in this area is that in sensational knowledge, desire (*yiyu*), through intuition, creates *yiwei, jingshen*, and *qushi*; while in rational knowledge, desire, through intuition, creates theories (*lilun*).

68. *Ibid.*, 412–13. Not only does Liang believe that motion is an illusion he also considers that such things as color and substance do not exist objectively but are peculiar to individuals. Liang's views in this respect follow in the tradition of *Weishi*. For example, the *Cheng weishi lun* states: "objective spheres of color and so forth are not colors but appear to be color, and are not external but appear to be external" (Wing-tsit Chan, *A Source Book*, 390–1); and, for different people "the same thing perceived . . . appear[s] differently" (*idem.*, 387). This is also similar to Wang Yangming's views. In the *Record of Instructions* it says: "You say there is nothing under Heaven external to the mind. What relation, then, do these high mountain flowers and trees, which blossom and drop of themselves, have to my mind? The Master [Yang Yangming] replied: 'When you do not see these flowers, they and your mind both become quiescent. But when you look at them, their color at once becomes clear. From this fact you know that these flowers are not external to your mind.'" Quoted in Feng Youlan, *A History of Chinese Philosophy*, vol. 2, 609.

69. Liang Shuming, *Dong-xi wenhua ji qi zhexue*, 485–6; Zhu Yilu, "Liang Shuming," 7.

70. Zhu Yilu, "Liang Shuming," 7.

71. I believe this is the best translation of Liang's notion of *lixing*. It is the principle of feelings as opposed to the detached scientific reasoning of *lizhi*. *Lixing*, however, can also be translated as rational in a purely epistemological sense.

72. Liang Shuming, *Xiangcun jianshe lilun* in *Liang Shuming quanji*, vol. 2, Shandong: Shandong remin chubanshe, 1994, 314.

73. *Ibid.*, 185–6.

74. Zhu Yilu, "Liang Shuming," 13. For Liang, however, the scope and function of *lixing* is extensive. One of its principal functions is to maintain social order. It is the reason humans are different from nonhuman animals; it is the distinguishing feature, strong point, and inherent spirit of the Chinese people; it was responsible for shaping the education, etiquette, and customs of traditional China. Liang also believed that rural reconstruction had to begin with *lixing*; and an ideal, new social organization had to be sought from it.

75. Liang Shuming, *Zhongguo wenhua yaoyi* (The Essence of Chinese Culture), in *Liang Shuming quanji*, vol. 3, Shandong: Shandong remin chubanshe, 1994, 260.

76. *Ibid.*, 281, and *Xiangcun jianshe lilun*, 181. In *Zhongguo wenhua yaoyi*, Liang reiterates what he said about *lixing* in *Xiangcun jianshe lilun*. For example, he says that it gives significance and value to human life; it is the mainstay of society, the support of the old order and what holds the new society together; it is both a characteristic of humanity, in general, as well as something characteristic of the Chinese people; it has given rise to a particularly Chinese attitude to life; it enjoins people to direct power inwards. It is an innate capacity that was only recognized in traditional China. It is the *li* (reason) of *li* (rites); the traditional rites are therefore an expression of *lixing*. It is *xin*, that is, people's subjective consciousness; it is also the *tianli* (heavenly principle) of Song Confucianism and so on (*Zhongguo wenhua yaoyi*, 137).

77. In this work Liang returns to a theme he elaborated in *Zhongguo wenhua yaoyi*. *Lizhi* involves people directing power outwards. The object confronting them is the objective natural world and what is pursued is science. *Lixing* involves people directing power inwards. The objects confronting them are people. In this instance, it is directed toward moral ideals and the rich emotional world this involves.

78. The Buddhist terms indicate that this is the stage or mode of knowledge that Liang understands as *biliang*.

79. *Mencius*, 11.7

80. Li Yuanting (comp.), *Liang Shuming jiang Kong Meng*, 43–5.

81. *Mencius*, 13.15.

82. Quoted in An Yanming, "Liang Shuming and Henri Bergson on Intuition," 125.

83. Li Yuanting (comp.), *Liang Shuming jiang Kong Meng*, 51, 46.

84. An Yanming believes that the disappearance of *zhijue* (replaced by *lixing*) in Liang's thought is not an academically trivial problem. He comments on two approaches. The first is that of Guy Alitto and the Chinese "Marxists" who maintain that Liang abandoned the notion of *zhijue* because it had gone "out of fashion." The second approach is exemplified by Zheng Dahua who maintains that there is some overlap between the notions of *zhijue* and *lixing*. An considers both of these approaches and his own strategy (which goes beyond Zheng's) as answering the question of the abandonment of the notion of *zhijue* ("Liang Shuming and Henri Bergson on Intuition," 339). I do not, however, regard this issue as one of abandonment but as one of development. Bergon's original contrast was between intellect and intuition. Liang adopted or focused on this contrast in the light of a similar one he saw in the epistemology of *Weishi* (between *biliang* and *feiliang*). Moreover, *zhijue* is not a Chinese term but an adopted neologism. As Liang developed the meaning of this term it obviously appeared to him to be somewhat limited. As his agenda increasingly became one of using *zhijue* and *lizhi* to distinguish between Chinese and Western cultures, respectively, his focus correspondingly shifted to demonstrating the distinction between the intellectual and the ethical emphasis of these two cultures. *Zhijue* cannot really do this whereas *lixing* can. The word *lizhi* 理智 is represented by the characters for "principle" and "intellect;" *lixing* 理性 is represented by the characters for "principle" and "(human)

nature/character/disposition." Although *lixing* can also be understood as the faculty of reason (*li*), judging by the importance Liang placed on the etymological function of principle (*li*) in other concepts (see following note) he used, it is probable that the former rather than the latter interpretation of *lixing* appealed to him. Consequently, I believe that we should understand Liang's notion of *lixing* as principally referring to ethical reason. With this understanding we can see Liang as anticipating the current Western interest in evaluating people in terms of their "emotional intelligence" as well as their I.Q., and the attention currently given by ethicists to the question of the "rationality of the emotions."

85. Taking Liang's works as a whole, there are four principal notions underpinning his epistemology. The first two consist of the pair *lizhi* (intellect) and *wuli* (the principle of things). *Lizhi* is a purely rational (non-emotive) faculty of the mind directed to understanding the principles at work in the objective and external world (*wuli*). The second two consist of the pair *lixing* (ethical reason) and *qingli* (the principle of feeling). *Lixing* is a faculty of the mind concerned with people's subjective feelings (*qingli*). Liang explains the distinction between *wuli* and *qingli* as follows. In the world there is *wuli* (principle of things) and *qingli* (principle of feeling). When we observe evolution and natural selection in the animal and plant worlds, we notice that they are characterized by the strong dominating the weak and so on. This is also true of the human world. For Liang, this is indicative of the principle of things. Emotionally, we find this state of affairs repulsive. We sympathize with the weak and demand fairness and justice. For Liang, this is indicative of the principle of feelings. See Liang's "Chu Hsi's Contribution to Confucian Learning and Flaws in His Theoretical Thinking," in Wing-tsit Chan (ed.), *Chu Hsi and Neo-Confucianism*, Honolulu: University of Hawaii Press, 1986, 29.

86. Wang Ruoshui caricatures the opposing positions of Hu Shi, Liang, and the Marxists with the following tale. The wheel of history is rolling along steered by a worker. The road it must travel is winding and rugged and it has to overcome many obstacles, hardships, and dangers. It keeps moving forward because the further it travels, the more the masses push it forward; it does not lose direction because it is guided by Marxism. Despite everything, the wheel of history moves forward with ever increasing speed. Arriving at a crossroads it finds the way blocked by two men—Hu Shi and Liang Shuming. Hu Shi advises the worker who is pushing the wheel of history to take the road that travels west; Liang Shuming advises him to take the eastern road. The worker ignores both and pushes the wheel of history forward. See "Liang Shuming he lishi de chelun 梁漱溟和歷史的車輪" (Liang Shuming and the Wheel of History), in *Zai zhexue zhanxian shang* 在哲學戰綫上 (On the Philosophical Front), Beijing: People's Publishing House, 1980, 71-7).

CHAPTER 8
XIONG SHILI'S METAPHYSICAL THEORY ABOUT THE NON-SEPARABILITY OF SUBSTANCE AND FUNCTION[1]

NG Yu-kwan

Xiong's Position in Contemporary New Confucianism

Xiong Shili 熊十力 (1885–1968) commands a unique and superior position among the Contemporary New Confucians. To begin with, he was the first Confucian after Wang Yangming 王陽明 (1472–1529) to inherit and promote moral spirituality in general, and moral metaphysics in particular. This moral spirituality represents the *daotong* 道統 (traditional heritage of truth) within Confucian thought or traditional Chinese culture.[2] Second, Xiong had propounded a substantial metaphysics about the non-separability of substance and function based on the idea of the non-abiding and perpetually changing *benti* 本體 (ontological or original substance) promoted by Confucius and in the *Book of Changes* (*Yijing* 易經). This philosophy of the non-separability of substance and function is the foundation of New Confucianism. Third, Tang Junyi 唐君毅 (1909–78), Mou Zongsan 牟宗三 (1909–95), and Xu Fuguan 徐復觀 (1903–82)—commonly regarded as belonging to the second generation of New Confucianism—have substantially developed different aspects of Confucianism, widely influencing students of Chinese philosophy. They were all Xiong's disciples, being deeply indebted to him for the cultivation of a sophisticated philosophical orientation and a superior personality.[3] Fourth and most important, he was truly faithful to his own thought and teachings. He firmly upheld philosophical idealism throughout his life, never submitting himself to secular political authority to forsake his original ideology. This was so even after the Communist takeover of China in 1949. He was brave enough to declare that he could not accept the prevalent materialism and be brainwashed. It was said that he even dared to snub the highest Communist leadership.[4]

Mou Zongsan, Xiong Shili's most important disciple, provided the following evaluation of his teacher:

> When the sages speak of *ren* 仁 (benevolence), *xing ming tiandao* 性命天道 (the nature, orientation, and the heavenly way) and *liangzhi* 良知 (moral consciousness), these are not [regarded as] presuppositions, but are manifestations of true life. Such statements by themselves, however, are not sufficient since anyone can claim that he has realized the truth. Therefore, we need teachers and friends to witness these manifestations in actual life. Only Xiong has sufficient qualifications to do this in the contemporary world. No one else has sufficient [qualifications]. Therefore, Xiong is a *zhenren* 真人 (true human).[5]

The term *zhenren* originally comes from the Daoist philosopher, Zhuangzi 莊子, and the Linji School 臨濟宗 of Chan Buddhism. Its ideal personality, *wuwei zhenren* 無位真人, refers to the highest subjectivity, which transcends space and time as well as secular norms, and to one who has attained enlightenment. Mou used the term to refer to one who had manifested moral consciousness as well as existentially identified with the highest truth. For him, it could be applied equally well to Confucianism, Daoism, and Buddhism. Moreover, we can say that not only did Xiong have an existential understanding of the truth, but also he was able to put into practice the Confucian moral principles and values of neither fearing nor submitting to political power and authority. His personality is even more exceptional when compared with other contemporary Chinese scholars who hung onto men of influence and followed the steps of the ruling authorities, such as Guo Moruo 郭沫若 (1892–1978) and Feng Youlan 馮友蘭 (1895–1990). In a nutshell, it is unquestionable that Xiong holds a superior position in contemporary New Confucianism.

General Comments on Xiong's Life and Thought

Here, I will briefly describe Xiong's life, thought, and his scholarly works. Xiong came from a poor peasant family, helping to graze cattle when he was young. After studying in a village school for half a year, he did not have the opportunity to receive further education. He was largely self-educated. His thought was influenced by his father at an early age. His father was a Confucian who was committed to preaching Confucianism and regarded being involved in every secular affair as his responsibility. As a result, Xiong formed a good impression of Confucianism when he was young. As a young man, he joined the army and participated in the Wuchang Uprising 武昌起義, which occurred just before the establishment of the Republic of China in 1911. Afterwards, he felt strongly that the members of the Revolution Party lacked moral consciousness and a sense of responsibility for the nation, fighting only for personal gain. He felt that if one were to start a revolution, it would be best to purify and cultivate the people's minds before revolting. Therefore, he gave up his career in the army and began his academic life. At that time, he was already thirty-five years old.

At first, he studied Song-Ming Confucianism, but was not at all satisfied. Consequently, he traced Confucian teachings back to the Six Classics, but was still not satisfied. He then turned to Daoism—Laozi, and Zhuangzi in particular. In the beginning, he was delighted, but later grew dissatisfied. Then he turned to Buddhism, and studied works of the Vijñāna-vāda (*Weishi* 唯識 Consciousness-Only) of the Yogācāra School. Although at first he liked it, afterwards he found that he could not agree with it. This led him to investigate the thought of the *Prajñāpāramitā* literature, but found its indulgence in the realm of quiescence objectionable. At last, he gave up his investigation of the classics and turned to reflect on his inner life, with the hope of reaching an enlightenment about the truth of the universe and life. After endeavoring for a period of time he felt that he gained a truly existential understanding of these issues. He considered the perpetually creative (*shengsheng buxi* 生生不息) ontological substance (*benti* 本體) put forward by Confucianism, in particular *The Book of Changes*, to be the highest truth. (Xiong believed that *The Book of Changes* had been written by Confucius.) On the one hand, he was deeply impressed by *The Book of Changes*, which claims that the universe is perpetually and vigorously changing. On the other hand, he also absorbed the Buddhist idea of quiescence. As a result, he formulated the metaphysical doctrine of an ontological substance, which is both active and quiescent. In addition, he meditated on the nature of the original mind (*benxin* 本心), feeling that the original mind was where the ultimate truth was flowing and functioning. At this stage, he returned to investigate the Buddhist classics, such as the *Avataṃsaka-sūtra* (*Huayan jing* 華嚴經), *Laṅkāvatāra sūtra* (*Lengqie jing* 楞伽經) and *Parinirvāṇa sūtra* (*Niepan jing* 涅槃經).

He also read the literature of the Vijñāna-vāda, such as those written by the prominent masters Asaṅga (Wuzhu 無著) and Vasubandhu (Shiqin 世親). Furthermore, he reviewed the literature of pre-Qin philosophers, Song-Ming Confucians as well as the masters of Chan Buddhism. He felt that he could understand them individually and also, all of a sudden, he could comprehend them clearly as a whole, integrating them altogether. At that point, he felt consciously that he had grasped the essence of Confucianism, Buddhism, and Daoism. He also read Western philosophy, such as the intuitionism of Henri Bergson, grasping its profound meanings. Finally, based on the Confucian thought delineated in *The Book of Changes*, he created his epochal metaphysical system based on the non-separability of substance and function, which was explicated in his magnum opus, *Xin weishi lun* 新唯識論 (The New Theory of Consciousness-Only).[6]

When Xiong began to investigate into philosophy seriously, he started with Vijñāna-vāda or Yogācāra Buddhism. At that time, he studied the works of Asaṅga and Vasubandhu under the guidance of Ouyang Jingwu 歐陽竟無 at the Zhina Neixueyuan 支那內學院 in Nanjing. He was not satisfied with the empirical and rigid character of the Yogācāra doctrines. As a consequence, on the basis of the dynamism explicated in *The Book of Changes*, he articulated a new and sophisticated theory of Consciousness-Only in which substance and function are non-separable. Later, when he became a lecturer at Beijing University giving lectures on Vijñāna-vāda, he was in fact transmitting his new theory of Consciousness-Only. Gradually, he received due attention from academic circles and was considered to be a new emerging philosopher. In 1949, the political situation changed drastically and the Chinese Communist Party came to power. Xiong did not follow his students such as Tang, Mou, and Xu to go to Hong Kong or Taiwan, although he did have thoughts of going to America or India. Finally, in response to an invitation sent by members of the Chinese Communist Party such as Dong Biwu 董必武 and Guo Moruo 郭沫若, he decided to go to Beijing to continue his teaching career and also to participate in political affairs. At first, he was highly respected and regarded. He earnestly put forward proposals on a variety of matters to develop Confucian education and scholarly research, attracting the attention of Mao Zedong 毛澤東. Unfortunately, his proposals were taken to be superficial and impractical, and were not accepted. Deeply disappointed, he stayed in Beijing for several more years. Finally, unable to endure the severely cold weather, he moved to Shanghai and remained there until his death.

During the 1950s, Xiong was still quite dedicated and was allowed to continue to investigate philosophical problems and write books without being hindered by serious political pressure and ideological disturbances. During this period, his starting point was internal sageliness (*nei sheng* 內聖), which included the practice of the attainment of moral virtues and the existential realization of the heavenly way (*tiandao*). Based on internal sageliness, he developed external kingliness (*wai wang* 外王), which involved political, social, and charitable concerns. During this period, he wrote some of his important works, including *Yuan Ru* 原儒 (Tracing Confucianism) and *Qian kun yan* 乾坤衍 (The Explication of Creativity and Procreativity). He said:

> The *Book of Changes* of the ancient sages is comprehensive, nothing is not contained in it. The *Book of Changes* can be summarized into two aspects, namely internal sageliness and external kingliness. . . . The study of internal sageliness solves the important problems of the universe and life. This is what *The Doctrine of the Mean* refers to as "the learning leading to the establishment of the self." The study of external kingliness solves important problems in society and politics. This is what *The Doctrine of the Mean* refers to as "the study of the establishment of things." . . . The establishment of the self and things are nothing but the same act.[7]

During his last ten years, Xiong's health declined gradually.[8] His close friends either passed away or submitted to the Communist regime. Those having personal contact with him became rare. His greatest suffering was solitariness.[9] In 1966, Mao Zedong launched the Cultural Revolution and many people suffered from its mass destruction. As a classical philosopher, Xiong could not be exempted from its attack. He was beaten by the Red Guards and his property was confiscated. He was worried that Chinese culture would decline to the extent that the Chinese people would become slaves of Marxism for ten thousand years. He was deeply wounded both mentally and physically. He refused to eat any food in order to end his life sooner. Later, he was extremely grieved and depressed, and suffered a mental breakdown. Finally, he became ill but refused to take any medicine, suffering from high fever and serious heart pain. The great master at last died under these conditions, two years after the start of the Cultural Revolution.[10]

Xiong's scholarship and philosophic works can be divided into two types. The first is the system developed in *Xin weishi lun*, *Tiyong lun* 體用論 (The Theory of Substance and Function), and *Ming xin pian* 明心篇 (A Treatise on Understanding the Mind). The second is the system developed in *Dujing shiyao* 讀經示要 (Revealing the Main

Points of Reading the Classics) and *Yuan Ru*. The former discusses the problems of internal sageliness, while the latter is concerned with those of external kingliness. Finally, Xiong wrote *Qian kun yan* to synthesize these two systems of thought and render the inner and outer aspects consistent. Among these works, *Xin weishi lun* has been considered the most important in academic circles. It is a systematic work that represents the core of Xiong's thought throughout his life. It is based on the idea of a perpetually creative and ever flowing ontological substance as delineated in the *Book of Changes*, which Xiong used to develop his magnificent system, amply touching upon important problems regarding both the universe and life. In terms of the comprehensiveness and depth of its content as well as the compactness and strictness of his arguments, Xiong did this work superbly.[11]

Xiong was largely consistent in his thought before and after 1949. That is to say, from the theoretical standpoint, Xiong maintained his ideology throughout his life. The *Tiyong lun* and *Ming xin pian* reiterated the main points articulated in his *Xin weishi lun* and emphasized the aspect of internal sageliness. *Yuan Ru*, written after 1949, was based on the study of inner sageliness and supplemented by doctrines of external kingliness. *Dujing shiyao*, which was written before 1949, followed the same direction. *Qian kun yan*, as mentioned previously, revealed a broader synthesis. Xiong considered this work to be extremely important: "the final view of my declining years" (*shuainian dinglun* 衰年定論).[12]

The core of Xiong's thought is the theory of the non-separability of substance and function. Generally speaking, substance (*ti* 體) refers to the substance or essence of things, while function (*yong* 用) refers to the form or phenomenon of things achieved on the basis of the underlying substance. The two concepts are intimately related: substance is the substance of function and function the function of substance. Ontologically speaking, substance exists in the midst of functions; apart from functions, there is no independent substance. On the other hand, function is the manifestation of substance; apart from substance, there is no function. The non-separability of substance and function (*tiyong bu'er* 體用不二) refers to the existential or actual non-separability between them, to their mutual entailment. Regarding this non-dual relationship, Xiong usually explained it by the analogy of the relationship between a massive ocean (*dahai shui* 大海水) and its multiplicity of waves (*zhong'ou* 眾漚): the ocean itself is like the substance, while the ocean waves are like the function. The ocean exists in the midst of various waves; apart from various waves, there is no existence of the massive ocean. Also, the different waves are the manifestations of the massive ocean and their essence resides in the massive ocean. We cannot imagine that the massive ocean and various waves exist separately, so we cannot imagine the separate existence of substance and function.[13] Moreover, Xiong spoke of substance as perpetually creative and unceasingly changing. This is very different from the notion of substance in mainstream Western philosophy, which does not allow substance to embrace dynamism, considering it to be static and normative (such as Plato's Forms). According to Xiong, substance changes and transforms unceasingly to become function. Function has two forms. One form is integration (xi 翕), which tends to condense by itself and become entitative. The other form is development (pi 闢), which is the function of creation. Consequently, the former gives birth to what we call (physical) entities, while the latter gives birth to the mind. The complementary interaction between integration and development pertaining to substance, manifests a universe that contains mind and matter.

The theory of the non-separability of substance and function belongs to the category of internal sageliness. The aspect of external kingliness, expressed particularly in his *Dujing shiyao* can be regarded as a sequel to *Xin weishi lun*. In this work, based on the philosophical thought laid down in *Xin weishi lun*, Xiong annotated the classics, affirming the constant way (*chang dao* 常道) embraced in the Six Classics (*The Book of Changes* 易, *The Book of Odes* 詩, *The Book of History* 書, *The Book of Rites* 禮, *The Book of Music* 樂, and *The Spring and Autumn Annals* 春秋). They are the source of the fundamental spirit of Chinese culture. The development of the constant way had two golden periods. The first was the period during which the pre-Qin philosophers (sixth to third century B.C.) arose and blossomed, while the second was the period of development of Song-Ming Confucianism (eleventh to seventeenth century A.D.). The ideas exalted by Xiong were those of Lu Jiuyuan 陸九淵 (1139–93), Wang Yangming 王陽明 (1472–1529), and Wang Fuzhi 王夫之 (1619–92). The thought of the Lu-Wang School emphasizes an infinite mind that is identical to principle (*xin ji li* 心即理), or a moral consciousness that is identical to the heavenly principle (*tianli* 天理), while Wang Fuzhi emphasized the concrete problems of cultural constructions, reflecting on the negative aspects of historical and political traditions.

From Buddhism to Confucianism

In this section, we will investigate more concretely and in more detail Xiong's ideal of the non-separability of substance and function. Generally speaking, Xiong was not satisfied with Buddhism.[14] The fundamental standpoint of Buddhism is Nature-Emptiness (*svabhāva-śūnyatā*). That is to say, the essence or truth of all things is Emptiness. Everything exists in the form of dependent origination, without a perpetually unchangeable self-nature (*svabhāva*). Or we can say, there is not a single thing that has a substantive self-nature or essence and therefore everything is empty. Xiong always mentioned "emptiness" (*kong* 空) and "quiescence" (*ji* 寂) together and spoke of "empty quiescence" (*kongji* 空寂). On the other hand, based on its experiential identification of the Truth or true nature, Buddhism also emphasizes that a boddhisattva should manifest functions in the world to save all sentient beings. This is the highest ideal of Buddhism. The true nature of a bodhisattva, however, is "empty quiescence," which does not have a substance. How then is he able to produce effective functions to save all sentient beings? Xiong realized that only substance could produce power or function, otherwise there would be no functions. Consequently, the Buddhist theory of Emptiness or having no substance was untenable. This is by no means difficult to understand. We can explain it by giving a concrete example. For instance, it is necessary for a farmer to have a strong and healthy body in order to have the power and strength to plough and sow as well as to fulfill the basic needs in life. If the farmer does not have a healthy body or is ill, he cannot cultivate the land and work. Even though he forces himself to work, he will not have a good harvest. Relating this example to the problem of Buddhism referred to earlier, the farmer's healthy body is like substance, while the cultivation of the field is like function. Only substance can produce function. If there is no substance, there will also be no function. In this way, the relationship or association between substance and function will be untenable. Here, substance, as understood by Xiong, corresponds to the substantive spirituality (*Geist*) of Hegel, while function corresponds to Hegel's action of the spirit. According to Xiong, Buddhism could not hold either that substance produces function or that a substantive spirituality produces spiritual action. If it did have the concept of substance or substantive spirituality, then the fundamental Buddhist standpoint of the dependent origination (*pratītyasamutpāda*) of all things, and thereby its doctrine of Nature-Emptiness would have collapsed, since substance is an expression of or pertains to self-nature.[15]

This is where Xiong found Buddhist doctrines the most unsatisfactory and untenable. According to him, all things, including humans, are the manifestations of ontological substance. Substance contains a true content, embracing various functions. With these functions, it can condense itself and manifest the phenomenal world and carry out religious and soteriological actions of transforming sentient beings.[16] He considered the Confucian *tian* 天 (heaven), *tiandao* 天道 (heavenly way) or *yiti* 易體 (substance of change), and *qianyuan xinghai* 乾元性海 (primordial creativity and the unfathomable nature) described in *The Book of Changes* (which Xiong believed was written by Confucius), as representing a substantive spirituality. This spirituality is perpetually creative (*shengsheng buxi* 生生不息), flowing (*dayong liuxing* 大用流行), and ever changing (*biandong buju* 變動不居). Since it is the substance and essence of all things, they inherit its true attributes and virtues and become real. This contrasts with the Buddhist view that all things are false and illusory. It was exactly with this understanding that Xiong converted from Buddhism to Confucianism, and to the ideas of *The Book of Changes* in particular. He regarded Confucianism as propounding the authentic truth that settles the problems of life.

In the following, we will verify Xiong's changes in the direction of his ideas through textual studies. First of all, he affirmed the reality of truth or substance, saying that it embraced an infinite content: "*Zhenyuan* 真源 (the true origin) embraces all things which are infinite and boundless."[17] This reality of truth repudiates the Buddhist conception that all *dharmas* are empty or illusory. Moreover, substance is also dynamic in nature and is intimately related with the actual world. He also criticized Buddhism on this point: "The two schools [of Mādhyamika and Yogācāra] have a common, fundamental, and unyielding belief. That is, the substance (*dharmatā, dharmatva; faxing* 法性) of all things is devoid of creative creativity (*shengsheng* 生生), movement (*liudong* 流動), and change."[18] Actually, neither Mādhyamika nor Vijñāna-vāda speak of the substance (of all things). They only say that all things are empty or are "as such" (*tathā; zhenru* 真如). In fact, the meanings of substance and emptiness (or *tathā*) are exactly opposite. By interpreting the two schools as affirming the substance of things, Xiong's intention was to explicate his own view about substance and compare it with the two schools of Buddhism on the problem of truth. In his view, the substance propounded in Mādhyamika and Vijñāna-vāda did not have the function of creative creativity, while his substance did. He also said that "Daoism degenerates into nothingness (*lunxu* 淪虛), while Buddhism bogs down into quiescence (*zhiji* 滯寂). Degeneration into nothingness and bogging down into quiescence imply the weakness of forsaking all sentient beings."[19] Here Xiong also criticized Daoism. "Degeneration into nothingness" and "bogging down into quiescence" are very close in meaning. Whatever is "nothingness" or "quiescence" is spoken of in contrast to the reality and unceasing changeability of various phenomena and entities. Phenomena and entities, including humans, are things in the empirical world, are tenable within the forms of space and time revealed by sensibility, and are governed by the category of causality. This is the nature of what is "real."

Let us now further investigate Xiong's criticism of Buddhism from theoretical and conceptual points of view. The fundamental problem he put forward to challenge Buddhism is that function refers to the subtle function of spontaneous creativity and the changeability imposed on entities. This can only be manifested by a substance. Otherwise, how can function arise from nothing? Furthermore, he emphasized that if the substance was empty, quiescent, and lacking both creativity and transformation, then it was a dead thing, useless or unimportant.[20] He severely criticized Buddhism as "explicating (merely) substance but missing function" (tanti yiyong 談體遺用)[21] or "missing function in explicating substance" (yiyong tanti 遺用談體).[22] Between Mādhyamika and Vijñāna-vāda he criticized the latter most severely. According to Xiong, the shortcoming of Mādhyamika was that it established only an empty and quiescent ontological substance, which was static and devoid of content. It failed to identify an ontological substance that embraced dynamism, and so initiate functions of creative transformation. On the one hand, the Vijñāna-vāda regarded tathā 真如 (suchness) to be an ontological substance that did not possess any dynamism and as being incapable of action in whatever form. On the other hand, it established bīja (zhongzi 種子; seed) as the cause of actual things, which Xiong took to be an ontological substance.[23] Consequently, the Vijñāna-vāda had the drawback of having two different ontological substances. Since the ontological substance is ultimate and has absolute character, there can only be one ontological substance. This "oneness" is not a number, but conveys the meaning of absoluteness. If there are two different kinds of ontological substance neither can be said to be absolute or ultimate. So this kind of ontological substance is untenable and inauthentic.[24]

Xiong's position is very clear: function has to be based on a substance. A substance is needed to produce the function, which then establishes the phenomenal world. Substance or ontological substance is metaphysical, while phenomena are physical. The two of them need to be synthesized to form a unity. Within this framework, the ontological substance is capable of manifestation due to its dynamism, while function or phenomenon also has its ground. Since the concept of ontological substance in both Mādhyamika and Vijñāna-vāda is essentially empty, quiescent, and lacking dynamism, it could not produce functions to form the phenomenal world. Ontological substance and phenomena do not have an intimate connection and are not united. Instead, they are divided into two separate worlds. This leads to the bifurcation between the world of ontological substance and that of phenomena.[25] Obviously, Xiong considered that there should be a coherent and unobstructed relationship between substance and function, or between ontological substance and phenomena. He saw Confucianism—specifically identified as the thought delineated in *The Book of Changes*—as being able to do this.

In this way, Xiong introduced two antinomical metaphysical systems: one regarding substance and function as separate; the other regarding substance and function as non-separate. Xiong manifestly appreciated the latter and criticized the former, which he identified with Buddhist thought. Concerning this point, Xiong made the following comments:

> Mahāyāna Buddhism speaks of free and superior functions, but does not allow them to be the manifestation and movement of the true nature (*zhenxing liuxing* 真性流行), since they do not allow the true nature to manifest and flow. If we say that the true nature is movement, we can acknowledge free and superior functions, which are the development and manifestation of the true nature. In other words, substance and function are non-separable (*jiyong jiti* 即用即體). Now, Mahāyāna Buddhism speaks of the true nature, but it is devoid of action and creativity (*wuwei wuzuo* 無為無作). It acknowledges free and superior functions, which arise in dependence on the true nature, but are not themselves the manifestations of the true nature. In this way, substance and function cannot be non-dual.[26]

"True nature," here, refers to substance or ontological substance. As mentioned above, however, Buddhism cannot establish any substance that pertains to self-nature (*zixing* 自性). If we take the true nature or ontological substance as self-nature, using it to criticize the true nature and ontological substance of Buddhism as problematic, this is inappropriate. Xiong did not look into this point. He observed that Buddhism also spoke of the true nature and ontological substance, but criticized Buddhism for not understanding the movement of ontological substance and only knowing that it was empty and quiescent. If it were empty and quiescent, it could neither have flowed nor produced functions. It could only be "devoid of creativity" (*wuzuo* 無作). In this way, Buddhism could not account for the tenability of the phenomenal world. It could not establish the intimate relationship between substance and function or between ontological substance and the phenomenal world, nor could it speak of function or phenomenon as the manifestation and disclosure of the true nature or ontological substance. It could only say that functions "arise in dependence on the true nature." That is, functions depend on the true nature or ontological substance in order to arise. Therefore, the two are still separate. They are not "non-dual" but "two." Only when they are non-dual can we say "substance and function are non-separable" (*jiyong jiti, jiti jiyong* 即用即體，即體即用). From Xiong's point of view, only Confucianism—*The Book of Changes* in particular—pertained to the mode of thought in which substance and function are non-separable. Moreover, this non-separability of substance and function was coherent and perfect; it is where the highest value lies. As a result, Xiong gave up Buddhism and converted to *The Book of Changes*. He even used "the movement of heavenly virtue" (*tiande liuxing* 天德流行) to describe and praise Confucian metaphysics. He wrote: "The Dao of Confucians can be understood directly from the movement of heavenly virtue."[27] He also explained: "Heavenly virtue is called ontological substance. Buddhists are biased and only understand its quiescent aspect, so they do not allow the movement of the ontological substance. Confucians can perceive the vigor of creative transformability directly from this quiescence."[28] By this, Xiong meant that Buddhism only understood ontological substance to be quiescent and incapable of creatively transforming things. By contrast, the Confucian ontological substance was not only quiescent, but also dynamic, enabling it to creatively transform things. Confucianism considered quiescence and dynamism as one (*jidong yiru* 寂動一如).[29]

The Non-Separability of Substance and Function

In the following, I will explain in detail the meaning of Xiong's theory of the non-separability of substance and function. First of all, we need to delineate the precise meaning of "non-separability" or "non-duality" (*bu'er* 不二). After investigating various aspects of the above concepts, we will conclude that "non-separable" means "not separate" or "not two different things."

According to Xiong's understanding, "non-separability" does not imply "identity" (*tongyi* 同一), which means that substance and function are the same thing. Xiong only meant that ontological substance and function, or substance and phenomena, are at once united and not separate (*xiangji buli* 相即不離) and cannot be independent from each other. Here, we quote a few of Xiong's words to support our understanding:

> Substance is the internal foundational origin (*genyuan* 根源) of all things. It cannot be said that substance lies beyond all things. This is what is meant by the non-separability of substance and function.[30]

Beyond all things, there are not any independent substances. There-fore, the theory of the non-separability of substance and function is established.[31]

The non-separability of substance and function means that the substance does not lie beyond all things.[32]

Ti (體) is the abbreviation of *shiti* 實體 (substance). *Yong* 用 (func-tion) is nothing but another name for phenomena. By non-separability, we mean that substance is the substance of phenomena and we cannot recklessly guess that the substance is transcendent from the phenomena and becomes independent.[33]

The true origin (*zhenyuan* 真源) and movement (*liuxing* 流行) cannot be separated into two sections.[34]

Phenomena and substance are not two different worlds.[35]

The meaning of the above quotations is very clear and requires no additional explanation. Concerning the historical origin of the non-separability of substance and function, Xiong said modestly that he was not the first to discover the theory, but inherited it from Confucius. He also mentioned that from this mode of thought, it could be seen that Confucius greatly emphasized the actual world, which was firmly grounded on substance and did not arise from voidness and nothing-ness.[36] With regard to the *Analects*, which is most representative of the thought of Confucius, there is no mention of the non-separability of substance and function. The attribution of the theory to Confucius, according to Xiong, is of course due to *The Book of Changes*, the theme of which is the non-separability of substance and function. On the other hand, Xiong also mentioned that this theory of the non-separability of substance and function was obtained by his personal exis-tential verification.[37] This implies that this theory could not be perceived or understood by any conceptual, theoretical, or logical procedure, but could only be understood by one's own personal introspective experi-ence or practice (*gongfu* 工夫).

Here, I try to apprehend the precise meaning of substance and func-tion from the texts where Xiong spoke of them: "Substance obtains its name by its correlation with function. Essentially, substance is the sub-stance of function. It is not true that substance and function are mutu-ally separate and different. If function is not the manifestation of the substance itself, then substance is not the substance of function, but is separate and different from function and distinctly becomes a realm of voidness. In this way, the meaning of substance cannot be estab-lished."[38] In addition, he emphasized: "By function, we mean power or action. This kind of power or action itself is only a kind of dynamic tendency and is not a substantive or rigid entity. . . . Substance obtains its name by its correlation with function. However, substance manifests itself entirely to become diverse and magnificent functions. Therefore, it is said to be the ontological substance of function. It is absolutely false that substance is transcendent from its functions and becomes an independent existing entity."[39]

It is clear that Xiong spoke of substance and function in the context of "non-separability." That is to say, substance is the substance of function and function is the function of substance. Moreover, there is no substance apart from function and there is no function apart from substance. Furthermore, function must be the manifestation of substance. If substance is considered apart from its manifestation in functions, substance would become an empty realm without any content. In addition, function is a kind of dynamic tendency, the foundation of which is substance. Since function is only a dynamic tendency, the phenomenon or entity formed by its condensation cannot be rigid or unchangeable. They can be deconstructed as a result of the annihilation or dispersion of function.[40] In this sense, substance and function of course are of relative character: substance is substance with respect to function, and function is function with respect to substance. They are what Buddhism calls "provisional names" (*prajñapti*; *jiaming* 假名).

Functions arise from substance and therefore diverse phenomena are formed. Here, "phenomena" refers to the various things, which is simple to understand. What, however, is substance or ontological substance? What characteristics does it possess? Xiong spoke of substance in terms of virtues. That is to say, substance embraced various virtues. He has listed numerous items: truth, permanence, voidness (without form, without image, without contamination, without intention), sincerity, vigor, creativity, and transformability. They were expressed in a positive and bright style, unlike the way Buddhists speak of "ignorance" (*avidyā*; *wuming* 無明) as the primordial state of all things that conveyed a negative and illusive sense. This shows that Xiong was an idealist.

Now, I return to my main theme of the non-separability of substance and function in order to ascertain the relationship between substance and diverse phenomena. What Xiong meant is that the non-separability of substance and function is not spoken of in a strictly logical or linguistic sense, but is understood in a cosmological, and, in particular, an ontological sense. He clarified this when he wrote: "There is not a moment when substance does not change. That is to say, there is not a moment when substance does not manifest itself as function or phenomenon."[41] He also explained: "Constant change (*hengzhuan* 恆轉) becomes magnificent function means there is no substance which is separated from functions and exists independently."[42] "Constant change" refers to substance. It means that substance is constantly changing and transforming. There is not a moment that it is truly static and not moving. These two quotations express the same meaning: substance or ontological substance must exist in the form of function or phenomena and cannot exist independently or apart from the latter. That is to say, ontologically speaking (ontological) substance must manifest itself to become functions and phenomena. Not only can substance not exist apart from functions and phenomena, but it also can neither produce functions and phenomena nor exist independently.[43]

In connection with the point that ontological substance cannot exist independently and apart from phenomena, Xiong unreservedly criticized some philosophers who constructed a fictitious realm of extreme quiescence beyond "movement" (liuxing 流行) (this refers to the moving and changing world of phenomena), or a realm of extreme nullity beyond the actual world. He considered this to be a serious fault. At the same time, he criticized some philosophers who regarded the mere, isolated, and ever-changing phenomena as reality, because they did not understand that in the midst of the changing phenomena lies the reality of extreme quiescence (this refers to the quiescent ontological substance). There were even some who considered that what appeared before their senses in the form of various things was reality, but they did not know that these are the manifestations of extreme nullity, which is the true reality. He labeled the latter as materialists and denounced them as denying that there was any truth.[44] Here, we have to be careful to discern Xiong's precise meaning: we identify the reality or ontological substance within (and not outside of) the changing phenomena, but we cannot treat the mere changing phenomena themselves as real. There is a difference between the changing phenomena and the reality, the former being the manifestation of the latter.

Here, I intend to clarify further Xiong's meaning of the manifestation of substance, which is treated as the foundation of function and phenomena, so as to avoid any misunderstanding. Xiong said: "The change and action of substance is called function, which is at the same time called entities or phenomena. In this way, substance entirely undergoes change itself to become diverse entities or phenomena."[45] What Xiong meant is that substance embraces dynamism and activity. Any activity must involve change. Since active substance contains an essential content, it can produce power that constitutes function. There is, however, still one point missing in Xiong's explanation that can be supplemented by a quotation from one of his other works: "Every power or function (*gongneng* 功能) has the two dimensions of integration (*xi* 翕) and development (*pi* 闢). . . . These kinds of different dynamic tendencies (Xiong's commentary: integration and development) are mutually fused."[46] "Power and function" (*gongneng*) refers to the function of the substance. What Xiong meant is that the function of substance has two aspects: one is integration and condensation; the other is development. The result of condensation is the formation of physical entities, while that of development is the formation of mind. In this way, every phenomenon has two aspects: the phenomena of matter and mind. Xiong declared that these two kinds of phenomena were always fused and could not be absolutely separated. For some phenomena, the physical aspect is more prominent, while for others the mental aspect is more manifest. It is impossible to have physical entities without minds, or to have mental entities without physical content. This is the theory of the fusion of mind and matter. The two are finally unified within an identical substance.

Onto-Cosmology: The Assimilation of Substance and the Reversion to Functions

Based on the fundamental mode of thought pertaining to the non-separability of substance and function, Xiong started to construct his metaphysical system. This can be said to be a kind of "onto-cosmology" (*bentiyuzhoulun* 本體宇宙論)—a metaphysics in which the ontological substance transforms and permeates all things so that the ontological substance and phenomena are coherent.

Earlier, I noted how substance or ontological substance changes and becomes function, which consists of integration and development. But how do these two aspects perform and cooperate to constitute all things in the universe? Xiong summarized his answer as "Substance is function immediately (*jiti jiyong* 即體即用). After all, substance and function are not separate. . . . Regarding function, there are only the dynamic tendencies of integration and development. . . . The dynamic tendencies of integration and development are not substantive entities. Substance in every instant creates and annihilates continually. It flows rapidly and is manifest as traces and appearances, which are akin to the rotating wheel of fire. These traces and appearances we provisionally call the diverse entities in the universe."[47] What Xiong meant is that substance and function are not separate. Substance can manifest to become function, which has two forms of operation: integration and development. Neither of them are actual, substantive, and rigid entities.

Since both forms of operation continually take place at every instant, however, they continue to create and annihilate perpetually. In this process of creation and annihilation, it seems that there are various entities or phenomena existing; these are all the entities in the universe. Since all the entities in the universe are the results of the manifestations of ontological substance, which permeates and flows in the midst of them, we call this kind of theory, which emphasizes a coherent relationship between the ontological substance and all things in the universe, an "onto-cosmology."[48]

Furthermore, Xiong emphasized that the change and action of the ontological substance followed the laws of "mutual opposition and mutual complementarity" (xiangfan xiangcheng 相反相成). It is possible that he was influenced by the thought of Laozi: "Reversal is the motion of Dao" (fanzhe dao zhi dong 反者道之動).[49] Xiong's theoretical ground is as follows: change is not a "pure" (danchun 單純) matter. Dan 單 means "alone" without any opposition or confrontation. Chun 純 means "pure," suggesting that it is without any contradiction. Based on this, Xiong put forward the operations of integration and development. He held that the operation of ontological substance was achieved by the mutual and complementary interaction of the opposite forms of assimilation (sheju 攝聚) and development (kaifa 開發). Assimilation is integration; it is the tendency of ontological substance to assimilate, condense, and become various rigid entities. If this action continues to expand, it will finally form a physical universe. Therefore, during the process of assimilation and integration, there is simultaneously another vigorous and developing form of motion to balance it, or even to govern it, so that it does not allow the appearance of an object with a complete material basis. That is to say, it does not allow it to completely materialize (wuhua 物化) according to the action of integration.[50] According to Xiong, ontological substance requires the action of integration to condense and approach a definite form, so as to form the physical world. On the other hand, ontological substance also needs the action of development to hinder ontological substance from becoming completely materialized. Otherwise, it will become a world completely devoid of mind, spirit, and life. He considered the universe to be living and vital, and not as a stagnant or mechanical construction. After all, the universe is not a dead object.

It is, however, not easy to solve the problem of how ontological substance changes from an abstract state to become a concrete entity. This can only be explained by "pseudo-manifestation" (sixian 似現 or zhaxian 詐現). The presence of "pseudo-manifestations" indicates that substance condenses or degenerates before the senses to appear as a concrete entity. Ultimately speaking, such entities do not possess any reality or self-nature.[51] Moreover, both integration and development are equally forms of change and motion pertaining to ontological substance. These two forms are understood in the ontological sense. If we consider their literal meanings and understand them apart from ontological substance, Xiong's philosophy will have a dualistic inclination, which is not the monism typically emphasized by him.

Now, in connection with Xiong's onto-cosmology, I intend to discuss Xiong's orientation of thought. Between substance and function, philosophers can be biased toward substance and assimilate various functions into the substance, or make functions subordinate to substance. This stresses substance and disparages function. On the other hand, they can be biased toward function and assimilate substance into function, or make substance subordinate to function. This stresses function and disparages substance. Xiong called the former orientation of thought "the assimilation of function and the reversion to substance" (sheyong guiti 攝用歸體) and the latter orientation "the assimilation of substance and the reversion to function" (sheti guiyong 攝體歸用). Xiong placed great emphasis on the actual phenomenal or empirical world. Based on the non-separability of substance and function, Xiong adopted the orientation of the assimilation of substance and the reversion to function,[52] while he disparaged the other orientation. The reason for his dissatisfaction with the latter was that: "The ancient religions usually sought for an origin outside all things and recklessly conceived an independent heaven or various gods who transcended all things. This was simply to become lost in the mist of fictitious conceptions constructed by oneself. Philosophy usually established ontological substance by deduction. It did not experience the foundational origins of entities directly from those entities, but deductively sought a kind of real thing apart from the entities themselves which was called the ontological substance of the entity."[53] These comments are critical of the orientation of "the assimilation of function and the reversion to substance": it does not identify the ontological substance directly in the midst of all things or in the midst of functions, but deduces or constructs (fictitiously) a transcendent ontological substance, which is far apart from all things. What Xiong meant by "mist" (wu 霧) refers exactly to "the transcendent character" itself. This way is not "the assimilation of functions," but "the departure from functions" or even "the abandonment of functions."

In *Qian kun yan*, Xiong greatly appreciated the superiority of the orientation of the assimilation of substance and the reversion to function.

He summarized this mode of thought in two fundamental principles. He explained: "[A philosophical system should] ascertain the phenomena and all things as real, regarding them as its main theme. This is the first principle. It ascertains that the universe flows from the past to the present, rapidly approaching the future. It is a totality which never stops developing. . . . It is not appropriate to split up the phenomena and make selections from among them. For example, to insist that before a certain point of time there were no living things and conclude that there were no living or spiritual phenomena. This is an instance of splitting. This is the second principle."[54] Here, the first principle should especially be noted. He held that one should establish the reality of phenomena and all things with a positive attitude and should not regard them as illusive, as in Buddhism. Moreover, between phenomena and ontological substance, phenomena should carry the primary emphasis, while ontological substance is only secondary. This is very different from the tradition of Western philosophy, which usually emphasizes the ontological substance and disparages the phenomena. The second principle shows that he established his cosmology on the further theoretical basis of evolutionary thought.[55] He thought that the universe and the phenomena therein, as reality, were in a state of continual development. This had the implication of a process, that is, the reality of an entity was seen in terms of the process of its development. This is reminiscent of the philosophy developed by A. N. Whitehead in his magnum opus, *Process and Reality*. He proposed an organistic metaphysics, regarding process as a central theme in the theory of ontology, and emphasizing that process was immanent in any form of existence. Therefore, ontological substance cannot be unchangeable as emphasized by traditional philosophy, but is constantly in activity (*Aktivität*) and vitality (*Vitalität*). On the metaphysical side, we can observe that there are many similarities between Xiong Shili and Whitehead, especially concerning the concepts of process and change. Here, due to space limitations, the author cannot elaborate this point any further.

Regarding the assimilation of substance and the reversion to function, Xiong presented a concise summary: "The change (*yi* 易) pertaining to the sage is magnificent. It reverts and conceals the oneness (*yiyuan* 一元) of all things into all things themselves. It does not leave all things in the universe to establish an independent oneness that governs all things."[56] Borrowed from Confucius' *The Book of Changes*, he emphasized the immanence of ontological substance. That is to say, the existence of the (one) ontological substance (*yiyuan benti* 一元本體) was concealed within all things in the universe. It did not exist apart from or outside of all things. We could not establish the ontological substance under the presupposition that it existed apart from all things. Also, we could not regard all things as governed by the (one) ontological substance. This reminds us Plato's Forms. These Forms are ontological substances and are the perfect prototype, while all other things in the universe are their copies and are imperfect. All things in the universe exist in the sensual and empirical world, while Forms exist in Plato's ideal world. These two worlds are mutually separate, that is, the ontological substance and all things are separated. At the same time, from the axiological point of view, Plato considered the Forms as important but disparaged all things in the empirical world. Since the copies depend on the prototype, we can say that in Plato's viewpoint all things in the universe are governed by ontological substance. In contrast, Xiong did not agree that all things were governed by ontological substance; he was even inclined to regard ontological substance as governed by all things and considering all things axiologically more important than ontological substance.

The assimilation of substance and the reversion to function is a metaphysical proposition. It is also an activity or event in the ontological sense. Both the assimilation of substance and the reversion to function proceed simultaneously. It is not true that the assimilation of substance proceeds first in time, and then the reversion to function follows. Rather, the assimilation of substance happens on this side and the reversion to function manifests on the other side. By "this side" and "the other side" I do not intend to convey any sense of space and extension. Furthermore, from the viewpoint of the doctrine of the non-separability and identity of substance and function, the assimilation of substance and the reversion to function are nothing but different aspects or manifestations of the same thing. The most complete explanation is that the assimilation of substance and the reversion to function is the most suitable way of understanding the ultimate truth, which transcends space and time.

Overall Reflection and Evaluation

We have explicated Xiong's metaphysical theory of the non-separability of substance and function. Now, based on this kind of metaphysical theory, we will conduct an overall reflection and evaluation of Xiong's entire system of philosophical thought and his personality.

First, let us summarize the content of Xiong's entire philosophical system of thought. This can be divided into three aspects. The first is his onto-cosmology (*jinglun* 境論), the representative works of which are *Xin weishi lun, Tiyong lun,* and *Ming xin pian.* Part of the important work *Qian kun yan,* written in the later part of his life, can also be included in this area of study. The second is epistemology (*lianglun* 量論). He often remarked that he intended to write a special monograph or *Lianglun* 量論 to investigate the problems of epistemology. He died, however, before it was written.[57] The third is the "extensive theory of change" (Dayi guang zhuan 大易廣傳), in which his philosophy of life is developed. The main works treating this subject are *Qian kun yan* and *Yuan Ru.* Part of the following three works also were concerned with this subject: *Dujing shiyao, Shili Yuyao* 十力語要 (Essential Sayings of Xiong Shili), and *Shili yuyao chuxu.*

On the positive side, Xiong's philosophical system can be said to be comprehensive in scope and penetrating in depth, as well as full of original creativity. He skillfully absorbed important ingredients from the Vijñāna-vāda that became his primary method of thought in developing Confucian viewpoints of the perpetually creative and ever-changing ontological substance, in particular those pertaining to *The Book of Changes,* so as to create his own onto-cosmology. Whether judged in terms of depth and comprehensiveness in content or in terms of its theoretical vigor, Xiong's philosophical achievements are great, and can be compared with those of Western philosophers such as Aristotle, Leibnitz, Husserl, Heidegger, and Whitehead. In Chinese philosophy, his scope is on par with that of Zhu Xi 朱熹 (1130–1200) and Wang Fuzhi.

Second, the greatest value and achievement of his philosophical thought is the fusion of ontological substance and phenomena. Based on the non-separability of substance and function, he solved the difficult metaphysical problem of the separation between ontological substance and phenomena. This problem has annoyed Western philosophers from the beginning. This is the greatest weakness of Plato's philosophy, since his Forms, on the ontological idealistic level, and their copies, on the phenomenal level, cannot be essentially connected. In the philosophy of Kant, the relationship between things in themselves (*Ding an sich*) pertaining to the ontological substantial realm or *noumena* and the phenomena (*Phänomene*) could not be essentially established. Things in themselves were only regarded as a kind of postulate (*Postulat*) or a limiting concept (*Grenzbegriff*), which limits the scope of the function of our cognition within the realm of phenomena. It did not have an essential and positive content. This difficult problem could not be solved until Husserl proposed his phenomenology. He put forward the method of a phenomenological reduction (*phänomenologishe Reduktion*) to bracket or suspend all propositions that lacked the support of evidence

(*Evidenz*), so that one could perceive the essence (*Wesen*) in the phenomena or entities (*Sachen*). Husserl, however, still did not solve this problem completely.[58]

Third, Xiong's philosophical understanding—especially his understanding of the relationship of the non-separability of ontological substance and phenomena (spiritual and physical)—was based on an introspective and existential realization, and was not just a conceptual and theoretical construction. He often emphasized the following passage from *The Book of Changes*: "Observe things from far away and analogize closely in one's person" (*yuanguan yuwu, jinpi yushen* 遠觀於物，近譬於身). This was an existential and experiential verification to apprehend the truth of the universe and life. This is what is called "to respond to [the truth] through introspective self-realization" (*wei shi fanqiu shizheng xiangying* 唯是反求實證相應). Xiong's thought has a strong character of moral practice.[59] He reflected on this dimension in the following manner: "My learning begins with conceptual speculation and ends in existential identification. If learning does not ascend towards existential identification, it is in the end isolated completely from the truth."[60] With regard to the understanding of ontological substance and truth, Western philosophy has usually only emphasized conceptual speculation, but disparaged the method of existential identification of ontological substance and truth by personal life and practices. Xiong embraced both of them and especially emphasized existential identification. This is where his philosophy is superior to mainstream Western philosophy.

Fourth, to continue the discussion of the third point, from the existential identification of ontological substance and truth through personal and practical life, one perceives that ontological substance and truth are not independent and separated from humans. Rather, they are immanent in humans, so that ontological substance, truth, and humans are all connected and can communicate with one another, and even merge. Ontological substance and truth possess a bright, pure, and upright character, as humans also do. This is human dignity. Xiong observed this very precisely. His life and conduct were also very straightforward and upright. He could put his personal beliefs into practice, not yielding to the doctrines of Marxism and not bowing down to the powers of Mao Zedong. This kind of moral discretion is what was lacking in many modern Western philosophers, but was considered extraordinarily important by Chinese philosophy, especially Confucianism. From the Confucian perspective, if a philosopher does not put his beliefs or values into practice, but only constructs his system conceptually, this system is only regarded as a "showpiece" (*guangjing* 光景) devoid of any true meaning.[61]

Here, I will evaluate the negative aspects of Xiong's philosophical thought. First, the greatest weakness of his onto-cosmology is that onto-logical substance is a complex. Due to this complexity, it has the different orientations of integration and development, which respectively lead to the existence of the physical and spiritual worlds. (Xiong was fond of using the expression "pseudo-manifestation" (*wanran zhaxian* 宛然詐現.)[62] On the one hand, ontological substance is ultimate and cannot be reduced to anything more fundamental. On the other hand, in saying that ontological substance is a complex means that it contains complex ingredients. If this is the case, we can analyze and separate these complex ingredients from ontological substance. That is, we reduce onto-logical substance to its ingredients, which constitute it or make it tenable. In this way, the ultimate character of ontological substance is lost, since it can be reduced to more fundamental ingredients. In order to be ultimate, ontological substance has to be pure and not mixed. How can such a pure ontological substance lead to the existence of an abundant and brilliant world of mind and matter? In my own phenomenology of Pure Vitality (*Phänomenologie der reinen Vitalität*), I regard Pure Vitality (*reine Vitalität*) as the Ultimate Principle. Its activity of degeneration and condensation is manifest as the phenomena of mind and matter. In this way, one can avoid Xiong's conceptual difficulty caused by the complexity pertain-ing to ontological substance.

Second, there is an intimate relationship between Xiong's philoso-phical system and Buddhism. Its methodology is basically Buddhistic. Its understanding of ontological substance can be said to begin from the Buddhist quiescent ontological substance and then changes to the vigorous and dynamic ontological substance as described in *The Book of Changes*. We can simply call it the substance of change (*yiti* 易體). There is, however, a limitation in his understanding of Buddhism. What he meant by Buddhism is primarily the Mahāyāna Vijñāna-vāda and secondarily the Mahāyāna Mādhyamika. What he meant by Vijñāna-vāda is again confined to the doctrines of Dharmapāla (Hufa 護法) explicating the thought of Vasubandhu (Shiqin 世親). This is precisely the Vijñāna-vāda that blossomed in China. As for the other development of the thought of Vasubandhu, that is, the Vijñāna-vāda developed by Sthiramati (Anhui 安慧), Xiong knew nothing. This latter development was transmitted into Tibet, but was not transmitted into China. Xiong could only read Buddhist classics in Chinese transla-tions but not the original Sanskrit classics or any Buddhist classics in Tibetan translations. Concerning Mādhyamika, his understanding was based on his reading of Prajñāpāramitā literature, in particular the

Mādhyamika works of Nāgārjuna. Although he appreciated the use of Emptiness (śūnyatā) by Mādhyamika to eliminate our attachment to self-nature (svabhāva), he thought that this method caused one "to eliminate form and reveal nature" (poxiang xianxing 破相顯性). That is, Mādhyamika taught us to eliminate the phenomenal or actual world in order to reveal the ontological substance of Emptiness.[63] Xiong personally did not agree with this method. Actually, the elimination of forms and the revelation of nature are untenable in Mādhyamika, since form and nature or phenomena and ontological substance cannot be separated. The identity of form (rūpa) and Emptiness (śūnyatā) in the Prajñāpāramitā-hṛdaya-sūtra (Bore xin jing 般若心經) and the non-separability of the supreme truth (paramārtha-satya; zhendi 真諦) and the worldly truth (saṃvṛti-satya; sudi 俗諦) spoken of in Nāgārjuna's Mūlamadhyamaka-kārikā (Genben zhonglun 根本中論) explain this point clearly.[64] Form (rūpa) or saṃvṛti-satya corresponds to phenomena, while Emptiness or paramārtha-satya corresponds to ontological substance. In his classification of Buddhist doctrines, the Chinese Tiantai master, Zhiyi 智顗 (538–97), also discussed the method to identify Emptiness or truth. He understood the method of common doctrine (tongjiao 通教) to be "penetrating into Emptiness by experiencing the dharmas directly" (tifa rukong 體法入空). That is, Emptiness or truth is experientially verified in the context of preserving and embracing all dharmas or phenomena.[65] These viewpoints about Prajñā and Mādhyamika pertain to the common doctrine. Xiong is, thus, not correct to claim that the method of Mādhyamika is "to eliminate form and reveal nature."

In addition, as already mentioned, Xiong considered the substance or ontological substance of Mādhyamika and Vijñāna-vāda to have no creative functions. He maintained that Buddhist writings did not talk about functions and as a result the religious ideal of the salvation of all sentient beings could hardly be realized. As far as Indian Buddhism is concerned, there is some truth in Xiong's assessment, but it cannot be used to criticize Chinese Buddhism. In the latter, ontological substance was described in terms of Buddha Nature. The three important schools of Chinese Buddhism, namely Tiantai, Huayan, and Chan, all emphasized the functions of Buddha Nature. Tiantai spoke of "power and function" (gongyong 功用), Huayan spoke of "force and function" (liyong 力用), and Chan spoke of "action and function" (zuoyong 作用). These functions refer directly to the manifestation of functions in the secular world in order to transform all sentient beings.[66] In his works, Xiong did not mention the explication of functions given by these three schools. Apart from Chan Buddhism, Xiong did not have a deep understanding of Chinese Buddhism.

Third, Xiong was quite influenced by certain kinds of Western philosophy, especially Bergson's philosophy of life. Xiong regarded ontological substance as having a moving character that could undergo change, and this was clearly inspired by Bergson. The latter emphasized that duration was the spirit and will of vital creativity (*élan vital*). It itself was a current of creativity that advanced eternally and perpetually. It could not be understood by our wisdom, but could only be perceived by our intuition. For the metaphysical construction carried out in *Xin weishi lun*, Xiong inherited and assimilated various ingredients from Bergson's philosophy of life. In order to understand Western philosophical literature, however, he had to rely on translations and this often resulted in misunderstanding. In his understanding of Bergson's philosophy of life, he understood that Bergson's intuition pertained to instinct, which corresponded to *vāsanā* (*xiqi* 習氣) in his *Xin Weishi lun*. *Vāsanā* is the terminology of the Vijñāna-vāda and carries an empirical and sensational implication. Bergson's intuition, however, is intellectual and supersensible. The two are quite different in meaning.

Fourth, concerning the problems of authorship and textual studies related to various types of literature, and Confucian literature in particular, Xiong made many mistakes. On this matter, he often relied on subjective views to make his decisions, without paying much attention to objective textual proofs or to the rules of developments in the history of thought. For instance, he believed that *The Book of Changes* had been written by Confucius. From a historical standpoint, a mature onto-cosmological system of thought such as that described in *The Book of Changes* could not have been established in Confucius' time. This mature onto-cosmological thought was a product of the Han Dynasty, which was at least three hundred years later than the time of Confucius. The connection that Xiong drew between Confucius and the *Book of Changes* was not supported even by his most intimate students.[67]

In sum, although there are various weaknesses in Xiong's philosophy, this does not affect in any way his status as the founder of contemporary New Confucianism. His philosophical insights and originality of thought are exceptional.

Notes

1. This chapter was originally written in Chinese, during a period when my health was very unstable. I am obliged to Dr. Wai Hon-kit for translating it into English. I am also grateful to my colleague, Dr. Lauren Pfister, for refining and polishing the English translation. In view of the fact that

. I revised and certified the final pre-edited manuscript, I alone am responsible for any mistakes therein. I also wish to thank Dr. John Makeham for generously allowing me more time to complete the chapter.

2. On the subject of *daotong*, see also the discussion in chapter 2 of this volume.

3. Concerning the purpose and intention of his learning, Xiong concentrated on the explication and development of an onto-cosmology. His interests were always orientated toward metaphysics. Tang's emphasis was on the investigation of moral problems, in particular the establishment of the moral self (*daode ziwo* 道德自我) and moral reason (*daode lixing* 道德理性). When he spoke of heaven (*tian* 天), he spoke of it in terms of its virtues (*de* 德), namely the "movement of heavenly virtues" (*tiande liuxing* 天德流行). In his magnum opus *Shengming cunzai yu xinling jingjie* 生命存在與心靈境界 (The Existence of Life and the Realm of Mind), written just before his death, he spoke of Confucianism in terms of the movement of heavenly virtues, regarding this as the highest philosophic realm (*jingjie* 境界). Xiong had already referred to the objective realm of the "movement of heavenly virtues." See Xiong Shili, *Shili yuyao chuxu* 十力語要初續 (The First Sequel to the Essential Sayings of Xiong Shili), Taipei: Letian Publishing Co., 1973, 58. Mou was more interested in onto-cosmology than Tang. He was, however, concerned with many problems and onto-cosmology was just one of them. During the latter part of his life, he investigated the problem of perfect goodness (*yuanshan* 圓善), trying to establish a perfect realm (*yuanman jingjie* 圓滿境界) of moral significance. Xu was more concerned with political philosophy and the history of thought. His scholarship showed deep social and practical concerns. He was not so interested in the construction of a theoretical system or in the issues of ontology and metaphysics. As far as their relationship with Xiong is concerned, however, these three thinkers regarded Xiong as the one who inherited the spirit of Chinese cultural life and took it to a high level of development. They also regarded him as a true Confucian who was uniformly consistent in personality and thought.

4. On an occasion when all officials stood up to welcome Chairman Mao to join a gathering, Xiong did not stand up. Liu Shuxian 劉述先, *Dangdai Zhongguo zhexue lun: Renwu pian* 當代中國哲學論：人物篇 (A Treatise on Contemporary Chinese Philosophy: On Persons), River Edge: Global Publishing Co. Inc., 1996, 146.

5. Mou Zongsan, *Shidai yu ganshou* 時代與感受 (The Times and Sensibilities), Taipei: Ehu Publishing Co., 1988, 225–6.

6. Cf. Xiong Shili, *Shili yuyao chuxu*, 99–100.

7. Xiong Shili, *Qian kun yan*, Taipei: Xuesheng Books Co., 1976, 491.

8. Xiong was constantly ill during his life, especially in his later years.

9. Xiong had complained, "It was only when I was seventy years old that I came to Shanghai and I am now old and solitary. Living in a small house and facing its walls, ten years have passed quickly. There are no inquiring youth at all [coming to seek for guidance] and rarely any guests visiting me. There is no pain in the declining years greater than that of solitariness." Xiong Shili, *Cunzhai suibi* 存齋隨筆 (Random Notes from

Existence Studio), postscript by Wan Chenghou 萬承厚, Taipei: Ehu Publishing Co., 1993, 147.

10. Concerning the later period of Xiong's life and his death, his daughter-in-law Wan Chenghou has made a detailed record. See *Cunzhai suibi*, 306–8.

11. This work has three different versions. The first is an early version written in literary Chinese (*wenyanwen* 文言文). The second is a version written in the middle period of Xiong's life, using the modern spoken language (*yutiwen* 語體文). The final version is a revised version of the second, written after 1949.

12. Xiong Shili, *Qian kun yan*, 492.

13. The metaphor of a massive ocean and its waves was often used by Xiong to explain the relationship of the non-separability of substance and function. This metaphor could be found in almost all of Xiong's writings, whether written before or after 1949. Moreover, this metaphor was often used to explain the coherent relationship between principle (*li* 理) and events (*shi* 事) or between ontological substance and phenomena in the works of various Huayan 華嚴 masters, such as Dushun's 杜順 (558–640) *Huayan wujiao zhiguan* 華嚴五教止觀, Fazang's 法藏 (643–712) *Huayanjing yihai baimen* 華嚴經義海百門, and Chengguan's 澄觀 (738–839) *Huayan fajie xuanjing* 華嚴法界玄鏡.

14. The Buddhism mentioned here primarily refers to the Indian Buddhist thought of *Prajñāpāramitā*, Mādhyamika, and Vijñāna-vāda. It does not include the thought of *tathāgatagarbha* (*rulaizang* 如來藏) nor the Chinese Tiantai and Huayan Buddhism.

15. Actually, it is not true that Buddhism does not have any views about the relationship between substance and function. It merely does not entertain the kind of relationship between a substantive spirituality and the corresponding spiritual functions. Concerning this point, see my "Fojiao de zhenliguan yu tiyong wenti" 佛教的真理觀與體用問題 (The Buddhist View of Truth and the Problem of Substance and Function), in my *Fojiao de gainian yu fangfa* 佛教的概念與方法 (The Concepts and Methods of Buddhism), revised edition, Taipei: The Commercial Press, 2000, 504–29. See also Mou Zongsan, "Fulu: Fojia tiyongyi zhi hengding 附錄: 佛家體用義之衡定" (Appendix: The Evaluation of the Meaning of Substance and Function in Buddhism), *Xinti yu xingti* 心體與性體 (Ontological Mind and Ontological Nature), vol. 1, Taipei: Zhengzhong Books Co., 1968, 571–657.

16. The ontological substance (*benti* 本體) and substance (*shiti* 實體; *ti* 體) mentioned here have identical meanings. These terms were often employed interchangeably in Xiong's writings.

17. Xiong Shili, *Tiyong lun*, Taipei: Xuesheng Books Co., 1976, 50. Xiong's statement is quite similar to the idea of embracing the various *dharmas* with Buddha Nature or Middle Way Buddha Nature (*zhongdao foxing* 中道佛性) proposed by the Chinese Tiantai Buddhist master Zhiyi 智顗 (538–97). According to Zhiyi, Middle Way Buddha Nature was the Ultimate Truth. On this point, see my *T'ien-t'ai Buddhism and Early Mādhyamika*, Honolulu: University of Hawaii Press, 1993; Indian edition,

Delhi: Sri Satguru Publications, 1995, 75–83. Of course, Xiong's "True Origin" and Zhiyi's Middle Way Buddha Nature have different meanings.

18. Xiong Shili, *Tiyong lun*, 123.

19. Xiong Shili, *Yuan Ru*, Taipei: Mingwen Publishing Co., 1997, 14.

20. There is an important paragraph in Xiong's *Xin weishi lun* (the version written in modern Chinese), Chongqing: The Commercial Press, 1944: "Function is a subtle movement of creativity and transformation. If it is not manifest from a substance how can it arise from nothing? If substance is merely quiescent, empty, and cannot transform creatively, it is just a dead and useless thing." (This paragraph is quoted in Jing Haifeng 景海峰, *Xiong Shili*, Taipei: Dongda tushu gongsi, 1991, 167.) Similar passages are also found in Xiong Shili, *Xin weishi lun*, vol. 2, Taipei: Guangwen Books Co., 1962, 19.

21. Xiong Shili, *Xin weishi lun*, vol. 2, 25.

22. *Ibid.*, 55–6.

23. *Bīja* or "seed" is a cosmological concept put forward by the Vijñāna-vāda. This doctrine holds that everything possesses both states of actualization and potentiality. The state of actualization is revealed by concrete entities that we perceive with our sense organs, while the state of potentiality is the *bīja* that can develop into concrete entities. In other words, *bīja* is the state of potentiality that makes concrete entities tenable.

24. Xiong is correct to make the criticism that Emptiness of Nature (*svabhva-śūnyatā*) of Mādhyamika—regarded as an ontological substance—cannot produce function. Emptiness of Nature represents the true state (*Zustand*) of all things, because they do not possess any self-nature. It is not a substance that gives rise to functions. He is also correct to make the criticism that the *tathā* of Vijñāna-vāda lacks dynamism and cannot initiate creative transformation. Concerning the problem of two different kinds of ontological substances, as repudiated by Xiong, the *bīja* of Vijñāna-vāda is actually not an ontological substance and the Vijñāna-vāda never conceived it as an ontological substance, but merely as a potential state of actual things. According to the Six Meanings of *bīja* (*zhongzi liuyi* 種子六義) or the six rules governing the behavior of *bīja*, the first meaning states that the *bīja* arises and annihilates in every instant. The second meaning states that the *bīja* constantly changes to another state once it annihilates. As a result, *bīja* is constantly changing and possesses an empirical character, while according to the Vijñāna-vāda, ontological substance is a transcendental truth that does not arise or annihilate. So, Xiong's understanding of *bīja* as an ontological substance does not correspond to the original meaning of the Vijñāna-vāda.

25. This understanding can be reached by reorganizing what Xiong has said in *Xin weishi lun*, vol. 2, 10–17.

26. *Ibid.*, 23–4.

27. Xiong Shili, *Shili yuyao chuxu*, 58.

28. *Ibid.*

29. "Quiescence and dynamism as one" is not spoken in a relative context. If not so, it would lead to contradiction. In my opinion, ontological substance is constantly in dynamism. It is a dynamism or an activity itself

(*Akt, Aktivität*), and it is not in the state of absolute quiescence. When we understand it in terms of quiescence, it is only due to the incipient subtlety (*jiwei* 幾微) of the dynamism that we could not recognize it.

30. Xiong Shili, *Qian kun yan*, 328.
31. *Ibid.*, 333.
32. *Ibid.*, 334.
33. *Ibid.*, 236.
34. Xiong Shili, *Yuan Ru*, 44. Here, the true origin is the ontological substance, while movement is the function or phenomenon.
35. Xiong Shili, *Qian kun yan*, 251–2. "Two different worlds" means that the two worlds are mutually separated and independent of each other.
36. *Ibid.*, 169. This is reminiscent of a kind of philosophy in ancient India, which holds that events are causeless. Such a view is regarded as heresy by Buddhism. Since it violates the law of causality, of course, it is not correct.
37. Xiong Shili, *Qian kun yan*, 215–16.
38. Xiong Shili, *Xin weishi lun*, vol. 2, 41.
39. *Ibid.*, 1.
40. Concerning the formation of entities from the action of dynamic tendency, in Buddhism, and the Vijñāna-vāda, in particular, this is called "seeming manifestation" (*pratibhāsa*; *sixian* 似現), while in Xiong's terminology this is called "discovery" (*faxian* 發現), or "pseudo-manifestation" (*zhaxian* 詐現) of traces (*jixiang* 跡象) or seemingly possessing forms (*wanran youxiang* 宛然有相). All these claim that no one thing possesses a rigid nature of unchangeability. In Xiong's words: "The magnificent functions flow vivaciously. They develop and manifest (*faxian* 發現) to become diverse traces called "the myriad entities" (*wanwu* 萬物) (*Yuan Ru*, 521). He also said: "From its [this refers to the function pertaining to the substance] non-abiding changeability and its manifestation into various forms as if they are real, it is called phenomenon. As if they are real is used as an adjective. Although it possesses forms, they are not fixed" (*Tiyong lun*, 224). The term pseudo-manifestation appears in almost all of Xiong's philosophic works.
41. Xiong Shili, *Qian kun yan*, 237.
42. Xiong Shili, *Tiyong lun*, 28.
43. Chen Lai 陳來 has elaborated on this point: "According to this explanation of Xiong Shili. . . . there is not any substance that does not transform into functions. It cannot be said that the universe once had an epoch in which there was a substance that had not yet manifested into functions. . . . At any time, substance always exists in the form of function. . . . That substance becomes function is not like a mother giving birth to her child." See his "Xiong Shili zhexue de tiyonglun 熊十力哲學的體用論" (The Theory of Substance and Function in the Philosophy of Xiong Shili), in *Xuanpu lunxue ji: Xiong Shili shengping yu xueshu* 玄圃論學集：熊十力生平與學術 (Collected Essays and Studies from the Profound Garden: Xiong Shili's Life and Academic Works), compiled by Xiao Jiefu 蕭萐父, Beijing: Shenghuo-dushu-xinzhi sanlian shudian, 1990, 283.
44. Xiong Shili, *Xin weishi lun*, vol. 1, 47–8.
45. Xiong Shili, *Qian kun yan*, 308.

46. Xiong Shili, *Xin weishi lun*, vol. 2, 68.

47. *Ibid.*, 61.

48. Mou Zongsan has widely employed the term "onto-cosmology," especially in his *Xinti yu xingti*. Although Mou followed Xiong in interpreting this term, Xiong rarely used it. When Xiong stated that integration and development were not actual things, he meant that they were a moving process and devoid of self-nature or empty, as understood in Buddhism.

49. Wang Bi 王弼, *Laozi daodejing zhu* 老子道德經注 (Notes to Laozi's Daodejing), Taipei: Shijie Shuju, 1963, 25. For an interpretation of this statement, see my *Lao-Zhuang zhexue de xiandai xilun* 老莊哲學 的現代析論 (A Modern Interpretation and Analysis of the Philosophy of Laozi and Zhuangzi), Taipei: Wenjin Publishing Co., 1998, 8–10. See also Fang Dongmei, *Yuanshi Rujia Daojia zhexue* 原始儒家道家哲學 (The Philosophy of Primitive Confucianism and Taoism), Taipei: Liming wenhua shiye gongsi, 1993, 222–3.

50. Xiong Shili, *Xin weishi lun*, vol. 1, 56–9.

51. See note 40 for further discussions about "pseudo-manifestations." In Edmund Husserl's phenomenology (*Phänomenologie*), the intentionality (*Intentionalität*) of Consciousness (*Bewußtsein*) has the dual aspects of *Noesis* and *Noema* that are, respectively, the origin or foundation of the subjective and objective worlds. He did not, however, provide a cosmological explanation for how *Noesis* constructs rigid, three-dimensional objective entities. He did not propose the notion of pseudo-manifestations. Concerning this point, see my *Husaier xianxiangxue jiexi* 胡塞爾現象學解析 (An Analysis of Husserl's Phenomenology), Taipei: The Commercial Press, 2001, 139–41.

52. In *Xin weishi lun* Xiong originally regarded the orientation of the assimilation of function and the reversion to substance as the supreme truth (*paramārtha-satya*; *zhendi* 真諦) and considered the orientation of the assimilation of substance and the reversion to function as the worldly truth (*saṃvṛti-satya*; *sudi* 俗諦). This discrimination carries an axiological flavor; that is, the assimilation of function and the reversion to substance is higher in value than the assimilation of substance and the reversion to function. When he wrote *Yuan Ru* and, in particular, *Qian kun yan*, however, Xiong changed his viewpoint, promoting the assimilation of substance and the reversion to function, while criticizing the assimilation of function and the reversion to substance. This is because in the later period of his life, he especially opposed the views of Buddhism and Daoism, which are strongly inclined toward quiescence and nothingness, respectively.

53. Xiong Shili, *Qian kun yan*, 276.

54. *Ibid.*, 316–17. Xiong attributed to Confucius the idea of emphasizing the actuality while not stressing the ontological substance. He maintained that this kind of thought came from *The Book of Changes*, which he believed had been composed by Confucius.

55. That is, matter appeared first, then plants, later animals, and finally humans (animals of the highest class). This idea of an evolution or a cosmology explicated and constructed in terms of evolutionary theory is widely evident in his writings.

56. Xiong Shili, *Qian kun yan*, 339.

57. The writings of Mou Zongsan (Xiong's most eminent student)—*Renshixin zhi pipan* 認識心之批判 (The Critique of the Cognitive Mind), *Xianxiang yu wuzishen* 現象與物自身 (Phenomena and Things in Themselves), and *Zhi de zhijue yu Zhongguo zhexue* 智的直覺與中國哲學 (Intellectual Intuition and Chinese Philosophy)—can be said to gratify Xiong's wish in this aspect in a limited way. In my opinion, there are two main reasons that Xiong could not construct "the Theory of Knowledge" during his lifetime. First, his knowledge about epistemology was insufficient. With regard to the important works on epistemology in Western philosophy, such as Kant's *Critique of Pure Reason* (*Kritik der reinen Vernunft*) and Husserl's *Logical Investigations* (*Logische Untersuchungen*), Xiong had not read any of them seriously. Secondly, although his theoretical standpoint was Confucian, his methodology was based on the Vijñāna-vāda. His onto-cosmology, in particular his explication and understanding of the originative manifestation of phenomena, was deeply influenced by the latter. In order to establish his own epistemology, it was necessary to employ the epistemology of the Vijñāna-vāda as a strong foundation. It was only with Dignāga (Chenna 陳那) and Dharmakīrti (Facheng 法稱) or even later, however, that the epistemology of the Vijñāna-vāda developed significantly. The important epistemological works of Dignāga and Dharmakīrti were not translated into Chinese. They were either written in Sanskrit or translated into Tibetan. Since Xiong could read neither Sanskrit nor Tibetan, he could not absorb their epistemology. As a result, Xiong was relatively weak in epistemology.

58. Concerning this point, see my *Husaier xianxiangxue jiexi*, the last section in particular, 155–9.

59. Concerning "responding to [the truth] through introspective self-realization," Xiong referred to it many time in his works, especially in *Xin weishi lun*. On this point, he was very similar to the Northern Song Dynasty Confucian, Cheng Mingdao 程明道 (1032–85) who said, "Although my knowledge is inherited [from tradition], *tianli* 天理 (heavenly principles) are experientially identified by myself." See *Henan Chengshi waishu* 河南程氏外書 (The Outer Collection of the Cheng Brothers' Writings), vol. 12, collected in *Er Cheng ji* 二程集 (The Collected Writings of the Cheng Brothers), vol. 2, Beijing: Zhonghua shuju, 1981, 424. He also said, "*Yin yang* 陰陽 is also empirical and physical (*xingerxia* 形而下). . . . Now I finally understand that this is just *dao* 道 and we have to understand it in a silent and speechless way." (*Henan Chengshi waishu*, vol. 11, in *Er Cheng ji*, vol. 1, 118.) What he called "experientially identified by myself" (*zijia titie* 自家體貼) and "understand in a silent and speechless way" (*mo er shi* 默而識) are existential and experiential identifications. It is quite similar to what Xiong called "responding to [the truth] through introspective self-realization." What is experientially identified is, of course, the ultimate truth. Concerning the ultimate truth experientially identified by Cheng Mingdao, see my *Rujia zhexue* 儒家哲學 (The Philosophy of Confucianism), Taipei: The Commercial Press, 1995, 119–40.

60. Xiong Shili, *Shili yuyao chuxu*, 38.

61. Wing-tsit Chan (陳榮捷) wrote a chapter on Xiong's philosophy in his *A Source Book in Chinese Philosophy*. He praised Xiong highly for explicating his own system of thought in his book, *Yuan Ru*, without quoting any Communist slogans or mentioning Marx, Stalin, and Mao Zedong. At that time, only Xiong could do so. (*A Source Book of Chinese Philosophy*, Princeton, N.J.: Princeton University Press, 1973, 765.) This is reiterated in his article "Xiong Shili de xin weixinzhuyi Ruxue 熊十力的新唯心主義儒學" (The New Idealistic Confucianism of Xiong Shili), in Xiao Jiefu, *Xuanpu lunxue ji: Xiong Shili shengping yu xueshu*, 22. Liu Shuxian has also expressed this well: "He never doubted his learning and thought or lost enthusiasm in his entire life. . . . He was thoroughly converted to *The Book of Changes* and refused to accept the standpoint of materialism. He exalted Confucius throughout his life, and never changed his mind. This is the fundamental difference between Xiong and Feng Youlan who submitted himself to the power and authority of emperors." (Liu Shuxian, *Dangdai Zhongguo zhexue lun: Renwu pian*, 169.)

It may be objected that in his later works Xiong wrote that Confucius showed his support for socialism and promoted the idea of revolution, thus Xiong was not completely independent from the reality of politics. At first, I also agreed with this interpretation. I can remember in the summer of 1972, the first time I visited Beijing, China had just begun to open and the Gang of Four was still on the rampage. I was very happy that I could buy Xiong's book, *Yuan Ru*, in a bookstore located on one of the main streets in the city center. Later, in a train heading south, I spent a whole day and night reading *Yuan Ru*. I discovered that Xiong had written that Confucius supported socialism and the idea of revolution. When I came back to Hong Kong, I immediately asked my teacher, Mou Zongsan, about it. Mou was very depressed and answered, "Xiong knew that the Communist Party was going to destroy Chinese culture. Because Confucius is the symbol of Chinese culture, in order to save Chinese culture, it is necessary to save Confucius first. But how do we save him? In that atmosphere where the political campaign against Lin Biao 林彪 and Confucius was still continuing, the only way to save Confucius was to admit that Confucius supported socialism and the idea of revolution. In this way, Chinese culture can be saved. This was an expedient strategy and it did not represent his true understanding of Confucius." Because of this, I do not think we should use this instance to doubt Xiong's moral fortitude in not submitting to political power.

62. Reference to this kind of complexity pertaining to the ontological substance often appears in his works, especially those written in the later part of his life. So, I have not cited the sources in all those cases.

63. In most of his works, Xiong regarded "elimination of form and revelation of nature" (*poxiang xianxing* 破相顯性) as the character of Mādhyamika or its method of apprehending the truth. According to him, the nature (*xing* 性) as understood in Mādhyamika was ontological substance. Since Mādhyamika spoke of the empty nature (*xingkong* 性空), Xiong therefore

regarded Emptiness as ontological substance. Actually, it is highly debatable whether "Emptiness" is an ontological substance, especially in the sense of Western philosophy.

64. Concerning the identification of *rūpa* and Emptiness (*sekong xiangji* 色空相即), see my *Fojiao de gainian yu fangfa*, 33–4. Concerning the non-separability of the supreme truth and the worldly truth, see 70–3.

65. Concerning the problem of "penetrating into Emptiness by experiencing the *dharmas* directly," see my *T'ien-t'ai Buddhism and Early Mādhyamika*, 42–3; *Zhongguo Foxue de xiandai quanshi* 中國佛學的現代詮譯 (A Modern Interpretation of Chinese Buddhism), Taipei: Wenjin Publishing Co., 1995, 48–9.

66. Concerning the Tiantai discussion of "power and function," see my *T'ien-t'ai Buddhism and Early Mādhyamika*, 66–75; *Zhongguo Foxue de xiandai quanshi*, 62–71. For a summary on the discussion of function in Tiantai, Huayan, and Chan Buddhism, see my *Fojiao sixiang da cidian* 佛教思想大辭典 (A Comprehensive Dictionary of Buddhist Thought), Taipei: The Commercial Press, 1992, 200a–201a.

67. Concerning these problems, apart from my point that in Confucius' time it was impossible to produce a fully established theory of onto-cosmology like that of *The Book of Changes*, a number of scholars have made other criticisms. See, for example, Zhang Dainian 張岱年, "Yi Xiong Zizhen xiansheng 憶熊子真先生" (In Remembrance of Mr. Xiong Zizhen), in *Xuanpu Lunxue Ji: Xiong Shili shengping yu xueshu*, 35; Liu Shuxian, *Dangdai Zhongguo zhexue lun: Renwu pian*, 142; Jing Haifeng, *Xiong Shili*, 277–8.

NOTES ON CONTRIBUTORS

N. Serina Chan is a doctoral candidate in the Centre of Asian Studies, the University of Adelaide. Her research interest is in New Confucianism, with a focus on the thought of Mou Zongsan.

Sylvia Chan is a visiting research fellow of the Centre for Asian Studies, the University of Adelaide. Her research interest is in intellectual trends in contemporary China. She has published several articles in English and Japanese on Li Zehou. Currently she is also working on problems of democratization in China.

John J. Hanafin is a Research Fellow at the Australian Research Council Special Centre for Applied Philosophy and Public Ethics, Philosophy Department, University of Melbourne. He has published articles in major English and Chinese-language journals, such as the *Business Ethics Quarterly* and *Zhexue yanjiu* (*Philosophical Research*).

John Makeham is Reader in Chinese Studies, the Centre for Asian Studies, the University of Adelaide and specializes in Chinese intellectual history. Scholarly interests include Confucian thought, contemporary Chinese philosophy, and translating classical texts. Recent publications include *Balanced Discourses*, an annotated translation of Xu Gan's (170–217) *Zhonglun* (Yale University Press, 2002), and *Transmitters and Creators: Chinese Commentators and Commentaries on the Analects* (Harvard Asia Center/Harvard University Press, 2003).

NG Yu-kwan studied Buddhism and philosophy in Hong Kong, Taiwan, Japan, and Germany, and obtained his Ph.D. at McMaster University, Canada. He has been teaching religion and philosophy at the Hong Kong Baptist University since 1988. His discipline and expertise cover Buddhism, Confucianism, Taoism, Kyoto philosophy, and phenomenology. He has published 150 articles and 25 books, including *Yogācāra Phenomenology*, *T'ien-t'ai Buddhism and Early Mādhyamika*, and *A Comprehensive Dictionary in Buddhist Thought*.

Lauren Pfister is Associate Professor at Hong Kong Baptist University, teaching in departments related to religious, philosophical, and humanities studies. He serves as the Associate Editor for the *Journal of Chinese Philosophy*, and is on the editorial boards of several other journals published in China. His research interests focus on sinological, comparative philosophical, and comparative religious themes. Soon to be published monographs include a major work on the Scottish missionary-scholar, James Legge (1815–97), forthcoming from the Peter Lang Press, and a small study on the major twentieth-century Chinese philosopher, Feng Youlan, forthcoming from Harrassowitz Press.

Song Xianlin is a lecturer in Chinese Studies, Centre for Asian Studies, the University of Adelaide. She has published widely on cultural semiotics and Chinese literature in journals, including *Semiotica* and *Social Semiotics*.

Index

Lixing: as ethical reason, 202, 205
Lizhi: as cognitive reason, 203
  as intellect, 202, 218n. 85
Lu-Wang school/tradition, 66, 132
  at Beijing University, 175
  Cheng-Zhu school/tradition
    and, 49n. 43, 60–1, 66–7,
    77n. 57, 107, 113
  Feng Youlan and, 176
  as "idealist," 189n. 14
  Mencius and, 10, 19n. 12
  Mou Zongsan and, 19n. 12
  Xiong Shili and, 61, 176

Ma Yifu (1883–1967), 29, 34,
  45n. 9, 48n. 36, 60, 61, 65
Mao Zedong: Confucianism and, 89
  Feng Youlan and, 173, 177,
    181n. 16, 182n. 20, 183n. 23
  Xiong Shili and, 222, 223, 240
Marxism: Confucianism and, 94
  Feng Youlan and, 177
  Liang Shuming and, 191, 192,
    207, 209
  Mou Zongsan's opposition to,
    133, 135
  New Confucianism and, 2, 95
  tension between Confucianism
    and, 7
May Fourth Movement, 17n. 3,
  119, 151
Mencius (ca. 372–289 B.C.):
  attitudes of New Confucians
    to, 107
  daotong and, 56, 57, 58, 63, 64,
    65, 66
  on empathetic compassion
    (*ren*), 146, 156
  four incipient virtues of, 137
  on human nature, 107, 112,
    141, 146, 147
  Liang Shuming on, 205
  Lu-Wang tradition and, 10, 19n. 12
  moral metaphysics of, 9
Mind: true (*xinti*), 137, 138, 143
  discriminating, 137, 138, 139, 143
  ontological (*benxin*), 66, 67

School of, 107
Mou Zongsan, 11, 26, 27, 34, 166,
  170, chapter 5 *passim*
  appropriation of Buddhist
    paradigms by, 10, 11
  on China's modernization, 152
  criticisms of, 105, 154–6
  on culture, 135
  daotong and, 5, 58, 61–6
  1958 Declaration and, 27, 169
  Du Weiming and, 41
  on Feng Youlan, 170, 181n. 16
  Kant and, 19n. 16, 132, 133, 148
  learning of the mind and the
    nature and, 29, 61–2, 67
  Lin Anwu on, 70, 150, 154–5
  Liu Shuxian and, 68
  on Marxism, 133, 135
  moral metaphysics of, 146, 151, 177
  Neo-Confucian thought and, 150
  on profound learning (*xuanxue*), 149
  on *ren*, 157–8
  on subjectivity, 140, 151
  syncretistic thought system of,
    9, 10, 149
  "three-unities" proposal of, 151–4
  on transcendence and
    immanence, 9, 15, 70
  on two-tier mind paradigm, 9,
    136–9, 141, 159
  writings of, 134
  Xiong Shili and, 5, 7, 9, 31, 39,
    60, 105, 119, 120, 132
  Zhu Xi and, 9, 61

National Studies craze (*guoxuere*),
  5, 6, 81, 98, 99
Neo-Confucianism: New
  Confucianism and, 2, 7,
    37–9, 60–1, 120
  Feng Youlan and, 35, 170
  "learning of the mind and the
    nature" and, 169
  Xiong Shili and, 60
  See also Cheng-Zhu school
    tradition; Lu-Wang
    school/tradition

Spiritual pollution campaign
(1983–4), 84
Subjectivity (*zhutixing*): Chinese
thought and, 63
highest form of, 220
Li Zehou on, 109, 119
Mou Zongsan on, 140, 151
Substance and function/structure
application (*ti-yong*), 15,
20n. 23, 20n. 24, 236
Xiong Shili's paradigm of non-
separability of, 133, chapter 8
passim

Tang Junyi (1909–78), 10, 11, 26, 27,
33, 34, 68, 100, 166, 219
conference on, 40
1958 Declaration and, 27, 29,
169, 170
as disciple of Xiong Shili, 14, 219
Ehu group and, 41
investigation of moral problems
and, 244n. 3
as student of Liang Shuming, 188
Transcendence and immanence,
20–21n. 25, 62, 120
in Mou Zongsan's thought, 9,
70, 138
the *ti-yong* polarity and, 15
unity of, 9, 141

Wang Bi (226–49), 15
Wang Fuzhi (Chuanshan; 1619–92):
daotong and, 65, 225
Lin Anwu and, 70
Xiong Shili and, 14, 239
Wang Gen (1483–1540), 13
Liang Shuming and, 188, 193
Wang Yangming (1472–1529),
10, 13, 14, 19n. 12, 64
daotong and, 74
moral mind and, 145
New Confucians and, 66
Xiong Shili and, 219
Weishi (Consciousness-Only)
Buddhism. See Yogācāra
Buddhism

Xianliang (direct perception),
199–200
Xiong Shili (1885–1968), 58, 92,
97, 166, 187, chapter 8 *passim*
Book of Changes and, 68, 219,
222, 229, 230, 240
Buddhist influences on, 11, 13,
48n. 34, 241–2
criticisms of Buddhism and,
226, 227, 228, 229–30
criticisms of Daoism and, 227–8
1958 Declaration and, 176
disciples of, 219
Feng Youlan and, 35, 59, 176,
220, 250n. 61
as founder of New
Confucianism, 11, 14, 29,
34, 66, 180n. 12, 188, 243
influence of Henri Bergson on,
68, 222, 243
influence of Yogācāra doctrines
on, 14
learning of the heart and mind
and, 29
Lu-Wang school and, 61, 176
Mao Zedong and, 222, 223, 240
Mou Zongsan and, 5, 7, 9, 31,
39, 60, 105, 119, 132
Neo-Confucian thought and, 60
Qian Mu and, 36
onto-cosmology of, 14, 15, 16,
234–8, 238–9
on ontological substance, 226,
228–9, 235, 236, 237–8
on the operations of integration (*xi*)
and development (*pi*), 234–5,
236
personality of, 156, 219, 220
as reviver of the *daotong*, 61,
64–5, 67, 219
spiritual legacy of, 5, 58–60, 219
two antinomical metaphysical
systems of, 229
Wang Yangming and, 219
A.N. Whitehead and, 237
writings of, 223–4
Yogācāra Buddhism and, 221

Xu Fuguan (1903–82), 10, 14,
26, 30, 33, 34, 36, 39, 68,
166, 220
1958 Declaration and, 27, 169
as disciples of Xiong Shili, 219
Xuanzang (600–64), 189, 195
See also Yogācāra Buddhism
Xunzi (298–238 B.C.), 106, 121
on human nature, 107
influence on Li Zehou of, 111

Yogācāra Buddhism: as alien to
the Chinese tradition, 190
Liang Shuming and, chapter 7
passim
Xiong Shili and, 14, 221
Xuanzang and, 189
Yu Yingshi: on *daotong*, 63–4
on definitions of New Confucian,
38–9
on Mou Zongsan's "three
unities" theory, 156–7
as a New Confucian, 40
on Qian Mu, 36
on "self-diremption," 119–20

Zeng Guofan (1811–72): as a
New Confucian, 38
Zhang Junmai (Carsun Chang;
1887–1969), 26, 29, 34, 36,
38, 50n. 54, 166
1958 Declaration and, 27,
169, 180n. 12
Ehu group and, 41
Zhang Zhidong (1837–1909),
110
as a New Confucian, 38
Zhijue (intuition), 202
Zhongyong (Doctrine of the
Mean), 63, 138
as one of the Four Books, 58
Zhu Xi's preface to, 57, 64
Zhu Xi (1130–1200): *daotong*
and, 57–8
Mou Zongsan and, 9, 61
Ziwo kanxian (self-diremption;
self-negation of moral
consciousness), 128n. 54
criticism of Mou Zongsan's
theory of, 119–20
Mou's theory of, 142, 150, 153

CPSIA information can be obtained at www.ICGtesting.com
Printed in the USA
LVOW120736041112

305738LV00003B/6/P